W9-BUW-887

WERTHEIM FELLOWSHIP PUBLICATIONS

WERTHEIM FELLOWSHIP PUBLICATIONS

Leo C. Brown, S.J., *Union Policies in the Leather Industry*, 1947

William Haber, *Industrial Relations in the Building Industry*, 1930

J. D. Houser, *What the Employer Thinks*, 1927

Paul H. Norgren, *The Swedish Collective Bargaining System*, 1941

Johnson O'Connor, *Psychometrics*, 1934

Wertheim Lectures on Industrial Relations, 1929

LABOR IN NORWAY

LONDON : GEOFFREY CUMBERLEGE
OXFORD UNIVERSITY PRESS

LABOR IN NORWAY

BY

WALTER GALENSON

ASSISTANT PROFESSOR OF ECONOMICS
HARVARD UNIVERSITY

CAMBRIDGE · MASSACHUSETTS
HARVARD UNIVERSITY PRESS
1949

WERTHEIM FELLOWSHIP PUBLICATIONS

In 1923 the family of the late Jacob Wertheim established the Jacob Wertheim Research Fellowship for ". . . the support of original research in the field of industrial coöperation . . ." The Fellowship was intended to enable men and women ". . . who already have expert knowledge of this subject, to pursue research that may be of general benefit in solving the problems in this field . . ." Fellowships are awarded annually by the President and Fellows of Harvard College on the recommendation of the Wertheim Committee.

The Committee undertakes to provide general supervision to the program of research of the Wertheim Fellow. When that research yields findings and results which are significant and of general interest, the Committee is authorized by the terms of the grant to Harvard University to recommend publication. The Jacob Wertheim Research Fellow alone has responsibility for the facts, analysis, and opinions expressed in this volume.

JOHN D. BLACK, *Chairman*
SUMNER H. SLICHTER
B. M. SELEKMAN
SAMUEL A. STOUFFER
JOHN T. DUNLOP, *Secretary*

FOREWORD

FEW BOOKS have explored the institutions and the policies of a country in their bearing on industrial relations and the role of labor in the community with such insight and thoroughness as Dr. Galenson's "Labor in Norway." Norway is an excellent subject for study, partly because its experience has been rich and partly because labor there has attained great power and has had to assume responsibility for the welfare of the country.

Many of the institutions and policies tried in Norway would not fit the American environment. Nevertheless, Dr. Galenson's study will be illuminating and suggestive to Americans. The efforts of the radical Norwegian labor movement of the early twenties to work out an understanding with the Third International are instructive reading today. Of great interest are the Norwegian experiences with the mediation of labor disputes, with the enforcement of contracts between unions and employers, with the problem of boycotts (and the unique "boycott court"), and with compulsory arbitration. The United States can learn much from Norwegian methods of mediation. Familiarity with Norwegian experience with compulsory arbitration will contribute to a more sophisticated view of that controversial subject. Four times within the last thirty-five years Norway has experimented with compulsory arbitration — sometimes with the approval of employers and in the face of opposition from unions and sometimes with the approval of unions and in the face of opposition from employers. Norwegian experience shows a use for compulsory arbitration which has received little attention — namely, the making of decisions "too hot" for collective bargaining to handle. It shows also that compulsory arbitration may be employed as a temporary device, superseding collective bargaining for a few years until conditions become more suitable for collective bargaining.

The most important part of the book is Dr. Galenson's penetrating discussion of the effect of power upon trade unions and the labor party. Ever since the end of the war the unions and the labor party have been the most powerful private organizations in the community. They have had to assume responsibility for the well-being of the country. Perhaps the effect of great power upon trade unions will not be the same in the United States as it has been in Norway. Nevertheless, the account of Norwegian experience is of great significance. Both the trade unions and the labor party have shown great capacity to see the interests of all employees in the community and, indeed, of all groups in the community, and to develop policies which reflect the community's concern for stable prices and more productive capacity.

Dr. Galenson's book will be found fascinating reading by all persons who are interested in social trends today and it will be found especially useful by all policy makers — whether in government, in trade unions, or in industry.

Sumner H. Slichter

AUTHOR'S PREFACE

THIS STUDY was first conceived while I was serving as labor attaché to the American Embassy in Oslo during 1945 and 1946. My work brought me into intimate contact with Norwegians from all walks of life, with a common interest in industrial relations. It also afforded me a unique opportunity to witness the inception of an interesting experiment in social and economic organization.

I could not hope to list in the space of a brief preface the names of all the Norwegians who contributed their time and counsel generously and patiently. Among the most helpful were *Fylkesmann* Alf Frydenberg, former permanent undersecretary in the Ministry of Labor; Mr. Paal Berg, former chief justice of the Supreme Court of Norway and of the Labor Court; Messrs. Christian Erlandsen, A. P. Østberg, and H. J. Darre Hirsch, respectively chairman, vice-chairman, and general counsel of the Norwegian Employers' Association; Messrs. Konrad Nordahl, Gustav Sjaastad, and Magnus Bratten, respectively chairman, general counsel, and press officer of the Norwegian Federation of Labor; Mr. Martin Tranmael, Editor of *Arbeiderbladet;* Mr. Gunnar Ousland, the venerable historian of the Norwegian labor movement; Mr. Petter Jakob Bjerve, of the Ministry of Finance; and Mr. Aake Ording, of the United Nations Secretariat. It is also a pleasure to acknowledge my inestimable debt to Mr. Haakon Lie, secretary-general of the Norwegian Labor Party, at whose cabin in Mylla I spent many instructive and pleasant hours, learning something of the Norwegian way of life.

Several American colleagues and friends were kind enough to read this study in manuscript and offer their advice. Whatever its shortcomings, it would have been much poorer without the penetrating criticism proffered by Professor Sumner H. Slichter of Harvard University. Professors Benjamin M. Selekman and John T. Dunlop of Harvard University, and Professor Abram Bergson of Columbia University, also made many valuable suggestions.

I am indebted to the Jacob Wertheim Fellowship in Industrial

Relations of Harvard University for financial assistance in connection with the preparation of this work. A grant from the Penrose Fund of the American Philosophical Society enabled me to spend the summer of 1947 in Norway, interviewing trade union officials and employers and going through the Archives of the Norwegian Labor Movement.

It is perhaps necessary to add two notes to the foregoing. First, all the translations of Norwegian documents quoted in the text and appendixes are my own. Secondly, in view of the official positions held by some of those whose aid is acknowledged above, it is incumbent upon me to accept sole responsibility for all statements of opinion expressed herein.

Finally, I must express my gratitude to my wife, without whose constant help and encouragement it would have been infinitely more difficult to complete this study.

WALTER GALENSON

Cambridge, April 27, 1948

CONTENTS

TABLES

LABOR IN NORWAY

CHAPTER I

INTRODUCTION

THE SMALL NATIONS that comprise the Scandinavian area constitute a social laboratory for the Western world. In recent years,
the attention accorded them by students of government and economics has been far out of proportion to their physical size and influence on world events. No phase of the Scandinavian experience
has aroused more interest than the experiments undertaken within
the field of industrial relations.

Despite what overly enthusiastic observers would have us believe, the Scandinavian countries have not discovered a panacea
for the alleviation of the labor problems that appear increasingly
to beset democratic industrial society. All have had their share of
labor strife in the past, and serious differences of opinion between
employers and workers still prevail. But there has grown up
through the years the recognition that mutual survival requires
mutual forbearance. More and more, force has been supplanted by
a highly organized system of collective bargaining governed by a
well-defined and widely accepted body of rules.

The three Scandinavian nations, while they have much in common institutionally, are nevertheless distinct entities in terms of
their history, traditions, and national temperament. The modern
Norwegian labor movement has tended to be somewhat more radical than those of Denmark and Sweden, and until recent years
Norwegian labor relations were more turbulent.[1] One of the purposes of this study will be to determine what gave rise to these
differences.

The basic aim of this analysis of Norwegian industrial relations,
however, goes beyond a mere history of how a small European
nation approached the solution of its labor problems. The fact is

[1] For a detailed and accurate account of the Swedish experience, see Paul
Norgren, *The Swedish Collective Bargaining System* (Cambridge, 1941), and
J. J. Robbins, *The Government of Labor Relations in Sweden* (Chapel Hill,
1942). There is no similar analysis in English of the Danish experience.

that despite the obvious disparity in the size of the two countries there are many illuminating parallels and contrasts between industrial relations in the United States and Norway. We tend to take our practices and institutions for granted, and it is often helpful in determining their origins and evaluating their contemporary desirability to have available a separate body of experience to serve as a control.

For this purpose Norway should serve admirably. The general framework within which labor problems have been posed is fundamentally similar in Norway and the United States. The Norwegian Constitution of 1814, for example, was strongly influenced by the Constitution of the United States.[2] The Norwegian people are as individualistic as the American and are equally resentful of dictation and regimentation. American visitors to Norway rarely feel that they are in an alien society, and the reverse is even truer in view of the great contribution Norwegians have made to American culture.

The opening chapters of this study deal with the history and structure of the Norwegian labor movement, both on the purely trade union and the political sides. Norwegian trade unions, though structurally similar to the American, are considerably more centralized functionally. This is in part due to the historical conditions in which Norwegian trade unionism first took root, and is in part a function of size.

The contrast between the political activities of Norwegian and American labor is even more marked. For many years, Norwegian workers have supported a labor party distinct from the traditional political parties, and in recent years succeeded in gaining governmental hegemony through this organization. Nonpartisan political action on the American style has been unknown in Norway since the beginning of this century. There is also the significant difference that the prevailing philosophy of Norwegian labor has been Marxism, and that class consciousness has been an important force in shaping both the organization and activities of the Norwegian

[2] Judge Christian Magnus Falsen, the "Father of the Norwegian Constitution," was well acquainted not only with the American Federal Constitution, but with the state constitutions as well. The measure of his debt to the American example is indicated by the names he bestowed upon two sons: George Washington and Benjamin Franklin. See Halvdahn Koht and Sigmund Skard, *The Voice of Norway* (New York, 1944), pp. 61–73.

labor movement — resulting, for example, in the relative unimportance of the concept of jurisdiction as an element in the trade union creed. Other significant reflections of this philosophy appear in such things as the character of labor leadership, the attitude toward government intervention, and trade union equalitarianism.

A related subject, treated in Chapter IV, is the manner in which Norwegian employers have organized for purposes of collective bargaining. Unlike American employers, who have generally insisted that labor relations are best handled by the individual firm, Norwegian employers have been willing to delegate this aspect of business management to specialized representatives. In view of the current American interest in employer organization, an account of the history, organization, and operation of the Norwegian Employers' Association may prove enlightening.

Following this discussion, Norwegian attempts to mitigate the effects of industrial strife through legislation are considered. This may well be one of the most informative aspects of the Norwegian industrial relations experience, for it includes methods of governmental intervention that have many advocates in the United States. The Norwegians have experimented with mediation combined with a brief "cooling off" period; compulsory arbitration of disputes arising under collective agreements, so-called disputes over "rights," through a Labor Court; and compulsory arbitration of "interest" disputes, that is, disputes concerning the determination of new terms of employment. They have gone a long way toward the solution of the perplexing problem of whether government employees should enjoy the right to bargain collectively. A separate chapter is devoted to the body of law built up by the Boycott Court, an independent tribunal established in 1933 to deal with a weapon of organized labor that has been as controversial in Norway as in the United States.

Against the institutional and legal background sketched in the first part of this study, the history and results of the industrial relations process are next considered. Bitter labor strife in the nineteen-twenties was followed by a decade of relative industrial peace, culminating in the conclusion of a Basic Agreement between the Federation of Labor and the Employers' Association regulating many of the aspects of collective bargaining and contract procedure. The American reader will be interested to learn that neither general employer acceptance of collective bargaining — the Employers' Association has never undertaken an anti-union drive, designed to destroy the trade unions — nor elaborate collective bargaining institutionalism has reduced work stoppages to a negligible amount.

Two sections which follow contain an analysis of the intricate pattern of industrial labor practices that have been embodied in the written collective agreements governing conditions of work for most Norwegian employees. Of particular interest are the two contrasting systems of wage payment most commonly employed, the minimum wage with personal increments and the standard rate; and the widespread extent of piece work, under which most building construction work, for example, is performed. The various types of wage differentials that have evolved from a long process of collective bargaining are also considered, as is the work of the Labor Court, a government institution that for thirty years has successfully arbitrated controversies between employers and trade unions concerning the interpretation of agreements.

The final part of the study deals with a range of subjects that is as yet alien to the American consciousness, but which nevertheless is of paramount importance in charting both our future domestic policies and our foreign policy: the impact of a labor government upon the labor market. This is prefaced by a description of the planned economy instituted by the Norwegian Labor Government in 1945, for it is only against this background of economic reform that the postwar policies of the labor movement are comprehensible.

An examination of collective bargaining and the settlement of industrial disputes in Norway since 1945 reveals clearly that the achievement by labor of political power implies a fundamental change in the essence, if not the form of employer-employee relations. Norwegian labor, for example, has espoused compulsory governmental arbitration of all labor disputes after decades of uncompromising opposition to such an arrangement, and it is not surprising to discover that the arbitration tribunal appointed by the Labor government, though technically independent, has actually applied governmental wage policy in its main outlines if not in every detail. The new political situation has also meant great augmentation in trade union bargaining power, and a corresponding diminution in the ability of employers to oppose trade union demands, raising seriously the problem of whether collective bargaining in the traditional sense has any meaning under a labor government with socialist aims.

Of even greater moment is the impact of labor's political victory upon the structure and functions of the trade unions themselves. It has already become apparent in Norway that the price of governmental power is a greatly increased measure of responsibility; that hoary trade union attitudes toward the strike weapon, toward scientific management, toward wage incentive plans and many similar matters must be altered if further economic progress is to be achieved. The chief threat to Norwegian labor's ambitious planned production goals is the difficulty involved in convincing the average worker that new times require a new outlook, and that the principal trade union function is no longer the extraction from employers of what the traffic will bear. It is to this range of subject matter that the final chapter constitutes an introduction, which may serve not only to present a problem of great immediate concern to European labor, but may also raise more general queries regarding trade union "responsibility."

A few facts about Norway will provide a frame of reference for the following pages. The total land area of the country comprises 323,000 square kilometers, about the size of Texas and Oklahoma combined. The population is slightly in excess of three million, making population density the lowest in Europe. This fact is deceptive, however, for 75 per cent of the area consists of barren mountainous land, 22 per cent is forest land, and only 3 per cent is cultivated ground. The bulk of the population is concentrated along the south and west coasts, and in the narrow sheltered valleys of the interior. Limited resources of arable land have been a problem since the days of the Viking, and each year small additional amounts of land are being brought under cultivation at considerable expense.

Up to the beginning of the present century, farming, fishing, and seafaring were the principal sources of livelihood for the Norwegians. Since 1900, industry has developed very rapidly, so that at the time of the last census (1930), 27.6 per cent of the population derived its income from manufacturing and industry and another 19.7 per cent from trade and transport, ranking Norway with Sweden from the point of view of occupational structure. The relatively tardy development of industry in Norway is attributable primarily to lack of coal, which was overcome when the technology of electricity made possible the exploitation of abundant resources of water power.

The major employers of industrial labor are the shipyards, saw-mills, paper and pulp mills, textile and leather plants, and building construction. Because of Norway's great reliance on foreign trade, such foreign-exchange-producing activities as the electrochemical and metallurgical industries, turning out aluminum, zinc, nickel, and ferro-alloys, possess a strategic importance out of proportion to the employment they afford. The same may be said even more emphatically of the merchant marine, the earnings of which in prewar years provided Norway with more than 25 per cent of her total *valuta*.[3]

It is important to recognize that Norway must be classified with the industrial nations of the world, and that industrial labor constitutes the largest single section of the population. The travel poster picturesqueness of fiords and snow-capped mountains should not obscure the fact that it was the growth of industrial capital which raised Norwegian living standards from a relatively low to a high level within a single generation.

[3] The unit of Norwegian currency, which is based upon the decimal system, is the crown (*krone*). This unit is divided into 100 öre. Since 1945, the *krone* has been stabilized at 4.97 to the dollar, representing a devaluation from the average 1939 rate of 4.315 to the dollar.

CHAPTER II

THE TRADE UNION MOVEMENT[1]

EARLY HISTORY

THE NORWEGIAN trade union movement traces its origins to the middle of the nineteenth century. In 1848 an unemployed school teacher, Marcus Thrane, founded an organization that had as its purpose the protection of small farmers and landless agricultural laborers against unemployment occasioned by the rise of agricultural rationalization. The organization grew rapidly, attaining a membership of 20,000 by 1851. Although some artisans and handicraft workers joined the Thranite movement, it was largely rural in character. At the time there were only 12,700 industrial workers in Norway, distributed among 3,300 separate establishments.

Thrane and his followers were interested primarily in obtaining legislation to protect agricultural labor standards. An additional goal was universal suffrage, which was destined to absorb much of the energies of the labor movement for fifty years. A few strikes were carried on under the auspices of the movement, and instances of violence occurred. As a result Thrane and his lieutenants were arrested and, in 1851, sentenced to long prison terms. The Thranite organization collapsed. Thrane himself, upon his release from prison, emigrated to the United States, where he worked as a photographer and engaged in political journalism.

During the next two decades the labor movement was confined to local associations of craftsmen largely philanthropic in character. Sponsored by clergymen and socially minded intellectuals, their main purpose was to further labor welfare through sickness and old age insurance funds, and coöperative purchasing. A good deal of educational work was carried on, and many workers' libraries were established. However, these organizations did not

[1] For much of the material in this chapter acknowledgment is made to the standard history of Norwegian trade unionism, Gunnar Ousland, *Fagorganisasjonen i Norge* (Oslo, 1927).

seek to bargain over wages and working conditions, and masters as well as artisans were admitted to membership.

It was not until 1872 that pioneer trade unions, in the modern sense, were founded. As a result of a rapidly rising price level, Norway experienced her first real strike wave. Out of the strike movement emerged the Oslo Typographical Union as a permanent organization. Cabinetmakers, upholsterers, paper hangers and bakers followed suit, but the recession of 1873 swept their organizations away; only the Typographical Union managed to survive. Some of the most active unionists joined the wave of emigration to the United States, a further setback for the labor movement.

For a decade thereafter, there was little attempt at new organization. In 1880, however, local associations of skilled workers began to appear once more, often as a means of protection against the steady stream of farm laborers who were migrating to the cities. During the eighties seventy local unions and two national unions were established — the Typographers in 1882 (the first national union in Scandinavia) and the Woodworkers in 1889. In addition, local unions in Oslo banded together to form the Oslo Trade Union Central Committee, the first of the city central trades councils.

Another significant event of this period was the formation of the Norwegian Labor Party under the leadership of a typographical worker, Christian Holtermann Knudsen. Theretofore the trade unions had been oriented politically toward the Liberal (*Venstre*) Party, whose program of universal suffrage and democratization of the army appealed to the workers. The first Liberal government of 1884 proved a disappointment, however, because of equivocation on the suffrage question and parliamentary opposition to a ten-hour-day law. Many workers turned to the new Labor Party, causing a serious political rift within the trade union movement that was not healed until after the turn of the century, when *Venstre* lost all its trade union support.

The years 1887 to 1889 were characterized by a sharp upward turn in the business cycle. Many strikes occurred, including a four-month stoppage by the Oslo printers, the longest and best organized strike that had yet taken place. Strikebreakers were imported from Denmark and Germany and meetings were broken up by the police. This served to strengthen the radical element within the unions and led to a division of the Oslo Central Labor Council, which had fifty local union affiliates, into rival Liberal and Socialist organizations. The Socialists took with them thirty-three locals and reconstituted themselves the Oslo Coöperating Trade Unions.

By 1889 there were only from 3,000 to 4,000 organized workers in Norway, most of them in Oslo. But the next decade witnessed more rapid trade union growth, and in 1899 there were 250 local unions in existence, with perhaps 20,000 members. A number of bitter strikes that occurred during this period pointed to the desirability of coöperation among local unions, and the necessity of establishing permanent strike funds. Local unions began to band together vertically and horizontally; the former type of organization gave rise to national unions of metalworkers, bakers, and tailors, while horizontal associations of local unions on the model of the Oslo Coöperating Trade Unions spread to other urban centers.

In this early period, with trade unionism confined to a few cities, it was natural for the city centrals to play an important role. They were more than the loose association that characterizes comparable organizations in the United States, or indeed than they later became in Norway. At this time they were a species of centralized federation, with considerable authority over the constituent locals. In their laws they embodied for the first time the important principle of the central strike fund, payable only if the purpose of the strike, and its procedure, were approved by the executive board of the city trade council. Ousland remarks that

the trade unions had now left their childhood, when strikes were based upon voluntary contributions, and were attaining a more permanent status, with an association of unions having the power to assess the coöperating unions to support strikers to the extent of a predetermined amount. This implied a widening of the association's power with respect to the leadership of labor disputes.[2]

Yet the organizational form that proved more durable was the national union of locals in the same craft or industry. Although there was considerable theoretical debate at the time over the relative merits of vertical and horizontal organization, in this sense, the spread of unionism beyond city lines made it more and more difficult for the city centrals to conduct negotiations and disputes efficiently. The dual organization often created friction, since

[2] Ousland, pp. 103–104.

strike committees had to consist of representatives of the national union, the local union, and the city central, who often differed on tactics and strategy. This stage of Norwegian trade union development is reminiscent of the rivalry between the amorphous geographical units of the Knights of Labor and the rising craft associations that were to join together in the American Federation of Labor.

The year 1899 is an important one in Norwegian labor history, marking the formation of the present Norwegian Federation of Labor. The tardy emergence of a national trade union center, thirteen years after the foundation of the American Federation of Labor, is to be attributed primarily to the fact that industrialization came relatively late in Norway. In 1900, only about 80,000 persons out of a population of two and a quarter million were engaged in industries subject to workmen's compensation laws, and many of these were handicraftsmen rather than industrial workers. It was only when the development of technical knowledge permitted the establishment of industry based upon electricity rather than coal that Norway's most important natural resource, the waterfalls, could be put to economic use.[3]

Although there had been some discussion of national federation in trade union circles, particularly among the socialists, what brought matters to a head was an inter-Scandinavian labor congress held in Stockholm in 1897, where it was resolved that "the national unions in the three countries, and the industrial local unions that are not affiliated with any national union, shall join together in a national federation with a common secretariat for each country." A Norwegian organizing committee was formed in 1898, among the most active members of which were the two socialists who had been most instrumental in the formation of the Labor Party in 1887, and very active in the trade union strife of the nineties: Christian H. Knudsen, who had originally been a typographer, and Carl Jeppesen, a Danish-born cigar maker who

[3] Primary power employed in industry rose from 315,000 horsepower in 1905 to 992,000 horsepower in 1914; a thousand kilometers of railroad and 3,600 kilometers of road were built from 1900–1910, a substantial amount for Norway in that period. In 1905 Norway had 664,000 tons of shipping, which had risen to 1,214,000 tons by the outbreak of war in 1914. Trond Hegna, "Norges økonomiske utvikling efter århundreskiftet," *Norsk Naeringsliv og Dets Problemer* (Oslo, 1938).

became the outstanding Norwegian labor journalist of his day.

The constitutional convention of the Federation of Labor which assembled in Oslo in March 1899, was attended by representatives of eleven national craft unions,[4] two city centrals (Oslo and Drammen), and a number of independent local unions. The delegates faced three principal problems: the status of the national craft unions versus the city central trades councils, the amount of central strike benefit payments, and the political affiliation of the new organization.

The organizing committee had prepared a draft constitution making national craft unions the principal structural unit, which was not at all to the liking of the city centrals. The Bergen city central, which was not represented, sent a communication to the effect that it would adhere to the Federation "only on condition that affiliation be exclusively on the basis of city central trades councils, and not as individual local unions and national craft unions." Although this extreme position had no support, there was some dissension as to the precise role to be assigned to the city centrals, which was finally resolved in the following form: "Local unions, whether or not affiliated with national unions, must join the local central trades council. However, the city central trades council may not accept the affiliation of any local union which is eligible to affiliate with a national craft union and has not done so." Thus the city centrals were prohibited from constituting themselves organizing bodies in rivalry with the national unions, but they were made an obligatory link in the organizational structure.

The second source of controversy was over the central strike fund, a matter of utmost significance for the future development of the Federation of Labor. The organizing committee proposed that each constituent national union establish a strike fund at the rate of ten öre per member per week, and that in addition the Federation of Labor be empowered to make an additional direct assessment of twenty-five öre per member per week in the event of labor disputes. The Federation was to be obligated to pay to each

[4] They were: the Stone and Earth Workers' Union; the Stonecutters' Union; the Metalworkers' Union; the Tailors' Union; the Typographical Workers' Union; the Tobacco Workers' Union; the Dock Workers' Union; the Woodworkers' Union; the Bakers' Union; the Painters' Union; and the Shoe Workers' Union.

striking member eight kroner per week, with supplements for families, an amount that equaled the total customary strike benefit at that time.

This provision was not satisfactory to a few of the weaker and poorer unions, for whom acceptance would have meant a substantial increase in dues. The wealthiest unions, on the other hand, feared that they might be called upon to subsidize strikes by the smaller unions. Moreover, since payment of Federation strike benefits was made contingent upon Federation approval of strikes, the latter were resentful of the potential power vested in the Federation; they would have preferred that a larger proportion of the strike benefits be paid out by the national unions, affording them a greater degree of independence in the conduct of negotiations. Despite these objections, the majority of the delegates to the convention voted in favor of the original proposal. One of the chief attractions of federation for them was the prospect of a pooled strike fund, which would greatly increase their bargaining power in anything short of a general work stoppage.

The third issue arose from a socialist proposal that all local unions be required to affiliate with the Labor Party. Although the presence of some *Venstre* adherents among the delegates made it impossible to secure passage of this resolution, it was resolved that the two organizations, the Federation of Labor and the Labor Party, should have mutual representation in their respective executive boards to coördinate common interests.

With these issues presumably settled, the formal aspects of union government proved to be no obstacle, and the delegates approved the constitution, elected officers, and proceeded homeward to secure ratification by their constituents. But there was more dissatisfaction than they had counted on. The two most important national unions, the Typographical Workers and the Metalworkers, refused to accept the conventions.[5] The executive committee of the latter stated as its reason:

The constitution is disadvantageous from our point of view, since it contains the provision that local unions shall also be affiliated with

[5] The Typographical Workers' Union had long been the backbone of the Norwegian trade union movement. As a pioneer, it had supplied the movement with some of its leading figures — Christian H. Knudsen, A. Buen, and Ole O. Lian. Its defection was thus disheartening from a moral as well as a financial point of view.

city central trades councils, where such exist. This is the same as saying that approval and leadership of wage disputes and similar internal matters shall be placed in the hands of the city central executive committee, thus making it impossible for our union to conduct its own affairs.[6]

The centralized strike fund provided by the constitution afforded another reason for its rejection by these and other organizations.

The result was that although 15,000 workers had been represented at the constitutional convention, the Federation of Labor began its existence as a federation of six craft unions and the Oslo central trades, numbering not more than 5,000 members in all. Even for Norway at that time this was a small number indeed, and the outlook for the future was not bright.

FIRST YEARS OF THE FEDERATION OF LABOR

Despite this inauspicious start, there was no lack of enthusiasm among the Federation's members. They proceeded to pursue the goals set forth in the constitution:

1. Through mutual coöperation among unions to achieve unity and strength in order to protect and advance the craft, social, and economic interests of the working class.

2. Through reports from member unions to obtain the best possible picture of trade union activity and development.

3. To support member unions in retaining gains and rights. To work for better wage and working conditions.

4. In coöperation with the political labor movement, to work for the socialization of production and commerce.

5. To carry on educational activities among the workers in coöperation with the Workers' Educational Association.

6. To maintain and expand international coöperation and work for mutual economic support between the Norwegian Federation of Labor and the trade union movements of other countries.

7. To coöperate in securing meeting places for the labor movement.[7]

Efforts to secure the affiliation of additional unions began to bear fruit. In 1901 the Laborers' Union, an organization of un-

[6] Ousland, p. 143.
[7] Arbeidernes Faglige Landsorganisasjon, *Lover*, 1946, Section 1.

skilled workers covering a number of industries, joined the Federation, though its request for a guarantee of jurisdiction over all unskilled workers was not met. The Federation did declare, however, that it looked with sympathy on the purposes and structure of the Laborers' Union. In the same year, the Bricklayers' Union also affiliated, raising membership to 8000.

The secretariat of the Federation,[8] from the very start, played an active part in labor disputes involving single local unions. It was able to do this largely by virtue of its control over strike benefit payments, for unions defying its wishes might find themselves cut off from this important aid. But the absence of a clear constitutional provision defining the limits of its authority made for some friction.

The second congress of the Federation in 1901 defined more precisely the power of the secretariat in labor disputes:

The secretariat has the right, whenever it considers it necessary, to intervene for the purpose of seeking the termination of a dispute through direct negotiation with employers. Before doing so, however, it shall seek the opinion of the executive board of the union involved in the dispute.[9]

In the event of a difference of opinion between the secretariat and the union, the Federation's next highest instance, the representative council, was made the final arbiter. The insertion of this provision in the constitution does not appear to have evoked much conflict; apparently the unions affiliated with the Federation were more interested at this stage in mutual protection than in particularist freedom of action.

That the problem of the rivalry between national unions and city centrals was not yet solved satisfactorily is evidenced by the fact that the Federation was obliged to call upon the city centrals "to circumscribe their activities so that they do not touch upon

[8] Although the structure of the Federation of Labor is dealt with in some detail below, it may be noted here that there are three principal policy levels in the Federation hierarchy: the secretariat, a small group of top leadership officials meeting weekly; the representative council, a body numbering about one hundred delegates at the present time and convening annually, as a rule; and the congress, the highest legislative instance, which met biennially in the early years of the Federation but now meets triennially.

[9] Ousland, p. 151.

wage disputes, since this portion of their activity in large measure restrains the development of the various national unions." The affiliated national unions were not yet strong enough to assert what they regarded as their legitimate authority in this sphere.

The third congress, held in 1903, considered for the first time the question of trade union jurisdiction. This was occasioned by the rapid growth of the Laborers' Union, which gave it forty-three out of eighty-eight convention delegates, and half the total membership of the Federation. The other unions, occupied until then with the organization of a field which seemed to provide room for all, began to fear the possibility of encroachment by this new organization of the unskilled. To curb any imperialistic proclivities on its part, they forced through an amendment to the constitution prohibiting local unions that broke away from a national union from affiliating with another member national union without the consent of the Federation. However, the congress rejected a proposal that would have vested in the Federation's representative council final authority to determine with which union a newly formed local should affiliate, in the event of conflict.

This congress also witnessed a further development toward centralization of authority. Faced with growing organization among employers, particularly within the new Norwegian Employers' Association, the national unions ceded to the secretariat of the Federation the right to declare sympathetic strikes, and to assume direct leadership over disputes in which more than one national union was involved. There were dissents, the Laborers' Union in particular maintaining the position that the secretariat should not be permitted to intervene in strike situations unless the unions concerned gave their consent, but the majority still feared the employers more than a possible loss of autonomy.

During the following year the Metalworkers' Union and the Typographical Workers' Union, which up to then had refused to join the Federation, finally decided to affiliate. According to Ousland,

what served most to secure unification of all the trade unions in Norway was the solidarity displayed by employers . . . The Federation of Labor and the Metalworkers' Union received an expression of that during the metal trades lockout in Bergen in 1903, and still more sharply in the molders' controversy of 1904, where the employers

threatened to lock out the other workers, and the Metalworkers'
Union sought to mediate. The strife that occurred among the unions
convinced the majority that practical and effective leadership of the
important disputes could be secured only after all unions were within
the Federation.[10]

But the entrance of these two unions raised again the problems
that had prevented their initial affiliation.

The 1905 congress of the Federation was the first in which the
majority of organized labor was represented: 15,600 out of perhaps 20,000 organized workers were affiliated through their national unions. It proved to be most controversial, and a split was
narrowly avoided. The center of the strife was a proposal submitted by the Metalworkers' Union that would have effected the
following changes: (a) altered the current system of direct representation of local unions at the congress to representation by national unions only, thus strengthening the latter vis-à-vis the
former; (b) increased the minimum levies that national unions
were required to make for their strike funds; (c) provided a fixed
payment to the Federation strike fund in place of its current
power to levy special assessments for this purpose; (d) reduced
the Federation's standard strike benefit payment from eight to
six kroner per week; (e) given the national union greater freedom in calling and conducting strikes. All these points had as their
purpose the further integration and strengthening of the national
unions at the expense both of their own constituent locals and of
the Federation of Labor.

The conflict that ensued was essentially one between the larger
and the smaller unions. A. Pedersen, a painter and the Federation's
chairman since 1901, agreed on behalf of the latter group to the
first three points in the proposal, but rejected vehemently the suggestion of a reduction in the Federation's strike benefit payments,
and any decentralization of authority in wage movements. He
pointed out that

through centralization it has proved possible to secure plan and per-
spective in wage disputes, and if now unions are permitted to engage
in disputes without Federation approval, we will no longer be masters
of the situation. And to reduce the strike benefits to six kroner will

[10] Ousland, p. 157.

put all the small unions, to say nothing of individual locals, in so difficult a position that the significance of the Federation for them will be illusory.[11]

By a vote of eighty-four to fifty-nine the resolution was referred to a committee with instructions that a new proposal be submitted to the next congress.

Fundamentally, these difficulties arose out of a transition in the basic character of the Federation of Labor. Originally, it had been a strict parent to small national and local unions, and it was understandable that a considerable degree of authority should be entrusted to it. But with the entrance of the metal and typographical unions, the growth of the Laborers' Union, and the increasing maturity of even the smaller national unions, the Federation assumed more the form of a coöperative of sovereign national unions. As a result of this development, the issues that had aroused so much controversy in 1905 were settled amicably two years later. Per capita payments to the Federation were raised to enable the accumulation of a central strike fund without resort to special assessments, and at the same time Federation strike benefit payments were reduced from eight to seven kroner per week — an action that had more symbolic than practical significance. The larger unions received another sop to their desire for greater autonomy through a constitutional change giving them greater freedom in minor wage disputes.

With the resolution of these problems, the Federation of Labor emerged from its infancy. The form of organization based on national as opposed to regional unions proved durable, despite a later syndicalist attack upon it. The authority entrusted to the central leadership of the Federation in the beginning left a permanent mark upon the organization, although the eventual distribution of power entailed retrogression from the original degree of centralization.

From the unity congress of 1905 to 1913, the power and influence of the Federation of Labor increased steadily. Table 1, which portrays the growth of Federation membership together with related factors of unemployment, labor disputes, and wages,[12] indi-

---

[11] Ousland, p. 162.

[12] There is unfortunately no consistent employment series going back for any considerable length of time.

TABLE 1

Trade Union Membership, Unemployment, Labor Disputes, and Real Wages in Norway, 1899–1947

Year	(1) Membership in the Norwegian Federation of Labor[a]	(2) Percentage of Unemployment among Trade Union Members[b]	(3) Man-days of Work Lost due to Labor Disputes (*in thousands*)[c]	(4) Average Daily Real Wages of Men (*1913 = 100*)[d]	(5) (*1914 = 100*)[e]	(6) (*1938 = 100*)[f]
1899	1,600	...	...	92.1		(53.7)
1900	4,800	...	...	84.2		(49.1)
1901	7,600	...	...	88.8		(51.8)
1902	7,500	...	...	93.4		(54.5)
1903	7,900	4.0	130	93.9		(54.7)
1904	9,000	3.9	45	92.5		(53.9)
1905	15,600	4.4	30	89.2		(52.0)
1906	25,300	3.2	95	86.1		(50.2)
1907	39,000	2.5	340	85.4		(49.8)
1908	47,200	3.0	380	89.7		(52.3)
1909	43,200	5.0	185	96.0		(56.0)
1910	45,900	2.9	179	96.8		(56.4)
1911	53,100	1.9	1,115	98.7		(57.5)
1912	60,800	1.3	446	94.7		(55.2)
1913	63,800	1.6	122	100.0		(58.3)
1914	67,600	2.4	156	101.5	100.0	(59.2)
1915	78,000	2.1	315		90.0	(53.3)
1916	78,900	0.8	720		82.4	(48.8)
1917	93,900	0.9	109		77.3	(45.8)
1918	107,500	1.4	187		89.9	(53.2)
1919	143,900	1.6	623		...	...
1920	142,600	2.3	1,199		130.3	77.2
1921	96,000	17.6	3,584			83.1
1922	83,600	17.1	91			75.9
1923	85,600	10.6	796			74.5
1924	92,800	8.5	5,152			73.3
1925	95,900	13.2	667			77.6
1926	93,100	24.3	2,205			85.3
1927	94,200	25.4	1,374			81.1
1928	106,900	19.1	364			82.6
1929	127,000	15.4	197			86.6
1930	139,600	16.6	240			89.1
1931	144,600	22.3	7,586			91.4
1932	153,400	30.8	394			95.3
1933	157,500	33.4	364			95.2
1934	172,500	30.7	235			95.2
1935	214,600	25.3	168			93.1
1936	268,300	18.8	396			93.7

TABLE 1 (Continued)

Year	(1) Membership in the Norwegian Federation of Labor[a]	(2) Percentage of Unemployment among Trade Union Members[b]	(3) Man-days of Work Lost due to Labor Disputes (*in thousands*)[c]	(4) Average Daily Real Wages of Men	(5)	(6)
				(*1913* = *100*)[d]	(*1914* = *100*)[e]	(*1938* = *100*)[f]
1937......	316,000	20.0	1,014			94.0
1938......	340,000	22.0	567			100.0
1939......	352,500	18.3	860			100.3
1940......	306,500[g]	23.1	...			93.0
1941......	293,800[g]	11.4	...			81.9
1942......	289,000[g]	...	...			78.5
1943......	280,500[g]	...	...			78.1
1944......	...	...	...			78.0
1945......	338,600	...	...			91.5
1946......	398,000	3.6	...			96.9
1947......	442,000	3.1	...			...

[a] *Statistical Yearbooks for Norway*, Central Statistical Bureau, for years 1899–1939; official figures of the Norwegian Federation of Labor for years 1940–1947.
[b] *Statistical Yearbooks for Norway*, based upon reports of the Norwegian Federation of Labor.
[c] *Statistical Yearbooks for Norway*.
[d] Calculated from "Average Daily Wages of Persons Subject to Workmen's Compensation," *Industristatistik*, Central Statistical Bureau, 1908 and 1915, deflated by "Farmands Wholesale Price Index," *Statistisk Oversikter*, 1926, Central Statistical Bureau. This series may be somewhat unstable because of the use of an index of wholesale prices, the only consistent price series available for the period, to deflate the wage series.
[e] Calculated from Morten Tuveng, "Arbeidsløshet," *Sak og Samfunn*, No. 13 (Bergen, 1946), p. 24.
[f] Calculated from wage and cost of living series in *Statistical Yearbooks for Norway*. The figures in parentheses were linked into Column 6 from Columns 4 and 5 to suggest real wage movements from 1899 to 1918. The reader is cautioned that they were calculated in a different manner from the data for 1920 and subsequent years.
[g] Excludes members of the Seamen's Union outside Norway.

cates that during this period membership rose fourfold. It was an era, as has already been noted, of rapid capital expansion. Employment remained at a relatively high level, and the general trend of real wages was in an upward direction.[13]

[13] The real wage data for the years 1899 to 1914 shown in Table 1 afford only a rough approximation of the actual movement of real wages during the period, since no cost of living index is available, and it was necessary to deflate the wage series (none too good for this period) by an unofficial index of wholesale prices. But the general conclusion appears to be correct: "During the years 1900 to 1905, when money wages remained about the same, prices sank; thus real wages rose — for workers who were not unemployed. Real wages probably increased more in this period than during the following decade. But from 1905 to 1914 they increased somewhat; on the average wages rose a little more quickly than prices." Edvard Bull, *Arbeiderklassen i Norsk Historie* (Oslo, 1947), p. 199.

The authority of the national unions and of the Federation of Labor was strengthened by the improvement of their financial status. They could now afford paid officials, serving to promote centralization. At the same time there were separatist tendencies at work, eventually resulting in division of the heterogeneous Laborers' Union along industrial lines. In 1912, for example, a group of local unions in the paper mills, dissatisfied with a collective agreement ratified by the Laborers' leadership against the majority will of the paper workers, seceded and formed an independent organization. For two years there was bitter rivalry between the two organizations, the Federation of Labor refusing to recognize the new union. A referendum conducted among the paper workers in both organizations resulted in 2,064 votes for the Paper Workers' Union to 2,063 for the Laborers' Union, and settled nothing. Finally in 1914 the Laborers' Union, faced with other problems, agreed to give the 7,000 paper workers their independence, thereby reducing its own membership to 17,000.[14]

A new element began to enter the trade union movement at this time, the workers engaged in the construction of Norway's expanding physical plant. Recruited largely from farms, on which their families had lived for generations, they were plunged directly into the boom-town maelstrom of the new industrial communities. They were enrolled originally in the Laborers' Union, but divided along individual lines as they settled down to man the newly constructed industries. These newcomers to industry lacked the roots and the craft traditions of the older trade unionists, and tended to become impatient with the gradualist methods of the Federation leadership.

MARTIN TRANMAEL AND THE RISE OF THE TRADE UNION OPPOSITION

The internal history of the Federation of Labor during the next decade can be written largely in terms of the struggle between the craftsmen and this new group of unskilled workers, between social democracy and semi-syndicalism. The struggle revolved around Martin Tranmael, the most controversial figure in Norwegian labor history.

Born in 1879, Tranmael was raised on a farm in the vicinity

[14] See *Opmarsjen: De Norske Papirarbeideres Historie 1878–1938* (Oslo, 1938), pp. 42, 49.

of Trondheim. Like many of his contemporaries, he was forced by economic circumstances to leave the farm and seek his livelihood in the city. At the age of fifteen he was apprenticed to a painter, and after qualifying as a journeyman, he joined the Trondheim Painters' Union. In 1899, at the age of twenty, he became a member of the editorial board of *Ny Tid,* a new socialist paper established by the Coöperating Trade Unions of Trondheim.

The next year Tranmael went to the United States for the purpose of studying the young American socialist movement. He spent a year with his two brothers, who had earlier joined the stream of Norwegian migrants to the United States and were living in Superior, Wisconsin. After learning English, Tranmael departed for Los Angeles, where he supported himself by working at his trade and made his first contact with the American labor movement through membership in the A. F. of L. Brotherhood of Painters.[15]

Tranmael spent four years in the United States, with a one-year break in 1902, when he returned to Norway. He lived and worked in many sections of the country, and had an opportunity to observe the development of the American labor movement at one of its most critical junctures. His ideas on the social functions of trade unionism began to take shape at this time. In 1904 he wrote back to his paper in Trondheim:

[American trade unions] are not as permanent and systematic as would be desirable. The Socialists have always urged the necessity of a more durable organizational form with political as well as economic aims. Trade unions, as representatives of social groups, will still be necessary under socialism. They will then be administrative departments rather than, as now, defense and fighting organizations.[16]

After attending the constitutional convention of the Industrial Workers of the World at Chicago in 1905, Tranmael noted:

This new organization is surely the most streamlined and modern movement we have thus far had in the economic sphere. Therefore,

[15] Among the things that impressed Tranmael unfavorably from his American trade union experience was the relatively high initiation fee ($25) that he was obliged to pay, and the difficulty of transferring from one union to another in shifting jobs.

[16] Aksel Zachariassen, *Martin Tranmael* (Oslo, 1939), p. 50.

its principles and methods are of international significance. It is broad enough to include all workers, but correct in not housing reactionaries and compromising misleaders in its midst.[17]

It will be recalled that at its inception the I.W.W. was not entirely a syndicalist movement. Not only were there strong advocates of political action among socialists, but the original participant groups included pure and simple trade unionists. Not until the split of 1908 did the organization fall under the domination of the syndicalists.

Tranmael was particularly attracted to the newly united Socialist Party, and was for a time a member of its Scandinavian section. He was struck by the importance which American radicals attached to individual freedom and to personal initiative on the part of the ordinary worker. The frontier spirit, so significant in I.W.W. ideology, found its way back to Norway through Martin Tranmael, and helped impart to the Norwegian labor movement the peculiar flavor which distinguishes it from the labor movements of its Scandinavian neighbors.

It would be an oversimplification to assert that Tranmael's American experience alone shaped the ideology of the Trade Union Opposition which he led. French syndicalism, with its emphasis upon mass economic action and rejection of parliamentarianism, had an important effect upon Norwegian labor thinking. This influence came in through Sweden, when thousands of young Swedish workers, black-listed after an unsuccessful general strike in 1909, migrated to Norway.

But the anarcho-syndicalists were never able to convince Tranmael that political action was futile. While he had seen the lack of political power of the American workers, and absorbed from them the lesson of direct economic action, parliamentary democracy was already a reality in Norway, and the first results of labor's political efforts were becoming apparent. Tranmael's early synthesis represented a compromise between social democracy and syndicalism: chief reliance was to be placed upon trade unions as the means of waging the class struggle, and upon mass economic action, but political action was by no means to be considered an illusory dissipation of working class energies nor an activity of purely secondary importance.

[17] Zachariassen, p. 50.

It was not fortuitous that the old trade union leadership and the Opposition should come to grips over union structure. The former represented primarily the craft unions, while the sinews of the Opposition lay among the unskilled, assembled mainly in the Laborers' Union. It was part of syndicalist theory that craft division weakened the labor movement, and rendered difficult the employment of the general strike.

Tranmael and his followers made their first bid for power at the 1910 congress of the Federation of Labor, in the form of a resolution favoring reorganization of the Federation of Labor along industrial lines. It was defeated by a wide margin, and Tranmael returned to Trondheim to lay the organizational groundwork for a more serious effort. Under his leadership the Trondheim Central Trades Council was formed, and at a meeting in 1911 formulated the now famous "Trondheim Resolution":

The Meeting declares that the labor situation demands that organizational work be based on a more revolutionary foundation than has hitherto been the case. The following program is proposed:

A. 1. Binding written collective agreements to be abolished.
   2. Union insurance funds to be discontinued.
B. As trade union weapons, chief reliance to be placed on the following:
   1. The strike.
   2. The sympathetic strike.
   3. The boycott.
   4. Obstruction.
   5. Sabotage.
   6. Coöperation.
C. Organizational structure to be altered as follows:
   1. The Federation of Labor to be the central, common organization.
   2. It shall be divided into departments corresponding to the basic industries and the industrial unions.
   3. There shall be established local central trades councils which, inter alia, will take over local organizational work and concern themselves with the determination of working conditions.[18]

This program is notable for its uncompromising rejection of collective bargaining, to the extent of advocating refusal to con-

[18] Halvard Lange, *Fagorganisasjonens Historie i Norge* (Oslo, 1934), p. 65.

clude collective agreements. (The term *coöperation* as used in the
resolution refers to coöperation among unions, not employer-employee coöperation.) It also constituted a challenge to the national
unions, since it proposed a considerable shift of power to city central trades councils, in accord with the syndicalist precept of regional industrial organizations of workers. A blow was struck at
the "gradualists" by the proposal to abolish union insurance funds.

Conditions created by World War I were favorable to Opposition propaganda. Workers faced a steeply rising cost of living,[19]
and shortages of staple foodstuffs hit the lowest income groups
particularly hard. The Opposition charged that the practice of
entering into collective agreements had the effect of preventing
necessary wage adjustments, and was unsuitable for a period of
rapidly changing prices. The first open clash occurred in 1915
when the government introduced legislation providing for compulsory mediation of labor disputes. The Opposition favored a
general protest strike, but the Federation leadership was opposed.
A year later, the government forced through the parliament a system of compulsory arbitration of interest disputes,[20] and this time
a general strike of a week's duration was authorized by the Federation. Tranmael condemned termination of the strike, proposing
instead that it be continued in defiance of law until the unions
secured satisfactory settlements of current disputes through direct
bargaining rather than compulsory arbitration.

Mass demonstrations took place against the high cost of living,
and the Federation took the lead in urging the government to
stabilize prices. In 1917 the government met those demands part
way, and the leadership of the Federation of Labor refused to accede to the Opposition program of a general strike to force full
compliance. This illustrated again the basic differences between
the two factions within the labor movement: the older unionists,
who had built up a large trade union apparatus, were unwilling
to take the risks involved in direct action of a political nature,
while the new element was impatient with pure trade union
methods and was looking for short cuts to the goal of higher living
standards.

[19] On the basis of the official index, the cost of living tripled from 1914 to
1920.
[20] See Chapter V.

The Opposition also promoted the formation of worker councils, modeled after those created in Russia following the communist revolution, under the slogan: "Seizure of all provisions and their sale at such reasonable prices that the entire population can afford them." The councils took up the cudgels for the eight-hour day, which was achieved by legislation in 1919. The Opposition captured the Labor Party in 1918 largely through the leverage of the worker council movement, although the failure of the "old guard" to take more vigorous action in pressing for control of the inflation was the basic economic factor in creating discontent.[21]

The Opposition pressed for its program with increasing vigor within the Federation of Labor. At the regular congress of 1916 and the extraordinary congress of 1917, its proposals were rejected by large majorities, but the tide was running in its favor. The most significant development was the increase in trade union membership from 80,000 at the time of the 1917 congress to 148,-500 at the 1920 congress.[22] The chief beneficiary of the flood of new entrants was the Laborers' Union, a stronghold of the Opposition, which numbered 25 per cent of the total Federation membership in 1920.[23] Other unions that increased their membership during this period were the Metal, Paper, Sawmill, and Transport Workers' Unions, all of which contained large numbers of unskilled and semiskilled workers who had fared particularly badly in the inflation and were attracted by the radicalism of the Opposition.

What had happened, in fact, was the transformation of the Federation of Labor, in a decade, from an organization representing primarily the craftsmen, with their long tradition of stable trade unionism and their belief in economic progress through the slow process of collective bargaining, into an organization in

[21] The worker council movement declined after 1918, partly as a result of the improved supply situation, partly because many of its functions were taken over by the Labor Party.

[22] These figures do not tally with the trade union membership data in Table 1 because the congresses were held in the early portion of the year, whereas the figures in Table 1 relate to the end of the year.

[23] Since representation at the Federation congress is roughly proportional to dues paying membership (see below, p. 34), the Opposition commanded an important bloc of delegates.

which the workers who manned the new industrial establishments constituted a majority. By 1920 the Typographical Workers' Union, originally one of the two most important members of the Federation of Labor, included but 2 per cent of the Federation's members. The older craft unions and their leaders resisted Tranmael and his followers, but they were overwhelmed.

The 1920 congress reversed the verdict of the earlier assemblies, and gave its approval to the Opposition proposals. By a large majority it accepted in principle the notion of a shift of power from national unions to central trades councils established on a regional basis, and set up a committee with instructions to prepare a concrete plan along these lines for presentation to the next congress. The formation of central trades councils was made obligatory "in each district, large town, or city," and the constitution was amended to give such organizations direct though limited representation in the Federation congress. The congress further declared itself for reorganization of the national unions along strictly industrial lines, and decreed specifically that the craft unions in the building trades were to join in a single industrial union.

Drastic as it was, this program was a good deal milder than the original Trondheim Resolution with which Tranmael had begun his trade union career. Sabotage was never employed as a trade union weapon, and the negotiation of collective agreements continued as the primary trade union function. Trade union benefit funds continued to operate as before. Even the modified form of the program to which the 1920 congress gave its assent met stubborn resistance among the workers when its practical implications for the future of the national unions, which had been built up laboriously and often at great sacrifice, became clear.

Edvard Bull attributes the failure of the Opposition program to materialize to the fact that it had been formulated in a period marked generally by a rising cyclical curve, while the downturn that commenced in 1920 cast another light upon it.[24] When prices began to fall, binding, long term collective agreements became desirable. Sabotage could not be effective in a period of high unemployment, with employers able to resort to the lockout. There was no incentive to eliminate union benefit funds when they were needed more than ever. And there was danger in forcing through

[24] Bull, p. 315.

changes in organizational form when union membership was falling.

REORGANIZATION

Between the congress of 1920, in which the Trade Union Opposition had triumphed, and the congress of 1923, at which the new leadership had hoped to see the concrete realization of its plans for reconstructing the trade union movement, there was a serious economic recession. The downturn came late in 1920, and the trade unions found their bargaining power seriously reduced. The percentage of unemployment among organized workers (Table 1), which had averaged 2.3 in 1920, rose to 17.6 in 1921. Trade union membership suffered a precipitous decline, from 142,600 to 96,000, the first real setback the Federation of Labor had ever experienced.

To make matters worse, from the point of view of the former Opposition, the unions that lost the most were the ones that had experienced the greatest increases during the war years, and within which the loyal adherents of the radical wing were to be found. Whereas the Transport Workers' Union lost half its members, and the Metalworkers' Union some 40 per cent, the Typographical Union retained over 90 per cent of its 1920 membership, and the Locomotive Engineers' Union, 95 per cent.

The position of the radicals was also weakened by serious ideological division within the political labor movement. The tide of European revolution was ebbing, and workers had to reckon with the hard fact that the existing social order was not going to be replaced by socialism in the foreseeable future. Loss of a general strike in 1921 made the Federation leadership cautious, and induced labor's parliamentary representatives to vote in favor of compulsory arbitration legislation in 1922, an unprecedented step.[25]

The committee set up by the 1920 congress to plan the reorganization of trade union structure moved slowly. National unions were requested to poll their members on the various questions involved, and by 1923 all had conducted referendums. Seventeen unions with a total of 41,200 members declared themselves against the structural changes recommended by the 1920 congress; fifteen unions with a membership of 46,700 favored the changes in gen-

[25] See Chapter V.

eral, though there was a good deal of doubt over the regionaliza-
tion project. In every union the vote was close, and it was evident
that a deep division of opinion existed within the ranks of labor.

Compromise was imperative if organic unity of the labor movement was to be preserved. It was proposed that the Opposition
program be put into effect only to the extent of establishing industrial national unions through amalgamations of crafts, and that
the central trades councils be retained merely as auxiliary organizational units. The syndicalists agreed to give up the ideal of regional syndicates, while the craftsmen ceded a measure of their
autonomy. This compromise was accepted by the congress, and
it was resolved that such reorganization should be accomplished
by June 30, 1924.

But again it proved easier to adopt a resolution than to effectuate it. As Ousland noted:

The difficulties arose from the tradition, concord, and good com-
radeship within each union. As with a living organism, any division
constituted a painful operation — an amputation of members who had
grown together and had become one flesh and blood. That things proceeded so readily within the Laborers' Union was due to the fact that
there was already a division along internal lines, so that fission was
more a matter of giving independence to those groups than real par-
tition.[26]

The fact that a good deal was actually achieved attests to the
firmness of purpose of the new trade union leadership. The various
building trades were assembled into a single Building Workers'
Union, with the exception of the bricklayers, who preferred to
withdraw from the Federation of Labor. (The Bricklayers' Union
was later readmitted on its own terms, as an independent organization.) Industrial unions of furniture workers, municipal workers, chemical, food, and textile workers were formed, transforming the Federation of Labor into an association of predominantly
industrial unions. But many crafts — bakers, molders, bookbinders,
locomotive engineers, postal workers — remained adamant in refusing to merge in these industrial combines.

The question of structure continued acutely to engage the atten-

[26] Ousland, p. 245.

tion of trade unionists, and every trade union congress debated the matter at length. The Federation of Labor adopted the following resolution at its 1934 congress:

The Congress charges those unions which should merge into industry or branch organizations immediately to commence negotiations concerning the practical accomplishment of merger. The negotiations, which shall be led by the secretariat, must be concluded before the end of 1936 . . . If agreement between unions is not attained the matter shall be submitted to the next congress for settlement.

Until merger can be effectuated the unions are obligated to establish cartels to handle all matters of common interest.[27]

By the next congress, in 1938, however, little progress had been realized. The chairman of one of the largest unions gave vent to the growing opinion that "there is beginning to be something trivial in these constant discussions of industrial union structure . . . At the congresses we take very radical positions, but when we go back to the workshops things are often different." [28] The chairman of the Federation of Labor was forced to admit that little could be expected in the way of additional fundamental structural alteration, and the congress restricted itself to the passage of a resolution calling upon the member unions to negotiate further, and established an organization committee to reconcile differences.[29] From the tenor of the debate at the next congress, that held in 1946, it was apparent that the proponents of craft autonomy, if anything, had gathered strength as a consequence of their wartime experiences.[30]

The result of this twenty-year debate was that by 1947, although 80 per cent of Federation membership was concentrated in twelve industrial unions, there were forty-one affiliated national unions in all, many of them insignificant in size. The Jewelry Workers, Harbor Pilots, Lithographers, Musicians, and Customs Officers had less than one thousand members each, while the Meat

[27] Arbeidernes Faglige Landsorganisasjon, *Kongressen 1934, Dagsorden og Protokoll,* p. 427.
[28] Arbeidernes Faglige Landsorganisasjon, *Kongressen 1938, Protokoll,* p. 54.
[29] *Ibid.,* p. 199.
[30] Arbeidernes Faglige Landsorganisasjon, *Protokoll over Kongressen 1946,* pp. 82–109.

Workers, Locomotive Engineers, Skin and Leather Workers, Stone Workers, and Tobacco Workers claimed membership of between one and two thousand each.

REORIENTATION AND RECENT GROWTH

It required a decade for the Federation of Labor to recover from the postwar debacle. The nineteen-twenties were marked by constant strife in the labor market that eventually exhausted both labor and management. Not until 1931 was there the beginning of more stable collective bargaining relationships, and with it greater stability within the trade union movement.

Despite the fact that the percentage of unemployed trade union workers remained high (see Table 1), union membership increased steadily, reaching 215,000 in 1935. This represented an extensive as well as an intensive gain in organization. While trade union membership in manufacturing increased by 75 per cent, organization among workers in lumbering, agriculture, road work, and transportation increased by 195 per cent. There was a similar development among white collar workers in both public and private employment. The base of the labor movement had been broadened considerably.

The growth of trade union conservatism during this period was to a certain extent a function of the cessation of rural-urban migration. After 1920 there were no longer annual increments to the industrial labor force from the farms, because of urban unemployment. The industrial labor force ceased to grow. Labor took root and acquired skills; the ferment of a migratory labor force no longer existed. Trade unions trained their sights once more upon small advances in wages and working conditions, and left revolutionary doctrine to intellectuals.

By 1939, Federation of Labor membership stood at an all-time high of 352,500. Amicable relationships had been established between the Federation and the Employers' Association, which were formalized in the conclusion of a master agreement between the two organizations. The Labor government that had come into power in 1935, hampered by its lack of an absolute parliamentary majority, and forced to rely for support upon the Agrarian Party, was engaged in carrying out an economic policy reminiscent of the New Deal, that had little in common with the revolutionary slogans of 1920.[31] It appeared that Norwegian labor was approaching the tempo of social change exemplified by the Swedish and Danish movements, under their venerable leaders, Per Albin Hansson and Theodore Stauning.

OCCUPATION AND LIBERATION

The German *Wehrmacht* invaded Norway on April 9, 1940, and an era came to an end. Many trade unionists were not immediately aware of the implications for democratic trade unionism of fascist rule. While some individuals followed the Norwegian government into exile, and others remained behind or returned to Norway in order to resist the invaders, there were not a few responsible union officials who believed in the possibility of a *modus vivendi* with the Germans.[32] Adding to the confusion was the "neutrality" policy of the Communist Party before June 1941, and the machinations of a small trade union group, including a former chairman of the Federation of Labor, which eventually went into the camp of *Nasjonal Samling,* the Quisling party.[33]

The first overt attack upon trade union independence came in September 1940, when the chairman and vice-chairman of the Federation were replaced by order of the occupying power, and all national unions were forced to declare their loyalty to the new leadership. Thereafter the situation deteriorated rapidly. Resistance began to take shape, culminating in a protest strike in September 1941, which ended with the execution of two leading trade unionists, Hansteen and Wickstrøm. Quislings were given leading positions in the national administration of the Federation of Labor, and lower officials were obliged to continue at their posts under threat of dire punishment.

A trade union underground organization was established to

[31] For a brief description in English of the policies of the Labor government during this period see Finn Moe, *Does Norwegian Labor Seek the Middle Way?* (New York: League for Industrial Democracy Pamphlet Series, 1937).

[32] See for example "Formannens samtale med Reichskommissar Terboven" in *Fagorganisasjonens Arbeidsprogram 1941,* in which Terboven is quoted as saying that the occupation authorities intended in no way to infringe upon trade union sovereignty.

[33] The events of this period were related at the first postwar congress of the Federation of Labor. See Arbeidernes Faglige Landsorganisasjon, *Protokoll over Kongressen, 1946,* pp. 136–212, 260–276, 356–371.

checkmate German efforts to use the trade unions for their purposes. This movement was directed by a committee functioning within Norway, though general policy was determined by secretariats in Stockholm and London.[34] An illegal newspaper, *Fri Fagbevegelse* (*Free Trade Union Movement*), was published regularly and attained a respectable circulation. A substantial portion of the funds needed to finance these activities was provided by agencies of the American Federation of Labor and the Congress of Industrial Organizations.

Although membership declined during the occupation, the structural framework of the trade unions remained intact. The Quisling officials dissipated union funds, but they were never sufficiently in control to realize their aim of a labor front on the German model. When liberation came in May 1945, the trade union leaders who returned from exile or concentration camps were able to step into going concerns and begin operations almost immediately. The transition from war to peace was accomplished with astonishing lack of friction. There was far less turbulence than after World War I, despite five years of oppression. Strikes were few in number, and mass demonstrations, and worker councils conspicuously absent.

Nonetheless, there were some deep-seated changes within the labor movement. There was a new urgency to achieve the social goals for which the trade unions had always stood in theory. In contrast to the years after World War I, this time worker protest was translated into concrete organizational effort, and harnessed to the task of building a political and economic machine capable of achieving fundamental social reform. The fact that this upsurge was disciplined made it all the more effective.

By 1947 the Federation of Labor had risen to a position of preëminence in Norwegian society. With well over 400,000 members, and with former trade union officials installed as prime minister and foreign minister, and occupying a majority of the other cabinet posts, the Federation faced the problem of charting its future course largely unhampered by considerations of employer

[34] The Stockholm committee was led by Martin Tranmael, while the London committee, which worked closely with the government-in-exile, was under the chairmanship of Konrad Nordahl, the constitutional chairman of the Federation of Labor. The Seamen's Union, which worked effectively in the service of the Allies, also had its headquarters in London.

bargaining power. The main lines of its decisions are reserved for later discussion.[35]

EXTENT OF TRADE UNION ORGANIZATION

The degree to which Norwegian labor may be considered organized depends in the first instance upon where the perimeter of the organizable portion of the labor force is drawn. Accepting as a first approximation manufacturing, mining, the skilled trades, transportation, construction, and lumbering, it was estimated that there were 438,000 workers in this group on December 31, 1946.[36] Trade union membership was approximately 400,000, which meant that the percentage of organization was slightly over 90.

This indicates a very high degree of organization within a limited industrial sphere.[37] In manufacturing establishments of any size, complete unionization is not unusual, although the union shop as such is not found in establishments affiliated with the Employers' Association. The railroads, which are government owned, are 100 per cent organized, as are other forms of inland transport, shipping, and the construction industry. Only among handicraft workers, in lumbering and in smaller manufacturing establishments are there any significant groups of unorganized workers.

However, the Norwegian trade unions have not yet approached the upper limits of their expansion. The National Planning Budget for 1947 estimates a total labor force of 1,356,000 persons during 1947, with Federation membership standing at 450,000 at the close of the year. The estimated labor force includes all the gainfully employed, many of whom are not eligible for union membership — farm owners, fishermen, entrepreneurs, supervisors. But there is still a large number of persons, mainly among white collar workers in industry and commerce, civil servants, and agricultural laborers that the Federation of Labor is anxious to bring

[35] See Chapter XIII.

[36] Finans- og tolldepartementet, *St. meld. nr. 10*, 1947 (Om nasjonalbudsjettet 1947), pp. 8, 9.

[37] The chairman of the Federation of Labor indicated to the writer in August 1947 that, in his opinion, 90 per cent of "industrial" workers were currently members of the Federation, or 85 per cent if white collar workers in industry were included.

into its ranks. Total insured employment in 1946 was about 500,-
000,[38] so that even under this concept of the organizable labor
force there is still considerable room for trade union expansion.

TRADE UNION STRUCTURE

The Norwegian Federation of Labor is more highly centralized
than its Swedish[39] or Danish counterpart. The Federation itself
enjoys an unusual degree of authority in the determination of
trade union policy, while the national unions in turn supervise
their local affiliates to a much greater extent than is true of the
American labor movement.

The governing body of the Federation of Labor is its congress,
which holds regular meetings triennially. Four-fifths of the three
hundred delegates to the Congress are elected by the national
unions, and one-fifth by the central trades councils. Specific representation in each instance is based upon dues-paying membership.
The congress is the final arbiter of general trade union policy,
disputes between affiliates, and controversies over the interpretation of constitutional provisions and bylaws.

Between regular meetings of the congress, the highest legislative authority of the Federation of Labor is the representative
council (*representantskapet*). Every national union and central
trades council elects one member of the representative council; in
addition, each national union with more than 3000 members is
entitled to a second representative, plus another representative for
each additional 4000 members up to a maximum of four representatives. Of 101 representatives at the 1945 representative council meeting, 50 were appointed by 13 national unions, while 20
represented central trades councils. The council meets once a year,
as a rule, although it may be convened at more frequent intervals.

Executive authority is vested in the secretariat, a body of fifteen, four of whom are full-time officials (the chairman, vice-
chairman, secretary, and treasurer). The secretariat meets every
week, and holds additional meetings whenever necessary. Members of the secretariat are elected for three-year terms by the con-

[38] Agricultural workers, domestic servants and self-employed persons are
normally not covered by the social insurance system in Norway.

[39] Recent constitutional changes have resulted in a greater degree of centralization within the Swedish Federation of Labor, but probably not to the
same extent as in Norway.

gress; the four paid officials must receive an absolute majority, while the remaining members can be elected by plurality vote. No more than two members of the secretariat may be from the same national union, and in practice it is usual to find that each of the larger unions is represented by a single member.

The administrative functions of the Federation are executed by the elected officers with the assistance of statistical, legal, auditing, and economic departments. A monthly journal, *Fri Fagbevegelse* (published before 1940 as *Landsorganisasjons Meddelelseblad*), publicizes the official views of the Federation.

National union structure parallels that of the Federation, in general. Each union has its national convention (*landsmøtet*), meeting almost invariably triennially, its representative council, and its executive council or secretariat. The number of paid executives and the size of the administrative staff vary from union to union.

The basic unit of organization is the local union (*fagforening*), chartered by the national union[40] where there is sufficient membership (usually a minimum of ten). Local union jurisdiction depends largely on the structure of the industry and the historical development of the national union. In the industrial unions covering factory industry, such as the Chemical Workers' Union, there is one local for each large establishment. The Laborers' and Lumber and Agricultural Workers' Unions tend to set up locals on an area basis. The Building Workers' Union, created by a merger of crafts in 1923, has preserved craft separatism to the extent of having separate locals in each of the larger cities, for example, in Oslo, where there are locals of painters, plumbers, iron workers, and so on.

Many union constitutions forbid the creation of more than one local in the same area. The Textile Workers' Union is typical in this respect:

There can only be one local at each factory. Nor can there be more than one local union in the same city or locality without permission of the executive council and the existing local.[41]

[40] There are now no local unions affiliated directly with the Federation of Labor, although in the first decade of the Federation's existence this was quite common. During the depression of 1929–1935 locals of unemployed workers were chartered by the central trades councils, but they have all since disappeared.

[41] *Lover* for Norsk Tekstilarbeiderforbund, Section 2(2).

In the unions that are amalgams of distinct crafts, this is usually modified to prohibit more than one local for each craft in a locality. Where there is no local, workers desiring to join the union are generally permitted to affiliate directly with the national office until such time as a local can be formed.[42]

There were 3986 local unions in Norway on December 31, 1946. The average size was subject to considerable variation. The Laborers' Union averaged only 50 members per local, the Lumber and Agricultural Workers, 35. The local unions covering manufacturing were substantially larger — 250 members in the Metalworkers' Union, 150 in the Chemical Workers' Union, and 140 in the Paper Workers' Union.[43] Few local unions are able to afford paid officials, although there is nothing to prevent it if the local is sufficiently large and wealthy.

Local union affairs are directed by an executive committee, the size of which depends upon the number of members in the local. This committee, as well as the local officers, is selected by the local's general meeting (*generalforsamling*), held regularly once or twice a year. Other membership meetings, primarily educational in purpose, are held at more frequent intervals.

Larger locals may be broken down into smaller administrative units. The Metalworkers' Union, for example, has established clubs (*klubber*), covering all union members within a plant, and groups (*grupper*), consisting of the members within a department of the plant. Both are headed by elected steering committees, and are important cogs in the machinery for enforcing agreements and adjusting grievances. The Oslo Stone, Earth, and Cement Workers' Local Union, an affiliate of the Building Workers, has its 5000 members divided into groups for cement layers, explosives workers, asphalt layers, excavation machine operators, and lathers.

Some coördination of trade union activities is secured through twenty central trades councils, so long a bone of contention. Formally, their current functions are:

To defend and advance the trade, economic, and social interests of the workers; to seek the establishment of local unions where possible,

[42] The Metalworkers' Union permits the formation of clubs (*klubber*), administered from the national office, until there are enough members for a local.

[43] These figures are calculated from Arbeidernes Faglige Landsorganisasjon, *Beretning 1945,* pp. 124–125.

to aid in disputes, to conduct local propaganda and educational work, and in general to improve the organization to the greatest possible extent.[44]

When the Trade Union Opposition failed in its efforts to establish these councils as basic organizational units, they tended to gravitate toward the fringe rather than the center of authority. The larger national unions continued to resent trades council interference, and often set up parallel organs at the local level. Resistance on the part of the trades council officialdom to recent proposals that would subject them to stricter Federation control produced a sharp admonition by a special committee established by the Federation to consider their future functions:

The local central trades council was never meant to be an independent organization. It has always been a source of assistance to the Federation of Labor and the national unions in the districts. It has had definite tasks, but could never make decisions that imposed obligations upon the membership without Federation approval. It has never had the right to enter into binding agreements for national unions and the Federation of Labor without the approval of these organizations. Nor has it had authority to terminate agreements . . . Since the central trades council is financed by the Federation of Labor, the Committee on Organization deems it reasonable that the Federation's representative council shall have the deciding word with respect to the selection of council officials . . .[45]

The central trades councils are thus limited increasingly to educational and welfare activities, and to the promotion of collaboration between local unions on noneconomic questions. Some national unions with more than one local within an area require these locals to form joint boards (*industrigruppene*), which are more directly concerned with trade policy questions of mutual concern. In sum, the tendency toward further centralization of authority in the national unions, almost an inevitable concomitant of the rise of industrial unionism, has been accentuated at the expense of the local central trades councils, which are beginning to show signs of atrophy.

[44] Arbeidernes Faglige Landsorganisasjon, *Lover,* 1946, Section 4.
[45] *Organisasjonskomiteens Instilling Angående De Faglige Samorganisasjoner* (mimeographed, 1947).

When it became apparent that complete industrial organization could not be achieved, the Federation of Labor authorized the creation of departments (*karteller*) to promote industrial coöperation. Such departments exist for the metal trades, the graphic trades, and the food, shoe and leather, and woodworking industries. They act in an advisory capacity only, and never supplant the national union in collective bargaining.

TRADE UNION GOVERNMENT

The considerable central authority enjoyed by the Federation of Labor is based upon constitutional provisions buttressed by financial sanctions. These relate primarily to control over collective bargaining procedure and strikes.

All wage demands not purely of local significance require the approval of the secretariat of the representative council of the Federation of Labor before they may be submitted to an employer or an association of employers. The national union may cut itself off from the important financial assistance that the Federation can render unless this is done. Although the Federation may not be represented at the initial bargaining conferences between the parties, it is generally represented at the mediation proceedings that almost invariably precede the conclusion of important agreements. If several national unions are involved in a single proceeding, a not unusual occurrence, the Federation's representatives conduct the negotiations for the union side.

In the event of a strike situation, if the national union concerned desires financial assistance from the Federation, or "if it can be assumed that the dispute in its further ramifications will be broadened or will affect other unions," approval of the Federation's secretariat must be obtained in advance of calling the strike. Should more than one union be involved in the strike, the secretariat assumes active leadership; once this occurs, none of the participating unions may agree to a settlement without the approval of the secretariat. The latter may also take over control of a strike when it tends seriously to affect the livelihood of workers outside the union directly involved. When leadership thus devolves upon the secretariat, it is empowered to take whatever steps are necessary to bring the conflict to a successful conclusion, including the ordering of sympathetic strikes by other affiliates. In a real sense, the secretariat of the Federation is the general staff of the labor movement. In the event of disagreement between the secretariat and a national union with respect to the terms of a proposed settlement, the representative council is the final arbiter.

When a national union has followed the prescribed procedure with respect to securing secretariat approval, it is entitled to the payment of strike benefits from the Federation strike fund amounting to one krone per day for each striking member, beginning with the eighth day of the strike. Payments may be somewhat greater if more than 40 per cent of a national union membership is out on strike at one time. Failure of a national union to comply with the constitutional provisions outlined above may lead to withdrawal of the right to receive strike assistance, at the discretion of the secretariat.

National union control of the activities of local unions is often more stringent. The constitutional provisions of the Building Workers' Union are fairly typical:

No work stoppage may take place until the matter has been laid before the national executive committee. If the national union's economic support is desired, its advance approval must be secured. Excepted are disputes arising out of employer harassment and wage cuts.

If a local union seeks to secure a change in labor conditions, the matter must first be prepared by the local concerned, then sent to the national union through the local joint board. If the contract concerns several locals, the matter must be handled first by the local joint board, and thereafter by the local unions . . .

In order that the national union may secure economic assistance from the Federation of Labor in furthering a local's wage demands, they must be sent to the national executive committee two months before they are presented to the employer . . .

A strike may not be called off before the interested local has recommended its termination. A local may not call off a strike unless the approval of the national executive committee is secured.[46]

Some national unions impose even stricter conditions upon their locals. The Printers require that if a dispute arises between a local union and its employer, the national executive conduct an immediate investigation and either seek to negotiate directly with the employer, or approve a work stoppage.[47] The Clothing Work-

[46] Norsk Bygningsarbeiderforbund, *Lover,* 1946, Section 15.
[47] Norsk Centralforening for Boktrykkere, *Lover,* 1945, Section 40.

ers' constitution provides that where "the national executive committee, on economic or other grounds, cannot acquiesce in a stoppage proposed by a local, or cannot permit the local to seek realization of desired reforms, the local must bow to its decision." [48] Under the rules of the Transport Workers' Union, the national executive takes over negotiations where the local cannot or will not bargain with the employer; thereafter the local is precluded from negotiating. Here, too, the "national executive committee has the right to determine that the framing of demands or the inception of work stoppages by a local union shall be postponed, if it finds that the time for such action is not appropriate." [49] The national executive committee of the Sawmill Workers' Union "has the right in all cases to negotiate directly with the employer on behalf of its members, or designate who shall negotiate." [50] The Tobacco Workers' Union prohibits strikes entirely unless the national union has sufficient funds to meet stipulated strike benefit payments for two weeks, and denies to local unions the right to enter into collective agreements covering working time or wages, or to submit to mediation or arbitration, without permission of the national executive. It may be said that in general the local union enjoys little independence, and often not even nominal control of wage policy.

The penalty for violation of these ordinances is usually the withholding of strike benefits, a serious matter in view of the fact that few local unions have their own strike funds. In extreme cases, refusal of a local to abide by constitutional regulations or decisions of the national executive is punishable by revocation of its charter, in which event all its property reverts to the national union.

The amount of strike benefits payable to striking workers by the national union, through the local, is stipulated in all union constitutions. There is considerable variation among the unions, depending largely upon the average earnings in the industry concerned. The Bricklayers' Union pays 6 kroner per day to married workers, with an additional 0.75 krone for each dependent child, up to a maximum of 10.50 kroner per day. The Woodworkers' Union, on the other hand, pays only 3.50 kroner a day plus 0.40

[48] *Lover* for Norsk Beklaedningsarbeiderforbund, 1945, Section 11.
[49] *Lover* for Norsk Transportarbeiderforbund, 1947, Section 8.
[50] *Lover* for Norsk Høvleriarbeiderforbund, 1945, Section 17.

krone for each child under fifteen years of age. Most other unions lie between these extremes. There is generally a waiting period of one week before strike benefits become payable.

Membership dues are relatively high, although their failure in recent years to keep pace with wage and price increases has reduced their incidence. Each national union is required by Federation constitution to put aside an annual sum of 20 kroner per member into a strike fund. Otherwise, the national union is free to determine its dues requirements, which again vary with the relative affluence of the members, as well as the types of benefit funds set up by the unions. A metalworker pays 2 kroner per week (about 1¾ per cent of his earnings in 1946) to his local union, which remits 1.50 kroner to the national union and retains 0.50 krone. The national union places 0.25 krone into a life insurance fund, pays 0.30 krone to the Federation in per capita dues, and retains the balance for its administrative purposes.[51] The Printers' national union collects 4.10 kroner per week from each member (local unions are permitted to require additional dues payments for their own purposes, a common provision, although often coupled with prescribed maximum or minimum amounts), of which 2.20 kroner go to an assistance fund, covering burial, life insurance, and old age and invalidity grants, 0.10 krone to a sickness insurance fund, and the remainder to the national treasury.

Under certain conditions, members may be excused from dues payments. In the Building Workers' Union, those who become unemployed, or are engaged in a strike or lockout, are excused automatically. Moreover, the national executive committee, upon recommendation of a local, may free from dues payments, wholly or partially, members who receive substandard wages as a result of age, sickness, or disability, and have held membership continuously for twenty years.

Union dues are collected directly from the members by the shop

[51] Most unions divide members into two or more classes for purposes of dues and benefit payments. The Metalworkers, for example, distinguish between Class A members, who earn at least the minimum journeyman rate, and Class B members, who receive less than that rate. The former pay dues of two kroner, the latter one krone per week. A Class A member is entitled to 20 kroner per week in strike benefits, a Class B member, to 15 kroner. In all other respects, however, Class A and Class B members enjoy equal rights within the union.

steward, and never checked off by the employer. The Norwegian unions consider that the administrative expense involved in direct collection is outweighed by the advantages of the constant contact between union officials and workers thus afforded. The worker is given an opportunity to voice any grievances he may have at the time he makes his financial contribution to the union. Besides, union dues are regarded as purely an internal union affair, with which employers are not properly concerned.

There is attached to the Federation of Labor an audit department, the director of which is elected directly by the congress. The books of each national union are audited at least once a month by the audit department, while a check is made of cash and securities on hand twice a year. Local unions may also avail themselves of the department's services, on request. Every union is required to elect a control committee empowered to determine whether union funds are being disbursed in accordance with the rules of the organization. As a further check, national union constitutions limit the amount of cash that may be held by national and local treasuries (5000 and 500 kroner respectively are common limitations), and some require bonding of officials empowered to handle money.

Initiation fees are customary, although they are relatively low, averaging from three to five kroner. Fines ranging up to one hundred kroner may be levied against members found guilty of violating union rules. In serious cases, a member may be expelled from the union, but generally only after a two-thirds vote of the local union, with the right of appeal to the national executive committee and the convention.

The use of the referendum is widespread in the Norwegian trade union movement. The Laborers' Union constitution provides, for example, that a referendum is required on all "important questions" that arise between conventions. As a matter of custom, this includes all new or renewed collective agreements, so that practically all Norwegian labor contracts, after they have been agreed to by the union negotiating committee, must be submitted to a vote of the workers covered. Local membership strike votes are a universal requirement, and some unions (the Clothing Workers, among others), require a two-thirds majority before any work stoppages may legally be initiated. Such matters as changes in dues or benefit payments and agreements with other unions are also customarily submitted to referendum vote.

TRADE UNION CENTRALIZATION

The degree to which authority over collective bargaining and the determination of wages and other conditions of labor is centralized in the Federation of Labor, as distinct from its national union affiliates, has already been remarked. The extent of this authority is made clear by a directive recently addressed by the Federation to its affiliates, the purpose of which was to prevent inflationary wage demands:

In conformance with Section 10(2) of the constitution of the Federation of Labor, the representative council declares that no collective agreement may be terminated, and no wage demand raised, unless the approval of the secretariat is secured in advance.[52]

In this respect the Norwegian labor movement stands in sharp contrast to trade unionism in the United States, where in both branches of the labor movement the national unions enjoy almost complete autonomy on purely trade questions. There is a similar distinction between the Norwegian Federation of Labor and its Scandinavian neighbors, particularly Denmark, where the trade union centers control the policies of their affiliates to a very limited extent.

To understand Norwegian trade union centralism, it is necessary to consider the early history of the Federation of Labor. It will be recalled that the trade unions which ratified the Federation constitution in 1899 were small and weak, and that the only two contemporary national unions possessed of real stability, the Metalworkers and Typographers, remained outside the Federation for six years after its formation. The charter members of the Federation felt themselves inadequate, as atomistic units, to deal with their employers, and federation for them was a quest for security.

In the circumstances, the affiliated unions not only did not ob-

[52] *Arbeiderbladet,* November 20, 1947. The section of the constitution cited reads: "If a national union desires the economic support of the Federation of Labor in furthering a demand or resisting an attack, or if a dispute may be expected to spread or involve other unions, the approval of the secretariat shall be secured in advance. If the situation involves a demand made by the workers for an improvement in wage and working conditions, the secretariat must be notified at least one month before the demand is raised or the collective agreement terminated."

ject to, but welcomed Federation intervention in their dealings with employers. This was particularly true of economic support during strikes, the significance of which appears from the fact that during the first ten years of its existence the Federation paid out in strike benefits 811,731 kroner (over $200,000 in current purchasing power), a sizable sum for an organization the membership of which did not exceed 50,000 during that period.

If the Federation of Labor had come into existence ten years later, when the national unions had become more firmly established and were less prone to cede their independence of action, the subsequent history of the Federation might have been different. As it was, by the end of ten years, under the constitution and in practice, the centralized authority of the Federation had become institutionalized.[53] Recalcitrant individual unions have since challenged the authority of the Federation on specific issues, but on the whole its decisions have been accepted loyally.

Initially, the principal disciplinary weapon of the Federation was its central strike fund. The original Federation strike benefit scale of eight kroner per week (reduced to seven kroner in 1907 to conciliate the larger unions) often constituted the entire amount that a striking worker might receive, since most of the unions had only small reserves of their own. The threat to withhold benefit payments was thus sufficient to quell an incipient rebellion.

The importance of this means of enforcing compliance with Federation decisions has diminished with the decrease in the Federation's relative share of total benefit payments. As the national unions became more affluent and raised their scale of benefit payments, the seven kroner per week that the Federation continued to pay became a less significant factor in their calculations. At the present time few national unions are financially dependent on the Federation.

It is not unlikely that the development of national unions would have presaged decentralization of authority had it not been for two closely related phenomena, the growth of worker class consciousness and the close relationship of the political labor movement to the trade unions. The first of these was a partial antidote to the occupational particularism that seems to prevail wherever workers organize voluntarily. It was not an entirely effective an-

[53] "Centralization was clearly one of the most important tendencies within the trade union movement in the period before World War I." Bull, p. 205.

tidote, as evidenced by numerous examples of stubborn resistance on the part of workers to the loss of their craft identity.[54] Nevertheless, the strong class consciousness shaped by a tradition of syndicalism and Marxian socialism undoubtedly had the effect of creating closer identification between the Federation of Labor and the average Norwegian worker than is generally true in other countries.

The Labor Party has also constituted a unifying force, except for a period after World War I when it was rent into three parts by ideological dissension.[55] With minor exceptions the trade union leadership has been closely identified with the Labor Party, preventing schisms on political objectives. There is thus a dual allegiance to the concept of a unified working class that has helped to prevent the growth of craft consciousness.

Two additional observations are pertinent in accounting for the success of trade union centralism in Norway. In the first place, the central power was always used with moderation. Rarely has any union been compelled to accept conditions displeasing to the majority of its members, and in the few instances in which compulsion was employed, the Federation was almost invariably obliged to reverse itself later. Persuasion rather than force has been the keynote of Federation policy.

Finally, the relatively small scale of Norwegian trade unionism has been conducive to central policy making. The entire Federation of Labor, after all, has fewer members than many individual national unions in the United States. While the industrial pattern of Norway is by no means simple, and Norwegian trade union problems in no sense uncomplicated, there is not that tremendous size and diversity of conditions that would render comparable centralization within the American labor movement pragmatically dubious.

However one may account for the strong tradition of trade union centralism, the fact that it exists is of the utmost signifi-

---

[54] For example, the Bricklayers' Union, despite a tradition of radicalism — it was the only national union with a communist leadership after World War II — refused to join the newly formed amalgamation of building trades in 1923, preferring to disaffiliate from the Federation of Labor. The Molders have always refused to merge with the large industrial union in their industry, and the same is true of the Locomotive Engineers.

[55] See Chapter III.

cance for the experiment in economic planning that the contemporary labor movement of Norway is conducting. This is considered in a later chapter.[56]

RESTRICTIONS ON MEMBERSHIP

Monopolistic tendencies were rare within the Norwegian labor movement before 1931. With depression and mass unemployment, however, some unions attempted to protect the jobs of their members by the introduction of strict seniority in hiring and discharge. Others tried to bar the doors absolutely to new entrants.[57] To stop this, the secretariat of the Federation sent a circular to all unions ordering discontinuance of the closed union.[58] Despite the unequivocal terms of this order, the practice continued.

A rising tide of complaint led to the adoption of a comprehensive resolution on the problem by the 1934 congress of the Federation of Labor. It merits full quotation, since in effect it represented a Federation-wide bill of rights for individual union members:

1. All organizations affiliated with the Federation of Labor are enjoined not to prevent workers from seeking or taking specified work. The only condition that may be set is that the work concerned be carried out under the conditions stipulated by the Federation of Labor and national unions concerned.
2. All workers who are in employment or who are offered work have the right to trade union membership through the local union having jurisdiction over their place of work. Excepted from this requirement are only those workers who have not acted loyally, or acted against decisions of the Federation of Labor or the national unions.
3. No local union has the right to deny transfer of membership from other local or national unions. Local or national unions may not deny a member's right to withdraw for the purpose of joining another local or national union. The condition precedent for transfer of membership is that the individual concerned has secured employment within the jurisdiction of the local union into which he desires to transfer.
4. A determination not to work together with unorganized workers

---

[56] Chapter XIII.
[57] For specific examples, see Socialdepartementet, *Ot. prp. nr. 71*, 1933, pp. 53–58.
[58] Arbeidernes Faglige Landsorganisasjon, *Kongressen 1934, Dagsorden og Protokoll*, p. 152.

when the latter wish to organize *is forbidden* unless the workers concerned have not acted loyally, or acted against decisions of the Federation of Labor or the national unions. Controversies shall be decided finally by the secretariat.

5. Contract provisions calling for the exclusive employment of members of a particular local or national union must not be employed to prevent workers belonging to other unions from seeking or taking work . . .

6. A union that desires seniority rules through contractual provisions must secure the permission of the secretariat before putting forth such demands. These rules must not be practiced in conflict with the present regulations.

7. With respect to rules concerning apprentices there shall be a reasonable relationship between the number of apprentices and journeymen. Contractual provisions desired must be submitted to the secretariat for approval in advance of presentation to the employer.[59]

It was reported to the 1938 congress that the new regulations had received general respect, a circumstance that was facilitated by increasing employment opportunities. Local unions of unskilled workers in the building industry complained that the new rules were too strict, and proposed that they be amended to permit "a reasonable relationship between employment possibilities and work applicants" in trades not protected by craft rules. This was voted down by the congress, after an acrid debate.[60]

JURISDICTIONAL DISPUTES

Although in Norway the jurisdictional dispute has never attained the intensity of bitterness that characterizes it in the United States, it has been a source of friction between national unions, particularly during depression years.[61] Work stoppages over jurisdiction have been rare, however. It is asserted that there have not been more than five true jurisdictional strikes in Norwegian history.[62]

[59] Arbeidernes Faglige Landsorganisasjon, *Kongressen 1934, Dagsorden og Protokoll*, pp. 749–750.

[60] Arbeidernes Faglige Landsorganisasjon, *Kongressen 1938, Protokoll*, pp. 377–390.

[61] See Socialdepartementet, *Ot. prp. nr. 71*, 1933, pp. 53–58.

[62] Interview with Gunnar Ousland, July 19, 1947.

The structural reorganization of the Norwegian labor movement undertaken in 1920 created a number of jurisdictional questions that the unions concerned were not able to settle by direct
negotiation. The precise jurisdictional boundaries of the Woodworkers' Union and the Building Workers' Union were hazy
under the respective charter definitions; the Textile and Clothing
unions disputed the right to organize hosiery workers; there was
some doubt whether road workers belonged to the Laborers' Union or should go into the Municipal Workers' Union; and the
Teamsters were engaged in a perennial dispute with industrial
unions over the proprietorship of truck drivers attached to factories.

In an attempt to grapple with the problem, the Federation of
Labor in 1931 created a disputes committee of seven members to
hear jurisdictional disputes and recommend solutions, subject to
appeal to the secretariat. It was provided that if the secretariat
could not reach agreement on appeal from the disputes committee,
it could name an arbitration board which would be empowered to
render a final and binding decision. Only when a decision of the
arbitration board could result in the exclusion of a union from
membership in the Federation was appeal to the representative
council possible.

A set of rules was promulgated for the guidance of the disputes
committee:

A. As soon as possible the committee shall draw up dividing lines be-
    tween the jurisdictions of individual unions.
B. The committee and the secretariat shall ensure that no union enters
    into an agreement with an employer covering workers where there
    are already contracts for the same type of employment, held by
    another union, unless the union holding such prior contracts is
    notified in advance. The interested union and the secretariat must
    be agreed upon the conditions provided in the new agreement. No
    agreements may be entered into which jeopardize the wage condi-
    tions of other unions.
C. Where there is a jurisdictional dispute over particular work, or-
    ganized workers who are referred to that work by a labor ex-
    change pursuant to its customary rules shall have the right to
    accept that work regardless of the union to which they belong, if
    labor conditions are in order and existing agreements in related

trades or industries are not debased thereby, and if the workers follow the Federation rules governing transfer of membership.[63]

From 1931 to 1934, fifty cases were handled by the disputes committee and the secretariat, and in only three instances did the unions concerned refuse to abide by the decisions, which were referred to the representative council of the Federation for enforcement. Nevertheless, not only was the 1934 congress of the Federation obliged to devote a major part of its time to this problem, but there were many unions that objected to continuance of the existing machinery. The Building Workers' Union appealed to the congress to review an award of jurisdiction over plumbers employed in a municipal gasworks to the Municipal Workers' Union, and proposed that in the future jurisdictional disputes be settled by boards consisting of two representatives of each of the disputing unions and an impartial chairman appointed by the secretariat.[64] This was supported by the Transport Workers' Union, whose representative declared that since the disputes committee did not include persons familiar with each local situation, "it had made horrible decisions." [65] The congress, however, upheld the decisions made by its subordinate bodies and refused to discard the disputes machinery.

In 1938 again jurisdictional disputes occupied a prominent place on the agenda of the congress. Despite considerable opposition, several long-standing controversies that had presumably been settled by the representative council were carried to the floor of the congress, and in at least one case decided by the congress. To forestall renewed attempts to establish an alternative system of adjudication, the secretariat revealed that it had established rules for the processing of disputes requiring direct negotiation between the parties prior to submission to the disputes committee, and providing for more exhaustive investigation by the disputes committee. By adopting the following resolution, the congress strengthened the secretariat in its role as final arbiter:

[63] Arbeidernes Faglige Landsorganisasjon, *Kongressen 1931, Dagsorden og Protokoll*, p. 399.

[64] Arbeidernes Faglige Landsorganisasjon, *Kongressen 1934, Dagsorden og Protokoll*, pp. 16–18.

[65] *Ibid.*, p. 576.

The congress declares that final determination shall be with the secretariat, either through direct decision or by naming a compulsory arbitration board. Decisions shall be binding and only in exceptional circumstances may they be appealed to the representative council. The congress has given the secretariat an absolute mandate to make binding decisions that must be respected by all parties.[66]

At the 1946 congress of the Federation, a combination of full employment and the presence of other pressing business relegated the jurisdictional problem to a secondary position for the first time in two decades. All outstanding disputes were referred to an organization committee of fifteen members with instructions to make appropriate recommendations to the representative council.[67] It seemed hardly dignified to argue over jurisdiction in the light of events during the occupation, and of labor's new political responsibilities.

Back of the various congress resolutions stood the power of the Federation to enforce its awards by expelling a recalcitrant member. On the other hand, a union could withdraw from the Federation if it refused to accept a decision, although a year's notice of withdrawal was required. But such contingencies have been few in number. The Electricians, the Locomotive Engineers, and the Bricklayers were out of the Federation for varying periods over attempts to interfere with their autonomy and jurisdictions, but were eventually reinstated on their own terms.

Jurisdictional controversy has not been a centripetal force within the Norwegian trade union movement largely because of class consciousness among workers. Jurisdiction was often defended tooth and nail within the labor movement, but insistence on craft jurisdiction to the extent of withdrawal from the Federation of Labor, as happened so often in the history of the American labor movement, was considered almost morally improper. A campaign of expansion at the expense of other trade unions would be entirely alien to Norwegian union mentality. It is in this ideology, rather than in formal machinery or sanctions, that the basis of Norwegian success in dealing with one of the most troublesome aspects of contemporary trade unionism must be sought.

[66] Arbeidernes Faglige Landsorganisasjon, *Kongressen 1938, Protokoll*, p. 289.

[67] Arbeidernes Faglige Landsorganisasjon, *Protokoll over Kongressen, 1946*, p. 325.

TRADE UNION DEMOCRACY

Despite their strongly centralized character, the Norwegian Federation of Labor and its affiliated organizations are democratic institutions. This conclusion is based upon personal observation of conventions and membership meetings, as well as upon examination and analysis of relevant documentary material. Some supporting facts may be adduced, classified in accordance with the scheme employed by Professor Slichter in an essay on American trade union democracy.[68]

1. Admission requirements. The principal restrictions on admission to membership in Norwegian trade unions are those which deny entrance to members of fascist political parties, a Federation requirement, and to persons who employ others. The Transport Workers' Union denies membership to owners of more than one automobile or truck; independent contractors are not accepted into the Building Workers' Union. Trade union members who go into business for themselves are generally permitted to retain their union cards if they so desire, but only as "passive" members, without the right to attend union meetings or to vote.

Employment in the trade or industry covered by the union is a universal admission requirement. Many occupations in Norway entail lengthy apprenticeships, but helpers and apprentices as well as journeymen are generally admitted to full membership, although craft unions often limit the employment of apprentices to a specified ratio of skilled workers. The closing of unions to new members, a depression measure occasionally undertaken, was ordered discontinued by the Federation of Labor.

2. The making of trade union policy. Sessions of the congress, the highest legislative authority within national unions, are scheduled regularly in all union constitutions. With few exceptions conventions are triennial, and except during the period of German occupation, they have been held at the appointed time. Most union constitutions provide for the calling of extraordinary congresses through initiation by a specified number of locals, and approval by a majority vote of the entire membership. Membership participation in congress debate is high; most delegates express their views on at least one issue, as evidenced by the fact that it is com-

[68] Sumner H. Slichter, *The Challenge of Industrial Relations* (Ithaca, 1947), Chapter IV.

monly necessary to limit debate to fifty speakers as a time-saving measure.

The inclusion of an intermediate policy making body, the representative council, between the congress and the national executive committee, provides a check upon the activities of the latter. The representative council meets annually at regular sessions and is small enough so that extraordinary meetings can be called whenever important issues arise, either on the initiative of the executive committee or of a specified number of locals.

Although the national executive committee inevitably becomes important in policy making, all decisions of any import must be submitted either to the representative council or to a referendum vote *before* being put into effect. Thus, new collective agreements require majority ratification by a secret vote of the entire membership. This is not merely a paper requirement; agreements concluded tentatively by negotiating committees are frequently rejected by the membership, perhaps too frequently for sound collective bargaining.

3. *The execution of union policies.* The execution of all major union policy is vested in the national rather than local officers. There is also considerable national control over local labor disputes, enforceable through the withholding of strike benefits in the event of local defiance.

Turnover in trade union office is fairly high, however, particularly in the large industrial unions, so that centralization does not necessarily imply loss of local democratic rights. The Federation of Labor has had seven chairmen since its formation in 1899, and the majority of the national unions have changed their leadership more often. It is a rare convention that does not see a genuine contest in the election of officers. Political divisions within the ranks of labor are the most common sources of opposition slates.

The salaries of trade union officials are low, and loss of office does not entail a serious decline in income. The chairman of the Federation of Labor receives only 10,000 kroner per annum, plus a cost-of-living bonus (the highest salary in the trade union movement), and most trade unions pay their officers only what they could earn at their trades. Union officers customarily live in workers' housing developments, and maintain a worker standard of living. Before the war the vice-chairman of the Federation, who traveled constantly, was severely criticized for buying a suitcase at union expense. It is not customary for the union leader to attempt to equal employer living standards, and there is in fact little social intercourse between trade union officers and the wealthier social groups.

Financial peculations are rare, largely as the result of the centralized audit control system. Most unions provide regular financial reports to the membership. The Building Workers' Union, for example, requires that the treasurer submit to the executive committee his annual financial report, covering a calendar year, by February 15 of the next year, and that it be distributed to the local unions for consideration at membership meetings. He must also prepare a summary of his regular quarterly report to the executive committee for local distribution.

4. *The power of union chairmen.* The chairman, or president of a Norwegian trade union, has general supervisory power over subordinate officers and employees, but the appointment of union employees is almost universally a function of the executive committee rather than the union chairman. There is a feeling among some union officials that the executive committee has more power in this respect than is consistent with efficient administration. Some unions require that all vacancies be advertised in the union journal, and that employees be chosen from among the trade union members who apply, provided they possess the necessary qualifications.

Union chairmen may not suspend or revoke local charters, or discipline or discharge national or local officers; these powers are vested either in the national executive committee or the representative council, with right of appeal to the congress. Any national or local union officer, including the national chairman, may be suspended from office by the executive committee or the representative council if, in the customary phraseology, he proves to be "incompetent to fulfill his tasks, or shows a lack of judgment in the exercise of his authority." The suspended official has the right of appeal to the next congress.

Actually the Norwegian trade union chairman is possessed of exceedingly limited authority by American standards. Partly as a result of constitutional limitations upon the chairman's power, the national executive committee maintains genuine independence of thought and action, and if the chairman's views are to prevail, it must be by persuasion rather than by edict.

5. Voting rights of members. Despite a differentiation of members for purposes of dues and benefit payments, there are no distinctions among active trade union members with respect to the right to vote in union elections and referendums. The only limitations are those which deny the franchise to members not actively engaged at their trades[69] for the duration of the inactivity, and which require of new members that they serve an initiation period (usually about thirteen weeks) before they may vote. Sickness, unemployment, or invalidity do not deprive a member of the franchise despite the fact that the payment of dues may be waived.

6. Administration of discipline. The grounds for disciplinary action against members are stated in union constitutions. The principal basis for suspension or expulsion is disobedience of union orders during a labor dispute. The following provision, taken from the constitution of the Chemical Workers' Union, is found in most national union constitutions, almost word for word:

Members who during a strike or lockout resume work before the local executive committee has declared the dispute ended, or who take work at blockaded or boycotted establishments, shall be expelled from the union. They are required to repay to the union all sums they have received in benefit payments in the course of the previous year, calculated back from the date of exclusion.[70]

Then there are certain general disciplinary clauses, the following being typical:

Expulsion of a member may occur when the person concerned —
1. Does not abide by the constitution or by the lawful decrees or resolutions of the national executive committee, the local executive or membership meeting.
2. Works in a blockaded concern.
3. Does not abide by contract terms, assists in contract breaches or persuades others to break contract terms.
4. Acts in a nonfraternal fashion or against the interests of the union.
5. Secures assistance from the organization's funds under false cir-

[69] Most union constitutions provide, however, that if a member leaves his trade for another in which there is no appropriate union, he may remain directly affiliated with his original national union.

[70] *Lover* for Norsk Kjemisk Industriarbeiderforbund, 1946, Section 10.

cumstances, commits embezzlement or other illegal acts against the union.[71]

Although there is scope for abuse in this broad language, there have been few complaints. It is impossible to protect membership rights by specifying precisely the offenses that are punishable. All that can be hoped for is the absence of arbitrary and capricious grounds for exclusion in constitution and bylaws, together with effective appeals machinery.

Fundamentally, the political morality of a country is reflected in all its institutions, including its trade unions. The deeply ingrained democratic tradition of the Norwegian people would make it difficult to establish autocratic rule within the labor movement.

Working class solidarity also undoubtedly played an important role in molding the democratic character of Norwegian trade unionism. The strong *esprit de corps* among workers has been both a leveling and a unifying force. Trade union leaders are acutely conscious of their responsibilities as stewards of the labor movement, and rarely attempt to exploit their positions for personal or family gain. There is no leadership cult, moreover, and opposition to the current administration of a union carries no dangerous consequences. Individual leaders have their following, rarely cohesive enough to justify the appellation of "machine," but they are by no means accorded unquestioning obedience.

Again, however, Norwegian trade union democracy is partly a function of scale. The relatively small size of trade unions facilitates greater individual participation in union affairs, and inhibits the growth of barriers between leadership and rank and file. Representative national meetings can be summoned quickly and at small expense. To this might be added the facts of population homogeneity and the almost complete absence of illiteracy among workers.

[71] Norsk Litografisk og Kjemigrafisk Forbund, *Lover,* 1946, Section 10.

CHAPTER III

THE POLITICAL LABOR MOVEMENT

VERY EARLY in its history the Norwegian trade union movement became deeply involved in independent political action. For the greater part of their existence Norwegian unions maintained close ties with the Norwegian Labor Party (*Det Norske Arbeider-parti*), without in any way surrendering their autonomy on purely trade questions. However, many fundamental internal controversies, such as that concerning union structure, had their origins in conflicting political philosophies. In recent years the growth of labor's political power has given rise to problems that are beginning to overshadow trade union preoccupation with the issues involved in collective bargaining.

The Norwegian political labor movement has been strongly influenced by the ideological winds that blew from the Continent, and even from overseas. In its early days the Labor Party was a typical social-democratic movement, similar to the German socialism that left a more indelible imprint upon the labor movements of the other Scandinavian countries. In the first decade of the present century, however, younger and less settled workers came under the influence of syndicalist thought, imported from France by way of Sweden, and from the United States through the contact that Norwegian radicals had with the Industrial Workers of the World. Communism as preached by Lenin and his disciples also found some adherents in Norway.

The end of World War I saw the rise to power within the political labor movement of the radical wing, and the ousting of the older social-democratic leadership. The decision to affiliate the Norwegian Labor Party with the newly formed Comintern in 1921 resulted in the first internal split the party suffered, when the social democrats withdrew to form an independent organization. But it proved impossible to reconcile even left-wing socialism with communism for long, and within two years there was still

another internal fission, resulting in the withdrawal of the Labor
Party from the Comintern and the establishment of an independent communist party.

Practical unification of the political labor movement was
achieved once more in 1927, when the social democrats rejoined
the Labor Party, leaving only a dwindling communist party outside. The Labor Party grew rapidly thereafter, and since 1935
it has constituted the government of Norway, losing in the process
of expansion and acquisition of political power much of the doctrinaire radicalism that had characterized its early history. It
emerged from World War II strengthened numerically and morally, though at the same time a general leftward shift of public
opinion revived the moribund Communist Party of Norway and
created an opposition within the political labor movement for the
first time in two decades. Although the present state of European
politics makes prediction particularly hazardous, recent trends
point to the decline of Norwegian communism and the recapture
by the Labor Party of its prewar monopoly of the allegiance of
Norwegian workers.

ORIGINS AND EARLY DEVELOPMENT OF THE LABOR PARTY

Toward the close of the nineteenth century, when trade unionism first began to take permanent hold in Norway, most workers
gave their political support to the Liberal (*Venstre*) Party, largely
on the basis of its advocacy of a broader franchise. The more radical trade unionists, led by Christian Holtermann Knudsen, believed that the Liberal objectives were too limited, and that labor
needed a political party of its own if permanent gains were to be
achieved. In 1887 a small group of trade unions and independent
political associations convened to undertake the ambitious task of
filling this need. Out of this meeting came the United Norwegian
Labor Party, as it was then called, an organization destined to
become a permanent feature of Norwegian political life.

Although the moving spirits behind the new party were socialists, influenced by the German social-democratic Gotha program
of 1875,[1] imported into Norway by way of Denmark, the first

[1] One of the leading political organizations participating in the constitutional
convention of the Labor Party was the Social Democratic Union, organized by
Knudsen in 1885. Its program was strongly reminiscent of that adopted by the
Gotha Congress, a mélange of Marxism and the ideas of Lassalle.

program of the Labor Party was mildly reformist in character, calling for the right of universal franchise, protective labor legislation, and progressive income taxation, and committing the party to support of "just and authorized strikes." The founders intended the new organization to be a trade union as well as a political party, and they were anxious to attract the more conservative labor groups to their fold.

The most immediate political issue at the time was the demand for extension of the franchise. Until property qualifications for voting were removed the Labor Party could hardly hope for any real success at the polls. The achievement of the franchise for all men over the age of twenty-five years in 1898 therefore marked a significant milestone in the party's history, and with good reason was hailed as "the dawn of a new day." [2]

Another obstacle to Labor Party growth was the universal contemporary political preoccupation with Norwegian-Swedish relationships. A majority of the Labor Party favored dissolution of the union that then existed between the two countries so that this issue, which aroused strong nationalistic feeling among workers as well as other sections of the population and lent itself to easy exploitation by conservative political groups, could be replaced by the social questions thereby relegated to a secondary position. Some members, however, were of the opinion that a labor party should not succumb to nationalism, and that the correct course was to disregard the problem of union with Sweden entirely. The Bergen socialists, for example, advocated that the government "make an end to the present crisis in any dignified manner, so that the work for internal reform to the gain of the people can commence." [3] The dissolution of the union in 1905 was another fortunate occurrence for the young Labor Party.

From 1887 to 1905 the Labor Party was, in the words of one of its leaders, a "practical, political people's party." It was absorbed with "the demands of the day and the realizable possibilities, the tactics of relationships with the Liberal Party and the possibility of establishing contact with the masses." [4] Although the Labor Party acted to a certain extent as a clearing house for

[2] Halvdahn Koht and others, *Det Norske Arbeiderpartis Historie 1887–1937* (Oslo, 1937), I, 193.
[3] *Det Norske Arbeiderpartis Historie*, I, 170.
[4] Håkon Meyer, *Den politiske Arbeiderbevegelse i Norge* (Oslo, 1931), p. 44.

affiliated trade unions, any possibility that it would serve the dual functions of political and trade union organization was foreclosed by the founding of the Norwegian Federation of Labor.

Despite its concentration upon daily events the Labor Party did not abandon socialist principles. It joined the Second International, and faithfully included the basic tenets of social democracy in its annual statements of policy. But socialism was primarily a slogan and a vague hope for the future. It was thus easier to reconcile divergent opinion within the Labor Party on questions of doctrine than on more practical issues of current political debate.

LEFTWARD TRENDS

After 1905 the Labor Party began to make rapid strides. In 1906 it polled a vote of 43,000, compared with 23,000 in 1903. The total rose to 91,000 in 1909, and 128,500 in 1912. The general elections of 1906 resulted in the return of a ten-man Labor group to the Storting, which increased to twenty-three in 1912.

Within the party, opposition commenced to develop against the cautious reformism of the leadership. There was considerable agitation among the younger socialists for espousal of the general strike as a political weapon, in line with their belief that the Labor Party should place greater reliance on direct economic action than on parliamentarianism. The depth of the schism was revealed by an incident that occurred in 1912. The leader of this radical opposition, Martin Tranmael, declared at a public meeting that striking miners ought to quit work at the agreed instant regardless of the fact that some dynamite might remain in the bore holes, and indicated that such action might give would-be strikebreakers food for thought. The phrase "dynamite in the bore holes" became the subject of widespread controversy, and led to a violent attack on Tranmael as an advocate of assassination by Carl Jeppesen, one of the more conservative Labor Party leaders.

The ideological impulses behind the leftward trend in Norwegian political thought were several. The younger generation of the Labor Party included followers of Georges Sorel and the Swedish syndicalist Alfred Jensen, as well as the important group centered around Tranmael which was strongly influenced by the rise of the I.W.W. in the United States.[5] The left wing of the

[5] The official history of the Labor Party states: "Trammael had acquired the principal features of his theory of trade union and political policy during a two-

Second International, of which Lenin was an influential leader, also had its adherents in Norway. Nor was the Fabian socialism of Great Britain without influence on Norwegian intellectual thought.

Fortunately for the young party, no single dogma gained exclusive sway. The principal leaders of the radical opposition, while they were strongly attracted by the militant aspects of syndicalist doctrine, nevertheless retained a belief in the importance of parliamentary action. Growing success at the polls would have been sufficient to convince a much less practical man than Tranmael that so promising an avenue should not be abandoned in favor of a political chimera. Syndicalist terminology was a useful weapon with which to attack the job consciousness of trade unionism, but it was never elevated to the position of an independent force.[6]

Behind the shifting center of gravity within the Labor Party, and explaining the fact that for several decades the Norwegian labor movement was politically to the left of corresponding socialist organizations in northern and western Europe, was the same development that gave rise to the Trade Union Opposition within the Federation of Labor, namely, the social upheaval resulting from industrialization. The transformation of an agricultural into an industrial economy has been associated with political radicalism in many countries, and in this Norway was no exception. But what distinguished Norway's industrialization process from that of every other country of western Europe was the rapidity with which it occurred once the reliance upon coal as fuel was lessened by the development of hydroelectric power.

Within a decade, sparsely settled villages far from urban centers had become the sites of chemical plants, paper mills, and metal refineries. The labor force to build and operate the new factories was drawn primarily from the farms. Farm boys by the thousands left their homes, drawn by the lure of adventure and chance, and the fact that industry offered wages far above the income of small

year stay in the United States from the end of 1903 to just before Christmas 1905." *Det Norske Arbeiderpartis Historie,* II, 77.

[6] Mr. Tranmael told the writer that he had always been too busy with organizational work to concern himself overly with the theology of Marxism and related doctrines. During his stay in the United States, however, he attended Marxist study circles and gained an extensive knowledge of political thought that served him well in his crusading years.

farm owners and agricultural laborers. This migration meant that people were plucked from the most deeply rooted and traditional of all milieus, a Norwegian village. Many of them were "rollers," who wandered from one place of work to another, never marrying and never putting down roots.[7]

Descriptions of Norway during this period remind one of the contemporary mining towns and lumber camps in the United States.[8] Both were characterized by a boom-town atmosphere, a frontier spirit that did much to determine the nature of the respective labor movements. It was not fortuitous that the Norwegian syndicalists were so strongly attracted by the structure and methods of the I.W.W., nor that the philosophies of the two movements should have so much in common. The greater success of the Norwegian left wing opposition may perhaps be attributed to the fact that in Norway the new industrial workers constituted a much larger proportion of the nation's total labor force.

Despite this growth in the industrial labor force, the old leaders might have been able to defeat the left wing challengers, as they did in Denmark and Sweden, had it not been for the conjunction of rapid industrialization with the chaotic conditions resulting from World War I. The faith of even the skilled workers was shaken by the failure of the trade unions to act effectively in the inflationary situation. The new recruits to the labor movement, more adversely affected, were completely dissatisfied with parliamentarianism and the slowness of collective bargaining. The decisive importance of the events of the first war years may be seen from the fact that while the 1915 congress of the Labor Party unanimously reëlected Christian H. Knudsen and Ole O. Lian as chairman and vice-chairman, and defeated the Opposition candidate for general secretary by a vote of 205 to 155, the congress of 1918, by a margin of 159 to 126 votes, elected an entirely new

[7] Edvard Bull, *Arbeiderklassen i Norsk Historie,* pp. 220–21.

[8] "In the lumber camps of the Northwest, the hop fields of California, the fruit- and wheat-producing areas on both sides of the mountains, the Pacific Coast industry, and elsewhere, thousands of migratory workers — men divorced from the stabilizing influence of permanent employment connection, property ownership, home life, social status, and the conventional forms of approbation, men who saw no reason why they should feel indebted to the established order of things — were ready to fight capitalism with the first weapons at hand." Millis and Montgomery, *Organized Labor* (New York, 1945), p. 116.

set of officers, Kyrre Grep, Emil Stang, and Martin Tranmael, the leaders of the Opposition.

This development, peaceful enough in comparison with the wave of revolution that swept over Europe in the wake of war, marked the rise of a new generation within the labor movement. Knudsen and Lian had stood at the head of the Labor Party for many years, while the new leaders were men in their thirties. The difference in their outlook is clear from the conflicting resolutions presented to the 1918 congress of the Labor Party. The conservative resolution read as follows:

The socialist society shall be built upon majority opinion, expressed through universal suffrage for men and women alike . . . Social democracy cannot recognize any dictatorship by force either on the part of the upper class or the working class.

The Norwegian Labor Party will of course not deny itself the right to invoke the general strike or revolution in a struggle against undermining of majority opinion . . .

The Congress is of the opinion, however, that it cannot advise a general strike or revolutionary mass action to advance demands for cost of living compensation, or as a part of a military strike to achieve abolition of military forces. Such action can only harm the interests of the working class in the light of present day economic and political conditions . . .[9]

The radical resolution, which carried, committed the Labor Party to the following statement of principle:

As a revolutionary class warfare party, social democracy cannot recognize the right of the ruling class to exploit and suppress the working class, even if such exploitation and suppression are supported by a parliamentary majority.

The Norwegian Labor Party must therefore reserve the right to employ revolutionary mass action in the struggle for the economic liberation of the working class.

However, the Congress is of the opinion that the Norwegian Labor Party as a political party ought in the first instance to work for unification of the working class to capture political power through elections.

But the party cannot remain indifferent to the struggles being waged by other organizations of workers. This Congress thus views

[9] *Det Norske Arbeiderpartis Historie*, II, 192–193.

with gratification the organization of councils of workers and sol-diers.[10]

THE DECLINE OF REVOLUTIONARY SOCIALISM

This party congress of 1918 and the two ensuing years marked the peak of revolutionary socialism in Norway. One of the first fruits was a joint manifesto issued in 1919 by the Labor Party and the Federation of Labor in which for the first time the sociali-zation of industry, banks, and large scale trade was programmed at the head of labor's immediate demands. At the 1919 party con-gress Tranmael declared that "the working class must today be-come aware that revolution and dictatorship are absolutely neces-sary," [11] and the executive committee was authorized to declare an election boycott, a parliamentary strike, or even a general strike if election laws were not immediately reformed to give workers greater representation.

The 1919 congress of the Norwegian Labor Party also resolved to sever all ties with the Second (socialist) International. It was the only one of the large, western European social-democratic parties to join the Comintern; the other western European sec-tions were comprised of small groups of communists that broke away from the traditional labor parties. This made for difficulties in adjusting to the Comintern requirements, which were set forth in twenty-one conditions for affiliation, the so-called "Moscow Thesis."

In several important respects these conditions ran counter to the practices of the Labor Party and to the political philosophy of the new leadership. Labor Party membership was based on the collective affiliation of trade unions, while the Comintern wanted strictly controlled individual membership. The Tranmael group favored a federative structure for both trade unions and party, diametrically opposed to the "democratic centralism" that char-acterizes all communist organizations. The Comintern demanded that any individual who did not accept its decisions unhesitatingly was to be expelled from the Labor Party, whereas the leadership of the latter was eager to avert a break with the conservative trade

[10] *Det Norske Arbeiderpartis Historie,* II, 193. The final paragraph of this resolution referred to revolutionary bodies then being organized in Norway on the Russian model.

[11] *Det Norske Arbeiderpartis Historie,* II, 214.

unionists. The principle of armed revolt espoused by the Comintern conflicted with the deeply rooted pacifism of Norwegian labor. Comintern insistence that the trade unions be subordinated to the political party was a practical impossibility if unity of the trade union movement were to be maintained. Finally, the unequivocal Comintern denunciation of parliamentary action was unreal in a country in which participation in parliamentary life had netted the labor movement real gains.

The right wing social-democratic element within the Labor Party refused to remain with an organization affiliated with the Comintern, and withdrew early in 1921 to establish an independent Social Democratic Party. The Tranmael group accepted the Comintern conditions, with some reservations, though not without misgivings. "The deciding factor was that they still believed that the tide of revolution was rising, that the 'phase of civil war' was approaching, and they wanted plainly to demonstrate their revolutionary will and their sympathy with the Russian Revolution." [12]

The reservations, however, were important. The Labor Party indicated that it would continue the practice of collective trade union membership, but as a concession to the Comintern amended its constitution so that members of collectively affiliated local unions who belonged to other political organizations or who did not accept fully the Labor Party's decisions were to be specifically excepted from party membership. The Labor Party refused to condemn parliamentary participation without qualification, and reaffirmed its conviction that the party and the trade unions must remain independent of one another. However, the old pacifist line was abandoned, with the following declaration:

Experience indicates the improbability of voluntary self-disarmament by the ruling class. The working class must understand that the *bourgeoisie* will use force to hinder the freeing of the working class and must prepare itself accordingly.[13]

The attempt of the Norwegian Labor Party thus to assert its independence quickly resulted in a deterioration of its relations with the Comintern. The latter conceived itself as the general staff

[12] Bull, pp. 280–81.
[13] *Det Norske Arbeiderpartis Historie,* II, 257.

for world revolution, and no more than an army command can permit subordinate units to question its decisions could the Comintern permit its sections to deviate from the line marked out. Tranmael at one point committed the unpardonable sin of refusing an order to come to Moscow for a discussion of some of the outstanding differences between the two organizations. This, rather than differences of principle, was the problem to be solved. "In reality, the strife was over whether the revolutionary class struggle in Norway should be led by the Norwegian party or by the executive committee in Moscow." [14]

The 1922 congress of the Comintern established a Norwegian commission under the chairmanship of Nikolai Bukharin to bring about compliance with its edicts. But the Labor Party executive refused to accept the commission's findings "out of regard to the party's unity and development, and confidence and coöperation within the party, as well as to relationships with the trade unions." [15] When its national committee convened early in 1923, Karl Radek appeared as a representative of the Comintern, and under his persuasive ministrations the following compromise resolution was adopted:

The Norwegian Labor Party will remain in the Communist International as an independent section, and recognizes the decisions of the communist congress and executive committee. The Party will execute these decisions independently, but acknowledges the right and duty of the executive committee to supervise the individual party's execution of world congress and executive committee resolutions and directives.[16]

But for all its artful phrasing, this resolution could not be more than a temporary truce. The Comintern and the Norwegian Labor Party remained at odds over basic organizational and structural questions. All of these were raised anew at the Labor Party congress of 1923, to which the Comintern sent a strong delegation led by Bukharin. The party leadership presented the so-called "Christiania Proposal," emphasizing the party's autonomy in all internal decisions, its organizational democracy, and equality

[14] Bull, p. 288.
[15] Bull, p. 315.
[16] Meyer, p. 101.

with rather than dominance over the trade unions.[17] The Comintern representative submitted a resolution that urged the necessity of building the Labor Party into a closely knit and disciplined group capable of leading a revolution and establishing a dictatorship in the name of the working class. After days of intense debate the Christiania Proposal was adopted by the close vote of 94 to 92.

This new split within the Labor Party manifested itself in an increasingly bitter struggle for control. New demands that the party could or would not accept poured in from the Comintern — adoption of the slogan "worker's and farmer's government," the requirement that all Labor Party leaders be avowed atheists together with the initiation of an intense antireligious campaign, affiliation of the Federation of Labor with the Red International of Trade Unions. Tranmael wrote that the Labor Party was facing the most severe crisis in its existence: "Shall it be a great mass party which will realize the communist ideal, or a narrow sect whose members renounce the right to have an opinion, and who let themselves be led intellectually by a self-appointed priesthood?" [18]

Throughout this struggle the Comintern exhibited a persistent interest in the "Norwegian question" quite out of proportion to Norway's importance in the European scene. The Norwegian Labor Party, however, was one of the strongest sections within the Comintern, the only one in western Europe with a mass following. Because of this it was able openly to express a resentment that was felt in many other sections of the Comintern against the necessity of accepting literally Comintern decisions that were plainly at variance with existing circumstances. Thus for the Comintern it was much more than merely quelling a revolt within one of its sections; the issue went to the very root of the communist conception of organization and discipline. Making an exception for the Norwegians would have been incompatible with the automatic obedience that Moscow expected of its adherents.

The difficulties between the Comintern and the Norwegian Labor Party came to a head late in 1923, when a special Labor Party congress was presented with an ultimatum, delivered by the

[17] Det Norske Arbeiderpartis *Landsmøter 1912–1933, Beslutninger og resolusjoner* (Oslo, 1934), pp. 64–66.

[18] *Det Norske Arbeiderpartis Historie*, II, 352.

German communist Edwin Hörnle, calling upon the Norwegians to agree "not to adopt any resolution that conflicts with Comintern decisions." Against this Tranmael, together with Torp, Nygaards-vold, and Madsen, members of his group, proposed the following declaration:

The Norwegian Labor Party is firmly resolved to consider the questions that confront it in a judicious manner. It is the right and duty of the congress to determine the party's policies in Norway in accordance with the will of the membership. The executive committee [of the Comintern] demands that we renounce this right and duty; therefore the congress cannot accept the ultimatum.[19]

By a vote of 169 to 103 the congress adopted the resolution proposed by Tranmael, whereupon the Comintern representative declared that the majority had read itself out of the International, and extended recognition to a minority group which withdrew from the congress and established itself as the Norwegian Communist Party. At the close of 1923, Norway thus had three separate labor parties. In terms of parliamentary strength the Social Democratic Party had eight adherents, the Communist Party thirteen, and the original Labor Party fifteen. The general elections of 1924 revealed, however, that the Labor Party had retained the loyalty of the majority of the workers, since it returned twenty-four candidates to the Storting, compared with six for the Communists and eight for the Social Democrats.

Although it broke with the Comintern, the Labor Party remained in theory a revolutionary organization. Its 1925 program contained the following declarations:

The Norwegian Labor Party is a communist party, and regards as its primary task the organization of the working class, and through the class struggle to defend the day to day interests of the working class and to carry the struggle further until the working people are master of the means of production and free of capitalist exploitation . . .

The gains that the working class can secure within the framework of capitalism should not obscure the ultimate goal. The working class must not devote its efforts to the attainment of such gains alone, but must make every effort to secure power, and through the dictatorship of the proletariat create a socialist society.[20]

[19] *Det Norske Arbeiderpartis Historie*, II, 360.
[20] Det Norske Arbeiderparti, *Landsmøter*, pp. 93–94.

Nevertheless, with the troublesome question of international relations settled, the way was clear for reconciliation with the social democrats. The collapse of revolutionary movements throughout Europe brought home the realization that while "dictatorship of the proletariat" might be an attractive slogan, it had little real content in the current situation. On practical domestic issues there was little difference between the views of the Social Democratic and Labor parties; both were essentially individualistic and democratic, committed to independent trade unionism operating through collective bargaining. A negotiating committee established in 1926 had little difficulty in preparing a program acceptable to both groups, and unity was achieved in 1927, leaving outside the fold only the communists, who through desertions had already been reduced to a small and ineffectual sect.

LABOR'S RISE TO POWER

Consolidation marked a new phase in the history of the Norwegian Labor Party. In its first years it had been a reformist, parliamentary party, in the tradition of German social democracy. The growth of syndicalist and revolutionary socialist thought led the Labor Party part way along the path of postwar communism, but unable to reconcile the theory and practice of Bolshevism as propounded by the Russians with existing political realities in Norway, it drew back. After 1927, the rise of fascism in Germany, the economic crisis, and the sobering effect of political power served to modify earlier revolutionary leanings. The Norwegian Labor Party became a staunch advocate of constitutional procedure, of a transition to socialism by peaceful and parliamentary means. It approached political and economic questions in a Fabian rather than Marxist spirit. After 1927 all reference to "dictatorship of the proletariat" was deleted from the party platform, nor did the Labor Party any longer characterize itself as a communist party.

The general elections of 1927, coming after a severe deflation, resulted in the return to the Storting of 59 labor representatives out of a total of 150 members; together with 3 communist members who later joined the Labor Party, they constituted by far the largest single political group in the parliament. Consequently, when the Storting convened in 1928, the first labor government in Norway's history was formed. It lasted only a month, being voted out of office by a combination of the non-labor parties over the issue of banking and fiscal policy, but was important in demonstrating to the workers that they could achieve political power through the ballot box, and to the public at large that labor could assume office constitutionally and govern without anarchy and chaos.

After a temporary setback in 1930, the Labor Party won a smashing electoral victory in 1933 under the slogan "labor majority and labor government," falling just short of an absolute parliamentary majority. This year was also notable in producing labor's first broad-gauged economic program aimed at achieving reforms within the framework of the existing system. The significance of this new orientation was described as follows:

The new economic policy of the Norwegian labor movement constitutes in fact a synthesis of the old reformist, gradualist view and of the revolutionary view, which previously characterized the party program. According to the old "revolutionary" view, the party could introduce socialism only *after* it had gained power. In the meantime it was its duty to fight for the daily interests of the worker. But it did not believe that through this daily struggle it could transform a capitalist society into a socialist society. In this traditional revolutionary view, the fight for socialism and the fight for the workers' daily interests were *two quite separate ideas*.

In the new policy, these two activities have been merged together. This was the natural result of its analysis of the crisis. It was led to lay stress upon what was formerly considered a reformist activity, the fight against the depression. But its analysis clearly showed that this depression was a crisis in the capitalist system itself and that it could be solved only by reforms in the entire structure of the capitalist society. Thus the fight for the immediate interests of the workers — the fight against the depression — was eventually tied up with the revolutionary task of changing the structure of society.[21]

The adoption of this program marked the end of one era and the beginning of another. The process of industrialization had been slowed, the footless migratory workers of an earlier period had settled in stable communities. "The workers no longer felt the correctness of the old battle cry that they had nothing but their chains to lose." [22] When in 1938 the Norwegian Labor Party

[21] Finn Moe, *Does Norwegian Labor Seek the Middle Way?*, pp. 33–34.
[22] Bull, p. 327.

joined the Labor and Socialist International, it could be said with justification that the economic factors which previously distinguished the Norwegian from the Swedish and Danish workers had largely disappeared.

In 1935, after various coalitions of the non-labor parties had failed to provide a stable government, the Labor Party succeeded in forming a government that remained in office until the German invasion. Its economic policy during these years is strongly reminiscent of the American New Deal: "pump priming" to stimulate business activity together with government public works to eliminate unemployment; introduction of old age and unemployment insurance; extension of credit facilities and price relief for farmers and fishermen.[23]

The labor government functioned as a government in exile in London during the war. Upon the liberation of Norway, it resigned to give way to a coalition interregnum, and was returned to office in the general election of 1945, achieving for the first time an absolute majority of the seats in the parliament. Thus armed, the Labor Party embarked upon a comprehensive program of state planning.[24]

STRUCTURE AND ORGANIZATION

At the base of the Labor Party's organizational pyramid is an extensive network of local clubs, which in turn unite to form city and county district organizations. The latter are responsible for the selection of candidates for local office, and have considerable autonomy in the determination of local policy.

The highest authority in the party is the national congress, meeting every third year, and composed of representatives of the local organizations in proportion to membership strength. The congress elects a national committee, which ordinarily convenes annually, and selects an executive committee of fifteen members to provide daily leadership. Unlike the custom of the British Labor Party, where the chairmanship rotates annually and is an honorary post, the chairman is the actual leader of the party. Since 1945 the prime minister of Norway has been chairman of the Labor Party as well.

Considerable importance is attached to the socialist youth move-

[23] See Olav Larssen, *Under Arbeiderregjeringen* (Oslo, 1938).
[24] See Chapter XI.

ment, which serves as a training ground for future leadership. Technically autonomous, in recent years this organization has been dominated by the Party, although in the past, particularly during the turbulence of the twenties, it was often more radical politically. There are special local groups within party clubs for women, but no independent women's movement as such.

The Labor Party's principal asset is the well-developed labor press. There are forty-two daily or semiweekly labor newspapers in Norway, many of them the chief paper of the locality. In general, they are well edited, and provide a sufficiently rounded news service so that workers are not obliged to, and customarily do not read other newspapers, a practice which is fortified by the fact that almost the entire Norwegian press is avowedly political. Labor papers are usually owned by the local party organization, which elects the editor and determines policy.[25]

Collective trade union affiliation provides a large portion of Labor Party membership; approximately 45 per cent of the party's 200,000 members (1947) are enrolled through their local trade unions (neither the Federation of Labor nor national unions affiliate as such). The system of counting-out is used, so that the individual union member must take affirmative action if he is to reserve himself from Party membership. An additional 15 per cent of the members are enrolled through youth associations.

Originally the Federation of Labor and the Labor Party were mutually represented in one another's executive committees. At the present time, however, there is merely a joint advisory committee linking the two organizations formally. Customarily, either the chairman or vice-chairman of the Federation attends all meetings of the party executive committee.

The constitution of the Labor Party specifies that "the Labor Party and the Federation of Labor each recognize the independence of the other." One of the features of the Norwegian labor movement is that despite the very close relationship that exists between the two bodies, each is completely autonomous, and neither is dominated by the other. With few exceptions national trade union leaders are members of the Labor Party, while the

[25] An important by-product of the press system is that the Labor Party has been able to provide employment for sympathetic intellectuals, who could also be used for educational and propaganda work in the numerous small communities of which Norway is composed.

party officialdom is largely drawn from trade union ranks. But the trade unionist makes his decisions according to his best judgment, and the political labor leader is in no sense a tool of a single or a dominant group of trade unions.[26]

Close collaboration between the two organizations is based upon mutuality of ideals, and the respect and confidence that intimate association engenders. Neither organization has secrets from the other; tactics have no place in their relationship. If the chairman of the Labor Party, in his capacity as head of the government, feels obliged to make a decision that may be unpalatable to the workers, he will discuss it with the trade union leaders but persist in his intention unless genuinely convinced that he is wrong. On the other hand, significant trade union demands are generally submitted to the Labor Party before being promulgated, but they are not withdrawn in the face of party or government disapproval if the trade union leadership considers them to be justified.

The Federation and the Labor Party have established several joint organizations: the Workers' Education Association, the Workers' Athletic Association, and the Workers' Justice Fund. The major portion of Labor Party funds is supplied by the trade unions through collective membership dues, lump-sum grants or continuing contributions, although again the relationships are such that control of the purse strings in no way implies parallel control of policy.

THE PHILOSOPHY OF THE LABOR PARTY

Norwegian socialism failed to produce an original body of political doctrine. The chief theoretical impulses were a mixture of orthodox and revisionist Marxism and syndicalism, imported from the United States and the Continent.

It is difficult to judge whether this proved a source of strength or of weakness. A clear, fixed goal that leaves no room for doubt and inspires fanatical devotion is undoubtedly of great assistance to a political movement at some stages of its career. But difficulty arises when doctrine becomes outmoded as a consequence of change in political and economic circumstance, and yet cannot be dis-

[26] This statement is based upon two years of close association with political and trade union leaders in Norway.

carded because it has attained the status of dogma. The lack of a Norwegian Kautsky or Bernstein may in the long run have redounded to the advantage of the Labor Party.

The Norwegian labor movement shares with the American labor movement a concentration of interest on specific and limited objectives, a capacity for stable organization, and an unwillingness to sacrifice small gains for attractive but tenuous goals of great magnitude. It is flexible and pragmatic, harboring many shades of political opinion and using constructively the energies that might otherwise be translated into futile independent action. Norway is one of the few countries in which syndicalism and social democracy were able to find a common roof. It was only with communism that agreement on a set of immediate, practical objectives could not transcend disagreement on future aims, however nebulous and improbable of achievement the latter.

It is usually asserted that Norwegian socialism is to the left of the main stream of European socialism.[27] While this was certainly true during the Comintern episode, it is not an accurate characterization of the movement during the last two decades. The Norwegian labor government of 1935–1940 cannot clearly be catalogued as more or less radical than its Danish and Swedish counterparts, both the latter being generally regarded as eminently moderate. The postwar program of the Norwegian Labor Party, approved by the party congress of 1945, is certainly one of the least drastic and most conciliatory of contemporary socialist credos, in terms of proposals looking toward the reorganization of basic social institutions.

And yet if a categorical assertion that Norwegian labor stands "to the left" proves untenable, it is equally misleading to characterize it as a "right" socialist movement. The difficulty appears to be that old symbols do not adequately describe a situation molded by the rise and violent fall of fascism, and the example of Marxism in practice offered by the Soviet Union. In the brief span of three years since its liberation, Norway has moved further toward a planned economy than any other western democracy, with a surprising degree of concurrence from those interests that are affected adversely. Moreover, the labor movement maintains a

[27] See, for example, Harry Laidler, *Social-Economic Movements* (New York, 1945), p. 539.

steadfast belief in the efficacy of socialism, which it is determined to achieve through constitutional means and without violence to the spirit as well as the letter of democracy.

A few illustrations may clarify some of these generalizations. On the crucial issue of nationalizing industry, the Labor Party had been officially committed since 1901 to "state socialism," that is, initial assumption by the government of key economic functions within the framework of a capitalist order.[28] The revolutionary upsurge of the twenties produced a demand for immediate nationalization of "banks and insurance companies, wholesale trade, shipping, power, and such natural resources as waterfalls, mines and woods, and industrial plants the economic and technical development of which make social direction particularly suitable."[29]

The program on which the labor government entered office in 1935 represented a pragmatic reappraisal of earlier policy in the light of immediate political prospects. It placed more emphasis upon regulation and control than upon government ownership, a tendency which was intensified in the following excerpt from the 1945 program:

The question of socializing the banks and the insurance system shall be investigated and effectuated to the extent deemed necessary.

. . . the government must coöperate with industrial establishments, workers, officials, and their organizations in order to secure planned construction, rationalization and a great expansion of industrial capacity.

Large forests that are not operated in conjunction with farms, when it is in the general interest, should be acquired by the state and placed under social administration.

Control of exports shall be maintained and expanded as required by new conditions . . . Imports shall be controlled through a system of licensing.[30]

In actuality the socialized sector of the economy has recently been expanded by government acquisition of property belonging to German interests or to disloyal Norwegians, and by the investment of public funds in new enterprises deemed essential to

[28] *Det Norske Arbeiderpartis Historie,* II, 243.
[29] Det Norske Arbeiderparti, *Landsmøter,* p. 46.
[30] Det Norske Arbeiderparti, *Arbeidsprogram,* 1945.

the economy. Since the Labor Party is not under the pressure of redeeming election pledges that call for immediate nationalization of industry, it is able to approach its ultimate goal by indirect though no less effective means, without alienating the badly needed coöperation of industrial management.

Similar eclecticism was displayed on other issues that could have been divisive or weakening. The Norwegian Labor Party is one of the few socialist parties with real influence in rural areas. No doubt this may be attributed in part to industrial dispersion, which places factory and farm in close juxtaposition. But of considerable importance is the fact that early in its career the party discarded the collective farm of orthodox socialism, and advocated instead the extension of small holdings combined with coöperative marketing, the only feasible organization of Norwegian agriculture, thus gaining the support of many small holders.[31]

The religious issue was another potential source of internecine strife. The first Labor Party program called for discontinuance of government financial support to the Lutheran Church, the state church of Norway, and the placing of all schools on a nonconfessional basis. Widening of the right of franchise in 1898 led many socialists to believe that a state church under more democratic control was preferable to uncontrolled sects. In 1901, the Labor Party dropped its demand for disestablishment, and in 1911 the plea for nonconfessional schools was modified by the qualification that "this program will not make the schools antireligious; education in the form of the history of religion shall be a part of the instruction." [32]

The religious question became more controversial with the growth of political radicalism. Conflicting resolutions were introduced at every party congress, resulting finally in the adoption, in 1918, of one that pledged the elimination of the teaching of Christianity in the schools, and the substitution of the history of church and religion as part of the regular history curriculum. This section was expunged from subsequent programs. When it was associated with the Comintern, the Labor Party refused to comply with an order calling upon it to propagate atheism, although the principal Norwegian leaders at the time were personally antireligious.

[31] Bull, pp. 179–184.
[32] Det Norske Arbeiderpartis Historie, II, 70.

Except for the guarantee of "freedom of religion and conscience," there has been no subsequent reference to the religious question in Labor Party programs. The state church has been administered by a socialist minister of education with no more than the customary friction.

The Labor Party long opposed militarism and espoused the cause of disarmament. The militance of the Comintern years was only skin deep. Even the growth of fascism could not eradicate the deep pacifist conviction held by most Norwegian workers. As late as 1939 the Labor Party advocated only the minimum of defensive armament necessary to preserve neutrality.

Norway's involvement in the recent war resulted in a considerable shift of opinion on this question. The 1945 congress committed the Labor Party to the thesis that "the nation's military forces shall be built up on the basis of wartime experience, so that they can defend the country and fulfill our international military commitments." The Labor government sent a brigade of troops to participate in the occupation of Germany. Nevertheless, the annual military budget still arouses considerable protest from the labor benches in the Storting, and the party whip generally leaves to the conscience of each individual member the way he shall cast his vote.

A final matter that has always played an important role within the Norwegian labor movement is the temperance question. The prime force in the temperance movement has been Martin Tranmael, who organized the Workers' Temperance League in 1932 and has been its chairman ever since. It is his conviction that the use of alcohol is incompatible with the attainment of complete mental freedom and the development of a sound physique. He and his closest collaborators, who now constitute the Labor Party leadership, are teetotalers.

Largely at Tranmael's instigation, the 1911 party congress proclaimed the struggle against alcohol to be of decisive importance for liberation of the working class, and pledged its support to the reduction and eventual prohibition of alcohol consumption. The adoption of a national prohibition law in 1920 after a referendum, and its failure to achieve the desired results, led the Labor Party to modify its earlier stand, to the satisfaction of many who considered the previous attitude puritanical. The most recent platform merely advocates intensified propaganda in the schools and within the labor movement to curb excessive drinking, which proved to be a particularly serious problem when the tensions of the occupation period were removed.[33]

A more complete review of Labor Party philosophy would lend additional support to the thesis that Norwegian socialism owes its prosperity to its ability to synthesize different shades of opinion by concentrating on immediate objectives. On every issue the majority, instead of insisting upon complete adoption of its views, endeavored to reconcile conflicting aspirations, particularly when the area of disagreement was primarily of theoretical import. The result has been internal democracy and freedom from dogma that are well suited to the individualistic temper of the Norwegian people, and provide the best long run guarantee of stability and unity of purpose.

[33] The postwar Labor government has also attempted, without discernible success, to reduce alcohol consumption by raising prices at the State Liquor Monopoly to near-prohibitive levels. One result has been an increase in bootlegging.

CHAPTER, IV

ORGANIZATION OF EMPLOYERS AND FOREMEN FOR COLLECTIVE BARGAINING

A DISTINCTIVE FEATURE of Norwegian industrial relations is the extent to which employers have joined together for purposes of bargaining on matters of wages and working conditions. Through their central organization, the Norwegian Employers' Association (*Norsk Arbeidsgiverforening*), they have delegated a large measure of authority in the sphere of industrial relations to specialists. The factors leading to organization, and the precise mechanism through which bargaining and, when bargaining breaks down, industrial warfare are conducted is of interest in view of recent trends in the United States in the same direction.

The manner in which the problem of the foreman's peculiar status in industrial relations has been approached in Norway may also offer some interesting contrasts to the contemporary American scene. There as here foremen have evinced a desire to bargain collectively, and there as here neither employers nor trade unions have acquiesced wholeheartedly in their independent organization for such purposes. But through persistence and persuasion the Norwegian foreman has been able to work out agreements with both labor and management, recognizing that he has interests apart from both.

THE ORGANIZATION OF EMPLOYERS

While the employer association movement can be traced back to the middle of the nineteenth century, it was not until 1886 that a national and representative organization of employers was established in Norway, with the founding of the Norwegian Association for Skilled Trades and Industry. This organization was not a collective bargaining association, however; it was primarily devoted to the promotion of matters of mutual interest outside the field of industrial relations. But it was a lineal ancestor of the present Norwegian Employers' Association in that the initiative for the formation of the latter came from certain elements within it.

In 1893 a committee of the Association for Skilled Trades and Industry began to plan for a functional association of employers in their capacity as employers. It was not until 1900, however, one year after the founding of the Federation of Labor, that the Norwegian Employers' Association was formed. The growth of trade unionism was undoubtedly the most important factor in the development of employer organization. A student of Norwegian labor put it as follows:

The Norwegian Employers' Association was founded in 1900. Both this and most other employer associations are directly a fruit of the labor movement. They were established as counter organizations to the trade unions. A single employer was at a disadvantage in a struggle with well-organized workers. With assistance from comrades in and out of the country several hundred workers could keep a strike going for a long time without hunger forcing them to give in. Therefore employers had to band together. They had to give one another economic support during conflicts, and they could answer a strike with a lockout.[1]

From the first, the Employers' Association enjoyed considerable authority in its dealings with trade unions. It is interesting that Norwegian employers should have been willing to delegate so much of the labor-relations function to a central organization in contrast with American employers, who have tended to guard jealously the control over relations with their employees. At least part of the explanation lies in the fact that the average size of the establishments originally affiliated with the Employers' Association was quite small, thus putting employers at a genuine disadvantage against workers organized on a national basis. In 1902 there were 876 establishments employing 34,150 workers affiliated with the Employers' Association, or approximately 40 workers per plant.[2] The industrial giants that faced the American trade union movement in its formative stages, on the other hand,

[1] Edvard Bull, *Arbeiderklassen i Norsk Historie*, p. 205. The present leaders of the Employers' Association give substantially similar reasons for employer organization.

[2] Axel Krefting, *Norsk Arbeidsgiverforening 1900–1910* (Oslo, 1910).

were generally possessed of greater bargaining power than their trade union opponents.

This is not to say that no large establishments have affiliated with the Norwegian Employers' Association, for there are plants employing several thousands of workers currently holding membership. But these were mainly products of the industrialization process that took place in Norway from 1900 to 1914, and they were confronted with the proposition of either joining a going concern and accepting established principles of operation or remaining independent. Most of them chose the former course.

There is another intangible but significant element behind the successful organization of Norwegian employers, that is, the relatively greater degree of stratification that characterizes Norwegian, and indeed European society in general, compared with American society. Norwegian employers are less inclined to be strong individualists than American employers, for there are fewer "self-made" men among them. The approval of the group into which most Norwegian employers were born means much to them, the need for approval being augmented by the small size of the Norwegian community. One is constantly impressed with the solidarity, almost class consciousness, that prevails among Norwegian employers.

The Employers' Association was always a federation of component organizations, although individual affiliation is permitted under certain circumstances. At its inception, the affiliated associations were organized both industrially and geographically. In 1907, for example, 613 establishments were affiliated through regional councils, and 199 through national industrial associations. The trend, however, has always been toward industrial organization: by 1916, some 1,042 establishments belonged to the industrial associations, and 618 to regional councils. In 1917 regional organization was abandoned entirely. This affords an interesting parallel to the early struggles between national unions and central trades councils within the Norwegian Federation of Labor, which eventually resulted in victory for the former.

The lack of an adequate historical account of the Employers' Association, and the reticence of its officials, make it difficult to assess the influences that conditioned its development. It is known that there was often internal strife between the affiliated organizations representing the skilled trades, such as printing and building, and those representing manufacturing, but differences were rarely aired in public. The Employers' Association has been fortunate in having forceful leaders who were able to impress their views upon the membership; among them may be mentioned Axel Krefting, C. Grøndahl, Lars Rasmussen, Finn Dahl, and the present chairman, Christian Erlandsen.

The growth of the Employers' Association through the years was steady though not spectacular. By 1946 it numbered 4,400 member establishments employing an estimated 160,000 workers,[3] compared with Federation of Labor membership of 400,000. But these figures alone do not portray the true measure of the influence exerted by the Employers' Association. By virtue of inclusion within its ranks of most of the important enterprises, the association's policies have ramifications that spread far beyond its actual membership. It has become the official spokesman for Norwegian employers in general, and since 1945 it has to a large extent bargained for nonmembers as well as members over terms of employment.[4]

Although the Norwegian Employers' Association has never had a direct competitor, there are several industrial associations of employers outside the NEA, despite periodic attempts to bring about their affiliation. They represent principally employers engaged in international trade — paper, lumber, shipping, whaling — whose interests and labor conditions diverge sharply from those of employers producing for the domestic market. There are also a number of small local employer associations that for one reason or another have refused to affiliate with the NEA.

PURPOSES AND STRUCTURE OF THE NORWEGIAN EMPLOYERS' ASSOCIATION

The purposes of the Employers' Association, according to its constitution, are:

[3] The latest official statistics are for 1944, when all employer associations, including those independent of the Employers' Association, were listed as having 3,274 establishments employing 119,540 workers. *Statistisk Årbok for Norge,* 1943–1945, p. 339. The figure of 4,400 establishments in the text was given to the author as a rough estimate by an official of the Employers' Association, while employment of 160,000 was estimated from the establishment-employment ratio prevailing in 1944.

[4] See Chapter XII.

(a) to maintain good and lasting relations between employers and workers and to attempt to avert and adjust disputes

(b) to give the members of the Association guidance as to working conditions and to assist them when they are subject to unjust conduct on the part of workers or their associations

(c) to promote coöperation among Norwegian employers and to assist them in establishing associations of industrial groups

(d) to deal with social questions of importance to industry, and other questions of mutual interest.[5]

The Employers' Association is a specialized labor relations agency, and does not concern itself with the range of questions that in the United States comes within the purview of such an organization as the National Association of Manufacturers. One significant result of this functional specialization is that the leaders of the Employers' Association tend to develop a more professional attitude toward the labor movement and labor problems generally than their associates who administer the more familiar type of business group. The man who headed the Employers' Association for twenty-four years until his retirement in 1947, and who had earned a reputation as a strong champion of employers' rights during decades of labor struggle, had this to say of his former labor opponents:

. . . I should like to say that the workers' organizations are led by clever men, competent in their trade and devoted to improving labor conditions . . . Even if we have had differences of opinion, they are always reasonable, and I do not think that I ever participated in negotiations or conciliation proceedings where they did not listen to our arguments and give them as much consideration as was consistent with their thousands of mandates. We have no interest in weakening their positions, and when we accord them confidence, we receive confidence in return.[6]

At the beginning of 1947 the Norwegian Employers' Association consisted of sixteen industrial associations, and a number of

[5] *Lover for Norsk Arbeidsgiverforening,* Section 1.

[6] "Direktør Finn Dahl's Avskjedstale," *Arbeidsgiveren,* January 17, 1947, p. 12. These views are reciprocated. Labor leaders told the author that Mr. Dahl was a hard but clean fighter, who had never once gone back on his word during a quarter century of negotiation.

directly affiliated concerns not eligible for membership in any of the constituent associations. All members of the latter automatically become members of the Employers' Association as well. Establishments belonging to constituent associations, with not more than two employees, or five thousand labor hours annually, may be exempted from the obligation to pay dues to the Employers' Association; in that event they have no right to participate in its councils, but are subject to its decisions. If a member controls more than one establishment of a similar character, he may be required to affiliate all his plants with the Employers' Association.

Some of the constituent associations are in turn subdivided into trade groups. The Skilled Trades Employers' Association (*Haandverkernes Arbeidsgiverforening*), for example, is composed of special sections for newspapers, bakeries, book printers, bookbinders, plumbers, master masons, and others. The constitutional provisions of the constituent organizations must be approved by the Employers' Association before affiliation is permitted.

The highest constitutional instance in the Employers' Association is the general assembly, which consists of delegates elected by affiliated organizations and direct members in proportion to the number of workers employed.[7] Annual meetings of the general assembly are attended by about 120 delegates. Between meetings of the assembly the association's highest authority is the central board (*Centralstyret*), a body of 45. For 1947 it included the chairman and vice-chairman of the association; 6 members elected directly by the general assembly; 4 representatives of district offices; 23 representatives of the constituent associations; 1 representative of a large direct member; and 9 representatives of groups of independent direct members. The central board meets as often as necessary, usually four or five times a year, and is for all practical purposes the policy-making organ of the Employers' Association. Six of its members, in turn, together with the chairman and vice-chairman, make up the executive committee of the central board, which supervises the daily affairs of the association.

There are three district offices of the Employers' Association, each governed by a district assembly, and separate city offices

[7] The constitution allows additional representation to firms with a high ratio of capital to employment, but this provision has rarely been invoked.

wherever the pressure of business makes them essential. They correspond to trade union central trades councils, and are responsible to the central board.

The administration of the Employers' Association is headed by a full-time chairman, who is elected by the central board. There are five negotiating departments, each embracing a sector of industry within which the association functions.[8] Customarily the constituent associations designate one or more members of the negotiating departments as their bargaining agent, and in effect each department consists of persons expert in the affairs of one or more industries. There are in addition legal, press, statistical, and industrial rationalization offices. During 1947 the administrative staff of the association numbered sixty-seven persons in all.

FINANCES

The chief source of Employer Association funds is an annual membership fee currently fixed by the general assembly at one per cent of the member firm's payroll. This represents a very large amount, the equivalent of what American employers pay as old-age insurance premiums. In addition, members are required to subscribe to a guarantee fund for an amount equaling three times their regular annual dues, payable on demand of the central board, with a 20 per cent fine for nonpayment within one month from the issuance of the call. This fund is used to render financial assistance to members who require such support during strikes or lockouts. Thus far, the guarantee subscriptions have been called in only three times, during the widespread work stoppages of 1916, 1924, and 1931.

In the event of a strike or lockout, the general assembly may authorize the central board to levy an extra assessment on members not affected by the strike, not to exceed half a year's regular dues for each month's duration of the work stoppage. This provision, too, has rarely been invoked. There is also an initiation fee equal to one year's regular dues, but it is payable only if the new entrant discontinues membership within five years, thus putting a premium upon stability of membership.

---

[8] The first department bargains for the skilled trades; the second for the metal trades and the hotel and restaurant industry; the third for the electrical and chemical industries; the fourth for shipping and transport; and the fifth for a variety of miscellaneous industries.

A small source of income is provided by fines for breach of association rules. While it has not often been necessary to levy fines, this has occasionally been done as a means of enforcing organizational discipline. During a strike in 1924, for example, a member was fined 100,000 kroner for signing an agreement terminating his strike without permission of the Employers' Association.

Ordinarily, small payments to members whose plants are closed because of a work stoppage are made from a so-called compensation fund, into which are placed initiation fees, annual dues not employed for meeting administrative expenses, fines, and special assessments. This fund is administered by the central board, in contrast with the guarantee fund, expenditures from which require authorization of the general assembly. Administrative expenses are limited constitutionally to 35 per cent of regular annual dues payments.[9]

The Employers' Association does not publish financial statements, and it is therefore difficult to assess the relative importance of the various sources of income and expenditure. It was estimated in 1935 that regular dues payments brought in between 1.75 and 2 million kroner per annum, while the static guarantee subscriptions amounted to between 5 and 6 million kroner.[10] These amounts have undoubtedly increased as a result of expanding membership and payroll expenditures, and by Norwegian standards constitute a very sizable sum.

Member firms pay their dues directly to the Employers' Association, rather than through their industry association. As a rule they do not pay fees to the latter, which are financed by grants authorized by the central board out of the dues payments of their members. This arrangement serves to strengthen the Employers' Association in its relations with subsidiary organizations.

THE CONDUCT OF COLLECTIVE BARGAINING

The undoubted success of the Employers' Association in bargaining for a heterogeneity of employers is due in no small measure to the concentration of decision-making authority in relatively few hands, and the means possessed by the central organization

[9] The central board, however, may authorize additional funds for administrative purposes to be paid out of the compensation fund.

[10] Viggo Hansteen, *Arbeidsgiverforeningen* (Oslo, 1935), p. 20.

to discipline recalcitrants. When a firm joins the Employers' Association it renounces its right "to enter into negotiations with trade unions or persons representing them in labor matters except through the appropriate national industrial associations or the central board." [11] This function is performed by specialists who, while they confer with individual employers, must nevertheless be guided by considerations of common welfare.

The exact negotiation procedure varies with the unit coverage of the proposed agreement and the status of the members who will be bound thereby. The majority of contracts negotiated by the Employers' Association are multi-plant or industrial in scope, and in that event policy is formulated initially by the interested employers under the aegis of their industrial associations. The latter are governed by their own rules, but in the absence of contrary provision all resolutions are adopted by a simple majority of employers present at formal meetings. Some associations dispense with meetings, however, and rely upon referendum votes.

The central board of the Employers' Association is kept informed of policy formulations, and in practice it exercises a right of veto over decisions running counter to national policy. On purely local matters the Employers' Association as such may be represented by a district officer, or it may not be represented at all, but in negotiations which may have national repercussions, a member of the appropriate negotiating department, and perhaps an officer of the central organization, will always be present. The constitution of the association gives the central board the right of representation in the manner it finds most suitable. If only a single plant is involved in negotiations the management will ordinarily be represented, but otherwise individuals are not entitled to separate representation at bargaining conferences. In industry-wide collective bargaining it is always the Employers' Association representative who assumes active conduct of the proceedings from the employer's side.

The power of the Employers' Association stems ultimately from the fact that neither an affiliate nor an individual member may enter into an agreement without the advance approval of its central board. On the other hand, the central board is bound to submit to the membership for approval agreements which its

[11] *Lover for Norsk Arbeidsgiverforening,* Section 22.

negotiators have accepted. The Basic Agreement between the Federation of Labor and the Employers' Association contains the following relevant clause:

When proposals for agreement are submitted to referendum vote, those members of the Employers' Association affected by the proposal shall participate. Voting shall be secret and written. For a proposal to be defeated, at least half of those entitled to vote shall have voted in the negative.[12]

In practice, a proposal accepted by the negotiator for the Employers' Association is almost never rejected by the employers themselves, unless the association desires its rejection for tactical purposes. There is a very good reason for this, apart from the prestige of the central organization: the Employers' Association is generally disposed to take a firmer view of a situation, and is less apt to temporize than is the individual employer.

If an employer or an industrial association desires to exercise its contractual right of altering or terminating an existing collective agreement, the central board must be notified in due time. Should the board find that such action will have an unfavorable effect upon other employers or industries, it may require formal discussion before cancellation is effected. In the event of an irreconcilable difference of opinion between the central board and the initiating organization or employer, the agreement may nevertheless be terminated, but in the event of a strike the members affected lose all right to the financial assistance of the Employers' Association. However, where the contractual alterations are initiated by an affiliated organization rather than an individual, the central board has the power to prevent alteration or termination where the decision to act was taken by less than a two-thirds majority of the organization members.

The central board itself may resolve upon the termination of an agreement binding its members. But to do this there must be concurrence by two-thirds of the board's members, and as a practical matter the interested parties are always consulted before any action is taken. It should be emphasized that only under very unusual circumstances will the Employers' Association override

[12] *Hovedavtale*, see below, pp. 192–197.

substantial opinion among its members, for it is, after all, a political as well as an economic institution, and its preservation and growth are contingent upon member satisfaction. The constitutional delegation of authority to the central board is designed to cover the extraordinary case where there is a conflict of interest between member employers requiring resolution by higher authority.

THE CONDUCT OF INDUSTRIAL WARFARE

Just as it leads collective bargaining, the Employers' Association captains the employer forces when negotiations break down and industrial conflict ensues. The individual employer delegates to the association, upon becoming a member, the right to decide for him when a strike is to be terminated, and whether he shall be obliged to assist his fellow employers through a sympathetic lockout.

The lockout has been an important weapon in Norwegian industrial relations. Because of the serious consequences entailed, the right of the Employers' Association to require its employment by members is carefully circumscribed. The central board is empowered to call a lockout involving less than 25 per cent of all workers employed by members of the association. If a greater number of workers will be affected, the general assembly must give its consent. Affiliated organizations may declare lockouts with permission of the central board.

Final decisions on the institution of lockouts can be taken by the general assembly only when at least half its members are present at a duly constituted meeting, or by the central board only when there is a quorum of two-thirds the membership. In each case a three-fourths affirmative majority is required for passage of a lockout resolution. A lockout called by the central board can be appealed to the general assembly by constituent associations or individual companies representing the employment of at least one-fourth the number of workers to be embraced by the proposed lockout, provided the appeal is lodged within twenty-four hours of the central board's action. Similarly, refusal of the central board to sanction a lockout may be appealed. Where the required three-fourths majority of the central board cannot be obtained, a simple majority of the board may request the general assembly to approve a lockout the declaration of which ordinarily falls within the jurisdiction of the central board.

Once a conflict has begun, whether it be a strike or lockout, no employer may engage in any activities that may affect the outcome of the controversy without the knowledge and permission of the Employers' Association. Obligations of association members during a labor dispute are indicated by the following constitutional provisions :

During a conflict involving members of the Norwegian Employers' Association no other member directly or indirectly may take any action against the interests of the association or of those involved in the conflict, such as undertaking work, delivering materials, engaging in transportation, and so on, that has been begun or contracted for by employers involved in the conflict, nor may he take over delivery or work of any sort that the members in question had contracted for prior to the dispute, without permission of the central board.

Every member must submit to decisions of the central board during a conflict involving a member of the Association, with respect to delivery of materials, transportation, and so on, in order to prevent workers who are on strike or who are locked out from obtaining employment during the conflict.[13]

An employer who sustains economic loss through compliance with the foregoing obligations is entitled to compensation to the extent permitted by the guarantee and compensation funds. The Employers' Association, however, does not undertake to make good in full the loss suffered, for millions of kroner may be involved in terms of canceled deliveries and sales, continuing overhead costs, and special strike expenses. There is a ceiling on its liability equal to .05 per cent of the employer's total payroll for the preceding year for each day the work stoppage remains in effect, after a noncompensable waiting period of six days. Thus an employer with 100 workers and an annual payroll of 500,000 kroner would be entitled to a maximum of 250 kroner per day in strike benefits.

Companies or industries against which the general compensation laws work a manifest injustice may receive additional compensation at the discretion of the central board. Employers sub-

---

[13] *Lover for Norsk Arbeidsgiverforening,* Section 25.

jected to extraordinary difficulties during a labor dispute may be granted loans upon proper application. On the other hand the central board may also reduce the benefits paid to an individual firm if application of the percentage formula results in an amount exceeding the firm's total ordinary operating expenses.

During a general strike or lockout the general assembly, by a three-fourths majority, may reduce or suspend entirely the payment of benefits to employers. By a simple majority it may resolve that for a future period not exceeding one year any member who becomes involved in a strike or lockout may forfeit the right to benefits. The purpose of these limitations is to protect the solvency of the association in time of widespread industrial controversy as well as to provide a means of enforcing discipline.

It is evident from the foregoing that benefits paid by the Employers' Association do not have the same significance as trade union strike benefits. In a sense, it is true, they represent emergency payments designed to tide the recipient over a period of stress, and to that extent the two are alike. But trade union benefits are designed to provide the worker with a subsistence minimum enabling him to remain away from employment almost indefinitely until the strike is terminated, and the ability of the union to continue benefit payments at a sufficiently high level may be a decisive factor in the outcome of the strike. Employer Association benefits, on the other hand, are not of sufficient magnitude in relation to the customary operating income of a firm to constitute a determining factor in the employer's decision to capitulate or to continue resistance. Of much greater importance is the general economic situation, the employer's business opportunities, his inventory and credit position. The employer, through the association benefit system, is assured only of a small amount of liquid funds to meet continuing expenses, but not sufficient to prevent failure in the event of a protracted struggle.

Withholding of compensation payments is but one of the disciplinary avenues open to the central board. If an establishment, whether or not it is affiliated with the Employers' Association, acts contrary to the interests of a firm tied up by a work stoppage, it may be subjected to an economic boycott as a "strikebreaker" for a period determined by the central board. Any association member found guilty of violating an association edict may be fined up to 200,000 kroner. Members against whom fines are levied may appeal to the general assembly, but they renounce recourse to the ordinary law courts in accepting the statutes of membership.

To assure organizational stability, no member may resign from the association before having completed two years of membership, and then only at the end of the quarter following one year's written notice of resignation. The minimum period of membership is thus 3¼ years. The central board, moreover, may refuse to accept a resignation during the pendency of a labor dispute, even if all other requisites have been complied with, in order to prevent any break in employer ranks in the midst of a battle.

The real strength of the Employers' Association lies not so much in formal constitutional provisions as in the attitude of Norwegian employers toward their collective bargaining organization, and in the strong solidarity that exists when industrial relations are at issue. There has never been any real difficulty in securing compliance with association decisions, and only on very rare occasion has the central board been obliged to invoke formal penal sanctions.[14] Norwegian employers view the ability of American trade unions to play one employer off against another with incredulity. It is highly unethical for a Norwegian employer to capitalize upon the labor trouble of a fellow employer by attempting to win away his trade, and any such effort is met with swift retribution.

There is always the danger, of course, that coöperation on labor matters may lead to restraint of trade and the growth of monopoly. The existence of a permanent government antitrust agency in Norway attests to the existence of this problem, but not to a greater degree than in countries where employers are less highly organized for collective bargaining. The Norwegian Employers' Association and its constituent organizations have confined themselves strictly to the sphere of industrial relations, and while conferences on labor problems may afford employers the opportunity to discuss trade practices as well, it is reasonable to believe that they would do so in any event if there is sufficient interest.

From its very inception the Norwegian Employers' Association accepted the principles of collective bargaining with trade unions and the written trade agreement. Although it opposed vigorously the demands of labor at many junctures, it never participated in a

[14] Statement to the author by the vice-chairman of the Employers' Association, July 28, 1947.

campaign aimed specifically at the destruction of trade unions. The same cannot be said of some independent employer associations, and in particular of organized employers in the lumber industry. As early as 1902 the Employers' Association entered into an agreement with the Federation of Labor providing for arbitration of controversies arising out of the terms of collective agreements. Indeed, in Norway the principal opposition to written agreements came from the syndicalist wing of the labor movement rather than from organized employers.

THE ORGANIZATION OF FOREMEN

The early development of stable collective bargaining relationships between employers and employees raised to prominence the question of the status of foremen. Desirous of remaining neutral in industrial conflicts, they often incurred the enmity of both sides. To protect their interests they organized at an early date a national association of their own, the Norwegian Foremen's Union, which still remains the object of suspicion.

Local organizations of foremen were beginning to emerge as far back as the beginning of the century. In 1910 representatives of some of these groups joined in the formation of the Industrial Foremen's and Work Leaders' National Union, which has since altered its name to the simple Foremen's Union. It began with only 131 members and, despite the open hostility of employers, managed to survive. In 1947 it claimed a total membership of 4000.[15]

The Foremen's Union is organized on the basis of local units, one for each industrial town or district. It is governed by an executive council of eleven, elected by a national convention meeting quinquenially. Membership is open to all supervisory personnel who (a) do not themselves participate in productive work, (b) are permanently employed on a weekly or monthly wage, (c) do not participate in piece work, and (d) are not independent employers.[16]

[15] The 1930 census put the total number of foremen in industry and building at 8,900. On the basis of the subsequent expansion of the industrial labor force, the total number of foremen in industry and building in 1947 might be estimated at 10,000.

[16] Norsk Arbeidslederforbund, *Lover,* 1946, Section 2.

The two principal problems that have faced the Foremen's Union from the very beginning concern the role of foremen in industrial conflicts and the right of foremen to bargain collectively. Although they regarded themselves as representatives of management, the foremen were anxious not to lose the confidence of the workers, and the ability to maintain shop discipline, by performing work during labor disputes that might be considered strike-breaking. Most of them, moreover, had belonged to trade unions before becoming supervisors.

At its 1911 convention the Foremen's Union adopted the following resolution on neutrality:

1. During a dispute each foreman or master shall supervise the workers that the establishment can secure.
2. If no workers can be secured, the foremen shall repair tools, machinery, or apparatus pertaining to our work.[17]

This resolution was sent to the Employers' Association, which had refused to discuss a pension system until satisfactory agreement on neutrality had been reached. It proved unacceptable, however, and after several years of intermittent negotiation, the following restatement was submitted for the approval of the Employers' Association:

In any dispute between employers and workers the masters and foremen shall remain in their positions and do what they can to enable the establishment to continue operations undisturbed. The employers, however, both out of regard for the establishment itself and for the foremen as future work supervisors, shall not request that any work be performed that may lead to conflict between foremen and workers, and prove harmful to future relationships.[18]

This again was rejected and the Foremen's Union was finally obliged, in 1919, to issue a unilateral declaration to the effect that "during recognized and lawful disputes between employers and workers the members of our organization must not perform work other than that performed under normal conditions." [19]

[17] *Norges Arbeidslederforbund 1910–1935* (Oslo, 1935), p. 78.
[18] *Norges Arbeidslederforbund 1910–1935,* p. 79.
[19] *Norges Arbeidslederforbund 1910–1935,* p. 82.

Further negotiation proved futile. Although at one point, there was a near meeting of minds on the neutrality issue,[20] the interjection of other matters prevented final agreement. The 1922 convention of the Foremen's Union revised its 1919 directive to the membership, somewhat amplifying the original one but making no change in principle. This directive stood the test of the general strike of 1931 and numerous subsequent disputes, but its thesis has never been accepted by the employers.

Trade unions, as well as employers, are reluctant to concede the neutrality of the foreman. There is a growing feeling within the labor movement that foremen belong in the trade unions. Foremen and supervisors in the state service are organized in the Municipal Workers' Union, while the Office and Commercial Workers' Union has indicated a willingness to admit to membership foremen in government-owned industrial plants. A recent editorial in the official organ of the Federation of Labor pointed out that when trade unions were primarily combative in character it was natural for them to exclude supervisory employees "many of whom felt themselves more closely allied with employers than with workers." But, it continued,

With the changed condition occasioned by the growth of trade unions and the increased political power of the working class, much of the reason for the old line between workers and supervisors has disappeared. To an increasing extent wage and working conditions are determined by trade unions and employer associations. Only in rare instances have supervisors anything to do with these questions . . . The old rationale for the maintenance of organizational separation between workers and supervisors is no longer valid.[21]

[20] The final proposal of the Foremen's Union read as follows: "During a strike or lockout foremen shall remain at their jobs and perform the work customarily performed as foremen, coöperate to the end that the shutdown shall be accomplished in a technically proper manner, perform guard duty, and see to it that as far as possible machinery, tools, and products are not damaged during the stoppage. However, they cannot be ordered to perform manual labor."

The employers' proposal was: "During a strike or lockout foremen shall remain at their jobs. However, they cannot be ordered to perform manual labor that may be considered production. On the other hand, they are obligated to perform that work they customarily perform, coöperate to the end that the shutdown shall be accomplished in a technically proper manner, perform guard duty, and see to it that as far as possible machinery, tools, and products are not damaged during the stoppage." *Norges Arbeidslederforbund 1910–1935,* p. 84.

[21] "Uniting of Forces," *Fri Fagbevegelse,* February 15, 1947.

With respect to the second major problem, the right of fore-men to bargain collectively, the Employers' Association originally manifested a firm belief that the relationship between an employer and his foremen was entirely individual. This attitude, together with the militant mood of Norwegian workers at the end of World War I, created some sentiment within the Foremen's Union for affiliation with the Federation of Labor, on the ground that only by such means could foremen secure the right to bargain col-lectively. Although the proponents of this step were in a minority, they succeeded in forcing a strong approach to the Employers' As-sociation.

In 1919 a proposed agreement was submitted to the Employers' Association embodying minimum wage rates, overtime provi-sions, and paid vacations. The Employers' Association agreed to consider the latter two demands in principle, but opposed the minimum wage, proposing instead a tripartite arbitration board to settle wage disputes between foremen and their employers. The negotiations broke down when the employers refused to concede the arbitration board jurisdiction to deal collectively with the fore-men in single plants, insisting that all wage questions would have to be handled on a completely individual basis.

The employers were more amenable when it came to the estab-lishment of grievance machinery. The discharge of foremen for insisting on the maintenance of neutrality during labor disputes was a continuing problem. Foremen were also often obliged to threaten resignation in order to secure serious discussion of their contracts. In 1932 the Employers' Association entered into a writ-ten agreement recognizing the right of foremen to organize, and providing for the settlement of contract disputes by the two or-ganizations if no agreement could be secured at the local level.

Not until 1946, however, was the Employers' Association will-ing to include wage provisions in an agreement with the Fore-men's Union. Under the terms of a contract concluded that year[22] the principle was established that foremen had the right to be paid for overtime work performed, and an annual vacation of two weeks and sick-leave pay were stipulated. No specific wage rates were inserted in the agreement, but the following general statement was included:

[22] *Avtale mellom Norsk Arbeidsgiverforening og Norges Arbeidslederfor-bund* (Oslo, 1946).

A foreman's wage shall be determined on the basis of his skill and his personal qualifications. As a general rule the parties agree that a foreman's wage must be at such a level that there is a significant difference between his and workers' wages.[23]

With this agreement foremen at last obtained full recognition of the right to bargain collectively. They also succeeded in working out standard arrangements with a number of trade unions whereby workers promoted to supervisory positions retain their rights in union benefit funds if they continue to pay contributions thereto, with a reciprocal arrangement when members of the Foremen's Union return to production work.

The leadership of the Foremen's Union professes to be satisfied with the status of foremen as determined by the 1946 agreement, though in 1937 the managing director wrote that "the foreman has not had the support and understanding he needs, nor the conditions that correspond to his responsibilities." [24] Yet it may well be that only a temporary equilibrium has been reached. Until recent years employer reluctance to differentiate the foreman from management was the greatest obstacle to the achievement of an independent status for him. The chief threat now appears to be from the labor movement.

[23] *Avtale mellom Norsk Arbeidsgiverforening og Norges Arbeidslederforbund,* Section 7.
[24] *Social Håndbok for Norge* (Oslo, 1937), p. 750.

CHAPTER V

THE LEGISLATIVE FRAMEWORK[1]

THE NORWEGIAN GOVERNMENT, at an early date compared with the United States, became a participant in labor relations. The character of its intervention was determined to a large extent by the bargaining strength of the contending parties. When the first Norwegian labor-disputes legislation was enacted in 1915, the inequality that gave rise to the Wagner Act in the United States had already given way to a situation in which the relative strength of workers and employers was fairly evenly balanced. The proponents of legislation conceived it to be the function of the state merely to serve as an arbiter in the interest of mitigating strife that would affect adversely social groups not party to disputes.

The cornerstone of Norwegian labor legislation is a fundamental distinction between disputes over rights and disputes over interests,[2] so often confused in the United States. This distinction actually predated legislation; in 1902 the Federation of Labor and the Employers' Association entered into an agreement providing for arbitration of disputes over rights at the request of *either* party, and arbitration of disputes over interests at the request of *both* parties. This agreement expired in 1905 and was not renewed, but most collective agreements subsequently concluded provided for arbitration of disputes arising thereunder.[3]

It was from the trade unions, interestingly enough, that the demand for labor disputes legislation first arose. They were mo-

[1] Legislation dealing with the labor boycott will be discussed in the following chapter.

[2] "Disputes over rights concern rights and obligations pursuant either to existing individual labor agreements or collective labor agreements. Disputes over interests are disputes concerning the establishment of new conditions of labor in the plants embraced in disputes. Disputes over rights are disputes over what *is* the law, disputes over interests concern what *shall be* the law between the parties." Paal Berg, *Arbeidsrett* (Oslo, 1930), p. 213.

[3] Socialdepartementet, *Ot. prp. nr. 54,* 1925, p. 2. (The abbreviation *Ot. prp.* designates legislative proposals or reports made to the Storting by government departments.)

tivated by the belief that their organization would be furthered by legislation imposing upon employers the obligation of settling controversies by negotiation. As the labor movement grew stronger, however, it reversed its previous position and opposed almost all the disputes legislation enacted prior to the debut of the Labor government in 1935. Employers, on the other hand, were cautious at the outset, but gradually veered to the support of an increasing degree of governmental intervention. But it was the Liberal Party, representing primarily professional and intellectual groups, rather than the Conservative Party, which spoke for the business men, that provided the impetus to legislation.

ARBITRATION OF DISPUTES OVER RIGHTS

The Act of August 6, 1915, Concerning Labor Disputes,[4] set the pattern of labor legislation in Norway and to a large extent governs the contemporary conduct of industrial relations. Its two major provisions were those creating the Labor Court (*Arbeidsrett*) and the mediation system.

The Labor Court consists of a chairman and six additional members,[5] appointed by the government for terms of three years each. Employer associations and trade unions of specified size nominate two members each, the Ministry of Labor selecting the individuals to be appointed from among the nominees. The chairman and one other public member must possess the qualifications required of a justice of the Supreme Court of Norway, and no member may belong to the executive committee of a trade union or employers' association, or be a permanent employee of either.

All disputes "between a trade union and an employer or association of employers concerning the validity, interpretation, or existence of a collective agreement, or involving a demand based

[4] The English text of this law is available in *Bulletin of the International Labour Office*, Vol. 10, (1915) p. 308. Further reference in this chapter to ILO publications indicates that the law in question has been translated into English.

[5] Originally the Court was composed of five members. In 1927, however, the number was increased to seven by the addition of two neutral members "in order to strengthen the Labor Court's authority." Socialdepartementet, *Ot. prp. nr. 54*, 1925, p. 11. It had been the experience up to that time that most cases were being decided by 3 to 2 majorities, the chairman casting the deciding vote.

The structure and jurisdiction of the Labor Court are treated more fully in Chapter X.

on a collective agreement" must be submitted to the Labor Court for arbitration. Strikes and lockouts over such disputes are forbidden, except when the Labor Court consents to a counter strike or lockout in the event that one party to an agreement has resorted to an unlawful work stoppage. Thus if a strike occurs in a particular plant over a contract interpretation, the association of which the aggrieved employer is a member may secure permission to close down other plants in the industry in sympathy.[6]

MEDIATION

The second major portion of the Labor Disputes Act of 1915 provided for the appointment of a State Mediator (*Riksmeglingsmann*) and district mediators (*kretsmeglingsmannen*). Originally there was also provision for *tripartite* collegial mediation boards, to which disputes might be referred on agreement of the parties, but this proved to be of no practical significance and was dropped in 1931.[7]

A trade union or an employer desiring to institute a strike or lockout in a dispute *over interests* must first notify the State Mediator of its intention. The notice must include detailed information regarding total employment in the industry, the number of workers involved in the dispute, the subject matter in controversy, and the status of negotiations. No strike or lockout may legally be called until four working days have elapsed from the date of receipt of notice by the mediator.[8]

[6] The provision for allowing counteraction was added to the law in 1927. It is based upon the notion that "when society's means of bringing a dispute to an end are not suitable in a given situation . . . it would be unjust if the injured party were barred from using force for the duration of the contract period." Socialdepartementet, *Ot. prp. nr. 54,* 1925, p. 13.

[7] There were several instances of collegial mediation during 1927 and 1928, when the government appointed three *neutral* mediators to intervene in stubborn conflicts. This action had no formal legal standing, however, and a subsequent proposal to enact it into law failed.

[8] Purely "political" or demonstration strikes; strikes of unorganized workers whose demands are not supported by any organization; and strikes of organized workers without permission of their union are not included within the definition of "strike" for the purposes of this section. See Paal Berg, *Loven av 5 Mai om Arbeidstvister og Tvungen Voldgift* (Oslo, 1928). However, even if a strike were thus excepted from the prohibition, and therefore from the penal provisions of the act, it could constitute breach of a collective agreement in appropriate circumstances.

The mediator (state or district) utilizes this period of grace to determine whether the threatened stoppage will "prejudice public interests in view either of the nature of the establishment or of the extent of the dispute." In the event of an affirmative finding, he notifies the parties that a work stoppage is prohibited until the termination of mediation proceedings.

As the law was originally written the mediation authorities could not intervene until they had received written notice of the stoppage from either of the parties. In 1934 the discretion of the mediator was broadened by giving him authority to intervene in the dispute at any stage of negotiations. The state and district mediators are now enjoined to follow closely the progress of all labor disputes within their respective jurisdictions, and mediation proceedings may be instituted before a notice of work stoppage has been received. The parliamentary committee that recommended this change expressed the belief that

it will be an important advantage if the State Mediator can have the opportunity of lending his assistance, as early as possible, toward the solution of the dispute. The parties will in general not have reached a situation in which a strike notice has been given and a stoppage is imminent, and the mediator will have a better chance of bringing about a peaceful solution.[9]

When a work stoppage prohibition has been issued, mediation must be undertaken without delay. In practice, the State Mediator himself handles the most vital disputes, particularly those involving national agreements, while less important matters are delegated to district mediators. The mediator may summon witnesses, subpoena books and records, and hear expert testimony, in fact perform all the fact-finding functions of an ordinary court of law except that he may not require testimony under oath. The proceedings are always conducted *in camera* to prevent the publication of material that might prove prejudicial to a settlement, and neither side may be represented by a lawyer without the consent of the mediator. As a matter of practice the principals themselves conduct the proceedings, though lawyers are occasionally present.

The conduct of mediation proceedings is an art that not all the

[9] Socialdepartementet, *Ot. prp. nr. 31,* 1934, p. 3.

Norwegian State Mediators, lawyers by profession without exception, were able to master with equal success. At first the mediator attempts merely to act in a conciliatory capacity, dealing with groups of from twenty to twenty-five people on each side, sitting in different rooms. When the issues have been narrowed, the mediator gets down to business and confers separately with the leaders on both sides in an attempt to find a real basis for settlement. The final settlement will usually be reached by joint meetings of a few leaders in the mediator's chambers.

The successful mediators, of whom Jens Michael Lund and Clausen may be accounted the most prominent, have been key figures in industrial relations. On the retirement of Mr. Clausen in 1945, the Federation of Labor gave the following valediction:

It is not easy to be a State Mediator. One minute he argues for one side, and the next minute he may have to take the other side. Often it is like balancing on the edge of a knife. It is rare that both parties are satisfied with a mediator's proposals. Usually, if one party is satisfied, the other damns it. Many times both are dissatisfied. State Mediator Clausen as a rule took the complaints of both parties good-naturedly . . . It is with sorrow that we face the fact of his resignation after so many years of activity. He had become so prominent a figure in all that had to do with wages and working conditions that we have many times asked ourselves what we would do when he retired.[10]

Ten days from the issuance of a work stoppage prohibition either party has the right to demand termination of the mediation proceedings unless it had refused to coöperate with the mediator. The proceedings must then be terminated within four days, leaving the parties free to pursue the dispute through whatever means they desire. The mediator may issue a public report and reopen the mediation proceedings, although without an accompanying prohibition of strike or lockout. If a work stoppage continues for a month, the act requires the mediator to bring the parties together once more for further negotiation looking toward termination of the stoppage. The mediator may not order the termination of hostilities, however.

Strikes or lockouts may thus be delayed for a period of fourteen days. This is a maximum, since the mediator may terminate proceedings and leave the parties to their resources at any time within

[10] *Fri Fagbevegelse*, January 1946.

the period. In practice, the full "cooling off" period is usually allowed to run unless agreement is reached earlier.

THE MEDIATION PROPOSAL

The mediator may formulate a proposal for settlement (*meglingsforslag*) during the course of mediation proceedings. In the hands of an experienced mediator this constitutes a powerful and flexible weapon. Since the mediator is always a person of considerable standing in the community,[11] rejection of what he considers to be a reasonable solution to a controversy may be prejudicial to the future chances of either party to the dispute.

After talking with the parties and ascertaining their minimum demands, the mediator is usually in a position to know whether there is any basis for compromise. He will almost never make a formal settlement proposal if he knows that both sides will reject it; the only problem is whether to issue it knowing that one party is opposed. Except under unusual circumstances, such as occurred during the general strike of 1931, the mediator will refrain from any specific formulation unless he is certain that it is acceptable to the immediate negotiators on both sides.

The real significance of the mediation proposal springs from the fact that mere agreement by the actual negotiators upon the terms of a new collective agreement does not constitute a binding contract. All collective agreements require ratification by the employers and workers who will be bound thereby. Employers rarely reject the proposals approved by their representatives, but in some unions refusal to approve agreements endorsed by the leadership has been commonplace, on the theory that better terms can be secured by holding out. It is not unusual for many weeks of difficult negotiation to be undone in this manner, particularly where political factionalism is involved. Yet the referendum procedure has become so fixed a part of the scheme of things that a trade union leader who flouted it, however logical his arguments, would be courting disaster at the next union convention. To the Norwegian worker the right to ballot on a proposed collective agreement is an integral part of his democratic rights.

The mediation proposal is in part a mechanism for bolstering

[11] District mediators, for example, are often the Norwegian officials corresponding to state governors in the United States. The recently retired State Mediator, Paal Berg, is a former Chief Justice of the Supreme Court.

the authority of the union negotiating committee and reducing the number of rejected agreements. If the union negotiators feel that the best agreement they can secure is likely to be unpopular among the workers, they can transfer at least part of the onus to the mediator by justifying their acceptance of his final proposal by their desire to avoid an unfavorable public reaction. Defiance of a mediation proposal is much more difficult from this point of view than mere rejection of a tentative agreement arrived at through direct negotiation between the parties.

In effect the mediation proposal occupies a position somewhere between mediation and arbitration,[12] and in the light of the fact finding that usually precedes its issuance, its impact is fairly close to that intended by the operation of emergency boards under the United States Railway Labor Act. But its strength, as compared with the American scheme, lies in its close relationship to collective bargaining. American fact finding, based upon the idea of an essentially objective judicial process, is often divorced from the actual situation to the extent that resultant public reports may become more a hindrance than a help to peaceful settlement of the dispute. The Norwegian combination of mediation and fact finding recognizes that in most labor disputes fact and opinion are merged to such an extent that only an individual familiar with the entire background of the controversy is in a position to separate the essential from the unimportant, to appreciate the nuances of opposing stands, and to arrive at conclusions that will reconcile rather than divide.[13]

[12] There is always a danger that the mediation proposal will tend to convert mediation proceedings into outright arbitration. To quote a former State Mediator: "Instead of being a confidential conference between the mediator and the parties' elected negotiators possessed of unlimited authority, mediation is apt to become a large debating assembly, where each of the parties seeks as best possible to present its case to the mediator. It is more and more common for people to expect that negotiation will not end without a proposal from the mediator . . . As State Mediator I have worked consciously to bring the form of negotiation more in consonance with the intent of the act, and to that end I often refused to frame a proposal unless the representatives of the parties declared publicly that they would ratify it." Socialdepartementet, *Ot. prp. nr. 54*, 1925, p. 36. This has been the policy of all mediators. Failure to exercise such restraint would jeopardize the institution of mediation.

[13] If fact finding conformed in practice to its literal meaning, these remarks might be irrelevant. American fact-finding boards, however, generally have as part of their mandate the formulation of recommendations, and even when this

The increasing importance of the mediation proposal led to the demand that its employment be subject to closer legal regulation. Lack of worker participation in referendums often enabled militant minorities to defeat a proposal that the majority might have favored. Although the Federation of Labor has always refused to divulge the extent of participation in contract referendums, 75 per cent would probably constitute an overstatement in most instances.[14] Employers maintained that acceptance of a mediation proposal by the union negotiators creates at least a presumption of reasonability that should be subject to rebuttal only by a clear showing of majority opposition. The trade union point of view, however, is that balloting procedure is purely an internal union affair, and that any attempt to codify the mediation proposal would destroy its usefulness.

The Act of 1915 contained no strictures on voting procedure. In 1927, however, the following provision was inserted into the law :

If a vote is taken in connection with a mediation proposal, the organizations concerned shall ensure that all members entitled to vote are acquainted with the full text of the proposal. If the proposal is rejected the mediator shall be informed in writing how many votes were cast against it and how many members were entitled to vote.[15]

More specific rules were enacted in 1934,[16] based largely upon Danish legislation. The chairman of the Federation of Labor was a member of the parliamentary committee that recommended the change, and his acquiescence in the new law was seized upon as a pretext to unseat him at the next convention, although actually the unions had no strenuous objections to the voting procedure adopted.

---

is not true, the facts are ordinarily cast in such a form as to lead to policy conclusions.

[14] It is asserted that in the voting on the first mediation proposal during the general strike of 1931, in which worker interest ran very high, only 28,000 votes were cast as compared with total eligibility of 50,000 (56 per cent). Some 27,300 votes (55 per cent) were cast in balloting on the second mediation proposal. Socialdepartementet, *Ot. prp. nr. 71, 1933,* p. 37.

[15] ILO *Legislative Series,* 1927, Law of May 5, 1927, Section 35.

[16] ILO *Legislative Series,* 1934, Act of June 26, 1934, Section 36a.

It was required that the ballot be in writing, recorded by a simple yes or no. A mediation proposal was deemed accepted unless the following number of votes were cast against it:

Percentage of persons entitled to vote actually voting	Required percentage of votes against proposal
75 or more	50
70–74	52
65–69	55
60–64	57
55–59	60
50–54	62
45–49	65
40–44	67
35–39	70
30–34	72
25–29	75

If less than 25 per cent of the persons entitled to vote actually voted, the proposal was considered accepted.

A year later this legislation was repealed,[17] largely as a result of labor pressure, but it was replaced by a private agreement between the Federation of Labor and the Employers' Association covering voting procedure both on mediation proposals and collective agreements reached through direct negotiation. The trade unions pledged that they would abide by the following rules:

In voting on collective agreements, all workers having the right to vote shall be assembled to hear the details of the proposal, and they shall then be given the opportunity to vote by secret ballot.

The ballots shall be sealed and preserved by the executive committee of the local union until voting in the district is concluded for all who shall participate. The executive committee or the committee on elections shall then count the ballots and enter the results in the minutes. The results shall be sent to the national union, and must not be published in any form until the two central organizations have given their consent. The ballots shall be sent to the national union if so requested.

All organized workers in the establishments covered by the proposal have the right to vote. In local unions in which workers constantly

[17] ILO *Legislative Series*, 1935, Act of March 29, 1935.

change their place of work (building, transportation, lumber and agriculture, seasonal work) all members have the right to participate in the voting. Where a proposal which will determine wage and working conditions for an entire trade is submitted to a local union, all members shall have the right to participate in the voting. All who have the right to vote have the duty to vote.

If there are so few votes cast that there is not an adequate expression of majority opinion, the national executive committee may require new balloting. This vote shall embrace all interested local unions and members. In plants where there is shift work, a meeting or meetings shall be held so that all members have the opportunity of voting.[18]

The agreement also provides, on the employers' side, that all members of the Employers' Association who are affected by a proposal may vote on it, by secret ballot. For a proposal to be defeated, a majority of those eligible to vote must vote against it. These requirements are not of practical importance, but were inserted primarily for the purpose of creating a balance of obligations as opposed to the one-sidedness of the previous legislation.

Both labor and management appear to be satisfied with the present operation of the voting regulations. There is some concern with relatively low worker participation in contract referendums since 1945, but no disposition to reinstate a more formal procedure.

A related provision in the 1934 legislation, not deleted in 1935, vested in the mediator authority to link various trades in voting on a mediation proposal, thus in a sense determining the bargaining unit. For example, if several allied crafts did not agree, he could issue a settlement proposal for each craft separately, or for any combination of them, whichever was more likely to lead to a peaceful conclusion of the dispute. The law stipulates, however, that "the mediator shall consult the central organizations before reaching a decision."

Before 1940, the mediator exercised this authority occasionally, though never without the consent of both parties. Since 1945, however, the voting unit has been coterminous with national union jurisdiction.

[18] These rules are quoted from the Basic Agreement between the Norwegian Employers' Association and the Federation of Labor concluded in 1947. The relevant provisions of the 1935 agreement were similar in all essential details, the 1947 revision having made only editorial changes.

THE COLLECTIVE AGREEMENT

Norwegian legislation contains requirements which collective agreements must fulfill if they are to furnish the basis of an action before the Labor Court, or are to be valid for other purposes of the labor-disputes legislation, and implies certain contract terms if they are omitted from agreements.

A collective agreement must be in writing; there must be a specified expiration date and termination notice. In default of a stated period of validity, a term of three years is presumed by law, and if no provision for notice of termination appears, an agreement is considered renewed for one year in the event of failure to give three months' notice.[19] Attested copies of all collective agreements are required to be filed with the State Mediator within fourteen days of final signature.

Collective agreements are deemed contracts between organizations as such, in contrast to the theories held by most American courts, and all individual rights are derived through them.[20] Collective agreements are superior to and supersede individual agreements. Therefore the terms of an individual contract between an employer and an employee which are contrary to a collective agreement, by which both are bound, are void. This is true even if the individual contract antedated the collective agreement. If a member of a trade union or employers' association resigns his membership, he is not relieved of the obligations in force at the time of his resignation.[21]

A collective agreement is legally defined as "an agreement between a trade union and an employer or employers' association concerning working and wage conditions or other conditions of

[19] This provision has been of little significance, since Norwegian collective agreements almost uniformly contain termination provisions.

[20] Individual workers thus have no standing before the Labor Court, and must prosecute their rights under collective agreements through their trade unions. See Berg, *Arbeidsrett,* p. 221.

[21] The Norwegians have not formally practiced the system of extension of collective agreements common in other European countries. The terms of a collective agreement do not *automatically* extend to nonunion workers in the plants covered by the agreement. Therefore an unorganized worker can not claim rights under the agreement. But the Labor Court has ruled that a trade union *may require* the extension of the terms of an agreement to all workers in the plant or industry covered, on the theory that the employer might otherwise undermine union standards.

employment." In order for a group of workers to be considered a trade union under the Act of 1915 it was required to have an elected executive committee and at least twenty-five members, or to be a constituent part of a combination of workers with twenty-five members or more. These requirements were deleted in 1927 as a means of preventing evasion of union responsibility;[22] at present any combination of workers seeking to protect the interests of its members against employers is deemed a trade union for the purposes of the law, and an agreement with an unorganized group may qualify as a valid collective agreement.

COMPULSORY ARBITRATION OF DISPUTES

The first attempt at compulsory arbitration of interest disputes, that is, disputes over the terms and conditions of new collective agreements, came in 1916 when Norway, though neutral in the European war, found herself hard pressed economically. During the winter and spring of 1916 a number of important collective agreements expired, and efforts to renew them through collective bargaining were unavailing. Mining activities ceased for four months, the metal trades closed down for six weeks. The Liberal government then in power introduced a compulsory arbitration bill that caused the union negotiators to make new concessions, and the bill was withdrawn. The workers refused to follow the recommendations of their leaders, however, and a sympathetic lockout of 70,000 additional workers was threatened by the employers. The bill was thereupon reintroduced and passed, despite a general strike of one week called by the Federation of Labor in a vain attempt to halt its enactment.

The law[23] empowered the government, if it considered that a labor dispute tended to endanger "important public interests," to decree the settlement of the dispute by arbitration. Work stoppages were forbidden in that event, and previous conditions of employment remained in effect pending the arbitration award.

A tripartite arbitration board of five members was established, three representing the public and one each employers and trade unions, with power to proceed "in any manner which the board thinks proper." Proceedings were to be public, unless otherwise

[22] Socialdepartementet, *Ot. prp. nr. 54*, 1925, p. 18.
[23] *Bulletin of the ILO*, Vol. II, Act of June 9, 1916.

determined by the board, which could subpoena witnesses and documents, take testimony under oath, and require evidence to be taken by any general inferior court of law. All decisions were to be by majority vote, and to be valid for a period not to exceed three years, with the same effect as collective agreements.

The Act of 1916 was by its terms limited to the duration of the war in Europe. In 1919, and again in 1920, it was reënacted for one-year periods over the opposition of the Labor Party.[24] When a Conservative government took office in 1921, however, it permitted the compulsory arbitration law to lapse. The principal reason was employer dissatisfaction with several 1920 arbitration awards. Organized employers had taken the position that while they were opposed to permanent compulsory arbitration, they would not object to it as a temporary expedient in emergencies.

The labor movement, weakened by the loss of a general strike in 1921 and by internal factionalism, feared the results of an employer offensive. When a minority Liberal government, which returned to office in 1922, proposed the reënactment of compulsory arbitration, labor gave its grudging consent. It hoped that the new law would provide a breathing spell and time to reform its disorganized ranks. The Conservative Party opposed the law, but it was passed by a combination of Labor and Liberal votes, in substantially the same form as the earlier legislation.[25]

This *volte-face* on the part of labor was short lived. When the act, by its terms, expired in 1923, the Labor Party joined once more with the Conservatives to prevent renewal. Substantial wage reductions imposed by the Board of Arbitration in 1922 had provided convincing evidence that such legislation was not a shield against economic fluctuation. From 1923 to 1927, compulsory arbitration was not practiced. In the latter year, after crippling strikes in the mining, textile, and shoe industries, the Conservative Party reversed its previous opposition and joined with the Liberals to enact a new compulsory arbitration law with a two-year term.[26]

The 1927 legislation contained several novel features. Taking

[24] Acts of April 4, 1919, and March 29, 1920.
[25] Act of March 31, 1922.
[26] ILO *Legislative Series*, 1927, Act of May 5, 1927. See also John Eric Nordskog, *Social Reform in Norway* (Los Angeles, 1935), Chapter IV.

cognizance of the increased importance of mediation, it stipulated that arbitration could be employed only upon the recommendation of the State Mediator, after mediation had failed. The Board of Arbitration was empowered to "refer disputed points which are laid before it to negotiation or mediation, provided that both parties agree thereto and declare that they are willing to coöperate in the settlement of the dispute without recourse to a stoppage of work." To allay employer fears of being burdened with uneconomic wage scales over long periods, it further provided that if, during the period covered by an award, material changes occurred in relevant economic circumstances, for example, a substantial rise or fall in the cost of living, either party could petition for reconsideration, although not before six months from the date of the award.

Successful trade union defiance of an arbitration award in 1928 undermined the prestige of the Board of Arbitration, and when the law expired in 1929 there was little sentiment for reënactment. Occasional attempts to revive compulsory arbitration during the early nineteen-thirties failed in the face of a solid trade union-employer front. In 1938, however, the Labor government secured the enactment of legislation providing for compulsory arbitration of a dispute involving transportation facilities in the northern part of the country. It was noted that

a continuance of the stoppage of sea transport in northern Norway and in the supply of foodstuffs to the various towns would in any circumstance entail serious consequences. In addition we are now awaiting the great Lofoten fishing season . . . Since important public interests are at stake the Ministry has found it necessary to consider the question of extraordinary regulations to bring the stoppage to an end.[27]

An arbitration board was established to decide this single dispute, with its jurisdiction limited to specifically named firms.[28]

This foreshadowed labor's attitude toward compulsory arbitration of interest disputes after 1945. The chairman of the Federation of Labor had the following to say with respect to this action, which ran counter to previous trade union policy:

[27] Socialdepartementet, *Ot. prp. nr. 14,* 1938, p. 1.
[28] Act of February 16, 1938.

In certain circumstances . . . it is fully defensible to accept compulsory arbitration in a contract dispute . . . Trade unionists must be aware above all of the great difference that lies between arbitration in which a labor government names the judges, and arbitration in which a bourgeois government names the judges. Political power opens great possibilities for advances that may otherwise cost thousands of strike days.[29]

TRADE UNION AND INDIVIDUAL LIABILITY

One of the more controversial aspects of Norwegian labor legislation concerns the extent to which trade unions should be held liable for the acts of their members or subsidiary organizations in violation of collective agreements and of the mediation and arbitration laws. It is the consensus that both trade unions and employer associations should be liable for damages when they fail to honor the terms of collective agreements. There is considerable difference of opinion, however, when it comes to requiring trade unions, particularly the national unions, to make good losses occasioned by their members. This is the key to enforcement of collective agreements, for as a practical matter an employer cannot hope to secure compensation from individual workers, whereas trade union treasuries are relatively easy to tap.

The Act of 1915 made a trade union liable for breach of a collective agreement or for an unlawful work stoppage by its members "when it is itself guilty either of pursuing conditions contrary to the agreement or an unlawful stoppage." The burden of proof was laid upon the injured party, who had to establish the affirmative guilt of the trade union. In fixing the amount of compensation the Labor Court was required to consider not only the extent of the damage but also the degree of trade-union culpability established and any improper act on the part of the injured party. Compensation might be forfeited entirely if extenuating circumstances were present. This proved an important qualification in the light of later developments.

Employers charged that these provisions were not effective in preventing contract breaches by local unions and small groups of workers, mainly in the form of unlawful strikes to secure terms of employment other than those stipulated by agreement. It was con-

[29] Olav Hindahl, "Fagbevegelsens samfundsmessige stilling," *Fagbevegelsens Økonomiske Problemer* (Oslo, 1938), p. 270.

ceded that national unions attempted in general to live up to their agreements,[30] but the employers argued that by sharpening the liability of national unions for the acts of their subordinate units and of individual members, there would be greater incentive to maintain internal discipline. The trade unions were not disposed to deny that there had been breaches of contract at the local level, but maintained that it was inequitable to impose constructive liability in so dynamic and difficult a field.

A 1927 amendment to the labor-disputes law had the effect of shifting the burden of proof, in the event of an alleged breach of collective agreement by workers, to the trade union side:

If a member of a trade union or employers' association breaks a collective agreement or is guilty of an illegal work stoppage, the union or association is liable unless it proves that it is not guilty, or that it sought to hinder the breach or continuation of the violation or the illegal work stoppage with the means that stood at its disposal.[31]

Even this did not prove satisfactory to employers, however, and in 1933 trade unions were made absolutely liable for contract breaches committed by their members, with disclaimer of liability forbidden. A distinction was made between unlawful strikes and other actions involving breach of contract, and those not involving breach of contract.[32] In the latter type of case, the union remained

[30] Referring to the Lumber and Agricultural Workers' Union, one of the newer and least disciplined unions, the Paper Industry Employers' Association remarked: "We must admit that by and large the aforementioned union has attempted to honor signed agreements as well as it could. However, we have had many instances of agreements that were difficult to administer because of the lack of economic responsibility in the local unions out in the country affiliated with the national union. Often there has been a feeling among the members when they are first organized that they can handle contracts, wages, and other conditions of labor as best they see fit." Socialdepartementet, *Ot. prp. nr. 71,* 1933, p. 60.

[31] Act of May 5, 1927, Section 4.

[32] There had been some doubt prior to this enactment whether the "unlawful work stoppage" of the Act of 1915 embraced all stoppages, or was confined merely to stoppages involving breach of contract. The Act of 1933 resolved this doubt by making a clear distinction between the two. See J. Øvergaard, *Arbeidstvist og Boikott-Loven* (Oslo, 1934), p. 51. Recourse to the ordinary courts was necessary to secure damages in other than collective agreement violations, since the jurisdiction of the Labor Court was limited to the latter.

liable in accordance with the 1927 provisions. Only when a strike or other action by members involved a contract violation did liability attach unconditionally to the union.

The Act of 1933 extended liability to any organization of which the union, union members, or employer involved in a contract violation was a constituent part, even though the superior organization was not a party to the agreement. To protect themselves, employer or worker organizations were authorized by law, regardless of their constitutions, to exclude members or subordinate bodies participating in actions that constituted contract violations for a period up to one year after the cessation of the illegal conduct, and to withhold strike or other benefit payments during this period.[33]

On its face, the liability section of the Act of 1933 appeared to open the way for damage suits against the Federation of Labor itself in the event of a breach of contract on the part of any individual member or subordinate union. However, the Labor Court declared in a unanimous decision of December 19, 1934, that although trade unions were absolutely liable as indicated, Section 5 of the Labor Disputes Act, adopted in 1915 and never repealed, required it to assess damages on the basis of actual guilt, and to waive damages entirely in appropriate circumstances. That this mitigating interpretation has resulted in a reasonable allocation of responsibility is evidenced by the fact that the trade unions have not seriously sought the repeal of Section 4, which remains upon the statute books in the 1933 form.

Turning to provisions for penal liability, the Act of 1915 set fines of from 5 to 25,000 kroner for violation of the sections dealing with "cooling off" periods for strikes and lockouts in interest disputes, and the prohibition of stoppages in disputes over rights. The following persons were made subject to penalty:

(a) Any person who initiates or continues a lockout or takes part in a strike contrary to law. A person who acts on behalf of an employer shall not be convicted unless the employer himself is convicted.

(b) The members of the executive committee of a trade union or an employers' association who coöperate in a strike or lockout contrary to law, by participating in a resolution to initiate, continue, or

[33] Act of July 6, 1933, Section 4.

approve a cessation of work or support it by payments from the association's funds, or who order such cessation of work, or collect or distribute contributions toward its continuance.[34]

The penal provisions of the labor-disputes legislation, as well as the contract-liability section, were strengthened considerably in 1927. Violation became punishable by prison sentences up to a maximum of three months, as well as by fine. The 1915 legislation was aimed primarily at trade union leaders, whereas the 1927 version extended liability to individual union members who engaged in the forbidden acts. In view of the more stringent penalties, however, individual workers who did nothing more than participate in unlawful strikes at the order of their leaders were absolved of penal liability. The law levied penalties against:

1. Any person who (a) supports a resolution for the purpose of initiating, continuing, supporting with contributions, or approving an unlawful strike or lockout, or coöperating therein, or
2. Incites another person to initiate or continue such a stoppage of work or supports it or collects contributions or distributes contributions when collected for the purpose of initiating or continuing such a stoppage . . .
Any person who (a) causes or endeavors to cause another person to lose or to give up his employment or to refrain from seeking or accepting employment, provided that this is done for the purpose of endeavoring to bring about a stoppage of work; (b) incites any person to commit any of the actions specified under (a) or contributes thereto; (c) causes or endeavors to cause an employer to take part in an unlawful lockout, or causes or endeavors to cause an undertaking to commit or refrain from any action in order to support an unlawful lockout, or (d) incites any person to commit any action under (c) . . .[35]

PROTECTION OF NONSTRIKING WORKERS

Since the beginning of the century there have been numerous legislative proposals aimed at affording special protection to workers willing to remain at their employment during labor disputes, but these failed of passage on the ground that the provisions of the

[34] Act of 1915, Section 40.
[35] Act of May 5, 1927, Section 40. Although these provisions remain on the statute books, prison sentences have never been meted out for violation of the labor-disputes law, and fines were imposed only in rare instances.

general penal code governing unlawful threats and force were sufficient.[36] In 1927, after several years of turbulent labor relations, a Conservative government succeeded in securing the enactment of an amendment to the penal code that imposed a fine of from 25 to 25,000 kroner, and/or imprisonment up to one year, for attempting to induce an individual not to work:

(a) by molesting him or members of his household by threats or violence or insulting or importunate demeanor;
(b) by following him from place to place;
(c) by publishing the names of persons who are working or have worked or sought work during a stoppage of work;
(d) by hindering such other person in his work or business by unlawful methods.[37]

No other piece of labor legislation aroused as much trade-union ire as this "jailhouse law," as it was commonly called by the workers. The Federation of Labor and the Labor Party created a joint fund for the purpose of defending persons prosecuted for its violation, and for paying their fines upon conviction. Several labor journalists were imprisoned for publishing the names of strikebreakers.

One of Norway's foremost legal authorities, after an exhaustive inquiry into the conduct of labor disputes, recommended the repeal of this legislation on the following grounds:

1. Regardless of the correctness of their belief, all workers were of the opinion that the law was one-sided, directed particularly against organized labor. This tended to create bitterness and class conflict. The administration of justice was being weakened by growing worker conviction of the class character of the criminal courts.

2. Other provisions of the penal law covering the use of violence and threats afforded sufficient protection to strike breakers.[38]

This recommendation was carried out in 1935.[39]

[36] The history of this debate is set forth in Jon Skeie, *Ulovlige midler i Kampen om Arbeidsvilkaar* (Oslo, 1931), pp. 351–466. See also Alf Frydenberg, *Kollektive arbeidstvister og deres bileggelse i Norge* (Oslo, 1927).
[37] ILO *Legislative Series,* 1927, Act of July 4, 1927.
[38] See Skeie, pp. 519–20.
[39] Act of June 21, 1935.

OTHER LEGISLATION

The Act of 1915 required every trade union and employer association to register with the Ministry of Labor the names of the members of its executive committee, its constitution and by-laws, and current membership data. The purpose of this provision was to supply the Labor Court and the mediators with information that might be of help in the performance of their duties. No benefits flowed from registration, nor was there any deregistration.

This requirement was reduced in 1927 to the submission of data "regarding the organization of the union, association, or federation and its membership," at the specific request of the Ministry of Labor or the State Mediator. The previous registration provision was repealed. Since Norwegian trade unions customarily publish financial and membership data regularly, this information requirement is of no practical importance.

Beginning in 1920 there were suggestions that all strike votes be hedged about with certain legal requirements. The parliamentary labor-disputes committee of 1933 proposed that strikes be forbidden unless a majority of the workers involved, both organized and unorganized, indicated their support in a secret, written ballot.[40] This was rejected largely on the basis of testimony offered by the State Mediators. The first, Valentin Voss, declared:

On the basis of my experience as State Mediator through four difficult years . . . I cannot subscribe to the belief that we would have had more labor peace in industry even if the law had included provisions concerning voting among workers and employers. I believe that the balloting we have had largely afforded a correct expression of individual opinion and that in any event no concrete case can be shown in which voting irregularities had a decisive influence on the outcome.[41]

The second mediator, Andreas Claussen, added:

Talk of force and undue influence during voting is more a slogan based on hypothesis than on fact. It is obvious that trade union leadership has significant influence upon the results of a referendum, but that is due to the advice that the leaders send out before the elections,

---

[40] Socialdepartementet, *Ot. prp. nr. 6*, 1933, Bilag, p. 89.
[41] Socialdepartementet, *Ot. prp. nr. 6*, 1933, p. 28.

and to organizational discipline. In general it should be said that no interest is served by weakening the influence of the leadership.[42]

While there was subsequent regulation of voting on mediation proposals, no further attempts were made to legislate strike vote procedure.

Picketing was not directly subject to regulation by national legislation, although it played an important role in industrial warfare during organizational campaigns. The effect of the boycott laws on the right to picket will be considered later. In general, if a strike were legal, peaceful picketing to notify workers and potential customers of the existence of the strike was equally lawful.[43] There were local police rules governing the number of pickets, the time that a picket could remain in the same place, and the conduct of the pickets — and considerable variation in the attitude of local courts toward these rules.[44] But even when parliament was considering the possibility of setting stringent limits to trade union activities, it was deemed sufficient to prohibit only "violent, offensive, or importunate conduct by pickets against those willing to work" [45]

COLLECTIVE BARGAINING IN GOVERNMENT SERVICE

Employees of the Norwegian government, both in the civil service and in nonclassified activities, enjoy a considerable degree of latitude with respect to their ability to influence wage and working conditions through collective bargaining. The civil servants are organized on three levels: the highest officials in the *Embetsmannsforbund,* the middle officials in the *Statstjenestemannsforbund,* and the lower officials in the *Tjenestemanns Kartellet,* a group of unions. Only the latter are affiliated with the Federation of Labor. Non-civil service employees belong to ordinary industrial or craft unions, for example, road workers are affiliated largely with the Laborers' Union.

The civil service law of 1918 [46] assured the right to strike in the public service (except for the highest category of officials).

[42] Socialdepartementet, *Ot. prp. nr. 6,* 1933, p. 28.
[43] Berg, *Arbeidsrett,* p. 245.
[44] Skeie, pp. 466–493.
[45] Socialdepartementet, *Ot. prp. nr. 6,* 1933, p. 12.
[46] *Almindelig Norsk Lovforsamling,* 1916–1919, Act of February 15, 1918.

No civil servant could leave work without first giving three months' notice, and the government, if it found that resignations were "by agreement or in common understanding, or will endanger important public interests," could ordain an additional three months of service. At the end of six months, however, a strike could lawfully take place. Pursuant to this law officials of the state-owned railways went on strike in 1920, the only strike of civil servants that has occurred since the enactment of the legislation.

The Act of 1918 provided that civil servants might establish committees within units that included at least ten employees, which in turn could unite into joint committees. Their functions were "to safeguard the interests of civil servants with respect to wage and working conditions and to express themselves on other service questions." The committees were given no specific negotiating right, and actually played but a minor role in wage questions.[47]

The growth of trade unionism among civil servants produced a demand for expansion of collective bargaining and union recognition. A parliamentary committee established to deal with this question rendered a divided report in 1925, the chief points of dissension revolving about the right to strike and the right of civil servants to appeal matters involving wage and working conditions to a neutral board independent of the government.[48] As a result no action was taken at that time.

In 1933 negotiations between representatives of the government and the civil-service unions produced the draft of a law which was promptly enacted by the parliament with few modifications and provides the basis for contemporary bargaining practice in the Norwegian government service. The strike provisions of the Act of 1918 were not modified, but an elaborate bargaining procedure was substituted for the earlier brief statement.

The Act of 1933[49] specified that civil servants have the right to negotiate on matters respecting changes in wages and working conditions. This right applies to three categories of organizations: (1) civil service unions within a unit or group of units determined by the government; (2) associations of such unions; and (3) groups of unorganized civil servants representing at least fifty per-

[47] Frydenberg, *Kollektive arbeidstvister og deres bileggelse i Norge*, p. 21.
[48] Justis- og Politidepartementet, *Ot. prp. nr. 85, 1933*, p. 1.
[49] ILO *Legislative Series*, 1933, Act of July 6, 1933.

sons. To secure the right to negotiate, a union must receive official recognition, which is accorded only to organizations that restrict their membership to civil servants in an appropriate bargaining unit,[50] and represent a majority of the employees within that unit.

Negotiations may be initiated by a single union or an association of unions, whichever is appropriate, or by a government ministry desiring to alter existing conditions of labor, and they must commence within fourteen days of the presentation of a formal demand. Ordinarily each ministry bargains separately, subject to a general policy laid down by the Wage Director in the Ministry of Finance. Careful minutes of all meetings are kept, the expense being shared equally by the parties.

When negotiations have proceeded for fourteen days, either party may request that they be terminated within three days. If an agreement is reached, it is submitted to the competent government authorities for ratification. The parliament must ultimately give its approval, but in practice it has never rejected agreements reached by this collective bargaining process, a consequence of the parliamentary system of government.[51] There are no formal agreements, wage scales being embodied in classified schedules.

If the parties are unable to arrive at an agreement, the government may require that its offer be submitted to a vote of the interested employees. The union, on the other hand, may demand that its proposals be submitted to higher authority within the government. The employee vote must be held within a month of submission by the government, while union proposals are to be taken up without unnecessary delay. If the employees vote to reject the government offer, they may presumably go on strike within a period of from three to six months after submission of quit notices.

The Act of 1933 also set up a Civil Service Court, consisting of five members appointed by the Chief Justice of the Supreme Court, three neutral and the other two representing each of the parties. In addition, two members are added on an *ad hoc* basis on nomination of (a) the government agency which the case con-

---

[50] This requirement applies only to local unions. Many national unions, such as the Telephone and Telegraph Workers' Union, include both locals of civil servants and non-civil service employees.

[51] A government could be overthrown, of course, because of parliamentary rejection of a civil-service agreement, but a political crisis over matters of this nature would be highly unlikely.

cerns, and (b) the union involved. The court has jurisdiction over "disputes between the government on the one hand and organizations of employees . . . on the other, respecting interpretation and application of the general conditions of remuneration and employment which are in effect." [52] It fulfills the same function for the government service as does the Labor Court for the general economy.

Very few cases have been brought to the Civil Service Court, most grievances being settled by direct negotiation. From 1934, the first year of its operation, to 1940, only thirteen cases were submitted, eight during 1934. Judgments were rendered in ten cases, the remainder being withdrawn.[53]

Government employees who are not classified as civil servants possess the same right to strike and bargain collectively as workers in private industry. They are subject to the general law on labor disputes, and their wages and working conditions are embodied in written collective agreements between their trade unions and the government agencies concerned.

A special law for the Government Liquor Monopoly was adopted in 1933, and remains in effect.[54] It is premised not only upon the injury the state, as employer, would sustain from a work stoppage, but also upon the fact that the important revenue from alcohol taxation would be cut off. All strikes are forbidden, disputes over interests that cannot be resolved through negotiation being submitted for arbitration to a special five-man board appointed by the Chief Justice of the Supreme Court. Disputes over rights go to the regular Labor Court for adjudication.

The foregoing sections set forth the essential details of labor relations legislation in Norway up to 1940, with the exception of the Boycott Act, which is the subject of the next chapter. Although much of this legislation remains on the statute books, the postwar superimposition of compulsory arbitration of interest disputes upon the prewar voluntary system built up since 1915 has inevitably changed the content, if not the form of the latter. A consideration of the changes that have occurred since 1945 will be reserved for later discussion.

[52] Act of July 6, 1933, *op. cit.,* Section 9.

[53] These statistics are from the annual reports of the Civil Service Court.

[54] Provisional Act of July 6, 1933; Act of June 7, 1935.

This analysis has been confined largely to a description of relevant legislation, and has avoided discussion of how successfully the institutions fostered by law have functioned to promote the settlement of labor disputes by peaceful means. The latter subject, too, will be deferred until it can be treated against a background of labor relations history.

CHAPTER VI

THE LABOR BOYCOTT

THE HISTORY of the labor boycott and legislative attempts to curb its employment in Norway merit a separate chapter. Determination of the appropriate use of this weapon was a matter of continual parliamentary investigation for several decades, resulting finally in comprehensive legislation. The history and the fate of that legislation may well be of interest to those concerned with similar problems in the United States.

In general, Norwegian courts and legislators shared with their American counterparts the basic notion that neutral parties should not unwillingly be dragged into labor disputes as a means of exerting pressure upon one of the disputants. However, they have not attempted any hard and fast distinction between primary and secondary boycotts, but instead approached the problem by inquiring whether the complainant in a boycott action was in fact a neutral, regardless of his formal relationship to the immediate parties to the dispute. Thus, for example, a retailer who deliberately purchased goods from a manufacturer engaged in a labor dispute in order to render him economic support was regarded as the legitimate object of a boycott. On the other hand, if the same retailer merely continued customary business relations with the manufacturer without intent to assist him in the prosecution of the dispute, then he was considered a neutral entitled to immunity from the boycott.

The Norwegian attitude toward the boycott springs logically from the solidarity previously noted as prevailing among both employers and workers. An American court would assume, as the New York Court of Appeals did in one of the leading cases on the labor boycott, that the retailer in the example cited was acting from commercial motives alone, and a link justifying trade union interference would have to be premised upon broader economic grounds, a "unity of interest with the manufacturer who is in the same business for profit." [1] But in Norway, where employers habitually act in concert in labor matters, the question of motivation is a pertinent one.

Given the fact of neutrality, however, a considerable degree of protection was afforded third parties. A retailer handling "unfair" material was given complete legal immunity from the boycott. But there was one major exception which again reflects the recognition given to group interests. A sympathetic strike, as contrasted, for example, with the refusal of workers to transport or work with unfair materials, was permitted under all circumstances. The logic was that if workers felt their responsibility to other members of the working class sufficiently keenly to make the personal sacrifice of leaving their employment, they should not be prohibited from doing so. Only when they attempted to discharge their "class" responsibilities by halfway measures, involving little or no sacrifice to themselves, was the employer entitled to protection.

Before considering in detail the Norwegian codification of boycott rules, it may be well to point out that the principal piece of legislation, the Boycott Act of 1933, was repealed in 1947 on the initiative of the Labor government, leaving the subject much as it had been developed by the judiciary prior to 1933. Nevertheless, it is well worth reviewing the Norwegian efforts to regulate the boycott not only because these efforts have inevitably had a permanent effect upon industrial relations in Norway, but also because through comparative analysis it may be possible to gain more insight into parallel American practice.

LEGISLATIVE BACKGROUND

The boycott, in both its primary and secondary forms,[2] was long used by Norwegian labor as a means of bringing pressure upon employers and nonunion workers. It assumed increasing importance after World War I, when the labor movement began to extend organization to nonindustrial pursuits.[3] Its employment

[1] Goldfinger v. Feintuch, 276 N. Y. 286 (1937).

[2] The distinction between primary and secondary boycott used here is that made in Millis and Montgomery, *The Economics of Labor* (New York, 1945), III, 581–599.

[3] During 1930 alone some 660 boycott notices appeared in the Oslo labor newspaper. Socialdepartementet, *Ot. prp. nr. 6,* Bilag, 1933, p. 26. The Norwegian Employers' Association catalogued 36 boycott notices that had been presented

was encouraged by the closely knit community life that characterizes so many of Norway's industrial towns, as well as by the
excellent labor press, which facilitated the dissemination of boycott information.

Prior to 1933 there was considerable judicial uncertainty over
the legality of the boycott. In general, neither a primary nor a
secondary boycott was in itself considered unlawful, though it
might become so when the object for which it was pursued or the
means employed were illegal.[4] Thus, boycotts that were instigated
merely as a means of inflicting punishment on someone, that were
aimed at inducing breach of contract, that accompanied an unlawful strike or lockout, or that had no reasonable relationship to the
interest sought to be furthered, were condemned by the courts.[5]
Similarly, boycott notices that contained false or misleading information were universally barred.[6] However, there was considerable doubt as to the legality of particular purposes and specific
means, as well as of the extent to which neutral third parties were
entitled to judicial protection.

The final impetus to anti-boycott legislation came from the
farmer rather than the industrialist. Boycotts were used primarily
in organizing new employers rather than in fighting those with
whom bargaining relationships had already been established. Boycotts of products or of customers were most effective in attaining
union purposes in sparsely settled rural areas, when labor unions
were attempting to organize dairies, lumber camps, and farm
workers, whereas in urban communities the strike, accompanied
by picketing, was the most practicable method of bringing pressure to bear on employers.

It was for this reason that the Agrarian government of 1933
pressed strongly for the passage of anti-boycott legislation. After
the introduction of a bill in parliament,[7] the Agrarian government
was defeated on another issue, yielding to the Liberal Party. Although the Liberals favored some limitations on the use of the

---

to its members in 1930, 69 in 1931, and 90 in 1932. Socialdepartementet, *Ot.*
prp. nr. 71, 1933, pp. 37–53.

[4] Paal Berg, *Arbeidsrett*, p. 251; Jon Skeie, *Ulovlige Midler i Kampen om
Arbeidsvilkaar*, p. 508.

[5] Skeie, p. 510.

[6] J. Øvergaard, *Arbeidstvist og Boikott-Loven*, p. 77.

[7] Socialdepartementet, *Ot. prp. nr. 6*, 1933, pp. 34–38.

boycott, their objectives were not as far reaching as those of the Agrarian Party. The legislation enacted represented a compromise of the two views.

The principal difference between the two lay in the breadth of the boycott definition. The Liberals proposed to define a boycott as an *appeal* to avoid economic relations with a concern or an individual for the purpose of coercion or inflicting punishment. The Agrarian conception, however, included participation in as well as incitement to boycott, and made equally guilty the passive participant and the active promoter. The draft finally adopted, which defined a boycott as an "invitation, incitement, joint decision, or other act that aims to prevent or hamper business intercourse between an individual or an undertaking and third parties with the object of coercing, injuring, or punishing anyone," [8] was ambiguous. In the parliamentary debate accompanying the bill Agrarian and Liberal spokesmen made statements that were flatly contradictory.[9] The Agrarians insisted, for example, that if a taxi driver should refuse to serve an individual against whom a boycott had been declared, such an act would fall within the scope of the law, while the Liberals held to their belief that mere passivity in a boycott situation was not comprehended within the definition. In the light of the law's legislative history and its later interpretation, the Liberal viewpoint appears to have been the better grounded.[10]

On one important point the Liberals were obliged to yield. In their proposal, blockade[11] of a place of work accompanying a legal strike was to be dealt with under the general labor-disputes provisions rather than the special boycott sections. The legislation as adopted made no exception for this type of activity.

The Boycott Act of 1933, which became section 6a of the Law

[8] Act of July 6, 1933, International Labour Office, *Legislative Series,* 1933.

[9] Øvergaard, pp. 31–34.

[10] Alf Frydenberg, "Arbeidstvister," *Social Håndbok for Norge* (Oslo, 1937), p. 776.

[11] A blockade "is always employed as an obvious and natural strike action . . . As a rule it consists in that a trade union, in connection with the publicizing of a strike, warns other workers not to seek work with the employer involved." Arnljot Engh, *Fagorganisasjonen og Loven* (Oslo, 1934), p. 72. The Norwegians use "blockade" as a general term to cover various means of keeping workers out of an establishment against which a strike has been declared, including newspaper advertising, circulars, picketing, and individual appeals to workers.

Concerning Labor Disputes, banned a boycott absolutely in the following circumstances, which corresponded generally to earlier judicial practice:

1. a. where it is undertaken without reasonable notice to the party boycotted, or without satisfactory explanation of the grounds for the boycott to the party against whom it is directed.
   b. where it is undertaken or continued through illegal means or in an unnecessarily provocative or offensive manner or by the use of false or misleading information.
   c. where it has an illegal purpose or will induce a breach of law if it achieves its purpose, or will impair essential public interests or operate unreasonably or where there is no reasonable relationship between the interest which is being furthered by the boycott and the damage which will result.

A second section banned boycotts under circumstances from which business concerns or individuals had not previously been protected unless the means or object of boycott were improper. Unless prior approval had been granted by a special Boycott Court, the new law made unlawful a boycott undertaken:

   d. because the person against whom it is directed has participated in or supported one of the parties to a labor dispute which has been brought to an end and which was accompanied by a lockout, strike, or boycott,
   or, because the said person or a person in his employ or with whom he has business relations is or is not a member of a labor union or an employers' association,
   or, in order to compel an employer or employees to join or leave an employers' association or labor union or to conclude or co-operate in concluding a collective agreement which none of the employees in the establishment concerned, or only a minority of such employees, has demanded,
   or, if in order to support one of the parties to a labor dispute, it is directed against a third party who is not connected with the dispute and has not taken economic measures in support of one of the parties to the dispute in connection therewith,
   or, if it is directed against a lumber-floating enterprise of considerable importance for the supply of timber to industrial enterprises.

It was further provided that in no event could a boycott be undertaken lawfully without the same notice as that required for the declaration of a strike, and the mediation procedure established by the Act of 1915 was extended to contemplated boycotts as well.

Two additional provisions were inserted to cover special situations. They rendered boycotts unlawful:

2. a. if directed against an employer who does not employ more than ten persons in addition to the members of his family. Brothers, sisters, nieces, nephews, and persons equally closely related by marriage shall be deemed to be members of the family, as well as husbands, wives, and relatives in the ascending or descending line

   b. if effectuated by a labor union or an employers' association which is affiliated with a central organization unless the central organization has given its consent in writing. This rule shall also apply to an employer who is a member of an employers' association.

The second provision accorded with existing practice, but the first was novel and of considerable importance. The Federation of Labor, in objecting to its inclusion, called attention to some of its implications:

These provisions will reach out a long way and will be of decisive significance for the trade union position in a number of areas of current activity. One can cite lumber and farming, the hotel and restaurant trades, and office work . . . To set a stipulated number of workers as a dividing line for legal and illegal boycotts is unreasonable, and will work arbitrarily for workers as well as employers. It will be possible to boycott an employer or business man who employs . . . eleven workers in case of a dispute, while his neighbor just across the street who has a larger business and a larger family to help him, will be protected from a boycott so long as he needs only ten workers.[12]

THE BOYCOTT COURT

The Boycott Court created by the Act of 1933 consisted of five members, three of whom represented the public interest, while one was required to be "intimately acquainted" with matters affecting employers, and one with matters affecting employees.[13]

[12] Halvard Olsen, "Arbeidernes syn paa lovforslagene om boikott," *Socialt Arbeid,* 1933, p. 192.

[13] In practice, the latter two members of the court were partisans of the respective parties, so that the court was actually tripartite. No member, however, could be a trade union or employer association official.

No plea for permission to boycott could be entered until conciliation had failed. The chairman of the court was empowered to
enjoin a boycott provisionally, pending a trial of the issues. Penalties for violation were fixed by the court and included fines of
from 5 to 25,000 kroner, or up to three months' imprisonment.

From its creation on August 1, 1933, to 1940, when it ceased to
function after the chairman and vice-chairman had been replaced
by quislings, some fifty-nine cases were submitted to the Boycott
Court. It rendered forty awards, the remainder of the cases having been withdrawn or settled. Out of eighteen requests for injunctions *pendente lite,* eight were granted, while four out of
six requests for permission to institute boycotts were similarly
granted.[14]

INTERPRETATION AND ENFORCEMENT OF THE LAW

1. The Concept of a Boycott. The Boycott Court was faced
with the formidable task of applying the vague definition of *boycott* to a variety of factual situations. The mere finding that a
boycott existed did not mean that it was necessarily unlawful. For
example, the boycott of an employer because he refused to conclude a collective agreement demanded by the *majority* of his
employees, if it did not run afoul of any of the specific prohibitions, was clearly lawful without prior permission of the Boycott
Court. But finding that a boycott did exist was a prerequisite to its
condemnation. The court was thus obliged to approach complaints
in two stages: it determined (a) whether the acts complained of
constituted a boycott, and (b) if so, whether such boycott was
unlawful.

(a) The blockade. The blockade of an enterprise with intent to
prevent the employer from securing labor and materials was held
to constitute a boycott, regardless of the fact that the blockade
accompanied a legal strike.[15] The court expressed no hesitancy on
this point, in view of the legislative history of the act.

In furtherance of the strike in the case cited above, the union

---

[14] Compiled from annual reports of the Boycott Court.

[15] Decision No. 1, 1933. The decisions of the Boycott Court were published
annually in *Dommer og Kjennelser av Domstolen for Boikottsaker.* Further
reference to decisions of the Boycott Court in this chapter will be by year and
decision number, except where decisions were not numbered, in which event
the number of the page on which the cited decision appears will be given instead.

had inserted the following announcement in local newspapers, typical of the public strike notice commonly employed:

Blockade. Since no agreement could be reached with Joh. Rasmussen & Racine A/S, a strike has begun. The company's goods, sea and land transport, and the loading of goods to and from the firm are blockaded. No honorable worker or employee should have any dealings with the firm until the dispute is settled.

Leaflets to the same effect had been distributed. Letters were sent to nonstriking employees with the following message:

Colleagues: You still have an opportunity to decide: Whether you will stand against the local union and the united trade union movement. Or whether you will stand side by side with the colleagues who have not violated the resolution which was unanimously adopted at the People's House. Let nothing influence your opinion of what you ought to do as a colleague and as a wage earner, who worked for a very low wage until *our* organization became involved. You are well aware of the cause of the wage increase recently granted. Or do you really believe that a union that runs the boss' errands *can* and *will* defend your interests? *Think. And decide correctly.* Everyone who stands with us is promised all the protection and support that a trade union movement with over 150,000 members can give. We accept no responsibility for the contempt, insults, and other disagreeable things which may be visited upon those who stand on the side of the lackey company union and act as strikebreakers.

Sympathetic strikes were also called against firms selling goods and supplying services to the complainant. These acts were held to constitute a blockade, and thus a boycott.

(*b*) *Newspaper announcements.* If a trade union, in advertising the existence of a strike, asserted specifically that a blockade was in force, the announcement was *ipso facto* a boycott. But there was some doubt as to the legal significance of the following type of notice:

A labor dispute began at Alfred Andersen's new building in Lillestrøm at the close of work on September 5, 1934. When the dispute is settled, announcement will be made.

The Boycott Court decided that since the notice did not urge any affirmative action, it was not sufficient to constitute a boycott.[16] This view was upheld by the Norwegian Supreme Court, on the sole occasion in which appeal was taken from the Boycott Court:

When a labor dispute first comes into existence it is not unusual for the trade union to publish the fact in an advertisement. This in itself does not establish that a blockade or a boycott has been called.[17]

However, anything beyond the mere statement that a labor dispute was in effect risked being labeled a boycott. For example, a trade union, after setting forth the facts leading to the calling of a transport strike, warned that

those who buy goods from the Hedmark dairy delivered by Kolbjørn Engh as a strikebreaker must therefore be aware of the consequences that may be entailed for the organized working class . . . It is suggested to consumers that when they make their purchases in the stores they make certain that the goods were not transported by a strikebreaker.[18]

The Boycott Court ruled that this constituted a boycott within the meaning of the Act of 1933.

(c) *Picketing.* The Boycott Law as finally enacted contained no reference to picketing as such, but its wording resulted in an ambiguous situation. The parliamentary committee that investigated the subject recommended that boycotts be forbidden if accompanied by picketing in the vicinity of the dwelling or place of business of the person boycotted.[19] This was deleted in the govern-

[16] *Dommer,* 1935, p. 22. Accord: 1933, No. 20; 1934, No. 16; 1937, p. 16.

[17] *Dommer,* 1936, p. 1. A minority member of the Supreme Court was of the opinion that such an announcement in itself established a boycott. "It is true that this contained only a notice that a labor dispute had commenced at Andersen's new building, and that there was no express declaration of a boycott. But it seems clear both that this notice had the effect of hindering access to organized workers, and that the Building Workers' Union must have been well aware that this would be the effect. In my opinion it must be conceded that the chief purpose of the repeated notices of the existence of a labor dispute clearly was to prevent Andersen from getting workers. Under these circumstances the notice must be considered to constitute a boycott."

[18] *Dommer,* 1937, p. 32.

[19] Socialdepartementet, *Ot. prp. nr. 6,* Bilag, 1933, p. 56.

ment bill on the ground that every strike would become illegal if picketing ensued.[20]

While it may be theoretically possible to distinguish picketing from a blockade, in practice the two tended to become synonymous, with the result that picketing *per se* came under the interdict of the Boycott Act. In the principal case in point, a strike occurred at a small restaurant, and pickets were placed before the premises with instructions to address would-be patrons and inform them of the facts of the strike. They were warned by their union not to urge the persons addressed to refrain from entering the restaurant.

Despite this attempt to limit picketing to the mere dissemination of factual information, the Boycott Court felt that

in determining whether a boycott existed, it is not sufficient to take into account *only the particular* words used. When one starts with the premise that the intent of the solicitation is to obstruct patronage, and that it could be thus construed, the posting of pickets and their demeanor must be judged as establishing a boycott, even though the pickets do not in so many words appeal to or urge anyone not to patronize the restaurant. The correctness of this opinion is strengthened by the fact that the picketing resulted in achievement of its purpose, since practically all patronage ceased during the period in which picketing was carried on.[21]

Only the fact that picketing has not been a major labor weapon in Norway, being largely confined to the relatively minor category of strikes against retailers, prevented the boycott legislation from assuming far greater importance than it actually did.

(*d*) *Sympathetic strikes and "unfair" lists.* The Boycott Act contained no limitation on the right of a trade union to strike, whether the strike was direct or in sympathy with other striking workers. The theory was that a sympathetic strike should be distinguished from a boycott in that it involved a sacrifice for the striking workers, and would therefore not be undertaken lightly, whereas a boycott may often be instituted with little risk.[22]

[20] Socialdepartementet, *Ot. prp. nr. 6, 1933*, p. 12.

[21] *Dommer*, 1933, No. 20.

[22] "The strike and lockout always represent a personal sacrifice for those who use these means of struggle. The striker loses the work on which he and his family live. He knows that the strike will mean privation, and often hunger. And he knows that he runs the risk that the job will not be open when he returns after the strike . . . It is different with an appeal to boycott. The ap-

But this distinction tends to break down in the case of the *conditional* sympathetic strike, that is, if the calling of a strike is made conditional upon the employer's acting or refraining from acting in a manner demanded by the union. This was argued by the Employers' Association, which proposed, without success, that the law be made more specific on this point.[23] The trade unions, on the other hand, contended that if workers who threatened to strike were willing to take the consequences by actually going on strike in the event that the employer refused their demand, they were not engaging in a boycott. In support of this they cited the instance in which workers might be unwilling to work with "unfair" material not primarily because they were seeking to put economic pressure on any employer, but simply to escape being considered strikebreakers by other workers. That this might lead their employer to cease economic intercourse with a firm involved in a labor dispute was only incidental to their main purpose.[24]

In an early case involving this question, a trade union had threatened to call sympathetic strikes among the workers of various establishments using materials produced by a firm engaged in a labor dispute, unless the threatened establishments ceased to use such materials. Similar representations were made to companies furnishing transportation services to the strike-bound plant.

The court held that this constituted a boycott within the meaning of the law, offering the following justification for its views:

The strike notice did not have as its purpose the calling of a strike to create a situation calculated to force a solution of the dispute with the plaintiff through an extensive and effective work stoppage at a large number of plants. What it was aimed at was to induce the employers in question to break off all economic intercourse with the plaintiff, and in the attainment of this purpose these employers, who stood outside the dispute, were threatened with a labor stoppage, and the assumption is that this threat would be sufficient to achieve the purpose: the breach of all economic relations with plaintiff.

---

pellant does not himself participate in the struggles, he does not take the risk and make the sacrifice . . . What makes the boycott so dangerous is just the fact that the instigator of it is not restricted by the limitations which are shaped by personal interests when one is asked to go out on strike."
  Socialdepartementet, *Ot. prp. nr. 71*, 1933, pp. 3–4.
  [23] Socialdepartementet, *Ot. prp. nr. 71*, 1933, p. 33.
  [24] Engh, *Fagorganisasjonen og Loven*, p. 71.

Therefore, in the opinion of the court it may be said justly that notice of the conditional sympathy strike was given not to support plaintiff's striking workers through a comprehensive sympathy strike directed against other employers, but to force the other employers not to have any dealings in plaintiff's goods.[25]

What this decision meant was that an "unfair" list constituted a boycott under all circumstances,[26] unless it was backed by an unconditional strike, in which case it became merely an incident of the strike. Clearly an unconditional sympathetic strike did not come under the ban of the boycott laws. This was clarified by a decision involving a strike called by the Paper Workers' Union at a pulp mill to force the company to sign a collective agreement with the Lumber Workers' Union for its lumbering operations. The court said:

The sympathetic strike at the Kistefoss mill must be considered a strike which the workers at the mill have undertaken in order to force a settlement of the dispute between the Lumber Workers' Union and the Kistefoss Corporation with respect to the company's operations. A sympathetic action has been started in one branch of the employer's operations in support of a demand for a collective agreement in another branch. This action is employed as a customary weapon in an interest dispute between the union and the employer, and has only this purpose.

The court cannot agree that the sympathetic strike has the character of a boycott. Its only purpose is to widen the scope of a conflict by a work stoppage, to create a situation aimed at forcing the solution of a dispute in another part of the employer's operations. It is not an appeal or a measure designed to hinder his economic intercourse with others. It is another thing that an effective strike can actually lead to such a result.[27]

The effect of these decisions was materially to reduce the incidence of conditional sympathetic strikes, which prior to the boycott legislation had been employed widely. The essential logic is clear, once the distinction between a strike and a boycott is recog-

---

[25] *Dommer,* 1933, No. 1.

[26] See also *Dommer,* 1934, No. 16.

[27] *Dommer,* 1933, No. 9. Mere reservation of the right to call a conditional strike in the future was not deemed a boycott. *Dommer,* 1933, No. 17.

nized. A full fledged sympathetic strike is a much more serious affair than a strike conditioned upon nonobservance of an "unfair" list, and is likely to be undertaken by a trade union only when the original dispute is very important. Moreover, the pressure generated by an outright sympathetic strike is much greater than that accompanying the conditional strike, since it will terminate only upon the settlement of the initial controversy. Suppliers and customers would be much more interested in the settlement of the dispute if they could not escape involvement merely by breaking off economic relations with the "unfair" employer, and thus there would be greater incentive to bring the conflict to an early end. An employer might continue to operate for some time despite a partial interruption in his raw material supply or sales, so that a boycott based upon an "unfair" list might in the long run lead to a greater disruption of economic life than a more widespread but shorter-lived sympathetic strike.

(e) *Discrimination in trade union or employer association membership.* On several occasions workers or employers who were refused admission to trade unions or employer associations appealed to the Boycott Court for help. The theory upon which they based their complaints was that refusal of membership, by restricting or preventing them from securing certain work, constituted a threat to their economic and commercial relationships with others, and thus constituted unlawful boycotts.

The Boycott Court concluded that mere refusal on the part of a trade union or employers' association to admit a person to membership did not in itself constitute a boycott. Thus the refusal of a local painters' union to admit to membership an unemployed opera singer who was supporting himself by part-time work in the trade was not a boycott, despite the fact that such action barred him from continuing to perform painting jobs.[28] A similar result attended the refusal of an association of paper-hanging contractors to admit to membership a painting contractor on the ground that "our group is a special group for paper-hanging work. Under our laws we can only admit contractors whose primary business is paper hanging." [29] A union's desire to "regulate the stream of labor" in order to protect the economic interests of its members

[28] *Dommer,* 1935, No. 8.
[29] *Dommer,* 1933, No. 7.

was held reasonable, provided no particular ill will had been demonstrated toward the complainant.[30]

On the other hand, discrimination with respect to membership, where it was shown to be part of a deliberate campaign calculated to interfere with the ability of an individual to earn a livelihood in an occupation in which he had long been engaged, fell within the boycott law. The leading case involved one Carl Welde, who was employed as the working foreman of a gang of longshoremen in Haugesund, a Norwegian port. He had first been hired in 1921 to replace striking stevedores, and remained as a permanent employee. In 1927 he took a leading part in the formation of a company union. The members of this union, with the exception of Welde, were admitted to the Transport Workers' Union in 1931. The latter organization, with which the employer was finally obliged to bargain, demanded the discharge of Welde. The employer refused, and a compromise was worked out whereby Welde was permitted to remain until the end of the contract period in 1935 (when he reached his sixtieth year), with the understanding that he would then be discharged.

Welde, however, refused to acquiesce in this arrangement. He endeavored repeatedly to gain membership in the Transport Workers' Union, but was denied entrance on the basis of his record of antiunion activity. The contract which was negotiated in 1935 provided that the company should choose its foremen from among the members of the Transport Workers' Union, but if it desired to hire a nonunion foreman, he could not participate in the work of loading. Since the company had no need of a nonworking supervisor, Welde was given his dismissal notice.

Before the Boycott Court, the union asserted that it was not attempting to shut Welde out of all employment, but merely from working as a member of the stevedore gang. The court rejected this defense in the following terms:

It is not a condition for a finding that a boycott exists that the appeal or action is unlimited—that it prevents *any* economic intercourse with others.

It is also a boycott within the meaning of the law to preclude one from engaging in or continuing work he has, and by which he has

[30] *Dommer,* 1939, No. 1.

hitherto supported himself, even if the boycott does not unconditionally prevent him from taking a position or work of a different sort.[31]

The union maintained that even though Welde was cut off from
his customary employment, it was the result of general union
policy which did not have as its primary intent to injure or punish
him, but rather to advance the economic interests of its members.
The court similarly rejected this argument, observing that "it
would constitute no significant detriment to the union or its members if Welde were permitted to continue in his work as a long-
shoreman in the same manner as before."

The final union argument was that Welde's difficulties resulted
from a valid collective agreement between the union and the company, and that any discrimination was incidental to the effectuation of the agreement. But the court found that "the fact that the
1935 actions impeding and making difficult Welde's economic
intercourse with others were initiated in contract negotiations and
took the form of a collective agreement, does not bar the conclusion that the action may be considered a boycott." [32]

As a consequence of this decision, the collective agreement was
modified to permit the hiring of a nonunion working foreman,
with the proviso that a full gang's pay, including a foreman's pay,
would have to be given to the union workers. Under the circumstances the employer was unwilling to hire Welde, since to do so
would have involved an extra wage cost. The Boycott Court, in a
new appeal by Welde, ruled that the new agreement represented a
continuation of the previous boycott in altered form.[33]

In another case, the refusal of the Office and Commercial Workers' Union to admit a clerk to membership was held not to constitute an unlawful boycott *per se;* but the acts of the union group
within the establishment which "systematically attempted to shape
a situation in which [plaintiff's] continuance in the position would
be impossible," together with the exclusion, were adjudged a
boycott.[34]

The question was raised in somewhat different form by the expulsion from the Seamen's Union of a ship's chief radio operator

[31] *Dommer,* 1936, No. 2.
[32] *Dommer,* 1936, No. 2.
[33] *Dommer,* 1936, No. 3.
[34] *Dommer,* 1936, No. 5.

for activities which were considered disruptive by the union leadership. As a result of the exclusion, the steamship company refused to retain the complainant in his former post, one of the most lucrative positions in the Norwegian merchant marine. The matter was brought to the Boycott Court which declared:

Exclusion from a trade union is not in itself a boycott, among other things because the "intercourse" between the member and the organization which exclusion seeks to cut off is not of an economic nature. On the other hand, the purpose of the exclusion may be to affect the plaintiff in his economic intercourse with others, which is a particularly obvious conclusion when a union is successful in restricting all work in the trade to its members.[35]

Since the plaintiff could have secured another position in his trade, although less lucrative, the court did not feel that the exclusion alone was a boycott. In fact, it held that the expulsion was justified on the basis of plaintiff's activities in the union. On the other hand, the court considered that further action taken by the union to prevent the plaintiff from continuing in his position, when membership in the union was not a condition of that employment, was unwarranted. It noted that "when expulsion in itself carries great peril for the excluded in this respect, one must be particularly careful not to contribute to such boycott." Here, on the contrary, the steamship company had been warned by the union that to rehire the plaintiff would be to risk trouble aboard ship.[36]

(f) *The union shop.* The question was also raised whether the exclusion of a nonunion worker from employment pursuant to some form of union shop agreement was necessarily a boycott. The court clarified this issue in considering a complaint brought by a truck owner against a union of which he was formerly a member. The union, which had a union shop agreement with local trucking concerns, had a bylaw under which no person who owned more than one truck could become or remain a member. When the plaintiff bought a second truck, he was expelled from the union, but

---

[35] *Dommer,* 1937, No. 9.

[36] There had been some hesitation by the lawmakers on this general question, for it was felt that a union or employers' association should have the power to enforce discipline even if individuals were injured. They resolved their doubts by permitting a disciplinary boycott to be undertaken with permission of the Boycott Court. Socialdepartementet, *Ot. prp. nr. 71,* 1933, pp. 18–19.

was permitted to operate one of his trucks with a union driver. The union asserted that it was not endeavoring to boycott him, but merely enforcing a rule deemed essential to the maintenance of full employment among its members.

The court pointed out that the effect of the union shop agreement was undoubtedly to interfere with plaintiff's "economic intercourse with others," but that it was not intended to "coerce, injure, or punish" him.

> The rule was adopted to defend the organization and its interests, it is not directed against [plaintiff] in particular. It was adopted and in operation long before the present conflict arose, and is not limited to plaintiff's district . . .
>
> The Court ruled in earlier cases that under certain circumstances there can be a boycott if it is sought through general provisions of a collective agreement to shut nonunion workers out of employment. That would be the case if in the rules concerning privileges or priorities for union workers there lay an individual action against a particular nonunion worker, whom the union sought "to coerce, injure, or punish." But according to the evidence this was not true in the instant case.[37]

The conclusion, then, was that enforcement of a union shop did not constitute a boycott if the purpose of the union shop was clearly to advance the economic interests of the union members, and not to "coerce, injure, or punish" nonunionists. The true motive of the union could be determined only from an examination of the relevant data in each particular case. Thus in the Welde case it appeared that a newly adopted rule was intended primarily to force the discharge of an individual with intent to punish him for past misdeeds, while in the trucking case there was no animus against the plaintiff, but merely a desire to enforce membership rules which had been in effect prior to the inception of the dispute in question.

This conclusion may have been somewhat at variance with parliamentary intent. The original committee report included the following statement:

> It cannot be left to private individuals or organizations, through use of the boycott weapon, to deny or seek to deny to a member of society

[37] *Dommer,* 1938, No. 4. Accord: *Dommer,* 1939, No. 1.

his right to a livelihood or the possibility of continuing the work or in the profession to which he has lawful access, on the ground that he is not a member of one or another private organization which seeks to secure a monopoly or preference to such work.[38]

Nevertheless, in its interpretations the Boycott Court was probably reflecting Norwegian public opinion. The wording of the Boycott Act would undoubtedly have permitted greater latitude in discrimination cases, if the court had cared to exercise it. However, in contrast with the preoccupation of recent American labor legislation, notably the Taft-Hartley Act, with the prevention of discrimination in employment for membership or nonmembership in a labor organization, discrimination has never been a major problem in Norway. The reason is twofold. In the first place, since the closed union has been rare, only in exceptional instances is an individual unable to acquire membership in a labor organization. Coupled with this is the fact that there is greater acceptance of associational structure in Norway and consequently less disposition to question the ethical justification of requiring trade union membership as a condition of employment. This acceptance carries the further implication that organizations of workers and employers, in order to function satisfactorily, must be permitted to exercise discretion in choosing and excluding members. It was only when exclusion was followed by what the court regarded as unwarranted persecution that it intervened, although even in those cases there were many who would have maintained that a course of conduct designed to deprive a worker of employment in a particular trade or industry might well be justified by the necessity of maintaining proper organizational discipline.

(*g*) *Antiunion discrimination.* On several occasions, trade unions attempted to turn the boycott law against employers whom they considered guilty of discriminating against organized labor in hiring and employment practices, but they were largely unsuccessful. One complaint concerned an application by three union members for advertised jobs. They were interviewed by a foreman and informed that while they had the necessary qualifications, the policy of the company was to hire only nonunion workers, and that they would not be taken on while they remained union members. Two of the applicants thereupon resigned from the union and were

[38] Socialdepartementet, *Ot. prp. nr. 6,* Bilag, 1933, p. 53.

hired, but the third refused to do so, and charged that a boycott had been instituted against her. The court disagreed with this contention and, in finding for the defendant, declared:

It is sufficient basis therefore to note that it is not proved from the evidence set forth that the foreman's remarks to [the three applicants] on the occasion of their inquiry about the advertised positions were designed to force them to leave the Union.[39]

In a second case, the Lumber Workers' Union complained that certain employers were systematically refusing employment to its members to punish them for having participated in a strike. As a condition of employment, applicants were required to join an association composed of both employers and workers, which did not admit union workers to membership. The court agreed with the plaintiff that the principal motive of the employer was to "coerce, injure, or punish" the organized workers and their union because of the strike.[40] Back of the court's decision was the notion that the employers had no interest in the formation of a joint management-labor association sufficient to justify the conclusion that exclusion of trade union workers was merely an incidental result of their policy.

Discharge for trade union membership presumably fell within the prohibitions of the Boycott Act only if there were a clear showing that the sole purpose of the discharge was to force resignation from the union. Where a union approached an employer with a request for an agreement to cover a newly organized worker, and the employer discharged the worker concerned, the court held that the employer's action could be construed as mere resistance to economic demands, and that "a discharge in connection with a wage dispute falls outside the law's definition of a boycott." [41]

Even when it was shown, however, that discharge was occasioned solely by opposition to the employment of trade union members, a complainant was under the additional necessity of proving that the object of the employer was to "coerce, injure, or punish" him for his union membership. In one case, the Office and Commercial Employees' Union had invited employees of a particular estab-

[39] *Dommer,* 1933, No. 18.
[40] *Dommer,* 1935, No. 9.
[41] *Dommer,* 1939, No. 12.

lishment to attend an organizational meeting; when the employer heard of the invitation, he demanded that each employee sign the following statement:

Each of my employees agrees herewith, by belief and law, not to join any union which is communistic or which is affiliated with the Federation of Labor.

One of the employees refused to sign the statement until she had taken the matter up at home. When threatened with discharge unless she signed immediately, she finally consented to do so. That same evening she attended the union meeting, although abstaining from joining the union. The next day she was discharged. The court held that the discharge did not constitute a boycott because the plaintiff had not proved that "defendant's purpose in discharging her was to 'coerce, injure, or punish' her, and not to rid himself of an organized or pro-union employee." [42] Thus in effect the court set up requirements for the successful prosecution of discriminatory discharge cases under the boycott legislation that could not possibly be met.

(h) *The secondary boycott.* The parliamentary committee report recommending the adoption of the Boycott Act proposed that the secondary boycott be made unlawful under all circumstances, on the following basis:

The tendency to widen the application of the boycott weapon in a labor dispute to embrace third parties who stand outside the dispute has grown steadily stronger. A dispute that has its origin in a trifling difference can thus be extended until it has significance for a large sector of the economy and exposes to significant injury third parties who desire only to remain neutral in the dispute.

The Committee is of the opinion that a special rule is needed for this type of boycott, that a third party who stands outside the original dispute and who takes the part of neither party has an absolute right to remain outside the conflict.[43]

The draftsmen of the final bill agreed in principle with the foregoing, but expressed the conviction that it was not always possible to draw a sharp line between true neutrals and those who were

[42] *Dommer,* 1935, No. 14.
[43] Socialdepartementet, *Ot. prp. nr. 6,* 1933, p. 13.

direct or indirect participants. They therefore refused to include an absolute prohibition against the secondary boycott, preferring instead to place it in the category of boycotts permitted only with permission of the Boycott Court.

It is interesting that the application of a "unity of economic interest" test, on the New York Court of Appeals model, as a means of defining the bounds of neutrality was rejected on the ground that appropriate economic categories were not readily distinguishable. No general standards could be applied:

The only certain distinguishing characteristic that offers itself in the determination of whether or not a secondary boycott should be allowed, is whether the third person is really neutral, that is, has not taken direct economic measures in support of one of the parties to the original dispute.[44]

The parliamentary committee stated that the mere maintenance of previous commercial relations with a strike-bound firm did not constitute a breach of neutrality. "On the contrary, it would be a breach of neutrality to break commercial relations with one of the parties to a labor dispute, or to refuse to enter into new relations, solely because of the boycott appeal." [45] The only safe course was for the third party to continue to act as though there were no labor dispute, with his own economic interests as a sole guide.

It was clear from the legislative background that all secondary boycotts instituted without advance approval of the Boycott Court were banned, where genuine neutrality was invaded. The broad concept of neutrality expressed by the parliamentary committee left the court little leeway. As a result complaints charging illegal secondary boycotts brought by firms buying from, selling to, or transporting goods for employers involved in labor disputes were sustained.[46]

(*i*) *Incidental boycotts.* In several instances unions were exempted from liability for the commission of acts that would otherwise have been considered illegal boycotts by demonstrating that damage was incidental to the enforcement of a valid collective agreement.[47] Thus a firm that had agreed to employ only union

---

[44] Socialdepartementet, *Ot. prp. nr. 6, 1933*, p. 13.
[45] Socialdepartementet, *Ot. prp. nr. 6, 1933*, p. 14.
[46] For example, *Dommer, 1933*, No. 14; 1934, No. 16; 1934, No. 20.
[47] *Dommer, 1935*, No. 8.

painters was subjected to a boycott when it began to operate on a nonunion basis. The court ruled that since the union's sole object was to force the complainant to live up to the terms of the agreement, the Labor Court rather than the Boycott Court had jurisdiction over the subject matter of the dispute.[48]

On the other hand, enforcement of an agreement was not a valid justification when it appeared that the union was motivated primarily by the desire to punish or coerce one not a party to the agreement.[49] Nevertheless, by introducing the subjective element of motivation, the court tempered the severity of the law.

2. The Absolute Prohibitions. It will be recalled that the Boycott Act set up two categories of unlawful boycotts, those unlawful under all circumstances, and those unlawful without prior permission of the Boycott Court. The first group included boycotts that the courts had tended to condemn before enactment of the special boycott legislation.

(*a*) *Reasonable notice.* A boycott "undertaken without reasonable notice to the party boycotted, or without satisfactory explanation of the grounds for the boycott to the party against whom it is directed," was made unlawful. Little difficulty was experienced in the interpretation of this section, since it was largely a matter of proof. When the employees of Supplier A refused without prior warning to load materials on a truck belonging to Enterpreneur B because B's employees were on strike, an illegal boycott was held to have occurred.[50] A strike against a general contractor in the building industry to induce him to cease dealing with a subcontractor, without direct notice to the latter by the union, was also condemned as without reasonable notice.[51]

(*b*) *Illegal means.* The conduct of a boycott through the use of "illegal means," in an "unnecessarily provocative or offensive manner," or through the employment of "false or misleading information" was also prohibited. A campaign undertaken to force the discharge of an employee, during the course of which the individual concerned was falsely charged with having misrepresented her qualifications for the job, was held an illegal boycott.[52] Hostile

[48] *Dommer,* 1937, p. 59.
[49] *Dommer,* 1936, No. 2; 1934, No. 20.
[50] *Dommer,* 1934, No. 19.
[51] *Dommer,* 1934, No. 20.
[52] *Dommer,* 1936, No. 5.

and threatening demonstrations against a nonstriking milk driver, and the dumping of several cans of his milk, clearly constituted illegal means.[53] However, dissemination of truthful information with respect to the existence of a strike, through newspaper advertisements[54] or orderly picketing, was considered reasonable means to employ in furtherance of a labor dispute.

(c) *General legal maxims.* The third class of absolute prohibitions covered a boycott

where it has an illegal purpose or will induce a breach of law if it achieves its purpose, or will impair essential public interests or operate unreasonably or where there is no reasonable relationship between the interest which is being furthered by the boycott and the damage which will result.

Each of these phrases is employed as a term of art, and presupposes general knowledge of Norwegian law. The term "will impair essential public interests," for example, was taken from antitrust legislation; the phrase "operates unreasonably," apparently intended to strengthen rather than to limit the accompanying language, also originated in the antitrust laws; while "illegal purpose" and "induce a breach of law" must be read against the background of numerous judicial decisions.[55]

The pitfalls involved in distinguishing between legality and illegality on the basis of such general maxims are apparent. The Federation of Labor, in its brief in opposition to the law, pointed out:

We face subjective concepts against which no objective standards can be placed. Any judge will be able to say to himself in a particular case that it is entirely unreasonable for John Jones to be subjected to a boycott, and judge the case on the basis of his subjective opinions and political and economic convictions. The result will be arbitrary and close decisions that will not exact any respect.[56]

These maxims thread their way through the decisions of the Boycott Court, although more by way of rendering support to the

---

[53] *Dommer,* 1937, p. 32.
[54] *Dommer,* 1935, p. 22.
[55] See Øvergaard, pp. 72–78.
[56] Socialdepartementet, *Ot. prp. nr. 71,* 1933, p. 89.

specific prohibitions than as independent factors. As an example, the doctrine that the interest furthered must exceed the damage inflicted (the only meaningful interpretation of the term "reasonable relationship") may be traced in some detail. Although this doctrine was not without precedent in Norwegian law, it is doubtful whether it had attained the status of a common law principle.[57]

From a mere perusal of Boycott Court opinions it is impossible to determine precisely the manner in which the two factors were weighed one against the other. What constituted a reasonable or legitimate act in a given situation appeared to depend primarily on the preconceptions of the individual judge, and upon current social mores.

The *sine qua non* for invocation of this section of the act was proof of loss or threatened loss. Such loss, however, had to exceed the trade-union interest measured by some social yardstick. If it did not, it was incidental to a socially protected activity, and had to be borne. It would appear, however, that mere proof of loss raised a substantial presumption of illegality in the mind of the Court.

When a trade union with no membership, or a small membership, among the employees in an establishment, engaged in a boycott to secure exclusive bargaining rights, its interest in the outcome of the dispute was considered by the court insufficient to outweigh severe losses inflicted upon the employer.[58] As a corollary, where organized workers had become involved in an unlawful strike and were replaced by nonunion workers, no legitimate union interest was deemed furthered by a boycott, since the strikers had lost their status as employees, and one of the conditions demanded by the union for the settlement of the dispute, replacement of the new workers by the strikers, was therefore not a reasonable demand.[59]

Still another situation involved a small producers' coöperative that had formerly been a private enterprise with a union agreement. The establishment had operated at a continual loss, and the owner persuaded his employees that a coöperative arrangement might yield better results. The union refused to acquiesce in the change on the ground that its real intent was evasion of the agree-

[57] Berg, *Arbeidsrett*, p. 252.
[58] *Dommer*, 1933, No. 1; 1937, p. 16.
[59] *Dommer*, 1933, No. 6.

ment, and called its members out on strike. They were replaced by others, who came in as worker-shareholders of the coöperative.

The court found that the union had carried out a boycott so successfully that the establishment would be thrown into bankruptcy if it were permitted to continue. The union interest in the boycott was held not sufficient to offset this loss on two counts: the new coöperative was not a nonunion shop, but was willing to admit union members as shareholders; and the demand for a union shop made by the union precluded any possibility of settlement, since it would have forced the withdrawal from employment of the nonunion shareholders.[60]

In the Welde case, the details of which are set forth above,[61] the harm inflicted upon an individual by a union boycott intended to deprive him of his customary means of livelihood was considered out of proportion to the benefits flowing to the union from the exclusion of one man from the trade.

The exact margins of this doctrine were not clear. In one case, where the court had refused to condemn a sympathetic strike against paper mills in support of striking lumber workers, it held that a boycott of the "unfair" lumber by transport unions was not in reasonable relation to the purpose served. The labor member of the court dissented sharply from this conclusion:

The Kistefoss Pulp Mill has refused to meet the workers' demand for a collective agreement covering its lumbering . . . despite the fact that the union has offered to submit the terms of the agreement to arbitration. The question of a collective agreement has such significance for the labor organization that it has fostered a month-long sympathetic strike with the economic sacrifices resulting therefrom for the union and the individual workers. In this serious situation it is obvious that the union must blockade transport activities to and from the pulp mill . . . In my opinion, this is an ordinary labor dispute situation.[62]

On the other hand, in an "intense controversy" between an employer and a trade union, a blockade of the place of work by the striking union was not deemed to affect the employer "unreason-

[60] *Dommer*, 1934, No. 16.
[61] Section 1, e.
[62] *Dommer*, 1933, No. 9.

ably." [63] Moreover, when the Federation of Labor requested permission to boycott a cannery operating on a nonunion basis with a wage schedule that was endangering the structure of union wages in the entire industry, the court assented in the following terms:

> The Boycott Court consents to a boycott (including a conditional sympathetic strike) by the Federation of Labor and its affiliated organizations of the transportation and supply of materials and goods in any form to Herøy Canning Corporation, of transportation of finished products from the plant, and a boycott of all goods and products purchased from Herøy Canning Corporation.[64]

It would appear that in an ordinary labor dispute, where the employer could show substantial loss, a secondary boycott against carriers of his supplies or products, or against his suppliers or customers, was presumed to inflict damage upon him out of proportion to the advantages accruing to the union. This presumption could be rebutted if the union showed that its interest in attacking the employer through a boycott was greater than the mere addition of one more establishment to the roster of organized firms. The interest yardstick made allowance for the necessity of protecting unionized establishments from dangerous nonunion competition.

Apparently, too, the degree of interest required of a union was somewhat smaller in the case of a primary boycott limited to a blockade of the establishment involved in the dispute. An interest in the organization *per se* of the particular establishment involved might suffice to outweigh the hardship inflicted upon the employer.

3. *Permissive Boycotts.* The theory of Section 1 (d) of the Boycott Act was that although certain boycotts were dangerous and should be controlled, there were circumstances in which their use was justified. The Boycott Court was therefore given authority to permit boycotts provided they did not run counter to the absolute prohibitions. There was some legislative sentiment against this provision on the ground that it would lead to numerous unfounded requests merely for the purpose of giving publicity to the facts of a labor dispute, but these fears proved unfounded.

[63] *Dommer,* 1934, No. 21.
[64] *Dommer,* 1935, No. 12.

Only eight requests were made to the Boycott Court for permission to institute a boycott, four of which were granted. The broadest license granted was in a case already cited.[65] The permissible limits of projected boycott action were always carefully circumscribed by the court. For example, the following permission was given in one case:

The Boycott Court . . . approves the request of the Norwegian Building Workers' Union, in connection with a dispute between it and Alfred Andersen, to urge union workers not to fill the places at Alfred Andersen's factory in Lillestrøm which twenty-three workers left on November 5, 1934, after notice of termination from Andersen. This permission does not embrace the undertaking of any other boycott action than the aforementioned blockade of the place of work.[66]

When this permissive boycott had been in effect for more than two years, Andersen asked the court to order its termination. The court refused to set any time limit on the duration of the boycott, but it did require the union, in its advertising, to state specifically that nothing more than a blockade of Andersen's plant was involved.[67]

The court emphasized that a request for permission to boycott had to be based upon one of the grounds specified in Section 1 (d) of the act. A union had requested the court's permission to boycott the products of an establishment by calling a conditional sympathetic strike against its carriers. The court pointed out that the boycott would not be directed against a "neutral third party" (in which case permission could be granted under the act, in an appropriate case) but rather against the employer engaged in the dispute, and that the law made no provision for prior judgment of such a boycott.[68]

It is somewhat puzzling that the court in this case did not rely for grant of permission upon another part of Section 1 (d), the provision that permission of the court is required, and may be

[65] See above, p. 147.
[66] *Dommer,* 1934, No. 21.
[67] *Dommer,* 1937, No. 2.
[68] *Dommer,* 1937, No. 6. A sympathetic strike is a *boycott* against the original disputant and a *strike* against the "neutral." This section of the act permits boycotts, in appropriate circumstances, against the neutral, but says nothing of the original disputant.

granted, when the boycott is undertaken "in order to compel an employer or employee . . . to conclude or coöperate in concluding a collective agreement which none of the employees in the establishment concerned, or only a minority of such employees, has demanded."

Here, union strikers had been replaced by strikebreakers, so that the union had no membership in the plant. The court had earlier held that where striking workers were replaced, they lost their employee status and therefore could not use the boycott without permission of the court, if their purpose was to oblige the employer to enter into an agreement with their union.[69] Thus where the circumstances were reversed, the striking workers would have seemed entitled logically to petition as strangers.[70]

The requirement that a trade union representing a minority or no employees had to secure advance permission to boycott was applied quite generally, however. This was true where the union had had previous contractual relations with the employer, interrupted by a labor dispute which deprived the union of its majority;[71] where the employees belonged to a rival union, even though it was company dominated;[72] or where the union, in its initial organizational activities, had not been able to induce a majority of the employees to join it.[73]

The legality of boycotts directed against third persons who had not ostensibly supported either of the original parties to a labor dispute was tested in a case brought against the Employers' Association. The plaintiff, a corporation engaged in the performance of electrical repair work, had been notified by the Employers' Association that since it was offering employment to electricians on strike against employer members of the association, no member of the association would have any business relations with it for the duration of the strike. As a result, the plaintiff was unable to secure necessary electrical supplies.

To plaintiff's contention that it was a neutral, and therefore entitled to the protection of the statute, the court pointed out that of

[69] *Dommer,* 1933, No. 6; 1934, No. 21.

[70] It may have been that in the case under consideration the striking workers were not demanding an agreement; the facts are not clear. It is reasonable to presume, however, that this was their aim.

[71] *Dommer,* 1933, No. 6; 1937, p. 32.

[72] *Dommer,* 1933, No. 1.

[73] *Dommer,* 1934, No. 19.

plaintiff corporation's 874 shares of common stock outstanding,
522 were owned either by the Electric and Power Station Workers' Union or by the Electricians' Union; that it had greatly expanded its business and employment since the outbreak of the
strike; and that under the circumstances it was hardly a neutral
"with a conditional right to be free from boycott." [74]

4. *Employers with Ten or Less Employees*. The proviso making boycotts illegal when directed against employers with ten or
less employees was of great importance because of the prevalence
of small scale enterprise in Norway. The fact that relatively few
complaints were brought under this section is not contradictory,
since the plain language of the act had the effect of discouraging
boycotts that might otherwise have been initiated.

Blockades were held illegal solely by virtue of the fact that the
affected employer was not of the specified minimum size.[75] In determining the number of employees in the hire of an employer, the
court limited the count to persons engaged in the activity affected
by the labor dispute, excluding personal servants and other employees in unrelated activities.[76]

One employer petitioned the court to revoke a boycott permit
on the ground that he had reduced his labor force to less than ten
employees subsequent to the grant of a permission to boycott. He
had earlier employed between twenty and twenty-five workers. The
court pointed out that the decline in his labor force was due largely
to the boycott, and concluded:

That the firm's employment after the institution of the boycott . . .
sank to a point below that stipulated in Section 6a (4) does not mean
that continuation of the previously legal boycott is unlawful. Any
other interpretation of the rule would lead to entirely unreasonable
consquences. It would mean, for example, that a lawful blockade of a
working place in connection with a strike (or lockout) involving a
wage dispute would become unlawful the moment the strike (or lockout) became effective.[77]

5. *Liability of Trade Unions*. Once the illegality of a boycott
was established, the court fixed the responsibility and assessed

[74] *Dommer*, 1937, p. 48.
[75] *Dommer*, 1933, No. 20; 1939, No. 13.
[76] *Dommer*, 1933, No. 17.
[77] *Dommer*, 1935, No. 6.

damages. Whether a local trade union, a central labor council, a national union or the Federation of Labor should be held responsible for the acts of individuals or groups of workers was not always easy to decide. It was a very practical matter because financial ability increased as the apex of the organizational structure was approached. An award against a local union might be uncollectible, but most national unions, and the Federation of Labor always, had the means to meet judgments levied against them.

The evolution of trade union legal responsibility for the acts of members or affiliates has already been outlined.[78] During the period of the Boycott Court's existence, the following provisions relating to financial responsibility were in effect:

If a member of a trade union or an employers' association is guilty of an unlawful work stoppage or an unlawful boycott, the union or association is liable, unless it proves that it is not guilty or that it has used the means at its disposal to prevent the violation or the continuation of the illegal condition. Provided that an association is a link in a more extensive organization with the same general purposes, the superior organizations are liable according to the same rules as in the first clause.[79]

The court's practice was to examine in each case the actions of trade union officials at various levels in order to determine whether efforts to prevent boycotts were genuine or merely *pro forma*. Usually only the organizational units that had participated in the underlying labor dispute were implicated.

How this was done may be seen from a specific example, using the Alfred Andersen case which has been mentioned before. Andersen, a small entrepreneur, had become embroiled with several trade unions over manufacturing and building operations. After the breakdown of lengthy negotiations, representatives of the Federation of Labor, the Building Workers' Union, the Transport Workers' Union, and the local central labor council met to determine ways of making the blockade of his factory more effective. It was agreed that no steps should be taken to broaden the action against Andersen beyond a blockade of his plant.

Despite this agreement, the local central labor council sent circular notices to similar bodies in other districts advising them

[78] Pp. 111–114.
[79] Act of July 6, 1933, Section 4.

that Andersen was producing certain brands of children's bicycles, and solicited their support. It also requested the Building Workers' Union to declare a sympathetic strike against Andersen's suppliers. This request was forwarded to the Federation of Labor, which sent the following reply to the offending central labor council:

The dispute at Alfred Andersen's is not the only labor dispute in Norway, and the council will find that the Federation will handle the matter in its proper turn, and judge what organizational step, at each stage, is possible and profitable for the organization as a whole. Planless individual actions are to be warned against. The council must realize that the consequences of this matter affect the organization as a whole. Under the circumstances it must be patient. We assume that the council will understand and yield on this matter.

The Oslo and Bergen central labor councils had acted upon the circular and induced local dealers to stop handling Andersen's bicycles. They, together with the initiating local council, were held liable for the boycott. On the other hand the Federation of Labor, after the circular was called to its attention, had notified all central labor councils that it was in conflict with Federation orders and that Andersen's goods were not subject to boycott; the court considered that the Federation had fulfilled its statutory duty.[80]

However, neither the Federation nor an affiliate was permitted to escape liability when it failed to act affirmatively in a situation of which it should have been cognizant, despite a disclaimer of knowledge. If aware of unlawful threats or acts by an affiliate, it was held the duty of a national union "to secure the requisite knowledge of the action's character and progress." [81]

The precise character of the obligation imposed upon a trade union varied with the circumstances. Where an employer demanded the recall of an illegal boycott, it was the union's duty "to make an unequivocal declaration that any boycott of the brick work's products and of the transportation to and from the plant is lifted." [82] Further, "it is required of an organization that it answer a query of whether a boycott has been suspended clearly and unequivocally, so that the person against whom the boycott has been

[80] *Dommer,* 1935, p. 22.
[81] *Dommer,* 1935, p. 22.
[82] *Dommer,* 1934, No. 2.

directed can transmit it to those to whom the original boycott appeal was addressed." [83] When a local union officer participated in a boycott without official authorization, the local was held to have ratified his acts because of its failure to disown them.[84]

In fixing the amount of monetary awards, the court attempted to estimate the actual loss suffered by claimants. If the boycott had been ineffective, no punitive damages were awarded. Some of the largest awards went to individuals who had lost their employment as the result of boycotts. The largest single award was paid to a chief radio operator in the amount of 8000 kroner, to compensate him for loss of earnings over the period of a year.

APPRAISAL OF THE BOYCOTT ACT

In the absence of statistical information on the incidence of boycotts before and after 1933, it is difficult to assess the effectiveness of Norwegian boycott legislation. It is generally agreed, however, that there was a sharp decline in the use of the boycott from 1933 on, and that the principal cause was the boycott legislation. On the other hand, the predominantly organizational character of the boycott weapon, coupled with the fact that the major portion of organizational work had been completed by 1933, must have contributed to the same result. The Boycott Act was thus not as damaging to the trade union movement as it would have been a decade earlier.

Members of the Employers' Association were not subjected to boycotts after 1933, and therefore had no occasion to invoke the legislation. However, members of the independent employers' associations in lumber, dairying, and agriculture did turn to the law frequently. Organized labor always evidenced intense hostility toward the Boycott Act, and maintained steadfastly that it promoted strife through the encouragement of sympathetic strikes to replace boycotts.

The Boycott Court appears to have administered the act more leniently than was the intent of the framers. Several instances of liberal interpretation were pointed out above. Another practice that worked to the same end was the use of the term "conflict" instead of "blockade" in referring to strike situations, thus avoiding the necessary implications of the act.

[83] *Dommer,* 1937, p. 16.
[84] *Dommer,* 1934, No. 20.

From a technical point of view the general prohibitions of the statute, by affording broad scope to subjective judicial interpretation, constituted one of the act's major deficiencies. It is interesting that trade union objections have been raised primarily against the specific prohibitions contained in the legislation, the court's use of the general legal maxims having been accounted as reasonable. But the basic defect remains; had the Boycott Court been less favorably disposed to labor, the general prohibitions would have constituted an effective bar to the employment of the boycott under most circumstances.

Whether this attempt to legislate out of existence one of the most controversial features of modern industrial warfare can be considered a success, on balance, depends upon one's evaluation of the factors that make for long run industrial peace. The Boycott Act undoubtedly changed union practice for the better by forcing the termination of abuses that would have redounded to the ultimate disadvantage of the labor movement. The conditional sympathetic strike, which could be undertaken lightly since it involved little risk, was one objectionable practice that was almost entirely discontinued after 1933.

On the other hand, the Boycott Act was viewed by the labor movement, with some justification, as "class" legislation. In the words of the Federation of Labor, "the Boycott Court is given a class character that is not good in a democratic society." [85] This feeling inevitably engenders suspicion as to the impartiality of the judicial system, and paves the way for partisan legislation in the other direction when the tide of political power turns.

POSTWAR DEVELOPMENTS

Subsequent to 1940, although the Boycott Act remained on the statute books, no complaints were brought to the court. In 1945 a tripartite labor-disputes committee was appointed by the government with a mandate to investigate, among other things, "revision of the boycott provisions of the Law on Labor Disputes based on the experience of the years during which the provisions were in effect." The committee made unanimous recommendations early in 1947 and legislation based upon these recommendations was proposed and enacted soon thereafter.

The chief finding of the committee was that "there is need for

[85] *Fri Fagbevegelse,* March 1946, No. 3.

certain boycott rules, but they ought not be limited to the labor boycott; rather, they should embrace all economic life." [86] It was therefore suggested that the boycott provisions be removed from the labor-disputes act and incorporated into the general legal code, thus removing the taint of "class" legislation.

The new law retains the absolute general prohibitions of the Act of 1933 (Sections 1a, b, c), but deletes entirely the conditional prohibitions (Section 1d). The special exemptions for small firms and lumber-floating enterprises are similarly absent. The Boycott Court is eliminated, and regular courts given authority to issue temporary injunctions against projected boycotts while their legality is being ascertained. [87]

In its decision to drop the conditional prohibitions of the Act of 1933, the labor-disputes committee confined itself largely to quoting the arguments that had been raised against the law at the time of its original passage. The boycott was given specific recognition as a legitimate weapon in certain strike situations, and as a last resort in the enforcement of organizational discipline. The blockade in the course of a strike was specifically excepted from the boycott regulations, as had been suggested originally. No special rules were set up for the secondary boycott, which became subject only to the same limitations as the primary boycott. The ban on boycotts for the purpose of securing minority collective agreements was deleted on the written promise of the Federation of Labor that "as a rule it will continue what has been the practice for many years, not to engage in a strike to secure a collective agreement when only a minority of the workers in a plant are organized." [88]

Surprisingly, the labor members of the committee raised no objection to the broad legal maxims of the earlier law, although in 1946 the Federation of Labor, in referring to the doctrine of interest furthered versus resultant injury, stated that "it is this provision that the Boycott Court has used with special partiality . . . The question of a boycott's legality under this elastic and indefinite rule is left to the arbitrary decision of the court, and hinges upon its composition and sympathies." [89] The committee merely

[86] Socialdepartementet, *Ot. prp. nr. 73,* 1947, p. 1.
[87] Justis- og politidepartementet, *Ot. prp. nr. 70,* 1947.
[88] Socialdepartementet, *Ot. prp. nr. 73,* 1947, p. 2.
[89] *Fri Fagbevegelse,* March 1946, No. 3.

noted that such general provisions had "their natural place" in the new law.

It was acknowledged that there were some advantages, from the point of view of uniform practice, in having a special court to deal with boycott matters. However, the expense of trying all cases in Oslo, and the fact that uniformity could be secured by permitting appeal to the Supreme Court from local court decisions, were considered sufficient reason for returning jurisdiction over boycotts to the ordinary courts.

Thus the Norwegian experiment in legislative regulation of the boycott has come to an end. The new law represents mainly a codification of rules developed prior to 1933 by the common law method. What effects this reversal of policy might have had upon labor relations must remain a moot question, for the rush of events, by removing the conflict between capital and labor to a different plane, has rendered the labor boycott largely obsolete.

CHAPTER VII

INDUSTRIAL RELATIONS IN THE INTERWAR PERIOD

THE HISTORY of industrial relations in Norway between the two world wars is characterized by sharp conflict between employers and trade unions up to 1931, and rapid improvement in bargaining relationships thereafter. Before this turning point was reached, few countries in Europe experienced as frequent and as lengthy work stoppages. Every minor dispute had potentially wide repercussions. While 1931 by no means marked a complete termination of hostilities, there was a perceptible change in the approach of both labor and management to the settlement of disputes.[1]

The industrial relations record of this period is shown statistically in Table 2. Man-days of work lost due to labor disputes were greatest during the deflation that set in during 1920, and continued, with only a two-year break in 1924 and 1925, until 1932, when the economic indexes began to move in an upward direction. The severity and persistence of that deflation, perhaps the most important determinant of labor relations during the period, are apparent from the data in Table 3. The official cost-of-living index declined about 50 per cent from 1920 to 1931, while wage rates were reduced by approximately 40 per cent.

[1] It is interesting to compare the records of Norway, Sweden, and Denmark, countries having basically similar economic and political institutions. (The populations of Norway and Denmark are roughly equal, and that of Sweden twice as large as each of the others):

Man-days lost due to work stoppages

	Norway	Denmark	Sweden
1921–1931	22,253,000	8,509,000	27,259,000
1932–1939	3,998,000	3,338,000	10,819,000

Source: International Labor Organization, *Yearbook of Labor Statistics.* During the decade previous to 1931, Norway's work stoppage record was almost as great absolutely as that of Sweden, despite the disparity in size of the two countries, and far in excess of the Danish. After 1931, the Norwegian and Danish experience was approximately parallel, while Swedish labor relations were characterized by a relatively larger loss of working days.

TABLE 2

LABOR DISPUTES IN NORWAY, 1916–1939

Year	(1) Number of Work Stoppages	(2) Total Workers Involved	(3) Man-days of Work Lost	(4) Membership in Federation of Labor	(5) Ratio of Workers Involved to Union Membership (Col. 2 ÷ Col. 4)	(6) Ratio of Man-days Lost to Maximum Potential Working Time of Trade Union Members (Col. 3 ÷ Col. 4 × 300)
1916.......	...	24,540	719,900	78,900	.31	.030
1917.......	...	5,445	108,700	93,900	.06	.004
1918.......	...	7,399	187,300	107,500	.07	.006
1919.......	...	25,121	622,600	143,900	.17	.014
1920.......	...	31,831	1,198,700	142,600	.22	.028
1921.......	89	154,421	3,584,000	96,000	1.61	.124
1922.......	26	2,168	91,000	83,600	.03	.004
1923.......	57	24,965	796,000	85,600	.29	.031
1924.......	61	63,117	5,152,000	92,800	.68	.185
1925.......	84	13,752	667,000	95,900	.14	.023
1926.......	113	51,487	2,205,000	93,100	.55	.079
1927.......	96	22,456	1,374,000	94,200	.24	.049
1928.......	63	8,042	364,000	106,900	.08	.011
1929.......	73	4,796	197,000	127,000	.04	.005
1930.......	94	4,652	240,000	139,600	.03	.006
1931.......	82	59,524	7,586,000	144,600	.41	.175
1932.......	91	6,360	394,000	153,400	.04	.009
1933.......	93	6,306	364,000	157,500	.04	.008
1934.......	85	6,364	235,000	172,500	.04	.005
1935.......	103	3,548	168,000	214,600	.02	.003
1936.......	175	15,286	396,000	268,300	.06	.005
1937.......	195	28,785	1,014,000	316,000	.09	.011
1938.......	248	24,045	567,000	340,000	.07	.006
1939.......	81	15,973	860,000	352,500	.05	.008

Source: *Statistical Yearbooks for Norway*, Central Statistical Bureau.

The peaks in the curve of work stoppages, during 1921, 1924, 1926–1927, and 1931, resulted from widespread strikes or lock-outs almost general in character. The disturbances had their inception in union resistance to money wage reductions. Once the long deflation had run its course and a slowly rising price level had supplanted it, the economic clime was much more propitious

TABLE 3

WAGES, COST OF LIVING, AND PRICES IN NORWAY, 1916–1939

Year	(1) Average Daily Industrial Wages of Men[a] (*in kroner*)	(2) Index of the Cost of Living (*1938 = 100*)	(3) Index of Wholesale Prices (*1938 = 100*)	(4) Index of Average Daily Industrial Real Wages of Men (*1938 = 100*)
1916...........	...	80.7	...	...
1917...........	...	100.0	...	...
1918...........	...	140.0	...	...
1919...........	...	150.3	...	...
1920...........	18.69	175.2	...	77.2
1921...........	18.58	161.8	...	83.1
1922...........	14.15	134.9	...	75.9
1923...........	13.10	127.3	151.6	74.5
1924...........	14.15	139.6	174.5	73.3
1925...........	15.21	141.9	165.3	77.6
1926...........	14.18	120.3	129.2	85.3
1927...........	12.17	108.6	108.9	81.1
1928...........	11.56	101.3	102.2	82.6
1929...........	11.59	96.8	97.0	86.6
1930...........	11.59	94.1	89.5	89.1
1931...........	11.26	89.1	79.3	91.4
1932...........	11.48	87.2	79.7	95.3
1933...........	11.31	86.0	79.5	95.2
1934...........	11.34	86.2	81.0	95.2
1935...........	11.34	88.1	83.1	93.1
1936...........	11.71	90.4	87.4	93.7
1937...........	12.59	96.8	101.	94.0
1938...........	13.82	100.0	100.0	100.0
1939...........	14.04	101.3	101.7	100.3

Source: *Statistical Yearbooks for Norway.*

[a] From 1931 to 1939 the wage data were calculated in consistent fashion. Prior to 1931 the Central Statistical Bureau employed diverse methods of computation. However, the discrepancies resulting are not believed to be of sufficient magnitude to render yearly comparisons invalid.

for harmonious industrial relations. The work-stoppage record of the decade before World War II was markedly different from that of the preceding decade, particularly when increased trade union membership is taken into account.[2]

[2] Since strikes among unorganized workers have not been common in Norway, the ratio of workers involved in strikes to total trade union membership (Table 2, Column 5) and the ratio of man-days lost to maximum potential working time of trade union members (Table 2, Column 6) are better measures of the degree of labor warfare than the unadjusted record of man-days lost.

WAR, DEFLATION, AND LABOR RELATIONS

An account of the history of Norwegian labor relations may be started conveniently with the year 1916, when the contemporary system of labor legislation first went into effect. The year began with a strike (or lockout)[3] in the mines, which spread to the metal trades a few months later. When the workers in these two industries rejected a compromise proposal approved by their leaders, the Employers' Association prepared to declare a general lockout that would have involved 70,000 workers. To prevent paralysis of the economic life of the country at a time when its foreign trade was seriously curtailed by the European war, a compulsory arbitration law was enacted.

The tripartite Board of Arbitration, to which the trade unions submitted their case with great reluctance, handed down awards that satisfied neither party. In the case of the metal trades wages were raised considerably above the level accepted by the trade union negotiators in the earlier bargaining sessions, but the miners received less than employers had been willing to concede. The logical basis for these differing conclusions has never been explained satisfactorily.[4] Opponents of compulsory arbitration long thereafter pointed to this result as an illustration of the uncertainties involved. The trade unions were led to conclude that "the best that can be said of compulsory arbitration is that it is a lottery." [5]

Once these disputes were settled, a period of relative calm commenced, lasting for three years. Prices were going up, and wages followed. Although strikes and lockouts occurred, none was considered of sufficient social import to warrant recourse to compulsory arbitration. Thus the Ministry of Labor, in proposing an

[3] In most instances it is difficult for the historian to distinguish between a strike and a lockout. When work stoppages are based on disagreements over wage scales, who the initiator of the wage movement is depends largely on the phase of the business cycle. Employers almost invariably refer to stoppages that are not clearly sympathetic lockouts as strikes, while trade union literature is replete with instances of lockouts. The neutral word "stoppage" will generally be employed unless the nature of the action makes it clear that one side or the other was the aggressor.

[4] See Inge Debes, "Erfaringer med Tvungen Voldgift i Norge," *Samtiden,* 1923, pp. 76–90, 151–160.

[5] Gunnar Ousland, *Fagorganisasjonen i Norge,* p. 362.

extension of compulsory arbitration in 1919, was somewhat premature in claiming that the legislation

> proved its worth in our country when it was employed to settle the great conflicts in the mines and metal plants. The trial had fortunate results, and the solution proved satisfactory to the great majority of the people . . . The wages set by the court were relatively good, and compulsory arbitration has not proved to be an obstacle in the path of the labor movement.[6]

The real test did not come until the twenties, when the rising price curve that had enabled employers to satisfy union demands for higher money wages was sharply reversed. During the first half of 1920 there was a rapid price increase, but thereafter prices fell. The cost of living rose by 16 per cent from 1919 to 1920, then dropped 8 per cent from 1920 to 1921. Inability to import during the war had resulted in a reduction of inventories and a surplus of purchasing power that was reflected in great pressure on prices. At the conclusion of hostilities there was a rush to import, and in a surprisingly short time the shortage of goods gave way to a surplus. Many enterprises began to find themselves in difficulty, bound by high interest rates and collective wage agreements; there were six times as many bankruptcies in 1921 as in 1919. The value of Norwegian exports was halved in a year, reflecting a collapse in world prices.

During the first quarter of 1920 work stoppages took place in construction, canning, transportation, and municipal employment. The government submitted these disputes to compulsory arbitration as tending to endanger important public interests. A newly appointed Board of Arbitration rendered fifty-eight awards, involving some 60,000 workers, during the year. The awards were almost uniformly favorable to the workers; the paid vacation period was extended, and the wage increases granted resulted in a substantial improvement in real wages. Since the awards were for a period of one year, as a rule, many employers were placed in serious economic straits when prices fell sharply toward the close of 1920. Consequently, when the life of the compulsory arbitration legislation expired in March 1921, organized employers joined with labor in opposing its extension.

[6] *Sociale Meddelelser,* 1919, p. 48.

It became apparent that wage rates would have to be reduced in 1921. The first important contract up for revision was that of the seamen, of whom the employers demanded a cut of 33 per cent. The State Mediator proposed a more moderate reduction but the seamen rejected it, and on May 8 those engaged in the coastal trade stopped work. A week later the remainder of the domestic transportation workers called a sympathetic walkout in support of the striking seamen.

Considerable sentiment in favor of a general strike developed within the ranks of the Federation of Labor where postwar revolutionary fervor still ran high. In almost all trades, employers and unions were far apart on the magnitude of the downward wage adjustment. Despite the efforts of the mediators, a general strike involving 120,000 organized workers began on May 26.

The government answered by requisitioning ships and mobilizing men to run them. Police protection was provided for strikebreakers. Slowly the men began to drift back to work and at the request of the Federation of Labor the State Mediator began negotiations anew. It was quickly agreed that all but the seamen and transport workers would return to their jobs on June 10. Subsequent negotiations for the latter trades resulted in an immediate wage reduction of 12 per cent when they resumed work several weeks later, plus a further cut of 5 per cent to take place in December 1921.

While this was less than the employers had demanded, it reflected the seriously weakened bargaining power of the unions. The general strike had achieved little, and when the paper and sawmill workers were locked out in the fall, they were forced eventually to accept wage reductions of 21 and 23 per cent respectively. Average daily wages of industrial workers fell from 18.58 kroner to 14.15 kroner during 1921–22, although the impact was softened by a decline in the cost of living.

Deflation had still not run its course. When agreements expired in 1922 the employers demanded additional wage cuts. Unemployment had increased to the point where 25 per cent of all organized workers were idle, and many of the remainder were working only part time. Fearing the consequences of an open test of strength, the Federation of Labor, by a close vote, decided to support the reintroduction of compulsory arbitration legislation. Although the employers, mindful of the unfavorable 1920 awards, remained adamant in their opposition, the Liberal and Labor parties mustered sufficient parliamentary strength to secure the passage of the bill.

During 1922 collective bargaining was largely supplanted by arbitration. The unions had expected that arbitration would soften the blow, but their hopes proved unfounded. As the result of some 111 arbitration awards, wages were reduced, in some industries by as much as 24 to 27 per cent, while the twelve-day vacation period, won through arbitration in 1920, was cut to eight days. The seamen, who had received a wage reduction of 17 per cent in 1921, were forced to accept an additional slash of 25 per cent. The trade unions could do nothing but comply with the awards, and several protest strikes were condemned by the Federation. However, when the compulsory arbitration legislation expired in 1923, labor sentiment in its favor had evaporated completely.

There is no doubt that work stoppages decreased in number as a concomitant of compulsory arbitration. During 1922 the loss of labor time due to strikes or lockouts was lower than in any other single year of modern Norwegian labor history. Only a little over 2000 workers, some 3 per cent of total organized labor strength, left their jobs during the year. But the achievement of this record cannot entirely be imputed to compulsory arbitration. The exhaustion of the trade union movement as a result of losing the general strike of 1921, ideological conflict within the political labor movement, and the considerable degree of unemployment that prevailed produced, independently, a sharp drop in labor militancy.

Some of the principal drawbacks of compulsory arbitration were pointed out by the person who was probably best qualified to assess its effects upon collective bargaining, the State Mediator. In his annual report for 1923, this official declared:

Under the compulsory arbitration law . . . it was assumed that arbitration would be employed only in extraordinary circumstances, in particularly significant disputes, as a way out when compulsory mediation proved ineffective. . . . For various reasons, the settlement of wage disputes through compulsory arbitration has become the usual procedure . . .

Arbitration procedure is in essence too summary. Procedure before a court cannot bring the parties into as intimate relationship with one another and with the government agencies as negotiation and conciliation. It does not help to say that the board of arbitration has a function going beyond pure negotiation, that it has the duty of bringing about the best possible outcome for the parties and the general public. The proceedings must nevertheless be summary, making it difficult to alter detailed contract rules.

This means that the board's action carries danger for both parties through the possibility of the imposition of new rules, and new principles, which can be particularly risky where their formulation was not preceded by direct negotiation between the parties.[7]

One of the principles introduced by the 1922 Board of Arbitration destined to have far reaching effects in future collective bargaining was the explicit tying of wages to the cost of living.[8] The State Mediator objected to it because of difficulties experienced in effecting the adjustments of October 1922 and March 1923. Downward index adjustments subsequently proved to be a source of major irritation in labor relations.

The year 1923 marked a temporary turning point in the postwar recession. Encouraged by the prospect of higher profits, employers generally abandoned their early intention of reducing wages still further and renewed agreements with little change. The metal-trades employers, however, insisted that their workers accept a reduction of 5 per cent on the basis of a similar fall in the cost-of-living index. Although the collective agreement in effect provided for this wage revision, the workers refused to accede and went on strike when the money was deducted from their pay envelopes. The strike was clearly illegal, in violation of a valid agree-

[7] *Norges Offisielle Statistikk,* Series VII, No. 145 (1924).

[8] The following is an example of the type of clause inserted in the 1922 awards:

"When the cost-of-living index number of the Central Statistical Bureau for October 1922 has been published, either party may demand a revision of wages, provided that the said index number has risen or fallen by more than six points as compared with the index number (254) for April 1922. In this event, the wages (time rates, piece rates and fixed wage schedules) which come into force immediately this award takes effect, shall be reduced or raised in the ratio of the index number for October 1922 to the index number for April 1922, so that the percentage fall or rise in the cost of living is accompanied by a corresponding percentage fall or rise in wages. If the parties fail to agree on the calculation, the dispute shall be settled by an arbitration board of three members, one to be appointed by each party, and a chairman elected by the two members. If the latter fail to agree upon a chairman, he shall be appointed by the government."

ment, leaving the Federation no alternative but to denounce it. When the workers persisted in their action, under the leadership of a rank and file "action committee," they were haled before the Labor Court and their leaders fined. But this failed to bring about a termination of the strike.

Coincidentally, trouble developed in connection with the renewal of agreements for harbor and transport workers. The Employers' Association demanded the insertion of a financial guarantee against unauthorized strikes in the agreement, which the Federation of Labor refused to consider. During the first week of 1924 the harbor workers went on strike. The employers countered by closing down the entire transport industry, whereupon the paper mill employees walked out in sympathy with the locked out workers.

Mediation proceedings were held intermittently, but the employers insisted that the *sine qua non* of a general settlement was the termination of the illegal metal strike. The State Mediator finally worked out the following three point proposal: (1) The metal strike to be terminated immediately. (2) The remaining strikes and lockouts to be ended thereafter. (3) Negotiations for new agreements to be commenced when work was resumed.

The employers agreed to this proposal but the unions rejected it on principle, insisting instead that all strikes and lockouts, including the metal strike, had to be terminated simultaneously, with the exception of the harbor and transport stoppage, which was only to be ended after a new contract had been signed. The Federation of Labor insisted in addition that the proposal would have to be approved separately by each union concerned.

The Mediator declared that this did not constitute a reasonable basis for settlement, and withdrew from the scene. Through the intercession of the Minister of Labor, the Employers' Association finally agreed to accept a simultaneous termination of all the stoppages with the exception of that in the transport industry, which was to continue pending further negotiations. Work was resumed on May 30, the metal workers having been on strike for thirty weeks. The net result of this struggle, which made 1924 the second worst year, in terms of total man-days lost, during the interwar period, was an increase of 5 per cent in transport wages and similar increases for other crafts.

In 1925 the index of wholesale prices began to fall, but it was

not until the following year that the general deflationary trend was
resumed. Although the causes of this persistent postwar deflation
were complex, the foreign exchange situation was certainly one of
the major factors, since foreign trade looms so large as an element
in the Norwegian economy. During the war the great demand for
Norwegian goods had driven the rate of the Norwegian krone up,
but the sharp reversal in the balance of trade after the war resulted in currency depreciation. Whereas the average rate of exchange in 1917 was 12.90 kroner to the pound sterling, the corresponding rate in 1924 was 32.60 kroner.

The government failed to take any positive position on the
question of exchange stabilization, although many argued that
maintenance of the lower krone value would stimulate exports and
offset depressive tendencies. Instead, the value of the krone was
pushed up steadily through the inward flow of foreign speculative
funds, for it was widely believed that the then director of the Bank
of Norway favored price deflation and opposed stabilization below
the prewar krone par. The result was that the krone reached its old
gold standard par in 1928, at which point gold payments, which
had been stopped during the war, were resumed.

This drastic appreciation, entailing in the course of four years
a doubling of the international exchange value of the krone, carried with it severe consequences for the economy. Bankruptcies
rose from 866 in 1924 to 1,292 in 1927; the number of farm mortgage foreclosures increased from 12,575 in 1924 to 15,614 in
1927. Unemployment also rose, until 25 per cent of all union
members were out of jobs by 1927. It was not until 1928, when
the krone reached a stable level and a halt was called to progressive deflation, that Norway began to experience the cyclical upswing that had begun three years earlier in most other countries.
This respite was short lived, for a few years later the general
world depression engulfed the Norwegian economy.

These economic circumstances were sharply reflected in labor
relations. When prices began to fall in the latter part of 1925, the
Employers' Association proposed a general reduction of 25 per
cent in the expiring metal, textile, shoe, mining, and building
agreements. The State Mediator, in April 1926, found the parties
so far apart as to render any proposal on his part useless. In addition to wages, the contract term was at issue, the union insisting

that wages should be fixed for a minimum of one year with the employers determined to leave the way open for revision before then if prices continued to slump.

The Mediator then proposed the appointment of a board of mediation to act as a fact-finding body. Both parties agreed and a three-man public board, with the State Mediator as chairman, was established. The board recommended that the 1925 increases be cancelled; that the unions accept a further cut of 10 per cent; and that the contract remain in effect for one year, with reopening in August 1926 should the cost-of-living index fall 10 per cent or more.

Neither the Employers' Association nor the Federation of Labor was prepared to endorse these terms, and a work stoppage involving 30,000 workers began. When the men had been out for a month, the State Mediator, in accordance with the provisions of the labor-disputes act, called the parties together for further discussion. By this time the unions had despaired of averting a wage reduction, and an agreement was concluded along the lines of the mediation board proposal.

This dispute illustrates the desirability of automatic resumption of mediation when a strike has run for a month. For prestige reasons neither party could afford to take the initiative in resuming negotiations, but both knew that at the end of a certain period they would be obliged to reconsider their positions. After the initial test of strength the trade unions could appraise more realistically the resistance that employers were likely to offer in the future, and to assess their own resources. A month's stoppage was also likely to take the edge off rank and file ardor, which may have previously stopped the leadership from reaching agreement.

From 1922 to 1926, wages tended to follow living costs. Both labor and management had more or less accepted the principle that wages should rise and fall with the cost-of-living index, though labor was successful in raising real wages about 12 per cent in this period through its resistance to proportional wage reductions. In 1927, however, the Employers' Association decided that competitive conditions in foreign trade required a reduction of wages in excess of the fall in the cost of living, which amounted to about 10 per cent since 1926. It therefore proposed a general wage reduction of from 25 to 27 per cent.

The unions replied that they could not compromise their real wage level, and on February 11, 1927, the metal, textile, shoe, and mining industries were tied up once more. The State Mediator tried first to secure agreement on another board of mediation, but the employers refused. He then suggested voluntary submission of the dispute to arbitration, without success. Finally he repeated his proposal for a mediation board, and this time the employers acquiesced.

The mediation board found in the existing circumstances justification for a wage reduction in excess of the fall in the cost of living. It recommended a figure of 15 per cent (5 per cent more than the cost of living decline) and a two-year contract term, with two interim index adjustments. This proposal was rejected by both parties.

The complete breakdown of collective bargaining, and the seeming impossibility of averting annual work stoppages in large segments of industry, produced renewed public demands for compulsory arbitration. Wage adjustment by force had become too costly a process. When employers finally became convinced that direct negotiation could lead to no further result, they threw their support behind legislation, and accepted government intervention once more.

When the Arbitration Act of 1927 was adopted, the work stoppages were terminated. It occasioned no great surprise that the arbitration board resolved upon a wage reduction of 15 per cent, following closely the recommendations of the mediation board which had attempted to compromise the dispute earlier. For the remainder of the year, all expiring agreements of any importance were renewed through arbitration, the board rendering 57 awards covering 46,000 workers, and applying the 15 per cent wage reduction formula in the majority of cases.

The cost of living continued to fall during 1928, and employers came before the arbitration board with requests for further wage reductions. In May, the court rendered a series of eighteen awards, covering the building, graphic, and tailoring trades, which contained a wage reduction of 12 per cent (the decline in the cost of living from 1927 to 1928 was 7 per cent). The Oslo building trades unions refused to abide by their award, however, and on May 25 they struck all jobs where the contractors belonged to the Employers' Association. At the same time they concluded agreements with unorganized contractors on considerably more favorable terms than those continued in the award.

The strike was of course illegal, and the Federation of Labor followed the letter of the law by calling for a resumption of work. Actually, "within the ranks of labor there was full unanimity as to the justifiability of the strike." [9] Emboldened by the success of the building workers, and the inability of the government to bring effective sanctions to bear, the graphic trades joined the walkout.

When the men had been out for a month, the Federation of Labor was called before the Labor Court to answer for the illegal actions of its constituents, under the sharpened liability clauses of the Act of 1927. The chairman of the Labor Court, Mr. Paal Berg, convinced the parties that it would be better to effect a compromise than to force the issue. As a result, the terms of the arbitration awards were improved by agreement; the wage reduction was split into two parts, 8 per cent to go into effect immediately and 4 per cent in May 1929, with the possibility that the latter change would be rescinded in the event of a rise in the cost of living.

This marked the virtual end of compulsory arbitration, although the legislation did not expire until 1929. Public confidence in the effectiveness of the board of arbitration was undermined. Although the Liberal Party continued to insist that "compulsory arbitration, on the basis of experience, must be deemed to have justified its position as a necessary step in legislation for the avoidance of labor disputes," [10] there were no tears shed by either employers or workers when the Storting in 1929 refused to extend the law.

The years 1928 to 1930 were relatively good ones from the point of view of labor relations. The krone was finally stabilized, and while prices fell slightly, there was not the same precipitous deflationary movement that had characterized the preceding quinquennium. Most employers waived the downward index adjustments to which they were entitled, since the business outlook was favorable and they were desirous of avoiding labor trouble.

By 1930, government mediation had become firmly established as a customary feature of Norwegian industrial relations. Table 4 indicates the extent to which mediation was employed in attempting to avert work stoppages and to stimulate the peaceful

[9] Halvard Lange, *Fagorganisasjonens Historie i Norge*, p. 117.
[10] Socialdepartementet, *Ot. prp. nr. 35*, 1920, p. 4.

solution of labor controversies; mediation was instrumental in paving the way for a major portion of the collective agreements reached during this period.

TABLE 4

MEDIATION IN NORWEGIAN LABOR DISPUTES, 1921–1929

	(1)	(2)	(3)	(4)	(5)	(6)
		Number of Work Stoppages Preceded by Mediation		Number of Workers	Number of Workers Covered by	Ratio of Column 4
	Number of Work			Involved in	Agreements at	to
Year	Stoppages	Number	Per Cent	Mediation	End of Year	Column 5
1921.........	89	38	43	58,271	91,162	64
1922.........	26	a	a	a	125,202	a
1923.........	57	24	42	59,710	100,560	59
1924.........	61	28	46	68,480	111,400	61
1925.........	84	37	44	98,672	121,095	81
1926.........	113	59	52	88,547	105,920	84
1927.........	96	31	32	81,899	122,536	67
1928.........	63	10	16	68,645	122,756	56
1929.........	73	16	22	53,933	141,500	38

Sources: Columns 1, 5, *Statistical Yearbooks for Norway;* Columns 2, 4, Annual Reports of the State Mediator.

a Not available.

The tendency toward a decline in the number of mediatory efforts from 1927 to 1929 was due in part to deliberate policy on the part of the State Mediator. In his report for the year 1926 the State Mediator noted that the district mediators were invervening in too many disputes: "The parties in recent years have been more and more inclined to reduce direct negotiations to a short exchange of views, and then await compulsory mediation, even in trivial disputes." He therefore sent the following circular to the district mediators:

It has in recent years become the practice to employ compulsory mediation in almost all conflicts where notice of a work stoppage is received. I understand Section 31 of the Act of 1915 to mean that there was no intention of employing mediation in trivial disputes. It is therefore my opinion that the present practice should be altered, since it both involves needless public expenditure and gives the parties to disputes the impression that all disputes are to be settled with the assistance of the mediator.

So that district mediators shall be kept informed of the disputes which occur in their districts, I will continue to advise them of each notice of work stoppage which I receive. But each case should be judged separately to determine whether there is any basis for mediation. In this respect, notice must be taken of local interests, and whether the dispute, even if it embraces only a few workers in the first instance, can lead to such serious consequences that the state should intervene. Ordinarily, the number of workers involved will be the prime criterion. I assume that mediation will not usually be employed where less than fifty workers are involved.[11]

Some gauge of the importance of the strike-delaying provisions contained in the mediation legislation can be secured from Table 5. Mediators did not find it necessary to invoke this power in more than one-third of the cases under mediation at any time, and

TABLE 5

Operation of the Norwegian Mediation Law, 1916–1929

Year	(1) Number of Disputes in which Mediation Was Employed	(2) Number of Disputes in which Mediators Delayed Work Stoppage	(3) Ratio of Column 2 to Column 1	(4) Number of Disputes Handled Personally by State Mediator	(5) Per Cent of Total Workers Involved in Mediation Handled Personally by State Mediator
1916.......	39	7	.18	10	88
1917.......	73	8	.11	19	66
1918.......	122	11	.09	15	51
1919.......	154	16	.10	33	81
1920.......	195	46	.24	55	83
1921.......	80	15	.18	25	68
1922.......	a	a	a	a	a
1923.......	112	20	.18	22	93
1924.......	137	34	.25	18	68
1925.......	163	46	.28	14	64
1926.......	204	47	.23	17	54
1927.......	147	49	.33	24	65
1928.......	100	30	.30	15	59
1929.......	97	30	.31	14	49

Source: Annual Reports of the State Mediator, 1916–1929.

a Not available.

[11] *Norges Offisielle Statistikk,* Series VIII, No. 38 (1927).

usually a much smaller percentage was involved. The "cooling off" period was thus not applied automatically, as had been feared in labor circles, but was used with considerable discretion.

Table 5 also indicates the personal role of the State Mediator. Although he participated in a relatively small number of disputes, they were the important ones. The Norwegian government was fortunate in its choice of a first State Mediator, Jens Michael Lund, to whom much of the credit for the subsequent success of compulsory mediation must go. Of Lund, the official trade-union history records:

For State Mediator the government chose the energetic, somewhat reckless but extraordinarily capable lawyer Jens Michael Lund, who soon gained the respect and esteem of both camps. He was robust and rough, with an unfailing energy that loosed itself upon the most difficult problems as in a game. There are many tales of his biting remarks and swift repartee. He earned an independent popularity— so great that he was known only under the name of "Jens Michael" in many circles, and that says much. When he wished to resign at the end of his term, both central organizations asked him to continue.[12]

THE WORK STOPPAGE OF 1931

The relative calm of the late twenties was shattered in 1931 by the most severe labor conflict in Norwegian history. Fundamentally it had its origins in the world-wide depression, first felt in Norway at the end of 1930. At the negotiation of the "spring" agreements[13] in 1931 the Employers' Association proposed a general wage reduction of 15 per cent. When the trade unions refused, a series of work stoppages commenced which at their peak involved half the members of the Federation of Labor.

The State Mediator had found the parties hopelessly far apart, since the unions demanded a wage increase, and a reduction of the working day as well. A month after the strike had begun, he intervened again, taking the unusual step of issuing a proposal for

[12] Ousland, p. 360.

[13] It has been increasingly customary to have collective agreements terminate in March or April. In 1941, for example, agreements covering 48 per cent of all workers bound by collective agreements expired during the first quarter of the year, an additional 25 per cent during the second quarter, with 21 and 6 per cent in the third and fourth quarters respectively. Most recent controversies have had their inception in renewals of the so-called "spring agreements," which tend to set the pattern for the rest of industry.

settlement without the assent of either party, embodying a wage reduction of from 7 to 10 per cent for the various trades. In the subsequent referendum on the proposal 95 per cent of the workers were opposed to its acceptance.

New mediation proceedings in June proved of no avail. Finally in August, when the workers had been out for more than four months, the Federation of Labor negotiators agreed to a mediation proposal calling for somewhat smaller wage reductions than the earlier proposal. In the balloting, however, the proposal was again defeated, this time by a narrow margin.

The strike then spread to newspapers, breweries, and the tobacco industry, which had not been involved before. The Federation of Labor, finding it impossible to settle the dispute as a whole, suggested to each union that it enter into direct negotiations with its employers to determine whether a better bargain could be obtained. When this had been done, the Federation asked and received from the executive committee of each union the authority to terminate the conflict on the basis of the last mediation proposal as amended in the individual bargaining conferences. On September 11, after five months, the strike was finally ended. It was only by virtue of financial assistance from Danish and Swedish trade unions that the Norwegian Federation of Labor held out for so long.

The general agreement called for an average wage reduction of 7 per cent and three-year contracts with a possible index wage adjustment on January 1, 1933. Under the circumstances this settlement was not unfavorable to the workers, real wages actually being increased slightly. Unemployment rose sharply, however, and between 1932 and 1935 about one-third of all trade union members were not working.

INDUSTRIAL RELATIONS FROM 1931 TO 1940

The general stoppage of 1931 marked the last great collapse of the Norwegian collective bargaining system. Thereafter a marked improvement in employer-union relationships took place, a fact that is borne out by the labor dispute statistics in Table 2. Both management and labor were tired of strife that periodically resulted in business losses and emptied union treasuries. There was mutual recognition that work stoppages such as those which occurred in 1921, 1924, and 1931 could not be repeated indefinitely without threatening the very foundations of the Norwegian economy.[14]

But even given this desire to avert further disturbances, whether there would have been so marked an improvement in industrial relations without the accompanying economic and political developments is problematical. The bottom of the depression was reached in 1931, and although it was several years before there was any real economic improvement, the important element for industrial relations was that it was no longer necessary to *reduce* money wages. The constant and irritating wage reductions of the twenties, resulting in a money wage decline of 40 per cent between 1920 and 1931, gave way to a slow but steady series of money wage increases.[15] The outcome of the 1931 general stoppage was a wage reduction sufficient to permit profitable operation, and thereafter prices rose steadily until the outbreak of the war.

The other important development was an accretion in the political strength of the labor movement, resulting in the formation of a labor government in 1935. It is one of the theses of this study that political power necessarily entails a greater sense of responsibility on the part of trade unions.[16] The growing soberness of the trade-union approach to economic problems in the late nineteen-thirties, as reflected in union publications and public utterances of union leaders, suggests that this was a factor in the improvement of industrial relations.

The course of trade-union membership during the period under consideration presents an interesting contrast to the American ex-

[14] It is impossible to assess precisely the economic losses entailed by these serious labor disputes. For example, national income or physical output comparisons would be influenced by the general level of business activity and employment, the state of foreign markets, and financial and monetary conditions, as well as by the deliberate withdrawal of a portion of the labor force from productive employment. It is apparent, however, that the loss of 7.5 million man-days of labor out of a potential 32.5 million man-days (1931) would have serious economic consequences, to say nothing of the fact that the portion of industry affected was generally the most vital to the economy as a whole.

[15] In contrast to the trend of money wages, real wages *rose* by 19 per cent between 1920 and 1931. The rate of increase during the following period was much slower, 10 per cent from 1931 to 1939. This offers striking confirmation of the observation that money rather than real wages are the important determinant of labor relations.

[16] See Chapter XIII.

perience. Like the American Federation of Labor, the Norwegian Federation of Labor suffered a serious decline in membership in the post-World War I recession.[17] During the depression after 1929, however, when the A. F. of L. experienced a further serious decline in membership (from 2.9 million in 1929 to 2.1 million in 1933), the Norwegian Federation of Labor actually increased its membership significantly (see Table 1), despite the existence of severe unemployment.[18] Efforts were made to keep the unemployed attached to the trade union movement by remission of dues and through the organization of local unions of unemployed workers, membership in which was open to unorganized as well as organized workers. The prevailing Ghent system of unemployment insurance, whereby benefits were paid out through union insurance funds, was also a factor in preserving the integrity of the trade unions.

The wage movements from 1931 to 1940 can be dealt with briefly. In 1932, the employers waived their right to a downward cost-of-living index wage adjustment in the major agreements in return for extension of the agreements to 1935. Both the money and real wage levels remained almost unchanged for three years. In 1935, there was a two-year renewal with a slight improvement in wage standards, but it was not until 1938 that any appreciable increase in real wages occurred as a result of money wage increases in excess of the cost of living.

A significant trend during this period was the increasing centralization of collective bargaining. The conclusion of a Basic Agreement[19] in 1935 between the Federation of Labor and the Employers' Association, covering many non-wage aspects of industrial relations, was a milestone in this development. The labor movement began to think in terms of a national wage policy, the so-called "solidaristic" wage policy, which implied that the well-paid crafts would refrain from securing wage increases fully commensurate with their bargaining strength in order that the poorly paid workers could be raised to a minimum decency standard.

[17] A. F. of L. membership in 1920 was 4.1 million, dropping to 2.9 million in 1924. Norwegian Federation of Labor membership for the corresponding years was 142,600 and 92,800.

[18] In December 1932, about 42 per cent of all trade union members were unemployed.

[19] See below, p. 192.

This did not occur without dissent within the trade unions,[20] but by 1940 the ability of the Federation to speak with authority on wage and other questions had increased greatly. The chairman of the Federation declared: "In negotiations, representatives of the workers, the national union, and the Federation of Labor may participate, depending upon the scope of the agreement. In important wage negotiations, national unions coöperate under the leadership of the Federation of Labor." [21]

In 1939 for the first time an extension of all the "spring" agreements was negotiated simultaneously. Some 350 agreements were extended for one year with little alteration. The manner in which this was accomplished led the State Mediator to remark that "whereas organizations met earlier as enemies at the bargaining table, the situation has changed. They do not meet as enemies, but as opponents with a will to peace." [22]

It was by no means true that absolute industrial peace had been achieved. On the contrary, Table 2 indicates the continuance of a high level of work stoppages. In contrast to the earlier pattern, however, the labor conflict of the nineteen-thirties was not primarily head-on strife between the central organizations of workers and employers. Rather, it was confined largely to industries in the process of organization where employers independent of the Employers' Association were determined to resist the encroachment of trade unionism upon their traditional prerogatives.[23]

Tables 6, 7, and 8 present a statistical picture of Norwegian industrial relations from 1928 to 1938, and when read in conjunction with the data for the preceding period shown in Tables 4 and 5, substantiate the conclusions reached above. Although the absolute number of labor stoppages increased, the average number of workers involved in each, and the duration, declined. Even omitting the peak strike year of 1931, total man-days lost due to stoppages from 1923 to 1930 inclusive were eleven million compared with four million in the eight-year period 1932 to 1939,

[20] See Arbeidernes Faglige Landsorganisasjon, *Kongressen 1938, Protokoll*, pp. 25ff.

[21] *Landsorganisasjons Meddelelseblad*, 1939–40, No. 12.

[22] *Landsorganisasjons Meddelelseblad*, 1939, No. 5.

[23] In 1938, for example, 42 per cent of total man-days of work lost due to work stoppages was in lumbering, and in 1939, 88 per cent. *Statistisk Årbok for Norge 1943–45*, p. 337. Lumber employers are independent of the Norwegian Employers' Association, in the main.

TABLE 6

MANNER OF SETTLEMENT OF LABOR DISPUTES IN NORWAY, BY
NUMBER OF DISPUTES, 1928–1939

Year	(1) Total Stoppages	(2) Number Settled by Direct Negotiation	(3) Number Settled through Mediation	(4) Number in Effect at End of Year	(5) Per Cent of Total Settled through Mediation
1928.......	63	31	26	6	41
1929.......	73	42	15	16	21
1930.......	94	54	26	14	28
1931.......	82	48	22	12	27
1932.......	91	57	22	12	24
1933.......	93	53	13	27	14
1934.......	85	52	14	19	16
1935.......	103	43	40	20	39
1936.......	175	107	49	19	28
1937.......	195	111	74	10	38
1938.......	248	157	67	24	27
1939.......	81	54	21	6	26

Source: *Tariffavtaler og Arbeidskonflikter*, annual publications of the Central Statistical Bureau.

TABLE 7

MANNER OF SETTLEMENT OF LABOR DISPUTES IN NORWAY, BY
NUMBER OF WORKERS INVOLVED, 1928–1938

Year	(1) Total Workers Involved in Stoppages	(2) Number Involved in Stoppages Settled by Direct Negotiation	(3) Number Involved in Stoppages Settled through Mediation	(4) Number Involved in Stoppages in Effect at End of Year	(5) Per Cent Involved in Stoppages Settled through Mediation
1928.......	8,042	1,091	6,730	221	84
1929.......	4,796	2,081	1,568	1,147	33
1930.......	4,652	2,763	1,491	398	32
1931.......	59,524	2,034	57,214	276	96
1932.......	6,360	3,078	3,023	259	48
1933.......	6,306	1,508	3,396	1,402	54
1934.......	6,364	1,927	4,118	319	65
1935.......	3,548	1,843	1,449	256	41
1936.......	15,286	5,028	9,978	280	65
1937.......	28,785	7,834	20,644	307	72
1938.......	24,045	7,707	15,847	491	66

Source: *Tariffavtaler og Arbeidskonflikter*, annual publications of the Central Statistical Bureau.

TABLE 8

MANNER IN WHICH COLLECTIVE AGREEMENTS WERE REACHED IN
NORWAY, 1928–1938

Year	With a Stoppage of Work				Without a Stoppage of Work			
	Direct Negotiation		Mediation		Direct Negotiation		Mediation	
	Agreements	Number of Workers	Agreements	Number of Workers	Agreements	Number of Workers	Agreements	Number of Workers
			(*In percentages of the total*)					
1928......	3.7	1.5	4.3[a]	10.6[a]	83.1	41.0	8.9[a]	46.9[a]
1929......	8.5	5.4	1.0	1.8	84.4	55.3	6.1	37.5
1930......	4.6	1.8	3.4	2.4	50.9	42.3	41.1	53.5
1931......	4.3	2.3	8.1	45.6	79.2	21.4	8.4	30.7
1932......	4.3	1.4	3.1	7.1	85.9	83.4	6.7	8.1
1933......	3.4	0.8	1.1	0.6	88.2	83.7	7.3	14.9
1934......	3.8	2.0	1.9	11.2	84.1	57.5	10.2	29.3
1935......	1.9	0.4	2.6	4.5	75.5	30.7	20.0	64.4
1936......	1.2	0.5	1.8	5.6	85.7	50.0	11.3	43.9
1937......	0.7	0.4	4.3	9.7	80.2	50.2	14.8	39.7
1938......	2.3	2.7	1.5	17.3	86.3	47.3	9.9	32.7

Source: Calculated from *Tariffavtaler og Arbeidskonflikter*, annual publications of the Central Statistical Bureau.

[a] Includes disputes settled by compulsory arbitration.

notwithstanding the fact that in the latter period average trade-union membership was double that in the former period.

These tables also present in some detail the role of government mediation in labor disputes. While the earlier policy of attempting to limit mediation to a relatively few major controversies[24] was not followed consistently, the tendency was to avoid mediation in minor disputes. Thus, the percentage of workers involved in stoppages resolved with the aid of mediation (Table 7, Column 5), is consistently higher than the number of stoppages in which mediation was employed (Table 6, Column 5). In 1937, for example, the government mediators settled only 67 out of 248 stoppages, but the 67 stoppages in which they intervened involved 72 per cent of all workers participating in work stoppages during the year.

Table 8 reveals that mediation was important in averting work stoppages as well as in helping to terminate them once they had begun. Although the great majority of collective agreements were

[24] See above, p. 170.

reached through direct negotiation without a stoppage of work, in the years when general contract revisions were undertaken (1935, 1937) mediation was active in the major contract negotiations. Once the basic pattern of adjustment had been worked out, numerous minor agreements could be concluded with little difficulty. It may be concluded that the Norwegian system of compulsory mediation by no means resulted in universal recourse to mediation as a substitute for direct bargaining between the parties.

GENERAL OBSERVATIONS

1. The prime determinant of interwar industrial relations in Norway appears to have been the business cycle. Least friction was generated when prices were rising and the workers pressed for corresponding increases in wages; the major conflicts occurred when employers were determined to reduce money wages.

When economic conditions were unstable, neither party was willing to commit itself to long-term agreements. Before 1914, two and three year contracts were normal. But with the sharp wartime price increases, contract terms were limited to one year or less, and in 1919 the Federation of Labor formally resolved that one year should constitute a maximum term.[25]

Beginning with 1924 a counter trend set in toward the extension of contracts to two years, with an automatic interim adjustment based upon the official cost-of-living index. By 1929 this had become the customary procedure, but the depression of 1930 caused a return to the one year agreement.

After the general work stoppage of 1931 the period of agreement duration began to lengthen under the influence of a more stable price level, but as Table 9 indicates, one year remained the most common term. The more important national agreements tended to run for two years, however, and Table 9 overstates the incidence of the one-year agreement, though by how much it is impossible to determine in the absence of relevant statistical data.

The cost-of-living index was employed widely during the entire

[25] The shortening of contract terms was very marked. In 1913, only 12.6 per cent of workers were covered by one-year agreements. The modal class was three years, embracing 51.9 per cent of workers. By 1919, 92.9 per cent of the workers were under one-year agreements, and there were virtually no agreements stipulating more than a two-year term. *Norges Offisielle Statistikk,* VII, No. 145 (1924).

TABLE 9

DURATION OF COLLECTIVE AGREEMENTS CONCLUDED IN NORWAY, 1932–1938,
IN PERCENTAGES OF TOTAL AGREEMENTS

Year Concluded	One Year	Two or More Years	Indefinite
1932	50	25	25
1933	40	33	27
1934	69	9	22
1935	59	39	2
1936	67	33	...
1937	61	30	9
1938	81	9	10

Source: *Tariffavtaler og Arbeidskonflikter*, annual publications of the Central Statistical Bureau.

interwar period both for bargaining purposes and as a means of reconciling the desire for wage certainty with fluctuating prices over reasonable periods of time. The choice of September as the month for reopening wage schedules in 1923, when the principle was first introduced, was unfortunate, since in Norway there is generally a seasonal drop in prices during that month. This made the labor unions initially suspicious of the entire procedure. Nevertheless, during the difficult years that followed, labor came to regard the index adjustment as an "emergency measure or a defensive weapon in wage policy during deflation. Wage regulation by the index means: mark time. It is a guarantee that the living standards won in good times will in no event fall." [26]

Upward index adjustments were always accomplished without difficulty, but time and again workers refused to accept downward adjustments to which employers were entitled by contract. For this reason employers were generally opposed to the index adjustment in principle, though they were obliged to accept it as the lesser of two evils when the alternative offered was a very short term agreement.

The trade unions refused to be limited by cost-of-living index considerations in the upswing of the business cycle, on the ground that improvements in real wages would thereby be precluded. That they were successful in this policy is indicated by the 25 per cent

[26] Johanne Reutz, *Indeksregulering,* Landsorganisasjonens Statistiske Special-undersøkelser (Oslo, 1928), p. 24.

increase in real wages that took place between 1920 and 1940 (Table 3).

Despite its drawbacks, the cost-of-living index adjustment was a useful arrangement for reducing the frequency of contract negotiations, and with it the possibility of industrial strife.

2. Contributing to the improvement in Norwegian industrial relations between wars was the increasing stability of the trade union movement. The revolutionary upsurge after World War I was accompanied by the belief, particularly among the unskilled, that collective bargaining was illusory as a means of effecting a permanent improvement in the worker's lot. The subsequent decline in membership left within the Federation of Labor a solid core of workers who were by and large habituated to the collective bargaining method, and the gradual rebuilding of the movement around this philosophy served to reduce tensions and antagonisms.

On the other side, the growing political power of labor was not lost upon employers. It became increasingly difficult simply to announce the necessity of substantial wage reductions and lock workers out when they refused to accept them. Initial bargaining positions tended to become more reasonable on both sides of the conference table, and the narrowed area between them made it easier for mediation to function successfully.

3. One of the characteristics of the period 1916 to 1940 was a great extension of industry-wide bargaining. In the opinions of officials of the Employers' Association, industry-wide bargaining cannot be said prima facie either to have increased or minimized industrial strife. What it did do, in their estimation, was to stabilize wage rates, which would otherwise have tended to rise more on the upswing and fall more on the downswing of the business cycle. Both the Federation of Labor and the Employers' Association favor industry-wide bargaining, the former partly as a means of preventing undercutting of East Norwegian standards by the less well organized West, the latter to promote employer solidarity and forestall union endeavor to play one employer off against another.

Employers are aware of the fact that industry-wide bargaining tends to create wage uniformities that may be undesirable from a competitive standpoint. They find, however, that many individual differences are perpetuated through separate negotiations when special problems are involved, affording sufficient wage flexibility.

4. Both labor and management are firmly agreed that the sys-

tem of compulsory mediation practiced since 1915 is a desirable form of government intervention in labor disputes. The automatic reinstitution of mediation one month after the beginning of a strike seems to have been a particularly effective feature of the system. There is no objection to the compulsory "cooling off" period, and the mediator's power to issue a formal proposal is regarded as an essential part of the process.

There appears to be little doubt that early fears of the weakening of direct collective bargaining through increased reliance upon mediation have materialized. Important agreements are generally concluded at the mediation stage rather than in the earlier direct bargaining between the parties, the latter tending to become a mere preliminary to the real bargaining in the office of the mediator. If mediation is regarded simply as a step in a continuous bargaining process, rather than as a distinct proceeding in itself, then it can be said to serve the useful function of lengthening the period available for discussion and at the same time setting definite limits to it.

Government mediation has become so integral a part of collective bargaining that its rationale is simply not open to question. By the pragmatic test of survival as a key institution of the labor market through many difficult years, compulsory mediation has established its suitability to Norwegian conditions. A major part of the credit for this development should go to the state mediators, who with few exceptions conceived the law as merely a very general framework within which advice and assistance could be distributed impartially and good humoredly.

5. Compulsory arbitration of disputes over interests was by no means equally successful. The Norwegian experience, however, cannot be employed as a general argument against the practice, for in contrast to the Australian type, it was always employed in Norway as an emergency measure rather than as a permanent method of settling disputes. There was stability neither of personnel nor of principle, so that the contesting parties were often faced with new and untried practices.

CHAPTER VIII

COLLECTIVE AGREEMENTS: NON-WAGE PROVISIONS

THE NUMERICAL GROWTH, the coverage and the complexity of
collective agreements reflect the increased influence of trade unions
on the regulation of wages and other working conditions. In contemporary Norway there is scarcely a field of economic endeavor
in which terms of employment are not directly determined or fundamentally affected by collective agreement. This and the two following chapters describe the contents of typical Norwegian agreements, the wage structure that they embody, and the manner in
which disputes over their terms are settled.

COLLECTIVE AGREEMENT COVERAGE AND THE BARGAINING UNIT

The first known collective agreement was concluded in 1873
between the Oslo book printers and a local typographical workers'
union. With the close of the eighties, agreements began to be more
common, and by the turn of the century it was commonplace to
find the skilled trades regulated by collective contract. The first
national agreement was negotiated in 1908 for the metal trades,
and by this time "the question was no longer whether there should
be an agreement, but rather what the form and content of the
agreement should be." [1] Table 10 shows the subsequent expansion
of the collective bargaining network in terms of the number of
agreements and the number of workers covered.

The data for 1922 and subsequent years reflect a consistent
tendency for the number of agreements to increase at a greater
rate than the workers covered, producing a decline in the average
coverage. There are several explanations for this phenomenon.
(a) Large scale manufacturing was generally the first to be organized, after the skilled trades, with expansion thereafter to units
and activities embracing fewer workers. From 1927 to 1932 hundreds of agreements were signed in lumbering, most of them
covering a few workers each. There was also a fragmentation of

[1] Gunnar Ousland, *Fagorganisasjonen i Norge*, p. 172.

TABLE 10

COLLECTIVE AGREEMENTS IN NORWAY, 1912–1940

Year	Number of Agreements	Workers Covered by Agreement	Average Number of Workers per Agreement
1912....................	705[a]	72,887	[a]
1917....................	888[a]	106,655	[a]
1922....................	252[a]	125,202	[a]
1927....................	846	122,536	145
1932....................	1,923	169,177	88
1937....................	4,545	341,000	75
1940....................	6,202	391,814	63

Source: *Statistical Yearbooks for Norway.*

[a] The data prior to 1927 with respect to the number of agreements are not comparable with 1927 and subsequent years because of changes in the method of compilation and computation. Before 1922 the Central Statistical Bureau relied upon data supplied by the Federation of Labor, but beginning with 1922 the annual compilations were based on the collective agreements filed with the State Mediator, as required by the Labor Disputes Act. From 1922 to 1926, the Bureau counted as one unit all agreements with unassociated employers identical in term with agreements concluded by employer associations. In 1927 and thereafter, all agreements with unassociated employers were computed separately, resulting in a fictitious increase in the number of agreements. In the printing trades alone there were 170 additional agreements listed as a result of this methodological change. However, agreements between unions and employer associations continued to be treated as a single unit, regardless of the number of employers bound thereby See *Norges Offisielle Statistikk*, Vol. VIII, No. 73.

collective agreements in the building trades, resulting from a tendency to break down national and regional agreements into individual employer contracts. After 1932, in addition to the further spread of trade unionism to lumbering, the primary growth of the collective agreement system was in trade and commerce, transportation, clothing, food, building construction, and agriculture (the last beginning with 1936), all of which are characterized by relatively small operating units. (b) Within each industry, the order of organization has generally been from the larger to the smaller firm, contrary to American experience in many industries. It will be recalled that large scale industry developed in Norway at a comparatively late date, when trade unionism in the skilled trades had become fairly strong, and when social mores more or less dictated acceptance of collective bargaining. Thus, the larger and more stable firms which constituted the Norwegian Employers' Association were from the start disposed to accept trade unionism, and there was no concerted effort to destroy the unions, as in the United States. It was mainly among the small, marginal estab-

TABLE 11

THE UNIT SCOPE OF COLLECTIVE AGREEMENTS IN NORWAY, 1922–1937

(*In percentages of the total number*)

Year	National		District		Local		Single Firm	
	Agreements	Workers	Agreements	Workers	Agreements	Workers	Agreements	Workers
1922......	14.3	78	a	a	a	a	a	a
1927......	4.7	59	a	a	a	a	a	a
1932[b].....	2.4	52.3	0.5	1.8	13.4	15.2	83.7	30.7
1937......	1.5	52.1	0.8	5.3	10.1	10.4	87.6	32.2

Source: *Tariffavtaler og Arbeidskonflikter*, annual publications of the Central Statistical Bureau.
a Not available.
b Excludes the lumber industry.

lishments, located in isolated communities, that resistance to union organization was to be found, for there rural individualism was strongest. In recent years, trade unions have devoted considerable effort to rounding out their organization by going after these small pockets of antiunionism.

The large number of separate collective agreements shown in Table 10 might lead to the erroneous conclusion that little uniformity exists in conditions of employment within individual industries. Table 11 shows, for selected years, the relative importance of national, district, local, and single-firm labor agreements. It indicates that although national agreements lost some ground in terms of the total number of agreements in existence, they still represented more than half the workers covered by agreement in 1937. The rapid proliferation of small agreements obscures the fact that, on the average, the coverage of the national agreements has grown. In 1928, the first year for which complete data are available, 40 national agreements covered 67,945 workers, an average of about 1,700 workers per agreement. A decade later, 77 national agreements covered 182,032 workers, the average rising to 2,360 workers for each agreement. It is estimated that in 1947 there were only 50 important national agreements in terms of their impact upon the economy as a whole.[2]

[2] Interview with Konrad Nordahl, Chairman of the Federation of Labor, July 24, 1947.

These data also tend to understate the actual degree of uniformity that prevails under present conditions of labor shortage, in that the majority of independent employers are obliged to accept the terms of employment contained in national agreements with employer associations. In 1946, for example, although the Office and Commercial Workers' Union signed an agreement with the Commercial Employers' Association for numerous small firms that formerly had individual agreements, the union entered into fifteen hundred separate agreements with independent firms following the pattern of the national agreement. If instead of the number of *separate* agreements in effect, the Central Statistical Bureau added the number of *different* agreements, the total would be much smaller than the published figures indicate.

Employer organization appears to be the most significant determinant of the bargaining unit. The normal pattern is a single agreement for all associated employers within an industry, and separate agreements for each independent employer. The establishment of differential conditions within the ranks of the associated employers is often accomplished by special clauses within the body of the main agreement, rather than through separate agreements.[3] The recent trend toward greater association of employers tends to reduce the total of individual contracts: as an example of this process the Building Workers' Union was able to replace 175 individual agreements with manufacturers of building supplies by a single agreement in 1946 when the manufacturers formed an association.

The intraplant bargaining unit has not been a major problem in Norway, owing largely to the organizational form of the labor movement. Large plants are usually covered by a single collective agreement for all the production employees, and while separate agreements for a few crafts — the bricklayers, electricians, and transport workers mainly — are not uncommon, it has been trade union policy that terms of employment for all workers within an industry shall depend upon conditions in that industry, rather than upon nationwide craft conditions.

The collective agreements in effect, and the number of workers

[3] For example, the national hosiery agreement for 1946 provided that employees of the firm Lauritzen and Sørensen should retain a certain bonus payment they had been receiving, which was not to be found elsewhere in the industry.

covered by such agreements in 1939, the last normal year for which such a breakdown is available, are shown in Table 12. Federation of Labor membership was 352,000 compared with agreement coverage of 388,000 workers, groups of nonunion workers in building construction, transportation, lumbering, and agriculture having been employed under union agreements.

The highly organized printing trades had but two basic agreements: one with the Printing Employers' Association, and a second, embodying more favorable terms, with the important Labor Press Association and the few independents. In the metal trades, on the other hand, there was a great variety of bargaining units. Recent statistics indicate that the 25 per cent of the industry's thousand-odd establishments belonging to the Employers' As-

TABLE 12

COLLECTIVE AGREEMENTS IN EFFECT IN NORWAY AT THE END OF 1939

Industry	Number of Agreements	Number of Workers Covered	Average Number of Workers per Agreement
Refining of metallic ores.......	16	5,220	326
Cement and stone............	140	9,450	68
Machinery....................	396	33,244	84
Chemicals....................	77	9,968	129
Fats and oils................	83	3,596	43
Electricity and gasworks.......	167	2,277	14
Woodworking................	422	11,761	28
Paper.......................	22	16,507	750
Leather and rubber...........	27	3,037	112
Textiles.....................	67	9,429	141
Clothing....................	316	13,338	42
Food.......................	458	19,604	43
Printing and graphics..........	12	4,365	364
Building and construction......	476	53,649	113
Transportation..............	701	39,320	56
Shipping....................	185	61,934	335
Lumbering and agriculture.....	249	40,549	163
Office and commercial work....	1,289	20,523	16
Hotels and restaurants.........	323	6,931	21
Miscellaneous...............	744	23,374	31
Total....................	6,170	388,076	63

Source: *Statistical Yearbook for Norway*, 194 ., p. 205.

sociation are divided into a number of sub-industrial groups, each with a separate agreement. The remaining firms have either signed individual contracts, or are covered through local independent employer associations.[4] Other industries occupy intermediate positions: sixty-five establishments in the textile industry are included in a single agreement, while there are forty-three independents bargaining separately; the Clothing Workers' Union has a single agreement with all large establishments, and separate or local group agreements with between four and five hundred smaller firms.[5]

LEGAL ASPECTS OF COLLECTIVE AGREEMENTS

To a far reaching extent the form and content of collective labor agreements are determined by legislation in Norway. The Labor Disputes Act of 1915, as amended, the Labor Protection Act of 1936, and the Vacation Act of 1947 are the chief sources of legislative standardization.

The Labor Disputes Act.[6] To be enforceable at law, collective agreements must be in writing and signed by both parties. An exchange of correspondence, as well as an agreement signed by only one party, have been held binding in special circumstances, but ordinarily a formal, properly attested document is necessary.[7]

In the event that an agreement does not contain a specified period of validity, it becomes legally binding for a period of three years. Contracts must also provide a date for notice of nonrenewal in advance of the termination date in order to permit new negotiations; in the absence of such a clause, the law imputes three-months' notice, and if this notice is not given by either party, the agreement becomes valid for an additional year without alteration.[8]

A trade union, defined as "any association of workers or workers' organizations which has as its purpose protection of the interests of workers against employers," is a necessary party to a collective agreement. Thus, some form of organization on the

---

[4] *Arbeiderbladet,* January 3, 1947.

[5] *Arbeiderbladet,* December 23, 1946.

[6] See above, pp. 98 ff.

[7] Paal Berg, *Arbeidsrett,* p. 165.

[8] Notice requirements in collective agreements vary from one to three months, with two months the usual period.

workers' side is a prerequisite to the consummation of collective agreements, though *ad hoc* organizations have been held to come within this definition. "Workers" are defined as persons in the employ of private employers or governmental units, with the exception of civil servants.

The Labor Protection Act. This legislation, enacted June 19, 1936,[9] under the sponsorship of a labor government, replaced some of the subject matter previously contained in collective agreements, in addition to establishing new basic labor standards. Many of the provisions are minimal, in that collective agreements generally contain more liberal conditions, while others embody standard practice and render unnecessary collective bargaining on the points they cover.

1. Night work. All work performed between 11 P.M. and 6 A.M. is deemed night work and, though generally forbidden, may be performed if necessary to prevent damage to machinery, materials, or plant, in transportation, retail trades, and building and construction, and in an occupation "that cannot be interrupted because of its nature." [10] The Ministry of Labor may grant other exceptions warranted by peculiar economic circumstances for a period not exceeding six weeks in peak seasonal operations.

2. Sunday and holiday work. No employer may offer and no employee may accept employment on Sundays or legal holidays except under the circumstances in which night work is permitted.[11] There are now eleven legal holidays in Norway, but hourly rated employees do not usually receive pay for holidays.

3. Overtime. Maximum regular hours are fixed at forty-eight weekly (including travel time in mines). The Ministry of Labor may extend the regular working time period in specified cases as, for example, in seasonal industries, where a regular fifty-four hour week is permitted in peak seasons provided average regular weekly hours for the entire year do not exceed forty-eight. Overtime is permissible only to the extent of ten hours a week, and for not more than thirty hours in four consecutive weeks for any indi-

[9] International Labor Organization, *Legislative Series,* 1936. The act does not extend to the merchant marine, fishing and whaling, agriculture, and the civil service.

[10] Another important exception is the provision that there may be two regular shifts between the hours of 6 A.M. and midnight.

[11] Building and construction work, however, is prohibited on Sundays though permitted as night work.

vidual, at a 25 per cent premium above the regular hourly wage rate.

4. *Rest periods.* If an employee works more than eight hours a day, he is entitled to one or more paid rest periods totaling forty-five minutes daily, which may not be spent at the work bench unless permission is secured from the labor inspector. The work week must be so arranged as to leave each worker free for a consecutive period of at least twenty-four hours.

5. *Termination of employment.* Unless there is a written agreement to the contrary, all workers paid by the hour, day, or week, or by the piece, must be given fourteen days' notice of dismissal, while those paid by the month or year are entitled to a month's notice dated from the end of a calendar month. Any employee in the former category is also entitled to a notice of a month if he is over twenty-five years of age and has been employed for five years in the same establishment. The notice requirement does not apply to justifiable disciplinary dismissal. The worker is required to give his employer similar notice if he resigns his position.[12]

Workers may not arbitrarily be discharged from employment; there must be just cause:

If an employee who has been employed for not less than three consecutive years in the same establishment after reaching the age of twenty-one years is dismissed for purely extraneous reasons, and without just cause based upon conditions directly involving the operator or owner of the establishment, or the employee, he shall be entitled to claim compensation from the employer.[13]

The question of what constitutes just cause is one for the courts to decide when the employee brings suit to recover lost earnings, which may not exceed one-half of his total earnings during the year prior to the discharge. A few cases may be cited as examples of how the courts have interpreted this section: [14] (a) Failure of an employer to prove that a discharged worker had acted to the detriment of the establishment, the alleged cause of the discharge, resulted in an award of back pay to the worker. (b) Proof that a

[12] This reciprocal obligation was inserted in the law to forestall allegations of one sidedness. It has been of no practical significance, however.

[13] Section 33 (3a).

[14] They are taken from Ferdinand Rømcke, *Lov om Arbeidervern* (Oslo, 1947), p. 106.

worker had several times refused to carry out the employer's orders was considered cause for discharge. (c) Discharge of a woman because of her marriage was not deemed good cause. (d) Discharge for refusal of the employee to accept transfer to a new position commensurate in salary with the old one was held valid. (e) A reduction in business volume was stated to be justification for discharging a worker.

A summary of what might reasonably be considered cause for discharge has been formulated in the following terms:

If a discharge is undertaken on the basis of reasonable judgment as to what is necessary to meet the demands of the establishment in the best possible manner, it must be said to be "just cause." For example, in the event of rationalization, merger, or shutdown on economic grounds, or lessening of trade or export possibilities, consequent discharges will be valid, even if the business is not unprofitable . . . It is not essential that the discharge shall be *necessary* to put the establishment on a sound basis. "Just cause" from the point of view of the workers' actions will be present not only when discharge is a result of so aggravated a situation that the employer is entitled to break the contract of employment, as in the case of disloyalty, willful destruction of company property, repeated intoxication during working hours, or complete inability to perform work, but can be implied also if the worker performs indifferent, slovenly or little work, or if on the basis of his entire attitude he shows that he does not fit into the establishment.[15]

Although it was originally proposed to give the worker a choice between compensation and the right to reinstatement, the law as enacted gives him only the former. To protect the employer from loss where he is not at fault, a qualification was inserted to the effect that no claim for compensation can arise if the discharge is attributable to pressure from other workers, or from a union, giving the employer reason to believe he will be subject to injury unless he effects the discharge.

6. *Working rules.* In establishments employing more than ten workers the employer is required to coöperate with an elected

---

[15] Rømcke, p. 107. Prior to the war the discharge provisions were of considerable practical importance, judging by the number of claims filed by workers. The postwar shortage of manpower has reduced their significance for the time being.

committee of five workers in the formulation of plant working rules not covered by collective agreement. These include such matters as the specific hours of work, smoking, hygienic conditions, and prohibitions against the use of alcohol within the confines of the plant.

THE BASIC AGREEMENT

The conclusion of a Basic Agreement in 1935 between the Employers' Association and the Federation of Labor constituted a significant advance in the extension of collective bargaining. This agreement remained in effect until 1947, when it was renewed with minor changes.[16] The Basic Agreement provides an important source of contract uniformity, since its terms are automatically incorporated into all agreements between affiliates of the signatory organizations, as well as because the provisions of collective agreements with unassociated employers are modeled after it. There are ten principal subjects, as follows:

1. Right to organize. The right of both workers and employers to organize for collective bargaining is given explicit recognition,[17] and the right of both to refrain from joining any organization is implied.[18]

2. Shop stewards (tillitsmenn). The second section deals with the representation of workers at the plant level through elected shop stewards. Employees select for this purpose for one-year terms at least 2 of their number "from among the workers generally acknowledged to be the most capable, with experience and

[16] The text of the 1947 agreement appears in Appendix A.

[17] "In our country the right to organize has always been recognized. There has been no legal obstacle to workers joining together to protect their interests against employers. However, the trade union movement, in its origins at any rate, was sometimes fought by employers. This led to the demand by workers for legal protection of the right to organize, and from 1893 to 1903 the matter was debated in the Storting, and again in 1906, but no legislation resulted. Finally in 1913 the Federation of Labor resolved to abandon the demand, and it has since remained in abeyance." Alf Frydenberg, *Kollektive arbeidstvister og deres bileggelse i Norge,* p. 2.

[18] In the 1947 negotiations the Employers' Association proposed inclusion of the following clause: "It is in conflict with the basic principles of coöperation between the central organizations that obstacles be interposed to employment because either the employee or the establishment is organized or unorganized." This proposal was dropped on assurance from the Federation of Labor that it was implied from the more general wording.

insight into the problems of the plant." In larger establishments additional representatives may be chosen up to a maximum of 10 when there are more than 750 employees, while each distinct craft with not less than 25 members is entitled to at least 1 representative.

The duties of the shop steward are listed in the agreement as follows:

1. Shop stewards together with employers and the representatives of employers are pledged to do their best to maintain peaceful and effective coöperation at the place of work. This holds true during work, during conferences between the employer and the shop stewards, in giving information to their organizations and in their demeanor toward the other party.

2. Shop stewards have the right to take up and seek to settle minor grievances that individual workers raise against management, or management against individual workers.

3. Shop stewards have the right within the terms of agreements to commit workers on matters that concern the entire labor force or groups of workers. It is assumed that the shop stewards, if they deem it necessary, will submit the matter to their constituents before committing themselves.

4. Shop stewards shall see to it that the obligations of the parties under agreement and law . . . are fulfilled. It is inconsistent with the shop steward's position of trust to stimulate or coöperate in unlawful work stoppages.[19]

Management is required to *consult* with the shop stewards before taking action in the following matters: (a) effectuation of or change in working rules, (b) significant operational changes that will result in a fundamental alteration in working conditions, (c) limitation of work that will reduce the labor force, (d) permanent transfers of groups of workers within the plant.

Shop stewards do not have authority to question these decisions, the purpose of consultation being merely to provide a means of apprising workers of prospective changes that may affect their employment.

The 1947 revision added the requirement that the employer maintain a responsible representative at the plant every day, with whom the shop stewards may deal. Another innovation gives the

[19] *Hovedavtale,* September 4, 1947, Section 5.

chairman of the shop steward's committee unrestricted access to all plant departments to the extent necessitated by his duties, and also permits him to leave his work upon informing his supervisor of the reasons therefor. The other shop stewards require the consent of their supervisors in a similar situation.

3. *Grievance and disputes procedure.* Disputes involving the interpretation of collective agreements are to be taken up first by management or its representative, and the appropriate shop steward. If a settlement is not reached, negotiations continue at the establishment between management and local union officials, in the presence of one representative of each of the two central organizations, and if necessary, the parties are pledged "to bring the dispute in for further negotiation with the national union concerned or the Federation of Labor or authorized sub-organizations." Meetings must be held within eight days of a written request therefor by either party. The final step in the procedure is submission of unsettled disputes to the Labor Court for arbitration.

There are no data on the percentage of grievances and disputes settled at each stage of the procedure, but the fact that relatively few cases are submitted to the Labor Court each year attests to the effectiveness of the machinery. The cornerstone of the grievance edifice is the shop steward. If he is an intelligent and responsible individual who is not interested in using his post for political purposes, few grievances will go beyond the first stage. The Federation of Labor has taken considerable pains to educate its stewards to their responsibilities. To quote the Federation's chairman:

To be a shop steward is a good school for trade union officials. There one learns the problems of working life to a much greater extent than do the workers who are not stewards. One is forced to learn that as a rule a case has more than one side, and that it is often wise to sacrifice the ideal for that which can be achieved immediately without so great a sacrifice. The shop steward's work is no bed of roses, and he is often misunderstood by his own fellow workers. He may be accused of running the employer's errands when after long negotiations he perhaps reaches conclusions that do not coincide entirely with the demands.[20]

The shop steward enjoys a certain degree of protection in employment partly by contract and partly by custom. He is entitled

[20] *Arbeideren og Bedriften* (Oslo, 1946), pp. 240–41.

to dismissal notice of four weeks in the event of an individual, as distinct from a general layoff. He may not be denied leave when called to meetings or negotiations. Some establishments lay off stewards on the basis of strict seniority, while others retain them unless an entire department or the plant is being shut down. With respect to the chairman of the shop committee, however, "that he shall be the last man to go is a battle cry, and by and large that is the practice." [21]

4. New members. The contractual obligations assumed by new members of the Employers' Association were clarified by the 1947 revision of the Basic Agreement because of numerous disputes that had arisen under the 1935 draft. Newly associated employers are bound by existing collective agreements *for plants of the same type,* if either central organization requests it, with disputes over interpretation of the italicized words being decided by the Labor Court. If there are several agreements in effect, national agreements shall apply if suitable, followed by city- or district-wide agreements, agreements for individual plants in the same locality, and finally other agreements for similar plants. In judging the character of a plant, the parties agree to take into account "its operation and working conditions and the type and execution of the work which comes under the agreement. The firm name is not deciding, and first and foremost that agreement shall be considered which from a production point of view is most natural for the plant." [22]

5. Employee status. When workers are temporarily laid off without notice because of lack of work or materials, they retain their status as employees, and have both the right and duty to resume work when it is again available.[23]

6. Work certificate. Every worker who resigns or is discharged from employment, regardless of cause, is entitled to receive from his employer a written certificate[24] containing the following information: his name and date of birth; the date on which he entered employment; the date on which employment ceased, without

[21] *Arbeideren og Bedriften,* p. 239.

[22] *Hovedavtale,* Section 11.

[23] Under Norwegian law strikers do not retain their employee status. When they return to work, however, it is customary to disregard the break in employment for all relevant purposes.

[24] However, employees who do not give the requisite legal notice of resignation are not entitled to work certificates.

reference to the reason; his trade, his wage rate and earnings at the time employment was terminated; date of last vacation or last receipt of vacation pay.

7. *Disloyalty.* Because of constant friction over complaints that individuals who acted in a disloyal fashion during the German occupation were being permitted to retain their positions in the shop or on management staffs, the 1947 Basic Agreement stipulated that workers are not obligated to work with or under persons "who have shown such improper conduct that they should be removed, from general social considerations." Disputes in individual cases are to be settled by negotiation and eventually by the Labor Court if agreement cannot be reached.

8. *Collective strike notice.* Trade unions desired to follow the practice of submitting the legally required strike notice to their employers collectively, without including the names of the individual strikers. The Supreme Court ruled in 1934, however, that an employer was entitled to strike notice from each employee individually. The unions objected to individual notice on the ground that it could lead to discrimination against active union members. The Basic Agreement waives on behalf of all employers bound thereby the right to receive individual strike notices, thus in effect nullifying the Supreme Court decision.

9. *Balloting on agreements.* The rules governing the manner of voting on proposed collective agreements set forth in the Basic Agreement are discussed in Chapter V.

10. *Sympathetic work stoppages.* The final section of the Basic Agreement contains the following clause:

The obligation to maintain peaceful relations shall not limit the right of either employers or workers to participate in a work stoppage in support of a lawful conflict, when consent of the Employers' Association or the Federation of Labor is obtained. Negotiations between the latter organizations must precede the granting of permission.

Far from encouraging resort to the sympathetic strike or lockout, this clause has the effect of limiting their employment through the requirement of prior central organization approval. A sympathetic work stoppage was never considered a breach of contract in Norway, on the ground that the participants were not breaking off relations to obtain any change in their employment terms.[25] It

[25] Berg, *Arbeidsrett*, p. 20.

may now constitute a contract breach if the necessary permission has not been obtained.

If the Federation of Labor declares a sympathetic strike against members of the Employers' Association in support of a strike against an independent unassociated employer, it is incumbent upon · the union under the Basic Agreement simultaneously to strike related independent employers in the same city or district, if there are such employers. The number of workers involved in the sympathetic strikes must be approximately equal for associated and independent employers.

A further qualification, introduced in 1947, prohibits sympathetic strikes against members of the Employers' Association in support of an independent's workers when the demands made by the latter exceed the terms of association agreements covering similar establishments. *Conditional* sympathetic strikes[26] are barred except under two circumstances:

a. When the underlying dispute involves the demand for a collective agreement, provided that at least half the workers in the establishment concerned are members of unions affiliated with the Federation of Labor; and

b. If the purpose of the strike is to protect the right to organize.

The significance of the Basic Agreement lay not so much in the particular provisions as in the fact that it implied the successful evolution of a method of dealing with labor problems on a national basis. The experience gained by both employers and trade unions in negotiating the first Basic Agreement stood them in good stead in paving the way for a smooth transition from occupation to constitutional government in 1945.

NON-WAGE PROVISIONS OF COLLECTIVE AGREEMENTS

The area of bargaining over the portion of collective agreements dealing with matters other than wages was reduced by the Basic Agreement. There are many subjects, however, that do not readily lend themselves to nationwide standardization, and these continue to be settled by bargaining on the industry or local level. While the trend is toward greater uniformity even here, much of this subject matter is a unique function of a particular set of operating

[26] For a definition of this term, see above, p. 132.

conditions, and can scarcely be brought within the framework of a single agreement.

"General" Provisions. Prior to 1920 it was customary to include in collective agreements so-called "general" provisions (*almindelige bestemmelser*) specifying the employer's right to determine the method of operation, distribute work, and hire and fire workers. During the 1920 negotiations the unions demanded that this clause be deleted and replaced by one giving to the workers the right to participate in management. When negotiations proved futile, this and other matters in dispute were submitted to governmental compulsory arbitration, the result of which was that the "general" provisions were omitted from the new agreements.[27] They have never been restored.

Hours of work. The basic work week since 1919 has been forty-eight hours. Failure to reduce normal working hours since then may be attributed partly to bargaining weakness on the side of labor, and partly to its concentration on other forms of labor welfare, rather than to deliberate choice. One of the spokesmen for the labor movement wrote in 1935:

The demand for shorter working hours has been raised and will be pushed with increased vigor, and as soon as customary working time in a somewhat wider sphere becomes shorter — thirty-six, forty, forty-two hours — than it is now, the working week to which the majority of trade unionists are bound by contract will become a general demand of the Federation of Labor.[28]

Some groups of workers, mainly in nonmanufacturing activities, already enjoy a shorter working week. Organized office employees have a forty-two hour week, shop clerks a forty-five hour week. Typesetters work forty-five hours on the day shift, thirty-six hours at night. The Federation of Labor refrained from taking advantage of its augmented political power to extend the reduc-

[27] A representative of the Employers' Association submitted the following comment to the author: "The Arbitration Tribunal excepted the provisions because a law to this effect was planned. The law issued (law of July 23, 1920, concerning production committees in industrial establishments) has never been of any importance in practice. I presume that the Federation of Labor will agree that the employers still have the right of determining the method of operation and so on, so far as legislation and collective agreements have not established a positive framework."

[28] Lars Evensen, *Tariffavtalen* (Oslo, 1935), p. 20.

tion of hours, however, out of consideration for the requirements of postwar reconstruction. It may be assumed that with the conclusion of the abnormal conditions created by the war, labor will resume its drive for at least a forty-four hour, and probably a forty-hour week.

Most agreements provide wage differentials for second and third shift operations. The 1946 agreement in the textile industry permits a second shift (between 2:30 P.M. and 12 midnight) of 42½ hours a week at 17 per cent above the day rates; the night shift in the metal trades carries a penalty rate of 25 per cent; in canning, the second shift premium is 16 per cent, the third shift 25 per cent; in the building trades, the corresponding rates are 25 and 40 per cent, while the airlines pay a premium of 15 per cent for work between 6 P.M. and midnight, and 25 per cent from midnight to 6 A.M. These illustrate the normal range of shift premium rates in Norwegian industry.

In a large Oslo plant which is typical of conditions generally, the regular day shift is scheduled from 7 A.M. to 4:15 P.M. with fifteen minutes for breakfast and one-half hour for lunch. On Saturdays the men work from 7 A.M. to 12:15 P.M. with only one fifteen minute break. Complaints that workers were coming late and quitting early led the Employers' Association to ask for the inclusion of the following clause in the Basic Agreement during the 1947 negotiations:

So that the working time fixed shall be effective, each worker is bound to abide by it punctually. When work is to commence he shall be at the work bench already dressed, and immediately begin to work. During the working day he may not leave the job without good cause. Work must not cease before the scheduled time, and before that time the worker must not make such personal preparations for quitting as changing his clothing or shoes, washing up, and so on.[29]

The Federation of Labor was not willing to accept this provision but it agreed to undertake measures to combat this and other forms of absenteeism.

In many small towns it is customary to schedule a somewhat longer lunch period, running up to two and a half hours in some cases, to give workers an opportunity to return home for lunch. During the summer months many establishments, by local agree-

[29] *Hovedavtale, Addendum.*

ment, commence work somewhat earlier in the morning and reduce the lunch period to the statutory minimum. Because of the high latitude of Norway, by quitting work at 3 P.M. a worker can enjoy over seven hours of sunlight at the height of summer.

Overtime. The flat 25 per cent penalty for overtime contained in the Labor Protection Act is exceeded in practically all collective agreements. The most common contractual rule is a 25 per cent supplement to regular rates for the first two hours after the end of the regular working day, and a 50 per cent supplement thereafter. Work on Saturday afternoons, Sundays, and holidays is usually compensable at double time.

Prior to the war, many agreements required overtime work to be offset by a corresponding amount of free time later, but labor shortages have since led to the adoption of the rule that workers may take compensatory leave at their option. The printing-trades agreement contains the following additional limitations on overtime work that have their counterpart, either in whole or in part, in other collective agreements:

For overtime work of two hours or more, there shall be a fifteen minute pause for eating.

Workers are ordinarily to be notified of evening overtime work in the morning. In continuous operations, or where workers are prevented from going home to dinner, notice shall be given the previous day.

If notice of consecutive overtime is given the same day, the worker shall receive 2.50 kroner for food if the overtime lasts two hours or more . . .

For performing overtime work at night or on holidays, journeymen are guaranteed a minimum wage of 10 kroner, helpers and apprentices, 5 kroner.[30]

Idle and waiting time. There are many types of guarantee against time lost through no fault of the worker. In the building trades and mining industry, among others, workers must be paid at hourly rates if work stops for lack of materials or equipment, unless (a) the stoppage is due to *force majeure,* or (b) the worker received three days' advance notice of the stoppage, or (c) the worker is offered other work bearing the same hourly rate. Can-

---

[30] *Overenskomst mellom Norsk Arbeidsgiverforening og Norsk Centralforening for Boktrykkere,* 1946, Section 4.

ning plants pay for time lost during repairs if no other work is available and, in the event that it becomes necessary to dismiss workers for the day, guarantee payment for the completion of the spell (morning or afternoon) in which the stoppage occurs.

Waiting time is often compensated along the lines of the following clause:

If workers appear for work without immediately receiving it, and are not sent away, but are required to wait, they shall receive waiting time at the average hourly rate. There shall be no payment for the first hour of waiting, however. If they are dismissed and summoned back to work on the same day, they are to be paid for at least one hour.[31]

Provision for call-in pay is not commonly found, however.

Travel time. Portal to portal pay is a common requirement where any considerable amount of time is required to go from the entrance to the site of the work, as in mines. For building workers who must journey outside city boundaries to reach their place of work, agreements specify that all time spent in travel without city boundaries shall be compensated, although it is not counted as part of the regular working day. If a worker must spend the night away from home, the building-trades contract gives the employer the option of furnishing board and lodging or agreeing in advance to an amount of money in lieu thereof. Travel time, as well as the cost of transportation, must be paid for journeys under contract; where sleeping quarters are supplied on trains or steamships, only the hours falling within the regular working day are compensable, otherwise the entire amount of time consumed in traveling must be paid for. The metal-trades agreement provides a supplement of 20 per cent for all work performed at a place where the worker cannot spend the night at home.

Vacations. Paid vacations constitute an area in which Norwegian trade unions have secured standards compensating in some measure for the long work week. Before 1920 the usual period was six days, but the compulsory arbitration awards of that year lengthened it to twelve days a year. There was a general reduction to eight days in 1922, an increase to nine days in 1935 and to

[31] *Overenskomst mellom Norsk Arbeidsgiverforening og Norsk Naerings og Nydelsesmiddelarbeiderforbund,* 1946, Section 6 (2).

twelve days in 1937. An analysis of collective agreements in 1939[32] revealed the following vacation provisions:

No vacation specified 13.4 per cent of all workers covered
8 to 11 day vacation   2.4 per cent
12 day vacations   65.3 per cent
Over 12 days   18.9 per cent

The vacation provisions of collective agreements between members of the Employers' Association and the Federation of Labor were largely enacted into law in 1947,[33] the principal alteration consisting of extension of the contractual two-week period to a statutory three-week period. The legal provision for vacation pay is based upon the principle that the worker shall receive an amount equal to his average earnings for the vacation period, whether he is paid by the piece or on time:

An employee who during normal working hours is paid exclusively by the year, month, week, or day is entitled to full compensation for the vacation period if he has been on the payroll of the establishment during the entire year . . . Employees who are not covered [by the foregoing provision] are entitled to vacation pay equal to 6.5 per cent of total wage earnings [in the base period].[34]

The vacation law measures the vacation year from May 16 to May 15, as in the previous collective agreements upon which the law is based, and provides that at least two of the three weeks of vacation must be given consecutively within the period May 16 to September 30. Persons employed for only part of a year are subject to a proportional reduction in their vacation pay, but no reduction may be made on account of illness up to three months, maternity leave, or compulsory military service.

[32] *Statistisk Årbok for Norge,* 1941, p. 205.
[33] Socialdepartementet, *Ot. prp. nr. 104, 1947.*
[34] The figure of 6.5 per cent of earnings is in excess of full pay for three weeks, and represents an arbitrary allowance to compensate for the fact that the previous collective agreements providing vacations of two weeks fixed the vacation pay percentage at 4.5 per cent of earnings, which was also in excess of a ratio based strictly on time. It will be noted that *hourly* paid workers are compensated at the fixed 6.5 percentage rather than on the basis of their actual earnings, in accord with prevailing practice before the enactment of the law.

By collective agreement, in every industry but the building trades the employer had been responsible for administration of vacation pay. In the building trades, because of the transitory nature of employment, a central vacation fund administered by the Employers' Association had been established, to which each employer was required to subscribe a certain percentage of his payroll biweekly, and corresponding credits were made to the accounts of individual employees. The Vacation Act of 1947 extends the latter principle by creating a State Vacation Fund, and requiring every employer subject to the act to purchase, through local post offices, vacation stamps to be inserted into employee vacation books at regular intervals. When the employee's vacation is to start (the exact date lies within the discretion of the employer) he is given his vacation book together with a statement from the employer as to the scheduled date of the vacation, and he turns the book into the post office for cash. The right to accrued vacation pay is almost absolute: if a worker is unemployed, he is entitled to receive the pay after August 1 provided he has proof of his unemployment from a labor exchange, and if he should die before taking the vacation, his wife and direct descendants, but not collateral relatives, are entitled to payment. To answer the objections of those who maintained that this system would create red tape, the framers of the law inserted a provision permitting employers to set up individual vacation funds by agreement with the trade unions, provided that there is a guarantee of payment deemed adequate by the Ministry of Labor.

The requirement that an employee produce attestation of his scheduled vacation period or unemployment before receiving vacation pay indicates the intent of the law that vacations shall be used as such, and not as a means of granting wage bonuses. To ensure the fulfillment of this desideratum it is further provided that no worker may accept paid work in his own or a related trade during a statutory vacation, and that if he does so the employer may withhold from his future wages an amount equal to his earnings during the vacation period.

There are many additional minor provisions designed to ensure prompt and complete payment of vacation benefits, also based largely on previous practice or developed through collective bargaining. Employer objection to the law centered rather on the extension of the vacation term to three weeks than on the principle of removing this important subject matter from the realm of collective bargaining.[35] This affords an informative example of the manner in which the common law of industrial relations, after standardization at the hands of two central collective bargaining agencies, becomes readily codifiable by the state without undue violence to prevailing conceptions.

Seniority. The general acceptance of trade unionism in Norway renders seniority in hiring and discharge largely superfluous as a union security measure. Considered as a means of distributing available jobs among workers, the labor movement has no unique concept of the seniority principle, as evidenced by the following citation from a handbook prepared for workers' education courses:

In times with uncertain and varying labor conditions provision [for seniority in layoffs and rehiring] may mean that the youngest workers, the last hired, approve their own layoffs by fighting for the adoption of this rule. For the youth, that signifies a handicap in competing for work. That such provision is not unqualifiedly advantageous for an organization can best be illustrated by the fact that the last trade union congress resolved that provisions concerning discharge by seniority may be inserted in agreements only with the approval of the secretariat [of the Federation of Labor].

To avoid misunderstanding, it should be recorded that the trade unions can never approve an arbitrary discharge system. Control of this factor, as in so many other things, will depend upon the union's strength.

A related question is that in layoffs account should also be taken of the family burdens of the individual. This principle has been less used, and in many cases it will be difficult for a trade union to permit the personal situation of the individual member to affect its general demands to the employer, even if in other respects a policy of encouraging families is followed.[36]

To prevent the use of seniority as a means of closing trades to new entrants, the Federation of Labor requires advance approval by its secretariat of all contract clauses embodying it in principle. It is worth noting that the resolution to this effect was adopted by the 1934 congress of the Federation when there was severe

[35] The Labor Protection Act of 1937 contained vacation provisions, but they were minimum rather than standard in character.

[36] Evensen, pp. 31-32.

unemployment.[37] As a matter of fact, although few agreements stipulate strict seniority, it is widely practiced in one form or another purely out of regard to good personnel policy. Employers recognize that complete disregard of length of service is likely to create unrest, and may eventually lead to union-imposed seniority. Since Norwegian plants are relatively small, the employer is usually in a position to strike a balance between equity to older employees with family responsibilities and his desire to rehire or retain the most efficient workers. Taken as a whole, relatively little industrial strife has arisen from this source.

Where trade unionism has not yet gained the full acceptance of employers, seniority provisions are to be found in collective agreements. The 1946 agreement for the lumber industry gives preference in rehiring to men previously employed at a particular location, and the employer is enjoined that "no account shall be taken of the fact that an individual is or is not organized." In the national agreement for office and commercial employees it is provided that when there is a reduction in force, seniority shall be taken into account so that in general the last hired are the first to be discharged. Excepted from this rule are employees with less than two years of experience and elderly employees working at the establishment for less than six months. The printed copy of the agreement distributed by the union appends a statement made by the employer representative during mediation proceedings to the effect that persons laid off owing to a shortage of work will, "as has been the practice," be the first rehired when business improves, provided they have the necessary qualifications for the vacancies. The 1946 agreement for unassociated (independent) automobile repair shops in Oslo contains a strict seniority clause, despite the fact that parallel agreements with shops belonging to the Employers' Association do not contain seniority provisions.

Union security. The general assembly of the Employers' Association, in 1907, resolved that "collective agreements providing for the employment of organized workers only are incompatible with the principle of freedom to work, and may not be concluded by members of the Employers' Association." The Federation of Labor never attempted to force repeal of this ban, and consequently the union security clause is to be found only in agreements

[37] Arbeidernes Faglige Landsorganisasjon, *Kongressen 1934, Dagsorden og Protokoll,* pp. 156–57.

with independent employers,[38] although there are no legal strictures on any form of union security.

Acquiescence of the Norwegian labor movement in maintenance
of the open shop principle cannot be attributed solely to acceptance
of trade unions by Norwegian employers. As late as 1933 a major
industry, lumbering, waged a partially successful campaign to prevent worker organization, and until labor's rise to political power
in 1935 many unorganized employers endeavored with all the
means at their disposal to combat unionism.

It is true, nevertheless, that the Norwegian labor movement has
never faced a concerted open-shop drive that threatened its very
existence. The stronger unions were not unduly concerned with
the problem of union security, and did not find it expedient to
engage in a pitched battle with employers on an issue about which
the latter held strong convictions. In 1907, the Metalworkers'
Union accepted a contract clause specifically embodying the open
shop, and although it has since been eliminated, the principle remains unchallenged. The solution reached in this and many other
industries is a happy one: the unions enjoy what is practically a
closed shop by virtue of almost complete organization of the trade,
while employers have not been obliged to yield on a matter of principle.

Another reason for the failure of the Federation of Labor to
press for formalization of the union shop, particularly in recent
years, has undoubtedly been its realization of the danger involved
for the trade union movement itself:

The [union shop] provision may be appropriate to ensure that all
workers are organized and that the employer thus has no interest in
hiring unorganized workers at wages lower than those fixed by agreement.

But the provision may also mean that work within a particular trade
is reserved for the members of a particular trade union. The provision
may thus degenerate into one of those recently considered by the labor
movement under the heading of monopolistic tendencies.

The Federation Congress adopted a comprehensive resolution providing that the union shop clause must not be used to prevent other
workers from seeking work within a certain trade, or to deny them

[38] See, for example, *Overenskomst mellom bilverkstedene i Olso utenfor
Norsk Arbeidsgiverforening og Norsk Jern og Metallarbeiderforbund*, 1946,
Protokolltilførsler, Sec. III.

trade union membership. It was made impossible to close trade unions and plead agreement provisions as an excuse for preventing other trade unionists or unorganized workers from securing work.

The union shop is unacceptable as a means of increasing the percentage of organization. Trade unions must always base their organization upon the principle that new members shall come in of their own free will and their conviction of the union's significance.[39]

The result is that the closed shop is not to be found in Norway, while the union shop is confined to independent employers, and generally stipulates only that the employer shall limit employment to members of the Federation of Labor as a whole.

New machinery and processes. Most agreements contain a clause providing that in the event of plant expansion, installation of new machinery, introduction of novel methods of work, or other changes in working conditions entailing an alteration in wage rates, or when new materials require pricing under a piece rate system, the initial negotiations must be held between management and shop stewards. If agreement is not secured at that level, the dispute may go as high as the central organizations, and to *private* arbitration as a last resort.

Apprenticeship. Some unions, particularly the skilled crafts, regulate the ratio of apprentices to journeymen, partly to limit entrance to the trade, but in recent years more to ensure adequate training. The following schedule is common in the building trades:

Number of journeymen employed	Number of apprentices permitted
1–3	1
4–6	2
7–12	5
13–20	8
21 and over	12

Individual contractors who work on their own account without hiring any journeymen are permitted one apprentice.

The skilled trades provide for tests of skill (*svenneprøve*) as a prerequisite for graduation into the ranks of the skilled work-

[39] Evensen, pp. 30–31. See also Arbeidernes Faglige Landsorganisasjon, *Kongressen 1934, Dagsorden og Protokoll*, p. 157; *Kongressen 1938, Protokoll*, p. 382.

ers. The agreement covering elevator constructors, for example, stipulates that a qualification test shall take place within ten weeks of the conclusion of apprenticeship, and that it shall consist of "installing a lift, freight, or passenger elevator complete both as to electrical and mechanical elements." The examining board, appointed for two-year terms, consists of one employer and one employee representative, with a chairman appointed by the State Technological Institute. The board is instructed to rate applicants as very good, good, acceptable, or not acceptable on the basis of their test. Achievement of any of the first three grades entitles the apprentice to work as a journeyman thenceforth.[40]

The electrical trades require elaborate qualifying examinations in both the theory and practice of the trades, supervised by local tripartite boards under chairmen appointed by municipal electric plants.[41] For the first time the printing trades, in 1946, in an agreement with the labor press, stipulated qualifying examinations within one year of the completion of apprenticeship, with a second examination six months thereafter should the first result in failure, and a third one year after the second, if necessary. Failure to qualify the third time bars the worker from entering the trade as a skilled craftsman.[42] Similar provisions are found in the baking trades, as well as in many branches of building construction.

Trade unions have been urged by the Labor government to accept greater responsibility for training young workers, and provisions of the type cited are likely to find their way into future agreements to an increasing extent. Also symptomatic of greater trade union interest in industrial training was a resolution adopted by the Federation of Labor at its 1946 congress advocating modernization and extension of the state vocational educational system and supporting a government plan for one year of compulsory vocational training for all youths who do not intend to pursue further studies after completing high school.[43]

Miscellaneous provisions. A few of the great variety of addi-

[40] *Hovedavtalen, Overenskomsten og Akkordtariffen i Heisemontørfaget,* 1946–1948.

[41] *Hovedavtalen og Landsoverenskomsten i Elektrikerfaget,* 1946–1948.

[42] *Overenskomst mellom Arbeiderpressens Samvirke og Norsk Centralforening for Boktrykkere,* 1946.

[43] Arbeidernes Faglige Landsorganisasjon, *Protokoll over Kongressen 1946,* pp. 505–508.

tional non-wage subjects covered by collective agreement may be cited briefly. Free work clothes are commonly required where the work performed is unusually dirty, where uniforms must be worn, or where special sanitary clothing is mandatory by law. The employer is often given the option of providing — or laundering — work clothes, or paying the workers an allowance to cover the cost. Office and commercial workers receive twenty-five days of paid sick leave and part pay for compulsory military service, but this provision does not apply to industry generally. The 1946 agreement for the airlines stipulates that in the event of a temporary lack of work, the available work shall be distributed so far as possible to avoid layoffs. This catalogue could be extended indefinitely by reference to peculiar conditions within industry.

CHAPTER IX

COLLECTIVE AGREEMENTS: WAGE PROVISIONS

THE WAGE SCHEDULE (*tariff*) is the focal point of the Norwegian collective bargaining system. A few basic principles run through the apparent complexity of the wage structure, unifying what would otherwise appear to be an illogical and inconsistent patchwork of practices.

Minimum and standard rates. The first distinction to be drawn is between minimum and standard (*normal*) time rates. A minimum rate, as the name implies, represents the lowest rate that may be paid a qualified worker within the bargaining unit. The standard rate, on the other hand, means that "all workers within a specified group shall receive the rate stipulated for the group." [1] Occasionally a third type of rate is to be found, the average wage, representing the minimum average rate to be paid a particular craft or class of workers.

The use of the minimum wage assumes that a system of personal rates is superimposed upon the minimum through the so-called "lift" paragraph:

The individual worker shall be paid wages higher than the minimum on the basis of skill and experience. Wages shall be determined through further agreement between management or its representative and each individual worker. [2]

If all workers, without regard to skill and experience, are held at the minimum rate, their employer is guilty, prima facie, of a breach of contract. [3] Increases must be bargained for individually, however, and the union may not demand a general wage increase or the maintenance of any particular level of wages during the

[1] Albert Jacobsen, *En oversikt over lønnsfastsettelsen* (Oslo, 1946, mimeographed).

[2] *Overenskomst mellom De mekaniske Verksteders Landsforening og Norsk Jern og Metallarbeiderforbund og Norsk Formerforbund, 1946,* Section 1 (c).

[3] Berg, *Arbeidsrett,* p. 176.

contract period. In fact, most agreements specifically protect the determination of personal rates from any interference by organizations of labor and employers.

To prevent wage decreases during the pendency of a collective agreement, it is often provided that personal rates in effect at the commencement of the agreement may not be reduced during the contract term. Any disagreement in the application of the "lift" paragraph must be settled through negotiation or arbitration.

The minimum wage system does not, as might be supposed, lead to an anarchic wage structure. There tend to be clusters of wage rates for various skill categories rather than the fine shadings that are theoretically possible;[4] equal pay for equal work is the only principle administratively expedient if a constant scramble for higher personal rates is to be avoided.

The operation of the minimum wage system in a large and representative metal-trades plant in Oslo illustrates the degree of uniformity established by custom. Before the war, workers started at the minimum and worked their way to a top rate, which was fixed by tacit agreement of the employers in the vicinity, in about fifteen years. The average worker received uniform personal step increases of five öre per hour each year. Since 1945, however, the manpower shortage forced more rapid promotion, so that the average length of time required to advance from the minimum to the maximum has been reduced to five years. Moreover, three-quarters of the workers are at the maximum rate, and in effect the minimum wage is being converted into a standard wage.

When a worker transfers from one plant to another, he generally carries his rate with him. In the state of overfull employment that has characterized the Oslo labor market since 1945, many workers have been shifting employment in order to advance their personal rates more rapidly. The original rationale of the minimum system, which was to provide incentive in the form of an annual personal wage increase, has been thus subverted. Another factor tending to break the minimum wage system down is the increasing size of the cost-of-living allowance which is added as a flat sum to wage rates, reducing the significance of the personal increment in its relationship to total earnings.

The tendency toward uniformity in personal rates within a

[4] Interview with Konrad Nordahl, Chairman, Federation of Labor, July 24, 1947.

single labor market area is illustrated by a comparison of wages paid in two Oslo shipyards:

Average Wage Rates in Öre Per Hour, February 1947

	Average	Highest	Lowest
Skilled Workers			
Akers	152	218	130
Nylands	152	220	122
Helpers			
Akers	132	198	110
Nylands	138	180	120
Apprentices			
Akers	65	110	45
Nylands	66	122	45
Average			
Akers	141	. . .	. . .
Nylands	144	. . .	. . .

Source: Norsk Jern og Metallarbeiderforbund, *Lønnsstatistikk for en del verksteder i Oslo* (1947, mimeographed).

Only for helpers was there any significant divergence of average wage rates between the two firms, despite the fact that in each, personal wage rates were determined by individual bargaining between the worker and management. Both management and trade union officials have expressed the opinion that there is sufficient knowledge of competitive conditions within the Oslo metal trades to ensure uniform wage rates for men of similar skill and experience within all like shops in the area. This was not as true during periods of unemployment, however, when the separate ideas of each firm on appropriate personal rates were more likely to be effectuated.

General wage increases are effected in the minimum wage trades by collective bargaining over minimum rates. Personal rates are ordinarily expressed in terms of absolute differentials over the minimum, so that increasing the minimum automatically increases the personal rate, though tending to reduce the percentage differential.

It is not customary to find personal time rates in the standard wage industries, although there is nothing in a standard wage agreement per se that prohibits the employer from paying above

standard rates.[5] To permit necessary wage differentials standard
wage agreements usually contain a greater number of wage classifications than minimum wage agreements, based on craft, age, experience, or a combination of all three.

The Central Statistical Bureau analyzed all agreements filed
with the State Mediator from 1922 to 1925, and found that about
80 per cent were based on the minimum wage principle, with the
remainder containing either standard rates or a combination.[6] Since
then there has been a trend toward the standard rate,[7] but to what
extent it is impossible to say in the absence of statistics. In general, the metal and graphic trades, the meat, wood products, shoe,
and mining industries, and commercial employers adhere to the
minimum wage, while the standard rate is to be found in the building trades (except for the plumbers and sheet metal workers), in
the canning, furniture, brick, textile, stone, and food industries,
and in agriculture and the merchant marine.

The principal reason for the trend toward standard rates is
trade union preference. Its advantages from the union viewpoint
are not difficult to appreciate. The minimum rate creates competition among workers within an establishment that expresses itself
in individual bargaining, over which the union has no direct control. Favoritism, although not a necessary concomitant, is facilitated if the employer desires to practice it, and there is always the
possibility that differential rates to individual workers may be
employed to discourage adherence to trade unions. For this reason the weaker unions have fought minimum wages the hardest.
The minimum wage, moreover, makes it difficult for the union to
gauge the effect of collective bargaining upon the average wage
level. Even though a bargained increase in the minimum rate is
presumably reflected in increases along the line to maintain differentials, there is no assurance that such a movement will necessarily
occur.

Though the minimum wage system preceded the standard wage
historically, many employers, particularly where their workers are

[5] In the case of a multi-firm agreement, however, the employer association
signatory to the agreement may prohibit individual firms from paying above
standard rates.

[6] *Norges Offisielle Statistikk,* Vol. VII, No. 105; Vol. VII, No. 145; Vol.
VII, No. 177; Vol. VIII, No. 2.

[7] Jacobsen, p. 4.

predominantly unskilled, have come to prefer the latter because of its simplicity and ease of administration. Where operations are not standardized, however, and particularly where sharp differences in skill are involved, the minimum wage is favored by employers, since individuals can be paid on the basis of their value to the establishment, and special incentives offered to the better workers. In a recent arbitration, representatives of small shipyards declared that

boat builders in western Norway have always found it most appropriate to employ minimum wage conditions. Most plants are so small that the workers employed must perform a variety of tasks. The most elastic wage system is therefore the minimum wage with personal supplements based on the nature of the work and the skill of the worker.[8]

The arbitration tribunal overruled this objection, and granted a standard wage "in order to secure the most uniform wage level possible, which under a minimum wage with personal supplements might be difficult to achieve." [9]

Economic conditions influence both employer and trade union wage system preferences to a certain extent. Since the minimum wage system tends to be the more flexible in both an upward and downward direction, employers are apt to prefer it when prices are falling, and trade unions when prices are rising. When faced with contracting markets, an employer may negotiate immediate individual wage reductions under the minimum wage system, but he can secure a reduction of standard rates only by collective bargaining at the expiration of existing agreements. On the other hand, in times of rising prices and labor shortages, the standard rate acts as a deterrent to continual individual demands for wage increases.

This factor has been particularly operative during the current labor shortage. The secretariat of the Federation of Labor pointed out to the 1946 Federation congress that standard wage industries had received since 1945 only the general cost-of-living allowances common to all workers, whereas the minimum wage trades had benefited from personal supplements as well. Future wage negotiations may have to be conducted on the principle that "wage

[8] Wage Board, Case No. 41, December 7, 1946.
[9] Wage Board, Case No. 41, December 7, 1946.

earners paid on standard wage schedules shall receive the same increases in income as those who have benefited from individual increases," else, "the workers and employees tied to the standard wage will be set back in an unreasonable manner." [10]

Piecework. Payment by results is widespread in Norway, although its importance varies sharply from industry to industry, as Table 13 illustrates. It is most prevalent in the metal and building trades, and in the mining, chemical, and clothing industries. The data in Table 13 tend to understate the use of piecework, since such occupations as watchman and cleaner, which require compensation on a time basis, are included. If data were available for production workers alone, the piecework ratios would be somewhat greater.

During the occupation period from 1940 to 1945 piecework was employed as a means of evading the general wage stop imposed in 1940. Statistics for the war years indicate that earnings based on piece rates increased more rapidly than earnings based on hourly rates.[11] Although the termination of the artificial wartime conditions led to a decline in piecework in some industries during 1945, the wage stabilization program undertaken thereafter caused renewed trade union pressure for piecework as a means of increasing earnings.[12] One of the principal arguments advanced by workers

[10] Arbeidernes Faglige Landsorganisasjon, *Protokoll over Kongressen 1946,* pp. 396–97.

[11] The indexes of time and piece-rate earnings of men in manufacturing and mining, based upon the first quarter of 1940, were as follows:

	Time-Rate Work	Piece-Rate Work
1940	99.4	98.0
1941	99.4	101.0
1942	101.3	105.4
1943	103.2	107.9
1944	104.5	110.4

Source: *Norges Offisielle Statistikk,* Vol. 10, No. 103, p. 9.

The occupation authorities winked at the use of piecework to evade wage stabilization regulations in industries they considered essential to their military program. In mining, for example, earnings of pieceworkers exceeded time rate earnings by 19 per cent in 1940; by 1944, the differential had risen to 36 per cent. For leather and rubber, the corresponding figures were 34 and 53 per cent; for clothing, 43 and 65 per cent; for food, 34 and 48 per cent.

[12] The chairman of the Building Workers' Union stated in this respect: "It is mainly in Oslo, Bergen, and partly Trondheim that the piecework system has been installed, but as a means of raising building workers' wages indirectly

TABLE 13

Extent of Piecework in Norwegian Industry, for Adult Males,
1940 and 1945

Industry or Trade	Ratio of Piecework Hours to Total Hours Worked	
	1940	1945
Mining and metal refining...............	28.4	34.1
Metal trades...........................	54.0	50.7
Chemicals.............................	34.4	48.1
Fats and oils..........................	7.8	3.1
Paper.................................	24.0	22.0
Leather and rubber....................	19.4	25.0
Textiles...............................	23.3	34.7
Clothing..............................	50.4	41.2
Food products.........................	9.0	7.6
Miscellaneous manufacturing............	21.2	25.6
Printing trades.......................	1.4	1.3
Building trades..,....................	38.9[a]	26.0[a]
Baking trades.........................	0	0
Total mining and manufacturing........	35.9	36.7
Total skilled trades..................	18.9	11.9

Source: *Norges Offisielle Statistikk*, Vol. 10, Nos. 62, 128.

[a] These figures are understated owing to incompleteness of the data.

seeking hourly rate increases is that they have no access to piece-work.

The schemes of piecework embodied in collective agreements vary considerably in detail. Some agreements call for straight piecework; others specify piecework with a minimum time guarantee (which may or may not be the same rate as that applicable to hourly paid workers); while still others provide only conditional time guarantees. A few examples will serve to indicate the manner in which piecework is applied.

1. The building trades. Much site work in building is performed

---

the national union and the congress believe that it is right to introduce piecework throughout rural areas as well. This would mean that even though hourly wages must temporarily stand still because of stabilization, earnings can be raised by the introduction of piecework, and the living standards of building workers raised." Peder Framnaes, *Tariffene og overenskomstene*, 1946 (mimeographed).

on the basis of individual or group piece rates. It is provided that if for any reason it is impossible to pay by the piece, workers are guaranteed a standard hourly wage, invariably set at a relatively high level. There is no time guarantee, however, where piece rates are embodied in permanent (*fast*) wage schedules, except when piece rates fall below specified time rates under circumstances that are clearly not the worker's fault.

Peculiar to the industry is the custom of permitting each local union to negotiate its own price list, subject to ratification by the national Building Workers' Union. The piece-rate schedules are exceedingly complex: the 1946 Oslo price list for painters contains 651 separate rates; the cement workers' schedule, 873 rates; while the carpenters operate with 909 rates. Price lists outside of Oslo are usually based on the Oslo rates, with uniform absolute or percentage increases or decreases. It would be manifestly impossible to renegotiate each rate separately in annual wage movements; in practice this is avoided by relating the price list as a whole to a specific hourly rate, and changing each piece rate by the same percentage as the negotiated changes in the basic hourly rate.

The procedure followed by Oslo painters is typical of normal piece rate operation in the building trades. The contractor must prepare for each job a rate ticket (*akkordseddel*) containing a description of the work to be performed, accompanied by a confirming statement of the architect, owner, or general contractor. Workers are thus afforded an opportunity to estimate their probable earnings, the difficulty of the work, the length of time involved, and other relevant factors. If more than one worker is needed for the job, a group is formed, all members of which receive the same rates.[13]

The rate ticket is in effect an agreement between the contractor and an individual painter or group of painters to perform a specified piece of work. If a portion of the work is not covered by any rate in the permanent price list, the individuals concerned bargain

---

[13] Some agreements provide for team bosses to represent the workers. The agreement for cement workers, for example, provides that where four or more men are engaged on a job, a boss shall be appointed who is entitled to extra pay of at least fifteen öre per hour. Even without contract provisions the workers may elect a shop steward to present grievances, under the Basic Agreement.

with the contractor without the intermediation of the union, although they are protected in this contingency by a minimum time guarantee. Once a rate ticket has been signed by both parties it is not subject to alteration except by mutual consent.

The crucial point in administering the piece-rate system is the measurement of results (*oppmåling*). The Building Workers' Union maintains district offices that perform this service for local unions desiring assistance, but many locals appoint their own surveyors. When a job is completed, it is measured by the union representative and the contractor or his representative, at a time mutually agreed upon. If either party fails to appear at the stipulated time, the conclusions reached by the other unilaterally are binding.

Should the surveyors find it impossible to agree, and no resolution of the dispute can be secured at the local level, the matter is taken up by a joint wage board of the Employers' Association and the Building Workers' Union. The few cases that cannot be settled at this level go to private tripartite arbitration, the neutral member of the *ad hoc* arbitration board generally being a district mediator.

For jobs of any considerable duration, measurement of piecework is performed at intervals agreed upon in advance. In the construction of an apartment house, for example, there might be tallying up at the completion of each story. During a measurement period the workers are paid weekly according to basic time rates specified in the collective agreement. These payments are deducted from total piece earnings calculated by multiplying the number of units completed by the appropriate unit rate, the excess (*overskudd*) usually being payable within two pay days after delivery and acceptance by the contractor. Some agreements permit the contractor to withhold a portion of this excess, usually 10 per cent, until the entire job is completed, as a guarantee against possible future overpayments to the workers.

Although the building unions are unanimous in support of piecework, many employers do not like it. A difficult problem arises in connection with work of a special character that cannot be estimated in advance, and for which the best men may have to be used. There is no alternative to paying workers on a time basis, which they are certain to resent unless they receive a bonus (*akkord avsagn*) to equalize their earnings with what they estimate retrospectively they could have secured through piecework. The result is that the contractor may not be able to estimate costs with any degree of accuracy.[14]

2. The metal trades. Piecework in the metal trades is based upon locally negotiated price lists, with a minimum time guarantee except where work is performed pursuant to permanent schedules. There is no national rate schedule by reason of the diversity of the industry's operations. To encourage the establishment of permanent as contrasted with *ad hoc* rates for each establishment, the following provision appears in the national agreement:

> For factory production and for work that lends itself thereto permanent piece-rate schedules shall be set up through negotiation between plant management or its representative and the workers or groups to be covered by the rates. If agreement cannot be reached at this level, the matter shall be submitted to negotiation between the local or central organizations.[15]

To stabilize piece rates it is further provided that price lists shall as a rule remain in effect during the entire period of the agreement, and may in no event be terminated by either party without a month's notice. Where new machinery or methods are introduced, however, alterations in piece rates may be demanded without notice. There is no limitation on the type of piece-rate incentive system that may be employed, but the agreement stipulates that before a new system is installed, the consent of the workers must be obtained.

As in the building trades, a job ticket is prepared for each separate lot if work is noncontinuous, specifying the nature of the work, its duration, and the applicable rate. For example, a particular operation in the construction of a ship may be farmed out to a group of workers at the flat sum of 1500 kroner, based upon previous experience with the length of time required to complete the work. While the job is in process the workers receive their respective time rates (the metal-trades wage scale is basically a minimum system with personal increments) which may in this case amount to 1000 kroner. The excess (*overskudd*) of 500 kroner

[14] It has also been alleged that the piece-rate system has hindered modernization of the building industry, since the powerful building trades unions often refuse to revise piece rates downward when new processes shorten the performance time of particular operations.

[15] *Verkstedsoverenskomsten*, 1946.

is paid out in the form of a 50 per cent bonus to each member of the group upon completion of the work, assuming that all members worked on the job the same number of hours. Thus the higher rated man receives proportionately more than the lower rated one, a means of reflecting different personal time rates in piece-rate earnings.

All previous rate experience in the plant is available for inspection by the workers. Temporary piece rates are generally arranged by the foreman and the group leader, and so well established is the system that disagreement is unusual. The managing director of Norway's largest shipyard, Akers Mekaniske Verksted, expressed the opinion that the piece-rate system is not only relatively easy to administer, but is absolutely essential to efficient operation.[16]

Manufacturing. The national agreement for the ready-made clothing industry[17] contains conditions for the performance of piecework that are to be found in more or less similar form in the manufacture of other standard commodities. To protect the inexperienced worker, it is provided that no individual may be taken off time work (the weekly wage is the industry's basic time rate) and put on piecework until he is able to earn 30 per cent above his time rate working by the piece at a normal rate of speed. Although the national agreement itself contains 460 separate piece rates, establishments may employ individual price lists that are more suited to their operations. These are determined jointly by the employer and an elected "shop steward for time studies," and the employer is obligated "to be of assistance in giving this shop steward the necessary knowledge of time study techniques." Disputes between the two are arbitrated by a neutral time-study expert appointed by the Clothing Employers' Association and the Clothing Workers' Union.

Many different systems of piecework payment are to be found in manufacturing establishments. A system commonly used involves time work with a production bonus after a specified output has been achieved.[18] Or a job may be rated at a certain number

[16] Interview, August 9, 1947.

[17] *Overenskomst mellom Norsk Arbeidsgiverforening og Norsk Bekledningsarbeiderforbund,* 1947.

[18] Before the war this system was to be found primarily in the paper industry. Since 1945 there has been a tendency to extend it to others as well, particularly the chemical industry.

of hours, the workers being paid a lump sum for completion of the job equal to their hourly rates multiplied by the standard time of the job, regardless of how long it actually occupies them. Various types of incentive systems initiated in the United States are also to be found in Norway. But almost invariably the following clause is either expressly stated or implied in the agreement:

Different types of piece systems may be used. Before new systems are introduced, there must be agreement concerning the rules and regulations thereof between the individual establishment and the labor group concerned, or between the central organizations.[19]

Despite the widespread employment of piece rates, time-study techniques have rarely been applied in Norwegian industry. This has been due primarily to trade union opposition, based on the fear that the result would be intensification of labor without compensating wage adjustments.[20] Prior to World War II, trade union rate-setting departments were unknown, and piece rates were negotiated by rule-of-thumb collective bargaining in which past experience provided the sole guide. The marked alteration in the trade union attitude toward scientific management that has occurred since 1945 is discussed in Chapter XIII.

Cost-of-living adjustments. Periodic adjustment of contractual wages by recourse to the official cost-of-living index has long been a feature of Norwegian collective agreements. The frequency of adjustment is six months or one year, with the six-month adjustment common in one-year agreements, and the annual adjustment in two-year agreements.

Adjustments are either automatic or in accordance with what the Norwegians call the "semiautomatic" principle, which is in effect a contract reopening. The latter makes negotiation a prerequisite to adjustment; the appropriate party may request an upward or downward wage revision in the event of a specified rise or fall in the cost-of-living index, but the change is not a matter of right. Usually, the initiating party has the option of terminating the agreement if the other party refuses to acquiesce in the adjustment. The principal advantage of the semiautomatic method is that it gives the parties an opportunity to consider the desirability of a

---

[19] *Hovedavtalen og Landsoverenskomsten i Elektrikerfaget,* 1946–1948.

[20] See, for example, Arbeidernes Faglige Landsorganisasjon, *Rasjonaliserings-Spørsmålet* (Oslo, 1929).

wage change in the light of existing conditions. During a recession, for example, employers might prefer to forego a wage reduction to which they were entitled by contract in order to avert labor
unrest. The present chairman of the Federation of Labor said of
cost-of-living adjustments that "we believe it to be significant that
the parties come together and talk with one another before changes
are made. We have no formal opportunity to do that in a fully
automatic adjustment." [21]

Beginning with 1939, nevertheless, the automatic adjustment
principle was widely adopted through union pressure. An agreement reached early in 1940 between the Employers' Association
and the Federation of Labor called for two automatic adjustments
three months apart, and a semiautomatic adjustment the following quarter. Although a national arbitration award in 1945 returned to the semiautomatic idea, the two central organizations
agreed upon the following provisions for all collective agreements
signed or renewed in 1946:

If the Central Statistical Bureau's cost-of-living index (based upon
1938) as of August 15, 1946, shows a rise or fall of five points or
more in relation to the index number for July 15, 1945 (155.8), all
cost-of-living supplements shall be adjusted by the following additions
or subtractions: (1) adult men and women, 1.5 öre per point, (2)
young workers and apprentices, a percentagewise increase or decrease
corresponding to the percentage rise or fall in the index.

The adjustment shall take place as soon as the index figure for the
aforementioned date is published, and will take effect on September 1,
1946, even though the index figure is published subsequently.

The year 1940 also witnessed the introduction of another essentially new principle, that all cost-of-living index wage adjustments were to be held separate from the wage rate and paid in the
form of cost-of-living supplements (*dyrtidstilleg*). Thus wages
consist of two separate sums — piece or time earnings and a flat
supplement for each hour worked. The nationally negotiated cost-
of-living supplements, which have been so important a feature of
the wage structure since 1940,[22] are paid in uniform amounts to
all workers in the same category (there are different absolute

[21] Arbeidernes Faglige Landsorganisasjon, *Beretning 1945,* p. 68.
[22] During the second quarter of 1946 cost-of-living supplements provided
24 per cent of average hourly earnings for men in mining and manufacturing.

amounts for men, women, and youthful workers) regardless of earnings, except for persons engaged in agriculture, lumbering, whaling, and banking, who are subject to special provisions.

The Federation of Labor intends to seek the incorporation of cost-of-living supplements into regular wage rates, in accordance with earlier practice. Employers prefer the present separate arrangement because psychologically a cost-of-living supplement is less "sticky" than the basic wage rate, while trade unions, with the same fact in mind, would prefer to have the two elements merged. The cost-of-living adjustment has created problems of wage administration, one of which, a general narrowing of wage differentials, is a concomitant not of the adjustment principle but rather of the manner in which the supplement is given: as a flat sum of money added to hourly rates. But it will undoubtedly continue as a customary practice until the return of a stable price level.

WAGE DIFFERENTIALS

Time and piece-rate earnings. Collective agreements which permit both time and piecework usually provide that piecework shall yield greater total earnings than work on time, and it is quite common to find a specified average percentage differential between the two. Thus, in woodworking establishments workers may demand revision of piece rates if they do not yield earnings 30 per cent in excess of stipulated time rates, while employers may demand revision if the difference in earnings is substantially greater. In the minimum wage trades the time basis is either the individual's personal rate or the performance of an average experienced worker, while in the standard wage industries the appropriate standard rates serve as the measuring rod.

Average hourly earnings of adult male pieceworkers during 1945 exceeded time-rate earnings by 34 per cent in manufacturing and mining. Although this magnitude partly reflected a means of avoiding wartime wage regulations, the fact that the comparable figure for the first quarter of 1940 was 30 per cent indicates that this differential is deeply rooted in the wage structure.[23]

[23] In the following sections the latest wage data available at the time of writing are employed in the statistical comparisons. Figures for 1940 are included primarily to emphasize the fact that the various types of differentials shown are not merely wartime phenomena, but existed in approximately the same degree prior to the occupation.

In the past it has not been unusual to find that within a single plant related occupations were subject to considerable variation in earnings on the basis of the method by which they were paid. The explanation of why workers were willing to accept this differential appears to lie in the universally held belief that piecework requires a greater degree of effort than time work. There is an oft told story of the carpenter with two saws, a larger one for piecework and a smaller one for time work. Employers favored piecework because it enabled them to maintain or increase output per worker with less supervision.

The tendency of piece-rate earnings to outrun time work earnings has created problems of wage administration in Norway, as in the United States. Some of the difficulty has been mitigated, however, by the common practice of bargaining collectively over time rates exclusively, and then specifying that piece-rate work shall yield on the average a certain percentage of earnings above the time rates, in effect putting a ceiling on earnings by the piece. Where workers within the same industry are paid some by the piece and some on a time basis, there is thus a commonly accepted differential which, though it may change slowly over time, provides a fairly stable standard at annual bargaining conferences.

There has been, of course, some piece-rate cutting, caused by marked technological change. Workers have tended to limit their output to the level yielding them the specified bonus above time earnings in order to avoid a reduction of piece rates resulting from intensified effort on their part. This factor is proving an obstacle to current endeavors by the Labor government to increase production. There is little doubt that a significant increase in output per labor unit could be achieved without technological change if piece workers were assured that they could retain the increased level of earnings permanently. But this would imply a further widening of the time rate–piece rate earnings differential unless time rates were increased correspondingly.

That any widening of this differential under current conditions of labor shortage would be dangerous is indicated by the fact that even under existing circumstances employers often face loss of their time workers unless they agree to pay unofficial equalization supplements (*akkord avsagn*), amounting in some industries to as much as 25 per cent of hourly rates. The only real solution, if inflationary time wage increases are to be avoided, is to convince piece-rate workers that rate cutting is essential in some cases. This is as difficult to do in Norway as in the United States, though the combined efforts of the Labor government and the trade unions may eventually overcome the disfavor with which workers regard an uncompensated speed-up.[24]

Sex differentials. With few exceptions, collective agreements specify separate wage scales for men and women. However, this reflects mainly occupational differences rather than pay distinctions for equal work. There is a fairly well-defined area of women's work, and it is rare to find men and women within an establishment, or even within an industry, engaged in identical work.

Where male and female occupations are identical, wage rates tend to differ if the system of wage payment is based upon a unit of time. If piecework is employed, however, the piece rates may be identical, although, of course, this is no guarantee of equal earnings.[25]

Taking the food products, textile, and clothing industries, in which 74 per cent of the total hours worked by women in mining and manufacturing were concentrated in 1945, collective agreements negotiated in 1946 set the wage rates for women workers at about 66 per cent of those for men. Relative earnings tend to be somewhat lower, however, as the following ratios of women's to men's average hourly earnings indicate:

	1940 (first quarter)	1945 (second half)
Food products	60	64
Textiles	58	59
Clothing	61	61

Sources: *Norges Offisielle Statistikk,* Vol. X, Nos. 35, 128.

The difference between wage rates and earnings is due to a combination of factors. The female-male ratio for earnings per *piece-rate hour* (second half 1945) was 53 per cent for food products, 55 per cent for textiles, and 60 per cent for clothing. Since

---

[24] See Chapter XIII.

[25] See Johanne Reutz, "Kvinnene i arbeidslivet," in *Fagbevegelsens Økonomiske Problemer* (Oslo, 1938).

piecework is fairly common in these industries, part of the wage
rates–earnings differential may be attributed to differences in piece
earnings, reflecting both lower piece rates in women's occupations
and lower female productivity. Another factor is the less frequent
access of women to overtime work in general, and in particular to
the progressively more remunerative overtime customarily required by contract if in excess of two or three hours a day. The
ratio of female to male earnings per *overtime hour* (second half
1945) was 50 per cent in food products, 52 per cent for textiles,
and 69 per cent in the clothing industry.

The comparison between 1940 and 1945 shows that the war
produced a narrowing of sex differentials. Much of this was due
to the imposition of cost-of-living supplements upon basic wage
rates, for in 1945 the amount paid women on this account was 67
per cent of the male supplement. The policy of the Federation of
Labor is to reduce the sex differential still further; it is symptomatic of the trend that the general cost-of-living increase effected in
1946 adopted for the first time the principle of equal absolute increases for men and women.

Age, experience, and skill. Contractual wage schedules for
learners and apprentices may be classified into three general types:
detailed wage steps varying over a specified time period, usually
four or five years; special wage classifications for "young" workers, that is, boys under nineteen years and girls under seventeen
years of age; and the mere provision of an age requirement for
attainment of the full journeyman wage scale.

Detailed apprentice scales are to be found primarily in the
skilled trades, for example, machinery repair, printing, meat cutting, building. The 1946 national agreement for the metal trades[26]
contains the following conditions:

Apprentices and learners shall be paid on the following scale:

1	2	3	4	5	6	7	8	9	10	half year
45	50	55	61	68	75	83	91	100	110	öre per hour

Other young helpers, for example, in mechanical shops:

Upon reaching	15	16	17	18	years of age
	43	55	73	95	öre per hour

[26] *Verkstedsoverenskomsten,* 1946.

The minimum hourly rate for skilled workers paid to the apprentice upon completion of his term is 1.22 kroner, rising to 1.30 kroner after a year's service as a skilled worker. The initial helper rate, which would apply to young workers who have not qualified as journeymen, upon reaching the age of nineteen years, is 1.10 kroner per hour, rising to 1.18 kroner in a year.

The scale for the textile industry, which does not require as high a degree of skill as the metal trades, is similar to that portion of the metal trades scale governing the wage conditions of youthful workers not undergoing apprenticeship:

Wages for young workers		*Kroner per hour*
Men:	15–16 years	0.55
	16–17 years	0.65
	17–18 years	0.75
	18–19 years	1.00
Women:	15–16 years	0.50
	16–17 years	0.60

Male workers over nineteen years graduate to the basic rate of 1.27 kroner per hour the first year, with increases to 1.35 and 1.45 kroner the second and third years respectively. The corresponding rates for women over seventeen years of age are .80, .85 and .95 kroner.

In the canning industry, which employs a great deal of unskilled seasonal labor, the agreement simply provides that workers over nineteen years of age (seventeen years for women) shall receive the basic time rate, while those under nineteen years are to be paid a lower rate.

Average hourly earnings of "young" male workers in 1945 were 50 per cent those of adult males in mining and manufacturing, slightly more than the comparable figure for 1940. Prior to 1946 this differential was maintained in nationally negotiated cost-of-living supplements, which were applied as percentage increases rather than flat sum additions to apprentice wage steps in order to prevent the narrowing of step differentials, resulting instead in widening the absolute differentials. The 1946 cost-of-living supplement provided the same absolute money increase for all workers regardless of age, resulting in some reduction of adult-youth wage differences. This was accomplished at the insistence of the Federation of Labor, the chairman of which declared:

We have good evidence of the results of the wage policy hitherto pursued. To a large extent it is impossible to secure apprentices for the various trades. Instead of entering practical trades, where there is such great need for young people today, they take irregular jobs where earnings are high, or enter commercial school. Recent statistics indicate that while there were 5,000 persons seeking admission to trades courses 20,000 were in various commercial schools and courses.[27]

Wage differentials on the basis of experience in an industry or occupation, either linked to an age requirement or independently, are almost universal, even where the work is largely unskilled in character. The number of grades and the amount of the differentials are roughly proportional to the degree of skill that must be acquired during employment at substandard rates. In canning, largely an unskilled industry, there are two experience grades with narrow differentials for production workers: 1.40 kroner per hour for workers over nineteen years of age and 1.45 kroner after one year of experience. For rotation press and stereotype helpers in printing, on the other hand, there are five steps:

	Kroner per week	
	Day work	Night work
First year	45	51
Second year	52	58
Third year	60	67
Fourth year	68	76
Fifth year	77	88

After ten years of experience, the minimum helper rate is equal to the journeyman rate, 86 and 97 kroner for day and night work respectively, regardless of a man's failure to qualify as a journeyman.

In the trades that draw a definite line between qualified journeymen and helpers, wage rates for the latter may either be fixed by agreement or left to individual negotiation between the helper and his employer. The latter alternative has been adopted for carpentry work. The metal-trades agreement, on the other hand, carries a definite wage rate for helpers, and provides that to qualify for the skilled rate a worker must be at least twenty-one years of

[27] *Konrad Nordahl's foredrag i Lønnsnemnda*, June 4, 1946 (mimeographed).

age and have fulfilled an apprenticeship. If he has not undergone an apprenticeship, he may qualify as a journeyman if he has reached his twenty-second birthday and possesses four years of experience in a recognized skilled trade. Should controversy arise over an individual's qualifications, he may demand a test of skill conducted by a board consisting of one worker chosen by him from among the recognized skilled workers in the shop, one man chosen by management either from within or outside the shop, and a third selected by the other two or, if they fail to agree, by the State Technological Institute. If the board decides that the applicant is not qualified he remains a helper, with the right to renew his demand for reclassification at the end of a year.

Statistical information on wage differentials between journeymen and helpers is available for the building, printing and metal trades:

Ratio of helper to journeyman wages
(average hourly earnings)

	First quarter 1940	*Second half 1945*
Building trades	73	91
Printing trades	75	75
Metal trades	85	91

Source: *Norges Offisielle Statistikk,* Vol. X, No. 35 and No. 128.

The effect of an acute wartime shortage of building and construction labor, induced by the German fortification construction program, is plainly to be seen in the narrowing of the journeyman-helper wage differential during the four year period 1940 to 1945. A high level of employment for construction workers during the period of reconstruction will probably result in continued upgrading of helpers in this industry. More moderate decreases in the wage differential ratio may be expected in other industries owing to the general labor shortage as well as the fact that cost-of-living supplements to wages are paid in equal amounts to skilled workers and helpers.

Geographical differentials. The Norwegian wage structure contains both geographical and urban-rural differentials. Geographically, the most important lines are those between the East and the West, and between the Oslo industrial area and the remainder of the country. The urban-rural differential cuts across both these divisions.

The geographical pattern of average hourly earnings of construction workers employed by independent contractors during the first quarter of 1940, before the disruptive effects of extraordinary military construction had set in,[28] was as follows:

	Kroner per hour	Relative
Østlandet (East)	2.45	109
Sørlandet (South)	2.00	89
Vestlandet (West)	1.87	83
Nordenfjelske (Northwest)	1.77	79
Nordland og Finmark (Far North)	1.82	81
Average for the country	2.24	100

Source: *Norges Offisielle Statistikk,* Vol. X, No. 35.

Geographical differential data are also available with respect to monthly wages of domestic servants, including board and lodging, for representative cities (1939):

	Kroner per month	Relative
Oslo (East)	60	122
Drammen (East)	56	114
Stavanger (South)	38	78
Bergen (West)	45	92
Trondheim (Northwest)	35	71
Average of 18 cities	49	100

Source: *Norges Offisielle Statistikk,* Vol. X, No. 35.

While the two sets of data are not precisely comparable because, among other things, the latter is influenced by city size as well as by geographical location, the East-West wage differential emerges clearly.

[28] The war-induced changes can be seen from comparable data for the second half of 1945:

	Kroner per hour	Relative
Østlandet (East)	3.02	110
Sørlandet (South)	2.40	87
Vestlandet (West)	2.23	81
Nordenfjelske (Northwest)	2.82	103
Nordland og Finmark (Far North)	2.97	108
Average for the country	2.74	100

Source: *Norges Offisielle Statistikk,* Vol. X, No. 128.

The influence of the Oslo urban area, which includes about one-tenth the entire population of Norway, can be seen from a comparison of average hourly earnings of male construction workers and printers in Oslo with similar earnings for the rest of the country (although the differentials for the skilled trades, printing in particular, are less than for manufacturing):

	All workers		Oslo		Rest of country	
	Kroner	Rela-tive	Kroner	Rela-tive	Kroner	Rela-tive
First Quarter 1940						
Building and construction	2.41	100	2.60	108	1.95	81
Printing trades	2.22	100	2.29	103	2.08	94
Second Half 1945						
Building and construction	2.58	100	2.74	106	2.39	93
Printing trades	2.90	100	3.06	106	2.63	91

Source: *Norges Offisielle Statistikk,* Vol. X, No. 35 and No. 108.

Wartime military construction along the south and west coasts had the effect not only of reducing drastically construction wage differences between Oslo and the remainder of the country from 1940 to 1945, but of diminishing the relative importance of the Oslo area as an employer of building labor as well. The printing trades experience is probably more typical of industry in general; the Oslo–rest of country differential tended to increase slightly during the period of the occupation.

Geographical and urban-rural wage differentials are often justified by reference to differences in the cost of living. That such differences exist appears to be confirmed by the results of an examination into workers' living expenses conducted in 1927 and 1928,[29] although it is not possible to state what the differences are with any degree of exactitude. A careful investigator of the problem concluded:

There seems to be a decided tendency for prices to be higher in Oslo and Drammen than in [Bergen, Trondheim, and Stavanger], that is,

[29] *Norges Offisielle Statistikk,* Vol. VIII, No. 103.

it is more expensive to live in the two eastern cities than in Stavanger, Bergen, and Trondheim . . .

. . . the difference between expenditures in cities and rural areas is due not only to lower prices in the country, but also to a real difference in the pattern of consumption.[30]

As a matter of general policy the Norwegian Federation of Labor has been opposed to zonal agreements, despite the favor with which they are regarded by the Swedish labor movement. "The rationale of our policy has been to secure members the same earnings and eliminate the possibility of disloyal competition by individual firms on the basis of a lower wage level than in competing firms." [31] One factor in this opposition was the great unpopularity of somewhat irrational geographical differentials in such government enterprises as the railroads, telephones, and roads, which have been largely eliminated by recent agreements.[32] There is some tendency to work for a reformulation of the Federation's views,[33] but officially the slogan remains "equal pay for equal work, regardless of where it is performed."

National policy notwithstanding, individual national and local unions permit zone differentials either from preference or at the insistence of employers. Unofficially, there is often a tendency for earnings to adjust themselves to the local cost of living through variations in piece rates. More openly, many collective agreements contain geographical differences in wage conditions. One of the most elaborate classifications is that in the 1946 national agreement for office and commercial workers, which applies to thousands of small concerns throughout the country. It is based partly on geography and partly upon community size: Oslo is in a separate class, while Drammen, a city of 25,000 near Oslo, is linked with Bergen (West, 105,000 population), and Trondheim (Northwest, 55,000). Stavanger, a southern town with a population of 47,000 is in a third class together with smaller southern and eastern towns. The ratio of the lowest to the highest wage class is 73 per cent. The 1946 printing agreement contains but two classifica-

[30] E. Storsteen, "Levemaate og Leveomkostninger i Norge," in *Social Håndbok for Norge,* 1937, pp. 92, 94.

[31] *Fagbevegelsens Økonomiske Problemer* (Oslo, 1938), p. 121.

[32] See for example, Norges Statsbaner, Hovedstyret, *Sirkulaere Nr. 322* (1946).

[33] *Fagbevegelsens Økonomiske Problemer,* pp. 121–125.

tions — one for all urban communities with more than 10,000 population, and the second for all other communities — representing a considerable narrowing of prewar differentials. The brick industry agreement of 1946, on the other hand, allows for a 19 per cent differential among three zones — Oslo, the remaining eastern districts, and the western districts.

The process of centralizing collective bargaining through the increasing prevalence of industry-wide agreements is complicated by the reluctance of both the national trade unions and the larger employers to establish differential wage zones and groups. Perhaps the greatest obstacle to expansion of the Employers' Association has been the fear of small employers, particularly in rural areas, that affiliation would wipe out the favorable wage differentials that they often enjoyed. The rapid increase in Employers' Association membership that occurred after 1945[34] may be attributed largely to the equalizing tendencies that set in as a consequence of inflation and a severe manpower shortage, which reduced the previous economic advantages to employers of bargaining individually or through local independent employer associations. The agreement for the office and commercial workers cited in the preceding paragraph indicates, however, that even at the present time further expansion of industry-wide bargaining may be contingent upon a reversal of customary trade union policy regarding geographical wage differentials.[35]

Export and domestic industries. It has often been argued by Norwegian employers that wages in industry producing for export must be lower than in industry producing for the home market, the implication being that such a differential was necessitated by the conditions of foreign trade. In analyzing the basis of this allegation, three general classifications of industry appear to be relevant: (a) Industry producing for the domestic market without foreign competition, thus enjoying a monopoly position relative to other industries. The building-construction industry and the printing trades may be cited as examples. (b) Industry producing for the domestic market but competing with imports. Such industries might of course be monopolistic from an internal structural point of view, but they do not enjoy a monopoly within the economy. (c) Industries producing primarily for the export market.

[34] See above, p. 81.
[35] Recent trends are considered in Chapter XII.

During the first quarter of 1940, average hourly earnings of male workers in the major export industries, compared with those producing for the domestic market, were as follows:[36]

Industry	Average hourly earnings, in kroner
Building, printing	2.27
Manufacturing and mining	1.74
Export industry:	
Electrochemicals	1.94
Metal mining	1.63
Paper and pulp	1.55
Canning	1.41

It is clear that no unique relationship exists between the wage level and the market.[37] The wage differences may rather be explained by a variety of circumstances. In the case of the building and printing trades, the high level of wages is due at least in part to the monopoly position enjoyed by these industries, although the relatively great strength of trade unionism and skill requirements also play their roles. If international trade in prefabricated housing were to develop, it might well be that building wages would fall to the average industrial level.

With respect to the export industries, the distinction appears to be one of relative efficiency. The electrochemical [38] industry is new, and competitive with the comparable industries abroad from the standpoint of costs. The paper and pulp and metal-mining industries, on the other hand, are inefficient compared with foreign competitors. The same is true of canning, with the added factor of a predominantly female labor force tending to depress the wages of men as well.

Why the trade unions in the paper, mining, and canning indus-

[36] *Norges Offisielle Statistikk,* Vol. X, No. 62.

[37] *Cf.* Karl Forchheimer, "The Role of Relative Wage Differences in International Trade," *The Quarterly Journal of Economics,* November 1947, p. 10, where it is stated: "It will be seen that there is a strong tendency for relative wages in any industry to be lowest in those countries which export the products of that industry." The statistical proof offered in support of this assertion is by no means conclusive; and in the case of Norway misleading conclusions might be drawn from its application.

[38] A complicating factor in the case of the Norwegian electrochemical industry is that in 1940 the industry was largely controlled by foreign companies, which may have had an influence on the wages paid.

tries have acquiesced in the lower wage level is another question. The answer lies partly in weakness of organization, partly in the acceptance of a situation sanctioned by tradition. There is evidence, however, that the trade unions are adopting the view that the cost of maintaining relatively inefficient industry vital to the economy should be borne by the economy as a whole rather than by the workers employed in such industry.[39]

Other Wage Provisions. Most agreements contain a clause to the effect that wages of employees whose working capacity is impaired by reason of age, sickness, or disability may be set below the minimum by individual agreement with the employee concerned, subject to the union's right of review. Before this may be done, however, there must be proof that the worker is incapable of performing a normal day's work.

Limitations are often found on the number of machines a worker may tend when he is paid on a time basis. For example, canning workers engaged in smoking fish are not permitted to tend more than six ovens. The metal trades and mining agreements specify that "if a worker is ordered to tend several machines simultaneously, he shall be paid a proportionate wage increase." In the absence of contractual limitation, custom ordinarily governs the amount of equipment an individual may be required to operate.

Payment in kind is widespread in agriculture and lumbering, and in other industries to a lesser degree. There are two wage scales for farm labor, depending on whether or not the worker receives board and lodging. Bakery workers are entitled to one or more meals during the day at the employer's expense, to consist of "good, nourishing, abundant food" — a carry-over from guild days. Oslo restaurant employees receive at least one warm meal a day, and two additional meals that include "coffee or tea, and $\frac{1}{4}$ liter of fresh milk daily."

Although the Basic Agreement provides a general framework for the settlement of disputes over contracts, many collective agreements establish special machinery for the determination of wage controversies. The Oslo tailoring trades[40] have a wage board consisting of two masters and two journeymen, elected for terms of one year each by their respective organizations, with a rotating

[39] See below, p. 299.
[40] *Overenskomst mellom Oslo Skredderlaug og Skreddersvennenes Fagforening,* 1947.

chairmanship. Wage decisions taken unanimously are binding, but in the event of failure to agree the disputes are returned to the organizations for further negotiation. A similar body exists in the clothing industry.

There are, in addition to the subjects covered in this and the preceding chapter, literally hundreds of provisions that adjust working conditions to special circumstances, built up through half a century of experience in collective bargaining. While the past fifteen years witnessed a consistent trend toward uniformity through nationwide bargaining, neither employers nor trade unions are disposed to rule out legitimate industrial differences when they appear necessary. Custom, moreover, is inevitably an important regulator of conduct in so stable a country as Norway, and in many establishments, particularly the smaller ones, habitual practice is of more significance than the written agreement. There are no signs of a bureaucratically imposed homogeneity threatening interference with experimentation and adaptation of general norms to unique requirements.

CHAPTER X

THE LABOR COURT

THE LABOR COURT (*Arbeidsrett*) was established in 1915 as a central agency for the adjudication of disputes over *contract rights* that could not be settled by the voluntary machinery provided by the parties themselves. In the three decades the court has functioned, it has earned the complete respect of both labor and management. It is no exaggeration to say that it is the cornerstone of the prevailing system of labor-management relations.

It is not possible to deal adequately with the work of the Labor Court within the confines of a single chapter. A meaningful commentary on the thirty formidable volumes of decisions rendered by the court would require separate and lengthy study.[1] All that is feasible is a brief account of the organization and procedures of the court, together with a few cases to illustrate the nature of its work.

Although part of the regular judicial system, the Labor Court is faced with special problems arising out of the relationship of the parties appearing before it. Almost every case is merely an incident in a pattern of continuing relationships between employers and employees. It is not sufficient to dispense justice impartially, letting the chips fall where they may; justice must be tempered by insight into the requirements of future harmony and coöperation. Dry legalism would doom a tribunal of this nature to failure.

The Labor Court consists of three members representing the public interest (two of whom must possess the professional qualifications required of justices of the Supreme Court), two members nominated by the trade unions, and two nominated by employer associations, all appointed by the government for terms of

[1] Unfortunately, no such commentary has been prepared in Norway. The experience of the Danish Labor Court, in existence since 1911, is the subject of two recent studies: Knud Illum, *Den Kollektive Arbejdsret* (Copenhagen, 1939), and Knud V. Jensen, *Arbejdsretten i Danmark* (Copenhagen, 1946). The first decade of Swedish experience is available in J. J. Robbins, *The Government of Labor Relations in Sweden* (Chapel Hill, 1942).

three years. In 1937, on the basis of an agreement between the Federation of Labor and the Employers' Association, the Labor Disputes Act was amended to permit submission of disputes not involving questions of principle, and primarily of local interest, to ordinary municipal and district law courts, with the right of appeal to the Labor Court. When trying labor cases, however, local courts must call in two associate judges, one worker and one employer representative nominated by the parties to the dispute.

The Labor Court has exclusive jurisdiction (with the aforementioned exception) of all disputes concerning "the validity, interpretation, or existence of a collective agreement or respecting any claim based on a collective agreement." [2] It has no jurisdiction over any other type of labor dispute. The court, for example, refused to consider a dispute arising out of the failure of parties to agree upon a subject that had been specifically reserved for further negotiation by the terms of a collective agreement.[3] Where an employer withheld wages from an employee who had missed work, the court remanded the latter's complaint to the ordinary courts because the collective agreement was silent on this point.[4] Strikes in contravention of valid collective agreements are the concern of the court, but all other strikes, and incidents arising therefrom, are not within its jurisdiction.

A case is initiated by a written complaint setting forth the grounds for the petition, the evidence that the complainant intends to offer, and the proposed time and place of trial. The petitioner must submit proof that negotiations looking toward a settlement of the dispute have taken place, or that he sought unsuccessfully to enter into such negotiation. If this is not done, the presiding justice is required by law to notify the complainant that "the court cannot consider the matter unless negotiations are conducted or sought to be conducted."

If the complaint is in order, a copy is sent to the defendant with the request that he submit an answer within a specified time. Upon receipt of the answer, or at the expiration of the time limit, the court fixes a date for trial. Normally, several weeks intervene be-

---

[2] *Lov om Arbeidstvister,* August 6, 1915. See *Bulletin of the International Labour Office,* Vol. 10, p. 308 (1915).

[3] Paal Berg, *Arbeidsrett,* p. 221.

[4] Berg, *Arbeidsrett,* p. 218.

tween filing of the complaint and the trial, but if a tense situation
is involved, a case will be given priority, and may under emergency
circumstances come to trial within two or three days of its initiation. Most cases are heard in Oslo, though the court occasionally
convenes at the scene of the dispute either to gather evidence or
as a psychological measure to assuage frayed feelings in a troublesome local situation.

Proceedings are open to the public unless the court decrees
otherwise. It possesses the same power as ordinary courts with
respect to summoning witnesses, subpoena of documents and records, and taking testimony under oath, though as a matter of practice witnesses are rarely sworn. The court may also inspect materials and require machinery to be operated as part of the evidence.
Litigants may be represented by attorneys, but each is limited to
three representatives. If affiliates or members of the Federation of
Labor or the Employers' Association are involved, attorneys for
these organizations usually conduct the case.

The opening session affords both sides an opportunity to state
their cases fully and without interruption — to "let off steam." At
the conclusion of the presentation, the presiding judge, if he feels
that any useful purpose would be served, may adjourn the trial
and attempt, either alone or in concert with other members of the
court, to mediate the controversy, taking care not to disclose his
views on the probable outcome of the case. This unusual procedure
has developed through custom rather than as a result of legislative
provision, and occurs in perhaps 25 per cent of the trials, mainly
those involving work stoppages rather than mere contract interpretations. Intra-trial mediation has proved increasingly successful in reducing the need for further litigation.

If agreement proves impossible the case proceeds to final judgment. The outcome is decided by a majority vote, with the court
required to render a decision within three days of the trial's conclusion; if it fails to do so, the cause of delay must be explained.
Appeal from Labor Court decisions is permitted to the Supreme
Court only on questions concerning the jurisdiction of the former,
and on certain minor procedural matters. In all other respects
Labor Court decisions are final.

The Labor Court's jurisdiction is limited to disputes over *collective agreements* between trade unions and an employer or an as-

sociation of employers. Thus, a trade union is always a necessary party to a Labor Court proceeding. If an employer wishes to prosecute a claim against an individual worker, he must sue the union signatory to the collective agreement on which the claim is based, at the same time naming the individual as codefendant. On the other hand, individual workers may sue only through their trade unions; if the latter are not willing to proceed, the individual has no recourse.

Similarly, in the case of a collective agreement signed by an employers' association on behalf of its members, the individual employer can proceed only through the association, and the association must be named as a party defendant in a suit by a union. However, in the case of an agreement signed directly by the individual employer, he may both sue and be sued in the Labor Court. It is important to note that claims based upon individual as contrasted with collective labor agreements must be prosecuted through the ordinary law courts.

It is provided by law that an interpretation of an agreement by the Labor Court is binding for all subsequent similar disputes arising under the same agreement. The rule of *stare decisis* is applied much more broadly, however. Principles enunciated in a case tend to be hardened into precedent, and are cited argumentatively by the parties.

Table 14 presents a statistical summary of the Labor Court's activities from 1916 to 1940. In all, some 1650 complaints were filed; of these, a little over 50 per cent were disposed of by formal judgment, 20 per cent were settled through court mediation, and the remainder were withdrawn before trial. The maximum number of cases submitted in any one year was 102, and in recent years the court has rendered from 35 to 50 decisions each year. The employment of mediation by the court tended to increase, 66 per cent of all cases concluded in this manner falling within the period 1931 to 1940.

Mr. Paal Berg, presiding justice of the Labor Court from 1916 to 1946, estimates that roughly 50 per cent of all complaints originated with employers (mainly members of the Employers' Association), and 50 per cent with trade unions, although in the later years union-initiated cases predominate.[5] Of the outcome of the cases, Mr. Berg has stated:

[5] Interview, April 29, 1947.

I have no figures on whether it is the workers or employers who have won most cases. It has not been our task to let the parties win alternate cases. But an indication that the trade unions do not consider it hopeless to go to the Labor Court appears from the fact that for several years most cases have been brought in by trade unions and not by employers.[6]

TABLE 14

NUMBER AND DISPOSITION OF LABOR COURT CASES, 1916–1940

	(1)	(2)	(3)	(4)	(5)
	Total Cases Submitted During the	Number of Cases	Cases Settled by Court Intervention without	Cases Withdrawn	Cases on Docket at
Year	Year	Adjudicated	Adjudication	before Trial	End of Year
1916–17....	52	39	6	...	7
1918–19....	99	57	44[a]	[a]	5
1920.......	45	28 }	13	19	{ ...
1921.......	88	46 }			{ 43
1922.......	86	61	8	21	39
1923.......	58	56	9	16	16
1924.......	56	30	12	17	13
1925.......	31	19	6	10	9
1926.......	52	26	7	15	13
1927.......	46	27	7	12	13
1928.......	65	31	8	14	25
1929.......	52	23	14	17	23
1930.......	77	30	19	25	26
1931.......	70	25	24	16	31
1932.......	93	43	14	26	41
1933.......	77	32	23	21	42
1934.......	86	38	27	35	28
1935.......	82	34	27	17	32
1936.......	102	45	18	31	39[b]
1937.......	102	50	17	37	35[c]
1938.......	95	36	25	28	32[c]
1939.......	99	51	25	29	22[c]
1940.......	39	24	7	9	18[c]

Source: Compiled from annual summaries of Labor Court decisions.

[a] The 44 cases include both cases settled and withdrawn.
[b] Discrepancy of one case between cases submitted and disposed cannot be reconciled.
[c] From 1937 to 1940, cases were disposed of by referral to lower courts, as follows: 1937, 2; 1938, 9; 1939, 4; 1940, 3.

[6] Paal Berg, *Arbeidskonflikter* (Sarpsborg, 1938).

The relatively high ratio of employer submissions, as compared with experience under private labor arbitration in the United States, is partly attributable to the court's practice of issuing declaratory judgments upon request of either party to collective agreements. This procedure affords employers a convenient means of securing interpretations of disputed clauses without initiating or waiting for the initiation of alleged contract breaches.

The Labor Court has no penal jurisdiction. It may award compensation for breach of contract or merely clarify the rights of parties to an agreement, but it may not punish violators by fine or imprisonment. This does not mean that work stoppages in violation of Labor Court decisions or, more generally, arising from disputes over the interpretation of collective agreements, are lawful, for the Labor Disputes Act specifically declares them illegal. However, imposition of penal sanctions in such cases is a function of the ordinary law-enforcement agencies.

Although the Labor Court will award damages in appropriate cases, "in the interest of preserving peace and goodwill at the labor site, the injured party often finds it to his advantage to let the matter rest with the settlement of the legal question and not demand damages."[7] While it is relatively easy to collect damages from trade unions against which judgments have been levied, there is considerable conflict over the feasibility of collecting from individual workers who have been adjudged guilty of breach of contract. Mr. Paal Berg expressed the opinion[8] that employers rarely receive from individual workers amounts awarded by Labor Court judgments.[9] On the other hand, officials of the Employers' Association declared that it has been the policy of the association to insist that its members assess individual workers, and that this has actually been accomplished by deducting small amounts from pay envelopes in agreement with the trade union involved.[10] The most accurate statement would probably be that while there

[7] Alf Frydenberg, *Norwegian Labor Disputes Legislation as of 1940* (Norwegian Information Services, New York, 1946).

[8] Interview, August 4, 1947.

[9] Alf Frydenberg, permanent undersecretary of the Ministry of Labor who has dealt with Labor Court matters for many years, concurred in this opinion (interview, July 31, 1947), as did the chairman of the Federation of Labor.

[10] Interviews with A. P. Østberg, vice-chairman, and Darre Hirsch, counsel to the Employers' Association, July 28, and July 30, 1947.

have been instances of damages paid by individuals, it is not customary for the employer to insist upon payment.[11]

In the event of breach of contract by an employer, he is liable to the union or its members to the extent of damages suffered thereby. In most instances such loss would be in the form of back pay, although other types of redress may be secured, for example, the employer may be ordered to perform specifically a non-monetary contract provision. There has been no undue difficulty in enforcing judgments against employers.

Before considering the elements that have gone into the Labor Court's successful career, it might be well to illustrate the type of situation with which it deals by reference to some significant cases of recent origin. The cases presented are in no sense representative of the wide variety of controversy in which the court is called upon to intervene; a really representative sample of the 1650-odd petitions filed with the court would require, as noted above, an elaborate commentary.

Request for back pay. Shortly after the restoration of constitutional government in 1945, the Labor Court encountered one of its most difficult cases. It arose out of a suggestion in April 1940, following the German invasion, made by the Employers' Association to the Federation of Labor, that a general increment of 12 öre per hour in cost-of-living supplements awarded prior to the invasion be canceled. This was done after a series of conferences, with trade union acquiescence. Sporadic strikes occurred during the summer of 1945 over the demand by groups of workers that the 12 öre reduction be restored retroactively, and political considerations soon made it a *cause célèbre*. The issue engendered so much feeling among the workers that the Federation leadership, despite its knowledge of the weakness of the labor case, was obliged to charge the employers with breach of contract. This exemplifies one of the deficiencies of the arbi-

[11] *Cf.* Section 301 (a) of the Taft-Hartley Act, permitting suits for breach of collective agreement to be brought in United States courts, and providing: "Any money judgment against a labor organization in a district court of the United States shall be enforceable only against the organization as an entity and against its assets, and shall not be enforceable against any individual member or his assets." In the light of the Norwegian experience with collection of damages from individual workers, this limitation appears to be a wise one from a practical point of view.

tration procedure: many cases initiated by trade unions are apt
to be based less on legal than on political considerations, and
if the Labor Court decides them without regard for intra-union
politics, it may be accused of proemployer bias.[12]

The union case was based upon the contention that the wage
reduction had been accepted only because the employers had asserted that the Germans were determined to reduce wages. Union
assent, allegedly based upon force, was therefore termed invalid.
The employers offered evidence to prove that the Germans were
not interested in reducing wages, but would have preferred to
reduce living standards by a price inflation. The amount of wages
involved in the suit was estimated at between five and six hundred
million kroner in back pay.

The Labor Court decided for the employers, holding that they
had been motivated solely by the desire to keep industry going in
the face of a wage-price squeeze. The majority opinion said in
part:

It is clear that the workers did not feel as free as they would have
under normal peacetime conditions . . . But this is not sufficient to
constitute the basis of a right to demand that the agreement of June 1,
1940, be revised with retroactive effect.

There is no proof that the Germans had used force to oblige the
labor representatives to comply with the mediator's suggestion, though
they knew that the Germans intended to reduce the Norwegian standard of living. If the negotiations had become stranded, the workers
would have risked even greater wage reductions, or the Germans
could have reduced the standard of living through inflation. This is
the reason why the Federation decided to accept the proposal . . .

The court could find no evidence to indicate any agreement that
the reduction was to be considered invalid or that the cost-of-living
supplement was to be repaid after liberation . . . The workers should
have notified the Employers' Association immediately of their intention to make this demand. Since this was not done, the court must
assume that the Federation's negotiators looked upon the agreement
as permanent.[13]

[12] The chairman of the Labor Court noted in this respect: "It has been said
that the workers cannot find understanding among the judges of the Labor
Court. We judge, it is claimed, according to the cold letter of the law, and not
by the meaning back of it. We represent the employer's point of view, the
charge goes . . ." Paal Berg, *Arbeidskonflikter,* p. 14.

[13] *Arbeiderbladet,* December 10, 1945.

A series of demonstrations against this decision was inspired by the Communist opponents of the trade union leadership in an effort to force the government to reverse the Labor Court's decision. The chairman of the Federation of Labor, however, made the following statement:

The negative court decree . . . was a disappointment, for we had anticipated some degree of understanding. But the decision is made and we must respect it. No one is more interested than the working class in protecting the Labor Court we have fought to retain.[14]

The Federation of Labor also sent a circular to all affiliates in which it declared: "The Court's decision must be respected. Any other alternative would undermine confidence in its independence, and would lead to chaos and anarchy." [15] These appeals proved successful, and the Labor Court emerged from the fray strengthened by the uncompromising support accorded it by the labor movement.

Above-contract wage payments. The Employers' Association filed a complaint in January 1947 involving a novel question of principle. The Building Workers' Union had accepted uniform rates for various crafts of workers on a nationwide basis in a series of agreements with the Employers' Association, but local building unions subsequently negotiated agreements with contractors not affiliated with the Employers' Association embodying more favorable wage conditions. It was the contention of the Employers' Association that in essence this constituted a breach of contract, since the prevailing shortage of labor deprived its members of labor unless they were willing to pay wages in excess of those provided in the national agreements. The Labor Court decided in favor of the union, stating:

The collective agreement with the Employers' Association contains no provision that the Building Workers' Union shall not be privileged to conclude collective agreements with unorganized contractors, at higher or lower wage rates than those contained in the agreement with the Employers' Association. If the Employers' Association . . . wanted the agreement to contain a new duty for the Building Workers' Union not to conclude agreements with unorganized employers at

[14] *Arbeiderbladet,* December 12, 1945.
[15] *Arbeiderbladet,* December 14, 1945.

different terms, it should have raised the point explicitly. It is clear that this was not done. Since there is no explicit declaration in the agreement, a new and unknown principle, namely, that the agreement should be binding for unorganized as well as organized contractors, cannot be inserted. It is possible that members of the Employers' Association will be forced to pay higher wages than those stipulated in the agreement . . . but nothing can be done about that.[16]

Refusal to perform overtime work. The crews of ferry boats operating in the Oslo fiord customarily receive higher overtime rates than are paid elsewhere in coastal shipping. In the national agreement signed by the Seamen's Union in 1946 this practice was continued, but the previous equality between the overtime rates of seamen and local longshoremen was destroyed. After ratification of the agreement, representatives of the Oslo crews approached their employers demanding restoration of equality with the longshore scale, which had moved relatively higher. When the latter refused, they voted not to perform any overtime work. As a result, many boats were either delayed or unable to operate.

The Labor Court ruled, on a complaint by employers, that refusal to work overtime constituted a breach of contract, and ordered the workers to fulfill their obligations,[17] which they agreed to do.

Seniority. In 1947 workers at a western brickyard went on strike to protest the employer's selection of workers to be laid off in a seasonal slowdown. At the Labor Court trial occasioned by the employer's suit, the union claimed in justification for the action of the men that: (a) two elderly men with a great many years of service had been laid off; (b) two workers with seniority of one-half year each had been laid off, while two other workers with less seniority had been retained; and (c) a worker who had accepted employment on German construction during the occupation was hired without first consulting the shop steward.

The Labor Court found that the two elderly men were incapable of performing the heavy work of loading required in off-season operations, and that it was reasonable for the two low seniority workers to be retained, since they had families, while the two laid off were young, unmarried men. Moreover, since the collective agreement contained no seniority provisions, "the establishment

[16] *Arbeidsgiveren,* February 28, 1947.
[17] *Arbeidsgiveren,* December 6, 1946.

must therefore have the right to determine which workers shall have winter work, on the basis of reasonable judgment." As to the third complaint, the court pointed out that the individual concerned had never been accused of disloyalty, and that the employer was therefore under no obligation to confer with the shop steward before hiring him.

The court found that the plaintiff had suffered damages of 20,000 kroner and ordered the Building Workers' Union, the local shop stewards, and the striking workers to make good this amount. The union was held liable because it had not "with all the means at its disposal sought to hinder the breach of contract or the continuation of the illegal situation." [18]

Strike to effect discharge of a foreman. Since the occupation, an important source of labor unrest has been worker objection to the continued employment of supervisors whose wartime loyalty they questioned. Such an incident arose in 1947 when five hundred employees of a machine shop in Sarpsborg left their work, and refused to return unless a certain foreman were discharged. The employer shifted him to other employment, but to no avail. Finally, a complaint was filed with the Labor Court charging the workers with breaking their agreement.

Although the national union to which the men belonged acknowledged that the strike was in violation of contract, the representatives of the men maintained that the dispute was concerned with a matter outside the agreement, and that they were therefore under no obligation to refrain from striking. This argument was rejected categorically by the Labor Court:

The Labor Court finds that the strike is unquestionably in violation of contract. It is a condition of the agreement that the employer has the right to determine which supervisors and workers shall be employed. Workers have no right to demand that a supervisor or employee be discharged or dismissed, and can certainly not seek to force such a demand by striking.[19]

The firm's loss was determined to be 85,000 kroner, and each striking worker was ordered to pay 200 kroner in damages.

The sequel to this decision is interesting. In spite of the adverse ruling, the strikers refused to return to their work, insisting that

[18] *Arbeidsgiveren,* April 11, 1947.
[19] *Arbeidsgiveren,* June 20, 1947.

the employer had violated an earlier promise to remove the complained-of foreman from any contact with the working force. The Minister of Labor prevailed upon them to accept the decision of the Labor Court and return to work upon the stipulation that the employer would agree to immediate arbitration of their alleged grievance. The arbitration decision upheld the employer in all but minor respects.

This case illustrates the difficulty involved in enforcing Labor Court decisions when workers are convinced that their claims have been treated unjustly. Although eventually the men returned to work in the situation just described, it is unlikely that they ever paid the damages assessed by the court (the union was absolved of responsibility, and was therefore not financially liable). An appreciation of the enforcement problem makes it all the more remarkable that the court has been able to maintain its authority unimpaired through so many years.

Unlawful work stoppage. In December 1946, dissatisfaction arose among plumbers in Trondheim with respect to the wage conditions embodied in existing agreements. The source of the difficulty lay in the fact that the wage standards in the Oslo plumbing trades were more favorable, leading the Trondheim workers to demand the application of similar standards to their work.

The association of master plumbers refused to consider a wage increase, since a valid collective agreement was in effect. The Plumbers' Union voted against a strike, but individual workers began to give quit notices. In the course of two weeks, 45 out of 134 journeyman plumbers in the city notified their employers that they were resigning.

The employers charged that this was actually a strike, despite the manner in which it was carried out, and sued the union and the individuals for breach of contract. Agreeing with this contention, the Labor Court noted:

Every worker has the right to leave his position and seek other work if his interests are served thereby. But workers do not have the right to quit work for the purpose of forcing solution of a dispute . . . The workers had discussed the matter [at a union meeting] and by a show of hands were unanimous that they should quit individually to compel a solution.[20]

[20] *Arbeidsgiveren,* November 24, 1947.

The court declared that the individual quit notices were in violation of contract and ordered the workers to resume their positions immediately. The union was fined costs, but no damages were assessed against individuals, the Labor Court taking judicial notice of the basic wage inequality as a condoning factor.

Acceptance of the Labor Court as a permanent institution by both employers and trade unions may be attributed to several factors:

1. A social institution is only as good as the men who compose it. In this respect the Norwegians were fortunate in the choice of Mr. Paal Berg as presiding justice of the Labor Court. Mr. Berg, who functioned in that capacity from 1916 to 1946, combines legal scholarship with a wide knowledge of industrial relations. During his tenure as a judge of the Labor Court he served a term as Chief Justice of the Supreme Court of Norway, and in the occupation period functioned as supreme leader of the Home Front, the underground organ of resistance to the Germans. Upon his retirement from the Labor Court in 1946, he was appointed to the post of State Mediator by the Labor government, a position he left in 1947 on attaining the age of seventy-five years.

Mr. Berg is a proponent of negotiation and compromise in industrial relations. He once declared that "the state must be cautious in forcing a settlement of a dispute that the responsible leaders on both sides do not approve as a natural and logical conclusion." [21] It was under his influence that the court adopted the unorthodox procedure of intra-trial mediation, and it is no accident that at several critical junctures in Norway's labor history, there was recourse to the Labor Court after all other means had failed, despite its lack of statutory authority.

Under Paal Berg's guidance, the court skillfully avoided extreme positions, but not at the cost of yielding on matters of principle that might have destroyed its reputation for impartiality. By steering a careful course between the Scylla of legal formalism, that could easily have rendered it inflexible and unsuited to the settlement of labor disputes, and the Charybdis of opportunism, the Court was able in a sense to remain above the conflict, and to step into the breach when a disinterested party was most needed.

Some years ago, in commenting upon the composition of the

[21] Berg, *Arbeidskonflikter,* p. 7.

Labor Court, the official historian of the labor movement wrote:
"As chairman of the Labor Court the government appointed a
conscientious and socially minded lawyer, Paal Berg, which has
undoubtedly been of the greatest significance in securing as un-
prejudiced decisions as possible under the leadership of a bourgeois jurist." [22]

More recently, the chairman of the Federation of Labor defended
an adverse decision of the Labor Court before the Federation
congress in these terms:

I have conferred with many lawyers who are associated with the
labor movement, and they agree that nothing can be said against the
Labor Court's decision. And certainly nothing can be said against
Paal Berg. He reached his decision on the basis of the evidence.[23]

In a valedictory statement upon the recent retirement of Mr.
Berg, the journal of the Employers' Association stated:

Both central organizations knew that by stating their cases before
the Labor Court with Paal Berg as chairman, they would have the
dispute considered and adjudged by a court whose chairman completely understood the conflict and the arguments the parties advanced, a chairman who had the desire and ability to render a judgment in full awareness of the consequences and couched in unassailable
juridical argumentation. It has been said that "Paal Berg is the father
of Norwegian labor law," and that is correct.[24]

2. The restraint exercised by the Federation of Labor and the
Employers' Association in submitting cases to the Labor Court
prevented its being swamped with a host of minor matters that
must surely have resulted in eventual impotence. Each year the
Employers' Association receives between three and four thousand
grievances and disputes over contract interpretation from its members, and yet the maximum number of complaints filed with the
Labor Court in any one year was 102. Thus at least in disputes
over rights, compulsory arbitration has not impaired direct bar-

[22] Gunnar Ousland, *Fagorganisasjonen i Norge,* pp. 359–360.
[23] Arbeidernes Faglige Landsorganisasjon, *Protokoll over Kongressen 1946,*
p. 415.
[24] *Arbeidsgiveren,* January 2, 1948.

gaining between the parties.[25] Most submissions to the Labor Court involve questions of principle that would probably require arbitration in any event.

3. Stability of personnel and application of the doctrine of *stare decisis* have been of great significance. To quote a labor source again:

The Labor Court handles a number of matters that possibly do not involve any far reaching principle, but where it is desirable to obtain as impartial an interpretation of agreements as possible. And in this respect the Labor Court, with its permanent composition, signifies an important advance over the earlier, more fortuitous arbitration. There is more unity and order in the decisions, and a certain tradition grows up which leads to the result that many disputes are settled before they come to the Labor Court, since the probable outcome can be determined on the basis of precedent.[26]

There is always a danger that *stare decisis* will result in the formation of a rigid code that stifles experimentation and prevents necessary adaptation to changing conditions. But this possibility hinges more upon the administration of the rule than on the rule itself, for there are always factual distinctions between specific cases that permit considerable latitude to the judge. Certainly it can be said that the Norwegian Labor Court was anything but inflexible, although for the greater part of its existence it was dominated by the ideas of one man. It is highly unlikely that a philosophy of *ad hoc* adjudication could have provided equal stability and continuity, or that it would have proved successful in the long run.

4. To be effective, a labor tribunal must act expeditiously. Nothing would be more fatal to successful functioning than long procedural delays, filing and refiling of documents, the taking of mountainous evidence, and procrastination in arriving at verdicts.

[25] The Federation of Labor was once warned by its general counsel to avoid unnecessary litigation: "Only when absolutely necessary should a case be brought to the Labor Court. Even one apparently insignificant case can have serious repercussions for the trade unions. I therefore repeat: Be careful in bringing cases to the Labor Court." Arbeidernes Faglige Landsorganisasjon, *Kongressen 1927, Dagsorden og Protokoll*, p. 232.

[26] Ousland, p. 370.

The framers of the Labor Disputes Act recognized this when they provided that the Labor Court must give a written explanation for delaying decisions beyond three days of a trial's conclusion. The court's chairman has defended its tempo of operation in the following terms:

> I mentioned the complaint that it has taken too long for cases to be heard by the Labor Court, and it has been said that this is ample justification for workers taking matters into their own hands. It has happened that a case was delayed because others were ahead of it. But if the parties wanted speed, the court always endeavored to satisfy them, and as the court is now organized, with the rules of procedure we have, a case is handled more quickly than in any other court in the country.[27]

This conclusion appears to be borne out by the facts. The court's docket was never in such a state that urgent matters, threatening work stoppages, could not be handled at once.[28] The procedural reform effected in 1937, whereby minor matters could be submitted to ordinary local courts convened in special sessions, served further to guarantee against strife-provoking procrastination.

5. There is general agreement that the tripartite character of the Labor Court is in large measure responsible for its successful record. Although dissenting opinions are quite common, many are meant primarily for the record, and a greater degree of unanimity exists than appears on the surface. Since the neutral members of the court are invariably lawyers, they rely heavily upon the technical advice of the partisan members. No one who ever sat upon a tripartite labor arbitration tribunal will minimize the importance of that advice in arriving at a correct evaluation of complex situations.

When, in the summer of 1947, I queried the chairmen of the Employers' Association and the Federation of Labor on their opinion of the Labor Court system, both not only expressed their general satisfaction, but indicated that it was perhaps Norway's most significant advance in the sphere of industrial relations. In the light of the record, it is difficult to disagree with their views.

[27] Berg, *Arbeidskonflikter*, p. 13.
[28] However, the court has refused to prosecute the claims of parties while they were engaged in unlawful work stoppages.

CHAPTER XI

THE PATTERN OF POSTWAR ECONOMIC STRUCTURE

MODIFICATION of the Norwegian labor movement's long hostility to compulsory arbitration and other fundamental alterations in the institutions of the labor market can be understood fully only against the background of the Labor Party's postwar economic program. Rather than risk any disruption of industrial production that might attend immediate efforts to create a socialist society, labor has elected to proceed via a system of controls imposed upon the inherited organization. This path nonetheless marks a sharp break with the previous order, and a considerable step toward the goal of a planned economy. Private enterprise has largely been assigned the role of executor of a governmental policy designed to reallocate national income among the social groups.

ECONOMIC EFFECTS OF THE WAR[1]

Except for the northern provinces, Norway largely escaped the capital destruction that blighted large areas of the European continent. However, five years of capital growth were lost while the apparatus of production was being worn out in the service of the German invaders. Large inventories built up in anticipation of economic isolation in 1940 were depleted. Thousands of workers were drafted for military construction, or were attracted voluntarily into work directly for German account by the lure of high wages. There were considerable additional withdrawals from the labor force for military service with the Allied armies or with the Home Front.

Direct war costs have been estimated at 13.5 billion 1939 kroner, compared with a national income of 4.7 billion kroner in 1939. This consisted of 8.5 billion kroner in reduced wartime consumption, and capital losses of 5 billion kroner. The index of in-

[1] The data in this section are from Odd Aukrust and Petter Jakob Bjerve, *Hva Krigen Kostet Norge* (Oslo, 1945), and *Statistisk-Økonomisk Utsyn over Krigsårene*, Statistisk Centralbyrå, 1945.

dustrial production fell from 115.4 (1938 = 100) to 65.9 from December 1939 to May 1945, and the constantly decreasing supply of consumer goods led to an enormous pressure on the price level. During the same period currency in circulation rose from 575 million to 3.039 billion kroner. Only by an efficient system of price control was a runaway inflation prevented; the price rise, though serious, was kept within bounds. The wholesale price index, based on 1938, rose from 131.3 to 178.1 during the occupation, the cost-of-living index from 114.3 to 155.0.

The most serious consequences of the war were industrial capital deterioration and a decline in labor efficiency, the latter partly a function of the former, but also attributable in part to a deliberate slowdown of working tempo as a means of thwarting the Germans. Output per worker in 1945 was only about 70 per cent of the 1939 level, while industrial capital, expressed as a percentage of 1939 capital, declined 26.7 per cent. The restoration of working speed proved in many instances to be a more difficult task than the rebuilding of plant and equipment, since new habits of work, once acquired, were difficult to change.

There were few who maintained that reconstruction could be achieved without a considerable degree of governmental participation. It was generally agreed that price controls would have to be retained, that wartime rationing would have to be continued, and that wages could not be permitted to move in accordance with the free play of economic forces.

There was a sharp divergence of opinion, however, on the precise limits of governmental control, and the manner in which it should be exercised. Labor pinned its hopes for speedy restoration of prewar living standards upon the government, while the conservatives felt that industry could better be rationalized and production increased through private enterprise. Labor wanted a planned economy with an increasing admixture of state ownership, while industry favored retention of the system of private capitalism. The issue was decided at the polls in 1945, when the clear-cut labor victory cast the die in the direction of planning and control.

The most dangerous immediate threat to the success of the reconstruction program was inflation. To prevent the dislocations attendant upon distortion of prices, and to stimulate the incentive to work, the government undertook to stabilize living costs as near as possible to the level prevailing upon its assumption of office. This was a goal of no mean magnitude, particularly in view of rising import prices, but it proved practicable. During the first two years of the Labor regime the cost of living rose by less than 5 per cent.

Part of the success in preventing price inflation may be attributed to the low level of labor efficiency prevailing immediately after the termination of the occupation in 1945. This made it possible to increase output rapidly with a minimum of technological improvement, which in turn permitted wages to rise without a corresponding effect upon the price level.[2]

Parallel with price stabilization there was a consistent endeavor to reduce income inequalities, not only from social considerations, but also out of regard to labor efficiency and optimum manpower allocation. Wage differentials were reduced by distributing the bulk of the "wages fund" to poorly paid industries, while earnings of business and professional groups were curtailed through salary and dividend limitations, and by taxation. Basic foodstuffs were heavily subsidized, financed by a sales tax on nonnecessaries. Family allowances were introduced and expenditures for social services increased to the highest level in Norwegian history.

NATIONAL ECONOMIC PLANNING

The Labor Party wants a definite plan and rational organization of our productive and economic life. We do not believe it to be possible without participation of the state. There is no ground for industry to look upon the state as an enemy, since the task of the latter is to further economic activity, and place it on a more secure basis. And those who regard social legislation as a revolutionary innovation would do well to remember that behind us there is a six-year war that created drastic changes in most European countries.[3]

[2] It may be noted parenthetically that like their fellows in the United States, Norwegian trade unionists maintain that the official cost-of-living index is not an accurate measure, owing to the changes in living habits that have occurred since the study on which it is based was conducted (1927–28). An elaborate survey of worker-family budgets has been under way since 1946 to provide the data for a corrected index. However, it is acknowledged that the major discrepancies occurred during the occupation period when prices rose rapidly and many consumer goods became completely unavailable. The index movements since 1945 are generally regarded as a fairly good measure of cost-of-living changes for that period.

[3] Speech of Prime Minister Gerhardsen, *Arbeiderbladet*, October 11, 1946.

The philosophy expressed in this quotation has been implemented by the so-called National Planning Budget (*Nasjonalbudsjettet*) prepared for the first time to cover the calendar year 1946. Thus far, the time unit of planning has been confined to one year, although a preliminary four-year plan for the period 1949–1952 was prepared at the behest of the Organization for European Economic Coöperation.[4]

The National Planning Budget of 1947,[5] the first comprehensive economic plan to be developed, was prepared by a technical group under the direction of a cabinet committee headed by the prime minister. The budget is prefaced by a methodological note in which the authors point out that they could have prepared it on the basis of any one of three principles: (a) It could represent simply a statistical summary of individual plans for investment, import, export, and so on, in which event a balance between national product and the total plan for its utilization would be unlikely to occur, so that some of the individual plans could not be realized; (b) a further step would be to prognosticate the probable magnitude of each factor, which would entail a comparison of the sum of individual plans with the objective possibilities of achieving them, thus affording a forecast of national product and its distribution for the year; (c) the third alternative was to regard individual plans as variable rather than as fixed magnitudes, and deliberately to adjust them to maximize total product.[6] The third alternative was chosen as being most consistent with the type of economic planning envisioned in the philosophy of the Labor Party, as expressed above.

The National Planning Budget of 1947 consisted of eight sections, covering, respectively, manpower, building materials, exports and imports, foreign exchange, production, private consumption, private capital investment, and state and municipal consumption and investment. It contained general policy statements for the guidance of administrators. Emphasis was placed upon the development of industries with a high ratio of capital to labor in order to offset the effects of declining population growth. The merchant marine, Norway's chief source of foreign exchange, was given high priority, together with residential housing. Imports for

[4] Utenriksdepartementet, *St. meld. nr. 54,* 1948.

[5] Finans- og tolldepartementet, *St. meld. nr. 10,* 1947.

[6] Finans- og tolldepartementet, *St. meld. nr. 10,* 1947, pp. 10–11.

which payment could be made in "soft" currencies were assigned preference over "hard" currency imports.

These general directives were supplemented by a series of specific programs. Taking manufacturing as an example, particular importance was attached to the development of electrochemical and metallurgical industries as the most profitable means of utilizing manpower. The wood products industry was to be rationalized by abandoning inefficient facilities and concentrating production in the larger and more modern plants.[7] Canneries were urged to iron out their strongly seasonal pattern by developing new products and introducing deep-freezing methods. The electrical-equipment and shipbuilding industries were slated for expansion, while textile-spinning capacity was to be increased to reduce Norway's reliance upon other countries for this operation.

Global resource allocation began with estimates of the national product, which for 1947 was calculated at 8.6 billion current kroner.[8] The estimated national product, plus the expected excess of imports over exports, was then allocated between consumption and investment. The allocation for consumption was subdivided into private and governmental consumption, the precise levels hinging upon the estimated availability of consumer goods. It was concluded that

because of reconstruction, housing, and other investment, the government has found it necessary to prevent excessive increases in consumption. In preparing the 1947 consumption budget, the aim was to hold total private consumption at about the level of 1946, or at any rate not significantly higher.[9]

Planned investment was also divided into private and governmental sectors. Information with respect to investment contem-

[7] This was in line with recommendations made to the government by the Sawmill Workers' Union. The latter pointed out that there had been an increasing tendency for small mills to follow the timber cut, with the result that the number of mills in operation had doubled during the war. It was estimated that concentration of production could result in a saving of 10,000 men. See *Arbeiderbladet,* January 27, 1947.

[8] The preliminary retrospective estimate for 1947 national product is 8.739 billion current kroner, or 1.6 per cent greater than the budget estimate, a remarkably close correspondence. See Handelsdepartementet, *St. meld. nr. 1,* 1948, p. 8.

[9] Finans- og tolldepartementet, *St. meld. nr. 10,* p. 93.

plated by private enterprises in manufacturing and construction was obtained from statements required of all such enterprises planning to invest more than 15,000 kroner during 1947, or planning to import investment goods for more than 5,000 kroner during the year. Estimated investment in agriculture was obtained from county agricultural agents, while municipalities were asked to file their investment requirements. Planned governmental expenditures, including those for the railroads, were available directly from the competent ministries, and estimates were prepared for the remaining sectors of the economy.

When these various statements had been collected, the following conclusions emerged:

The preliminary investment budget prepared in November [1946] which totaled 4 billion kroner, was considerably higher than the physically realizable amount . . . If these plans had been set in motion, the result would have been that a large proportion of the investment begun would have remained unfinished due to lack of labor and materials. In addition, there would have been undue pressure on the price and wage levels.

The problem was therefore to find that level of investment corresponding to real possibilities insofar as manpower, goods, and *valuta* were concerned . . . In setting up the investment budget the three central factors of labor, materials, and *valuta* were constantly kept in mind.[10]

This calculation, which revealed that private firms in manufacturing had planned to invest (gross) 878 million kroner in 1947 compared with the 458 million kroner finally allowed by the National Planning Budget, indicated that there has been no investment scare in Norway thus far. When I asked a leading Norwegian industrialist why he and others were willing to invest additional capital in view of strict control of profits and the avowedly socialist aims of the government, he listed three main reasons: (a) the constitutional protection of private property; (b) the hope of an eventual reversal in political trends; (c) the ability to evade some of the stringent legal limitations with respect to salaries and dividends.

The end results of the production-consumption-investment comparison are shown in Table 15, where the entire scheme is bal-

[10] Finans- og tolldepartementet, *St. meld. nr. 10*, p. 97.

anced through an ingenious double-entry system. The anticipated excess of consumption and investment over domestic production for 1947 (900 million kroner) is shown to be offset by the excess of imports over exports (production account). The manner in which the foreign trade deficit is financed is revealed in the foreign trade accounts. The final columns, the so-called income allocation account, represent a consolidation of the production and foreign accounts.

Inclusion in Table 15 of data showing actual economic events for the year preceding the planning year, 1946, enables the reader to understand quickly the basic policy decisions behind the plan. The plan for 1947 thus envisioned an increase in private consumption of 4.8 per cent, offset by a 9 per cent decline in government consumption. A summary of the distribution of the increase in real resources may be derived as follows:

Changes, 1946 to 1947	*Millions of kroner*	
Increase in national product	750	
Increase in imports of goods and services	700	
Total increase in goods and services available		1450
Increase in private and government consumption	200	
Increase in private capital investment	550	
Increase in government capital investment	550	
Increase in export of goods and services	150	
Total increase in allocation of goods and services		1450

It was recognized that many aspects of the plan were subject to alteration from causes that could not be foreseen — failure of import deliveries at the estimated prices, natural conditions affecting agriculture and fishing, unexpected developments in wages and prices. During 1947, for example, the value of agricultural production was 83 million kroner less than planned, while the fishing industry exceeded the plan by 74 million kroner and whaling by 89 million kroner. The most serious departure from the plan was in imports, due partly to the rise in world prices and partly to more rapid delivery of purchased shipping tonnage than had been anticipated.

The National Plan emphasized the necessity of flexible administration to meet any unforeseen developments. If, for example, unemployment developed as a result of the failure of private enter-

TABLE 15

GENERAL ECONOMIC PLAN FOR 1947 COMPARED WITH PRELIMINARY ESTIMATES OF OPERATING RESULTS FOR 1946

(in millions of kroner)

	Production Account				Foreign Account (Balance of Payment)				Income Allocation Account			
	Debit		Credit		Debit		Credit		Debit		Credit	
	1946	1947	1946	1947	1946	1947	1946	1947	1946	1947	1946	1947
Private consumption....			6,200	6,500					6,200	6,500		
Government consumption			1,100	1,000					1,100	1,000		
Private net capital investment....			1,000	1,550					1,000	1,550		
Government net capital investment..........			300	450					300	450		
Export of goods and services..............			2,300	2,850	2,300	2,850						
Import of goods and services..............	3,050	3,750					3,050	3,750				
National product, including customs duties.....	7,850	8,600									7,850	8,600
Net interest and dividend payments abroad.....							50	50	50	50		
Net deficit in the balance of payment or reduction in net claims on foreigners..........					800	950					800	950
	10,900	12,350	10,900	12,350	3,100	3,800	3,100	3,800	8,650	9,550	8,650	9,550

Source: *Nasjonalbudsjettet 1947*, p. 122.

prise to meet its investment quota, a reserve budget of public works was at hand to take up the slack. Excessive drains on foreign exchange reserves could be met by cancellation of outstanding import licenses and restrictions on the issuance of new ones. If the cut of lumber should fall below the estimated amount, building would be cut back.

It is inevitable that differences of opinion should arise on issues of planning policy. The basic decision on the allocation of resources between consumption and investment, the determination of which industries are to be permitted to expand, the distribution of available means within individual industries, are among the potential sources of dissension. The Norwegians have been fortunate in not yet having to meet these problems in their full impact, since their efforts have been devoted primarily to reconstructing a previous pattern of industrial organization.[11] It has been a cardinal policy of the economic program, for example, to bring the merchant fleet up to its prewar level. A much more difficult problem would have been whether to expand ship tonnage above the prewar level or to devote available resources to development of the metal trades. There is an awareness that the crucial stages of planning will be reached in 1950 or 1951, when reconstruction has been achieved and planning blueprints will have to be developed without the benefit of previous detailed experience.

The National Planning Budget of 1947 was a first approximation to the type of economic planning that Norwegian labor intends to install until a socialist economy can be achieved. That planning shall succeed is one of the most cherished objectives of the labor movement. Unless this is appreciated the current attitudes of Norwegian trade unionism on wage policy and other trade matters, and the concessions that have been made, can hardly be understood.

THE MECHANISM OF CONTROL

It is one thing to plan the orderly disposition of resources, but quite another to accomplish the plan without impinging upon

[11] This does not imply that pre-existing structure is being followed slavishly. A basic steel industry is being constructed for the first time, for example, in order that the country may be self-sufficient in respect to this material. But there are general notions of what should be done in terms of what has been done that influence strongly the managers of enterprise, and through them, the planning authorities.

democratic freedoms. The Soviet experience has made it clear that scientific techniques of control render a comprehensive national plan feasible. But Soviet plans are executed by fiat; the barrier to centralized allocation of labor and capital tends to be physical rather than institutional. Norwegian planners must face the fact that the great bulk of national output is produced by private entrepreneurs seeking their individual profit, and that the labor force possesses not only the theoretical right to strike against unpalatable planning decisions, but also the organizational and political capability of translating that right into reality.

The system of controls devised to channel individual initiative into socially desirable activities is neither as complete nor as authoritative as a planner might desire, although it is drastic by prewar standards. It reflects the weakness as well as the strength of democracy. Constructed by compromise among conflicting interest groups, it is in some respects a patchwork. The process by which agreement was achieved, however, was essential to the growth of mores that make it possible for the system to operate with a minimum of compulsion.

Staff Organization. Final authority for making planning decisions rests with a cabinet committee consisting of the prime minister and the ministers of finance, commerce, labor, and supply. The actual mechanics of preparing the 1947 plan were the responsibility of an interdepartmental technical committee reporting to the cabinet committee, but future plans will be prepared in a newly created ministry of commerce. The detailed statistical compilations required were and will continue to be farmed out to appropriate government agencies.

For advice on general economic policy the government relies upon the Central Coördinating Council (*Samordningsråd*), established in 1945 by executive order. This body is eclectic in composition, consisting of nineteen members headed by a government chairman and vice-chairman and including one representative each of manufacturing, handicrafts, commerce, the coöperatives, shipping, and banking; two representatives of agriculture; one each of fishermen and housewives; three representatives of the Federation of Labor; one from the Employers' Association; and one each of the Price Directorate, the Labor Directorate, and the Central Bureau of Statistics. The delegates of the various functional groups are selected by the most representative organizations therein.

The jurisdiction of the council extends to the following matters:

1. General proposals which should be adopted to regulate the economic situation after liberation and particularly to reconstruct and rebuild the economy.

2. General policy for the type of regulation which lies within the province of the Price Directorate, particularly in the case of the most significant regulations.

3. Proposals concerning measures to prevent or alleviate unemployment, as well as proposals for the consummation of emergency work and any general prohibition against plant closing or discharge.

4. Monetary regulation to the extent that such matters lie within the province of the Ministry of Finance.

5. Important alterations in the wage level to the extent that such matters lie within the purview of government ministries.

6. Questions concerning the nation's supply of raw materials, machinery, equipment, and other requisites for economic activity, and concerning the distribution of such goods. Other supply and rationing matters of particular importance for economic activity . . .[12]

Although the council may initiate policy, it has functioned largely as a sounding board for government proposals, affording the responsible officials an opportunity to judge in advance the reception that particular measures are likely to receive. The advisory opinions of the council, which are always well publicized, are an important public relations instrument, particularly if they are unanimous, as the majority have been. As the council has thus far been constituted, the government is certain of at least a majority for its policies.

The council has been called upon to consider a great variety of matters, among them the rate at which the Norwegian krone was to be stabilized, the appropriate relationship between wages and prices, tax policy, subsidies, and the validity of rigid price stabilization. Although there were dissents on specific matters, a surprising degree of unanimity has obtained in view of the many interests represented.

Supplementing the Central Coördinating Council is a group of

[12] Det Økonomiske Samordningsråd, *Beretning for året 1945* (mimeographed).

industry advisory committees (*bransjeråd*), established by parliamentary decree in May 1947. A joint program adopted by the political parties upon liberation of the country provided for such councils in all branches of industry,[13] but agreement could not be secured on their composition, industry insisting that they consist solely of labor and employer representatives, and labor maintaining that the government should be represented as well. The legislation enacted provided for tripartite representation, with each council to consist of as many members as the government deems necessary.[14] In the wood-working industry, for example, a council of eight has been established, three to represent management, one the white-collar workers, two the manual workers, and two the government.

The industry councils are expected to play a decisive role in the formulation of government policy. Their competence is broad, as the following statement of function indicates:

1. The utilization of the results of technical research in coöperation with the Norwegian Scientific Research Council and other public and private research organizations.

2. The allocation of tasks among establishments with the object of attaining the greatest possible utilization of plant capacity with regard to conditions of production and trade in domestic and foreign markets.

3. The establishment, expansion, alteration, or closing of plants.

4. Matters relating to the supply of raw materials.

5. Technical and organizational rationalization and other matters of significance for increasing productive and economic effectiveness . . .[15]

Business concerns will be required to supply the industry councils with the information necessary to enable the latter to discharge their functions. The councils are empowered to inspect plant facilities and other property, both real and personal. These provisions, as well as the broad grant of general power, were opposed strongly by industry, which charged that the councils could go so far as to recommend complete industrial reorganization. Labor asserted

---

[13] *De politiske partienes samarbeidsprogram for gjenreisningen,* 1945, Section II, 1. Only the Communist Party did not assent to the program.

[14] Handelsdepartementet, *Ot. prp. nr. 153,* 1945–46.

[15] Handelsdepartementet, *Ot. prp. nr. 153,* 1945–46.

that thoroughgoing reorganization would be necessary in some industries, and that the advisory councils were the most appropriate organs for the formulation of specific plans. It was also indicated that the government intends to consult the councils on rationing of materials, labor training, standardization of products, changes in accounting methods, and possibilities of joint purchasing and marketing. However, the councils are specifically enjoined by law from considering price or wage questions.

A third advisory organization at the staff level is the Monetary and Financial Council, under the chairmanship of the Minister of Finance and including representatives of the banks and other interested groups. As the name implies, its function is to advise planning authorities on technical matters relating to finance.

Administrative Organization. The system of economic controls operates primarily through special government bureaus responsible to the regular ministries. Although a permanent administrative organization has not yet been evolved, a brief catalogue of the more important units and their duties will serve to indicate the basic conception of the planning mechanism.

1. The Price Directorate. The most important of the special economic agencies is the Price Directorate, responsible to the Minister of Finance. This organization originated in 1917, when it was set up to curb the price inflation of World War I. In 1926 it was transformed into an agency for the regulation of monopoly practices, and operated as such until 1939, when its original price functions were restored and broadened.[16]

The principal function of the Price Directorate is the promulgation of maximum price regulations. All prices were frozen as of April 8, 1940, and prices in excess of this level are permitted only after the issuance of detailed price schedules[17] or regulations permitting the seller to calculate his own prices on the basis of specific formulas. In general, price increases are limited to actual cost increases, with profit margins fixed at the same amount per unit as prevailed before the war. Entrepreneurs are obliged to determine

[16] For a review of the history of the Price Directorate, see Sigurd Lorentzen, "Oversikt over norsk prisregulering," *Sosialt Arbeid,* 1946, pp. 257–276; *Pristidende,* 1946, No. 6.

[17] From May 1945 to September 1946 the Price Directorate issued 230 separate price orders, to supplement and replace the 600 orders that had been issued during the occupation period, which remained in effect until supplanted.

costs on the basis of actual outlays, rather than on replacement cost at the time of sale, serving further to retard upward movements. Virtually all commodities that are sold at wholesale and retail are subject to price control.

One of the most serious challenges to price stabilization has been the steady rise in import prices since 1945.[18] To dampen the upward pressure from this source, a program of subsidies has been evolved, financed largely out of special taxes on imports that yield above-average profits at domestic maximum prices, and on profitable exports. Importers are thus enabled to sell at prices which are often below cost, and to sell at uniform prices despite differences in purchase price.

Domestically produced commodities that are important in the cost of living of lower income groups have been heavily subsidized as a means of maintaining the price ceilings. The following comparison of prices prevailing in 1947 with estimated prices in the absence of price subsidies reveals the extent of the subsidy system:

	Actual maximum price	Estimated price without subsidy
Bread, per loaf	0.53	0.85
Sugar, per kilogram	0.80	1.80
Coffee, per kilogram	4.25	6.50
Margarine, per kilogram	1.50	2.50
Milk, per liter	0.47	0.61
Butter, per kilogram	6.45	9.67
Beef, per kilogram	6.00	8.45

Source: Finans- og tolldepartementet, *St. meld. nr. 43,* 1947.

The subsidy policy is not without administrative difficulties, nor without certain dangers to the continuation of an orderly process of production and marketing. Nevertheless, the economic planners regarded it as the only alternative to a price inflation that would have enormously complicated the task of planning. It constitutes, moreover, a step toward what might be termed the socialization of consumption, since the commodities subsidized are

[18] The critical nature of import prices stems from Norway's great dependence on international trade. In 1938, for example, Norwegian imports per capita were $109, the highest in Europe. The comparable figure for Great Britain was $100, and for France, $41. See *The Northern Countries in the World Economy* (Finland, 1939), p. 115.

relatively much more important to workers than to other social groups.

The Price Directorate also administers regulations limiting dividend payments. No corporation may pay dividends exceeding 5 per cent of its paid-in capital stock in any year without government permission. Moreover, any dividend payment must be consistent with the economic and financial position of the firm, and its reconstruction and modernization requirements.[19]

Although wartime measures directly restricting production have been relaxed, the Price Directorate continues to regulate certain industries in which existing productive capacity is considered adequate, in order to prevent the creation of excess capacity. The margarine, household equipment, and toy industries are in this category. There is also a prohibition against the establishment of new retail stores without permission.

In addition to the foregoing functions, the Price Directorate is empowered to exercise far-reaching controls under temporary regulations which were confirmed by parliamentary action in June 1947. No Labor proposal aroused more controversy than this so-called "Lex Thagaard," [20] named for the price director, which codified and extended previous emergency authority.

The most disputed portion of the legislation is Section 5, which permits the government to regulate:

(a) prices, earnings, and dividends of all kinds.

(b) production, commerce, and other economic activity for the purpose of preventing harmful competition or other economic conditions that are unreasonable or injurious to the public interest, or to promote rational organization of economic activity.

In pursuit of these objectives, the Price Directorate is empowered to take the following steps:

(1) Forbid an entrepreneur to curtail or cease production, commerce or other activity.

[19] *Pristidende*, 1947, p. 250. The regulations go into some detail with respect to calculation of the capital base. Ordinarily the Price Directorate does not permit excess dividends unless 5 per cent of the capital stock yields a sum which is less than $3\frac{1}{2}$ per cent of capital stock, surplus, and special reserves, excluding reserves for depreciation and pensions.

[20] Finans- og tolldepartementet, *Ot. prp. nr. 152, 1945–46.*

(2) Determine that new establishments may not be started and existing facilities may not be expanded without permission, or that production, commerce, or other activity be apportioned among plants in a specified manner, or that production within an establishment be reduced or halted entirely.

(3) Order entrepreneurs to manufacture certain commodities or perform specified operations at fixed prices and conditions. Such an order may be given only to the extent that it is logically relevant for the establishment concerned.

(4) Order entrepreneurs to pay levies for use in price regulation or as an aid in other regulation under this paragraph . . .

It is further provided that if a firm earns "substantially higher earnings than were given or should have been given as the price determination basis, or if the earnings are clearly unreasonable," they may be confiscated and the proceeds credited to a price equalization fund. There is a two-year statute of limitations on the power of the Price Directorate to inquire into excessive profits.

In commenting upon the bill, the Price Directorate acknowledged that it would be empowered thereby to close down marginal producers; standardize products; reduce distribution costs by eliminating advertising, promoting direct producer-consumer sales, requiring joint selling arrangements; or reduce the number of retail outlets.[21] But it is anticipated that such extraordinary authority will be employed sparingly, if at all. The Prime Minister promised that permanent legislation to succeed this temporary act would be in the form of two laws, one covering the noncontroversial aspects of price control, and the second, the disputed industrial rationalization provisions. The latter will be enacted only if an exhaustive parliamentary investigation reveals its necessity.

Price regulations are administered through local boards and enforced by a special price police. Violation is punishable by fine, imprisonment, loss of right to engage in business for a specified period, or by dissolution of a corporation or partnership. In the latter contingency, the business may be ordered transferred to different ownership if its continuance is essential to the economy.

2. *The Labor Directorate.* One of the principal limiting factors to the expansion of the Norwegian economy is manpower. Capital investment during 1947, particularly in building and construction,

---

[21] Finans- og tolldepartementet, *Ot. prp. nr. 152,* 1945–46, pp. 18–46.

had to be curtailed because of the lack of an adequate labor supply. It was estimated that desired public and private investment during the employment peak of 1947 would have required 1,438,-000 workers compared with a supply of 1,356,000 workers.[22]

The extent to which labor may be directed by a democratic state without impairing civil liberties is a nice question. It would appear logical to assume that with all other factors subject to regulation, the administrators of a planned economy could hardly afford to permit manpower to be allocated through free market competition, particularly when a condition of "overfull" employment places severe pressure upon the wage structure.[23] Yet there is an understandable reluctance on the part of socialists to curb the right of the worker to seek the employment he prefers.

The Norwegians have sought the solution of this dilemma through the establishment of a central manpower agency without compulsory authority. By an emergency decree of May 1945 the Labor Directorate, as the agency is called, was directed to supervise labor exchanges and to draw up plans for the unemployment it was feared would develop. Its status was formalized by an act of June 1947, which confirmed the previous authority and provided in addition for the establishment of local manpower councils to advise the labor exchanges.[24]

The law permits the Labor Directorate (a) to require employers to secure its permission before curtailing operations which may involve layoffs;[25] (b) to prohibit hiring of workers except after referral by the local labor exchange;[26] and (c) to require that

[22] *Nasjonalbudsjettet,* p. 50.

[23] The pattern of control over wages and salaries is considered in Chapter XII.

[24] Socialdepartementet, *Ot. prp. nr. 149, 1945–46.*

[25] Under regulations in effect from 1945 to 1947, no employer could discharge more than five employees in any one month without permission of the Labor Directorate. This was of little significance in view of the severe manpower shortage.

[26] The original draft of the law provided that "a worker may not be employed until after referral or approval by the labor exchange." The words "or approval" were deleted in committee to make it clear that the labor exchange could not limit the right of an employer to hire a particular worker, or of a worker to accept a particular job. *Storting Instilling O. XII,* 1947. However, a worker may be required, before taking a new job, to report to the labor exchange and ask to be referred. The exchange may not refuse to refer him, but at least it is aware of the transfer, and may attempt to dissuade the worker from effecting it.

all job seekers register with the labor exchange. The directorate is armed with knowledge of shifts in employment, but without the ultimate power to direct the flow of manpower through compulsion.

More stringent regulations proved necessary in a limited area of employment, the building and construction trades. Under a special act expiring December 31, 1949,[27] the Labor Directorate is authorized to decree that building and construction workers may not be employed without its permission. Work requiring not more than three employees, or performed as an incident to another type of economic activity by means of a permanent labor force, is exempted. The directorate is also empowered to set limitations on the duration of permissible employment and the number of workers of each craft who may be employed. To eliminate a persistent black market in building wages, it is provided that work may be required to be performed on the basis of the wages and other conditions contained in relevant agreements between the Federation of Labor and the Employers' Association or their subordinate organizations.

The only real objection to the general law on employment and the special legislation for the building industry has come from employers. The Employers' Association warned that government interference in the labor market might produce an uneconomic distribution of manpower:

We are entering a field where there should certainly be a warning that neither law nor a central organization can direct free people beyond certain limits. Such direction can only take place through natural forces over a long period, resulting from free economic forces and from motives that have a stronger grasp on the minds of men than that possessed by state intervention and decrees, which constantly require strengthening lest the entire complex fall about the heads of the builders.[28]

This line of argument has made no impression on the trade unions, which supported the legislation without reservation. The Federation of Labor declared officially with respect to the building law:

[27] Socialdepartmentet, *Ot. prp. nr. 63,* 1947, and *Storting Instilling O. XVII,* 1947.

[28] *Arbeidsgiveren,* April 25, 1947.

We regard the proposed legislation as one of the conditions that in our opinion must obtain before there is sufficient control over economic activity and production, and on this assumption the secretariat approves the proposal.[29]

To sum up, the Norwegian government possesses reserve powers through which the flow of manpower may be influenced, but apart from limitations on the right of employers to discharge workers, may exercise direct control only in the building and construction industry. If a greater degree of compulsory direction is considered essential in the future, it will undoubtedly be exercised in a similar fashion, that is, through limitations on the employer's right to hire rather than directly ordering a worker into specified employment.

3. The Directorate for Export and Import Control. Located in the new Ministry of Commerce, this agency maintains complete control over imports and exports through direct licensing and a system of foreign exchange permits operated in conjunction with the Ministry's *Valuta* Division. Subsidiary committees have been set up to rule upon special activities. Imports of ships, for example, are licensed through *valuta* allowances made upon recommendation of a committee consisting of representatives of the ministries of finance and commerce, and the shipowners. Exchange for repair of ships in foreign ports is granted by the Bank of Norway upon similar recommendation.

4. The Directorates of Rationing, Industrial Supply, and Housing. These agencies are responsible, respectively, for rationing consumer goods, industrial materials, and building materials for housing. Although the government has been de-rationing as quickly as possible, continuing scarcity of commodities has necessitated retention of wartime rationing for many items.

Rationing of industrial raw materials has been based upon a quota system under which each establishment receives a percentage of its consumption during a specified prewar period. The drawbacks of this scheme are evident: inefficient plants that would not survive under competition are kept going, while others that might put the material to better use are denied it. The government is relying heavily upon the industry advisory councils to recommend more effective allocation of available materials.

[29] Socialdepartementet, *Ot. prp. nr. 63*, 1947, p. 6.

The Building Directorate is in a sense the policeman of the investment program, insofar as it relates to the construction of new dwellings. It is its function to direct materials into the construction of the housing that can be completed most quickly and without delays occasioned by shortages of component materials.

5. *The Industry Directorate.* Thus far, this agency has been largely an advisory body with respect to the establishment and rationalization of plants. There are plans to equip it with legal authority to effectuate policy recommendations made by the industry councils and the Central Coördinating Council, by transfer of some of the functions of the Price Directorate.

SPECIFIC ECONOMIC POLICY MEASURES

The Labor government has employed two principal yardsticks in evaluating the desirability of alternative economic policies: would the measure in question contribute to increasing production, and would it tend to reduce inequalities in income or wealth? There has been a conscious endeavor to raise living standards of industrial and agricultural workers relative to other social groups, to the extent that this is feasible without jeopardizing the restoration of productive capacity. Measures that might appear inappropriate to cope with the ever present danger of inflation have a rational basis when viewed in this light.

Interest policy offers a case in point. On January 9, 1946, the Bank of Norway lowered its rediscount rate from 3 to 2½ per cent, causing rates on first mortgage obligations to drop to 2½ per cent.[30] It was reasoned that consumer demand, at least during the reconstruction period, would be independent of moderate changes in the rate of interest. Investment, which might be stimulated by lower interest rates and thus widen the gap between the supply of and demand for capital goods, could be controlled directly through rationing and indirectly through taxation.

Low interest rates, on the other hand, had the advantage of reducing the burden of national indebtedness, decreasing the cost of building and facilitating the maintenance of current home rental levels. "A reduction of interest rates will, on the whole, lead to the

[30] Interest rates had been maintained at an artificially high level during the occupation period. The decision to lower interest rates was in a sense a return to market determination of interest, but it did reflect conscious government policy.

result that capital receives less and labor more of the national income, as long as prices are regulated." [31]

The interest policy has had adverse consequences for insurance companies, social security and pension funds, banks and small savers. Some form of government support for, and perhaps nationalization of insurance is under contemplation. To promote individual saving, special government bonds were issued, paying a higher rate of interest than that obtainable from savings banks. Current interest rates are considered sufficient to enable commercial banks to operate profitably.

Although the major goal of postwar taxation was the reduction of purchasing power, the social aspects of taxation have not been forgotten. A capital tax, designed to confiscate the bulk of all increases in capital values between 1940 and 1945, was levied in 1946. The first 5,000 kroner capital increase was tax free, but beyond that the tax was sharply progressive, ranging from 30 per cent of the next 10,000 kroner to 95 per cent of all capital value increases above 70,000 kroner. For example, if a business man accumulated 200,000 kroner ($40,000) during the occupation, he would be obliged to return about 155,000 kroner ($31,000) to the government.

The tax was payable in a lump sum, and to insure payment all persons and corporations were required to register bank deposits and securities, a portion of which was frozen pending settlement. Unrealized increases in the value of both real [32] and personal property, with the exception of securities, were exempt from the levy, considerably simplifying the work of assessment.

Liberalization and extension of the social security system is another method of redistributing income that is being employed. It is estimated that 6.9 per cent of 1947 national income will go for social security payments compared with 6.2 per cent in 1939. The principle of increasing benefits in proportion to the decline in the value of money has been followed. In addition, family allowances were introduced in 1946, entailing an annual payment of 180 kroner for each child under the age of sixteen years with the exception of the first child.

[31] Aukrust and Bjerve, *Hva Krigen Kostet Norge*, p. 252.

[32] The exemption of real property does not produce the gross inequities that might be expected, because of the stringent price law that permits transfers of real property only at values not exceeding the prewar level.

SOCIALIZATION OF INDUSTRY

It was earlier pointed out[33] that although the Norwegian Labor Party is officially committed to socialism, its approach to the problem of nationalization is flexible, without dogmatic insistence upon the achievement of fixed goals regardless of cost. During the first two years of its administration, the postwar Labor government of Norway indicated its continued adherence to the tenets of socialism, but at the same time evidenced a desire to avoid disturbances to those sectors of the economy that were functioning effectively.

The relegation of nationalization to a secondary position, at least temporarily, is to a certain extent a function of the relatively high degree of government ownership that already prevailed in Norway before the war. The Norwegian equivalent of British coal, the waterfalls, are either state owned or will eventually revert to the state without payment under concession laws enacted in 1909, while the generation of electric power is largely a municipal function, as is the operation of gasworks. The railroads, telephone, and telegraph systems are state owned; bus lines and coastal shipping are partly nationalized; the airlines are operated by a private corporation in which the government owns a substantial share of the stock. The sale of agricultural and fish products is handled largely through producer coöperatives, while the purchase and sale of grains and alcoholic beverages are a state monopoly. Radio broadcasting is a government function and most moving picture houses are municipally owned.

Since 1945 there has been some expansion of the government-owned sector of the economy to manufacturing and mining. The principal sources of new acquisitions were German-owned or controlled property, and the investment of state capital in new enterprises. A majority of the stock of Norsk Hydro, the largest electrochemical plant in the country, was acquired through the enemy property office, together with a miscellany of other firms. Parliament authorized construction of a steel mill with government funds; the first in Norway, its annual capacity of 350,000 tons will cover a good portion of the domestic consumption. The government purchased from British interests the largest source of iron ore in the country.

[33] See Chapter III.

The tempo of socialization may be stepped up once the program of reconstruction is achieved, but the conclusion that can legitimately be drawn now is that the Labor government is unwilling to risk the economic dislocations that nationalization might entail, when it is straining every sinew to restore living standards.

CONCLUSION

Norway's postwar economic structure cannot be classified simply as capitalistic or socialistic. Formally, it remains private capitalism, for the ownership of capital is largely in the hands of individual entrepreneurs and private corporations. Yet the capitalist cannot gear his operations entirely to the maximization of individual profit. The materials he secures, the level of wages paid, the prices he may charge, are all determined by the state on the basis of what the dominant political group, labor, conceives to lie in the public interest.

Contemporary Norway is certainly not socialist, and even on the assumption that the Labor Party retains political power, it is not likely to undergo any rapid change in that direction. Rather, continuance of the present policy with its emphasis on nationalization of only those industrial sectors which it is believed the government can operate most efficiently may be anticipated.

But if Norway does not present an example of a collectivist society, there has certainly been a change from the prewar economy. In this respect it is important to emphasize the essential difference between regulation and control. The type of government regulation that prevails in the United States is negative rather than positive, and the ultimate efficiency of the system depends upon the correctness of individual entrepreneurial decision. To a large extent the Norwegians have substituted collective for individual judgment through national planning backed by compulsive governmental authority. The concept of property ownership has undergone a drastic change. The composition of the "bundle of rights and obligations" has been altered so that the Norwegian capitalist holds his property as a trust of which he may be deprived if he fails to employ it consistently with that concept of the general welfare which the majority of the people approve at the polls.

There are a number of broad issues, barely touched upon in the foregoing pages, that will be of crucial importance for the future of the Norwegian experiment in planning. The question of whether it will be possible in the long run to plan without compulsory direction of labor is one of great significance. The effects of government planning upon the establishment of new enterprises by domestic and foreign capital, particularly the latter, will be interesting to observe. There is also the possibility that enterprising individuals may find the economic atmosphere oppressive to their ambitions, and will resolve to seek their fortunes abroad.[34] But these are prospective matters, and definitive analysis of them will have to await the accumulation of more experience.

[34] Average annual emigration during the decade 1931 to 1940 was slightly in excess of 500. It is estimated that during 1946, 2000 members of the *labor force* left Norway, while 750 were expected to leave between July 1947 and July 1948. This indicates that while the postwar rate of emigration is substantially higher than the prewar rate, it is tending to slow up as the travel fever generated by wartime restrictions wears off.

This, of course, says nothing of the quality of those who continue to emigrate, and indeed it is very difficult to adduce any evidence to the point. It may be noted, however, that of 298 Norwegian students enrolled in American universities during 1947 who were queried about their future intentions, 84 per cent assigned a definite time for their return to Norway, less than one per cent indicated that they planned to remain in the United States permanently, while the remainder were undecided.

CHAPTER XII

POSTWAR LABOR LEGISLATION AND WAGE DETERMINATION

THE RAVAGES of wartime German occupation produced agreement within the Norwegian government-in-exile that for many years to come the principal problem would be reconstruction of the nation's economy. One of the prime requisites for successful reconstruction was a period of industrial peace, not an easy matter to achieve after so long a hiatus in collective bargaining. It was inevitable that liberation should bring in its wake the release of emotions that could easily lead to extremism.

Aware of the magnitude of the difficulties that lay ahead, the Norwegian government in London began to lay plans even before there was any certainty that constitutional authority would ever be restored. In 1942 it appointed the chairmen of the Federation of Labor and the Employers' Association a committee with the following functions:

1. To examine the question of how labor peace can best be secured after the war; to examine the relationship of organizations of employers and workers to one another and to the state.
2. To examine the relevant laws and regulations which the occupation authorities promulgated, and to present proposals for alteration.[1]

The committee submitted a draft proposal for temporary legislation on April 22, 1943. With minor revision, this draft became the basic labor disputes legislation of postwar Norway.

THE PROVISIONAL ACT OF SEPTEMBER 15, 1944[2]

As a condition precedent to the return to collective bargaining, the wages and working conditions in effect at the time of the

[1] *Lønns og arbeidsvilkårene i det befridde Norge* (Stockholm, 1944; pamphlet).

[2] Under the Norwegian legislative system, the government may promulgate laws without parliamentary approval when they concern "commerce, customs,

invasion were reimposed. All collective agreements in effect on April 9, 1940, were validated and in addition mediation proposal agreements that had not been finally ratified on that date were considered adopted. All wage reductions and increases effected during the occupation were cancelled with the exception of changes in personal rates under minimum wage agreements, which remained in effect.

Non-wage provisions of collective agreements as of April, 1940, were frozen for the time being. But it was deemed undesirable to treat wages similarly, and instead a procedure was adopted that bestowed quasi-governmental authority upon the Federation of Labor and the Employers' Association in controlling wage changes. The relevant portion of the act read:

An employer, association of employers or trade union desiring alterations in wage conditions which are determined by collective agreement . . . shall direct a request therefore respectively to the Norwegian Employers' Association or the Federation of Labor. If the appropriate central organization, on the basis of such request or on its own initiative, finds that there is adequate cause to effect a change in the wage conditions concerned, it shall submit a request to the other central organization, together with a full statement of the changes desired. A duplicate of the demand shall, so far as possible, be sent to the State Mediator. Negotiations between the central organizations shall commence within six days of receipt of the demand. Other interested parties may participate in the negotiations.

The Norwegian Employers' Association and the Federation of Labor have full power to make agreements with respect to the extension or change of existing wage agreements, binding upon both parties, after negotiations have taken place between the parties directly concerned.[3]

The effect of this provision was to require the funneling of all changes in the wage sections of collective agreements through the two central organizations, regardless of whether or not the petitioners were members. Moreover, nonmembers could be bound without their consent by action of the central organizations. This departure from prewar practice was defended on the ground that

trade and industry, and police." A provisional law remains in effect until the next session of parliament takes adverse action. If no action is taken, the provisional law expires at the adjournment of parliament.

[3] Provisional Act of September 15, 1944, Section 2.

since some form of wage control would be necessary immediately after liberation, it was logical to make use of the experience of the two main organizations in the wage field, and as far as possible to avoid direct governmental intervention in wage determination. Since the central organizations became quasi-agencies of government in this respect, it was appropriate that their authority extend to all workers and employers.[4]

The control mechanism was rounded out by giving to the State Mediator authority to promulgate regulations governing changes in compensation fixed by individual rather than collective agreement. This provision was aimed primarily at the prevention of increases in the higher salary brackets.

Both under the Provisional Act of 1944 and successor legislation, the mediator enters the scene when the central organizations are unable to agree upon requested wage changes.[5] Four alternative consequences may flow from the mediation proceedings:

1. The parties may themselves arrive at an agreement, in which case the proceedings are terminated.

2. If the parties are unable to agree, the mediator may notify the Minister of Labor to that effect, thus ending his responsibility.

3. The mediator may issue a proposal for agreement *with the consent of the negotiators*. This does not mean that the negotiators know in advance the precise details of the proposal. As the drafting committee pointed out, however, "in its broad features the negotiators will have some idea of how 'the land lies.' The differences may be so small that the parties place in the hands of the mediator the framing of a proposal. If that were not so, one or both parties would advise against the issuance of a proposal."[6] The proposal is then submitted to employers and workers for their approval.

4. The mediator may issue a proposal *without the consent of the negotiators*. This may be accepted or rejected by the negotiators. In the former event, it is submitted to a referendum vote; in

---

[4] This function of the central bargaining organizations has since undergone several modifications. See below, pp. 285–286.

[5] In the original act, representation in mediation proceedings was limited to a maximum of two persons for each central organization, three for the particular union involved, and three for the particular employer or employers, a maximum of ten persons in all. This limitation was subsequently deleted.

[6] *Lønns og arbeidsvilkårene*, p. 51.

the latter, the mediator may require that the individual employers or workers vote on it, or he may merely notify the Minister of Labor that his proposal has been rejected.

The significance of the course chosen by the mediator lies in the provision for compulsory arbitration of interest disputes that constitutes the heart of the act. In the third contingency above, that is, formulation of a mediation proposal with the consent of the negotiators, the mediator may *in his discretion* submit the dispute to the compulsory arbitration tribunal (Wage Board) for adjudication within two days[7] of the proposal's rejection by either party. In this event, the Wage Board is limited to approval or disapproval of the mediation proposal in its entirety; it may not modify the proposal in any way. Should the Wage Board approve the proposal, it becomes a binding agreement, while if it is disapproved, the mediator must immediately notify the Minister of Labor to that effect.

The mediator may not certify directly to the board if issuance of the mediation proposal does not have the prior approval of the negotiators; in such event, the mediator must report final rejection of the proposal to the Minister of Labor, together with an account of his efforts to bring the parties together.

The next move lies with the Ministry of Labor. Upon receipt of notice that mediation has failed, it has three (now four) days to decide whether or not to refer the dispute to arbitration. If the decision is negative, government intervention is at an end, and the parties may resort to a work stoppage. As a matter of fact, all disputes that occurred during the years 1945 to 1948, with a single unimportant exception, were referred to compulsory arbitration.

The arbitration board (literally Wage Board) created by the Provisional Act of 1944, and still in existence, is composed of seven members, three neutrals and two representatives of each of the parties. All decisions are by simple majority vote, but the two labor representatives cast but one vote between them, and the two employer representatives one vote. The public members are thus in the majority.

Strikes and lockouts are legal only when the Ministry of Labor has not referred the underlying dispute to the Wage Board, and then not until six days after the ministry announces its decision.

[7] Subsequently changed to four days.

Once the Wage Board takes jurisdiction of a dispute, its decision is absolutely binding upon both parties. Violations are punishable by fine or imprisonment, but to the time of the present writing penal sanctions have never been invoked, although infractions of the law in the form of wildcat strikes not approved by official trade union bodies have not been uncommon.

SUBSEQUENT DISPUTES LEGISLATION

Before its expiration the Provisional Act of 1944 was subject to several amendments. The most significant change was the broadening of its scope to include disputes over conditions of employment other than wages, accompanied by unfreezing the non-wage provisions of collective agreements. As originally conceived the 1944 legislation was to be of short duration, but when it began to appear that the period of its validity might be lengthy, it was necessary to remove the original ban on changes in working conditions.

Another important amendment was introduced when the life of the act was extended by Royal Decree in June 1946. The authority of the Employers' Association and the Federation of Labor over the wages and working conditions of nonaffiliates was deleted, independents thenceforth being free to deal directly with one another without the intermediation of the central organizations. Pressure for this change came from the trade unions, since the Employers' Association was endeavoring to use its statutory authority to prevent the consummation of collective agreements with unassociated employers on terms more favorable than those contained in agreements with member firms. This problem was particularly acute in the building trades, where a shortage of labor enabled workers to secure very favorable terms.

The Federation of Labor promised, in return for relaxation of the old rule, that it would instruct its affiliates not to conclude agreements with independent employers stipulating wage rates higher than those prevailing in associated shops, provided there was no customary differential. This promise proved difficult to effectuate, and additional legislation later proved necessary to cope with evasion of the Federation's intent.

The Provisional Act of 1944 was extended by administrative decree to June 30, 1947, but renewal beyond that date involved parliamentary action. A tripartite committee had been established in April 1946 to review the operation of the act and recommend successor legislation. The public and labor members advocated the continuance of compulsory arbitration on the ground that the need for industrial peace was as great as ever, and that the system had functioned in a satisfactory manner. The employer members, however, opposed the extension of compulsory arbitration for the following reasons:

The minority considers it beneficial and right that the parties themselves remain masters of and bear the responsibility for their collective agreements.

The minority has also learned that in practice it is much more difficult to arrive at a voluntary agreement through negotiation and conciliation when it is known that if unity is not achieved, the dispute will be settled through arbitration. Thus a compulsory arbitration law by its very existence can render more difficult that relationship and unity between the parties which we all regard as the most propitious form of renewing agreements.

In addition, in the opinion of the minority, the government today lacks legal and other means of ensuring that an arbitration award will be respected. This is true of voluntarily concluded agreements as well, but experience has shown that within the ranks of the workers there is a much stronger will to respect an agreement freely entered into, and ratified through referendum vote, than an arbitration award which is forced upon them. The minority cannot at all regard a compulsory arbitration institution as any certain subsidiary means of securing labor peace as long as society has not evolved rules that oblige individual workers who may be dissatisfied with awards to bow to the decision of a governmentally established tribunal. Experience with the arbitration awards of 1928 fully confirms this. The minority also points to the consideration that a board which arrives at a decision apprehensive of arousing opposition in certain quarters will not be respected.

The minority finally recalls that before the war the government, without having established any permanent arbitration institution, was obliged to resort to compulsory arbitration in particular instances when there was no agreement on new contracts, where vital social interests were threatened. This indicates that the authorities, without the continuation of a permanent wage board, have the same opportunity in individual cases to establish a court of arbitration, if social interests in connection with a concrete dispute render it necessary. Besides, both central organizations have agreed on contracts of two years' duration, so that there is no need to count on important contract revisions in 1947 . . .

Subsidiarily, the minority emphasizes that the draft of the temporary law lacks regulations for effective control of conditions in agreements with unorganized employers.[8]

The government's proposal was adopted by the parliament, although the validity of the new law was limited to the period ending December 31, 1947. It sharpened somewhat governmental control over the wage and salary provisions of individual agreements. For example, while the State Mediator had originally been given authority to regulate salaries, the penalties for violation were slight. It was now provided that an employer who raised salaries without the necessary approval became liable to fine, or imprisonment up to three months, or both.

One other substantive alteration is of interest. It concerned the qualifications of employer and trade union members of the Wage Board. The Provisional Act of 1944, in its original form, barred from appointment to the board, officers or permanent employees of employer associations or trade unions. This prohibition was deleted administratively in August 1945, and affirmed in the Act of 1947, on the basis of a joint letter from the Employers' Association and the Federation of Labor asserting that the Wage Board was thereby deprived of the services of persons most qualified to serve by training and experience. The Ministry of Labor noted that "the same requirements were established for members of the Wage Board as for members of the Labor Court, in the belief that it would strengthen the Board's objectivity and authority if the representatives of the parties were not as closely tied to their organizations as officers or permanent employees are bound to be." [9] The ministry yielded, however, to the arguments of the central organizations.

During 1947 mounting pressure on the wage level threatened the program of stabilizing prices and wages initiated by the government. In particular, the exemption of independent employers from the moderating supervision of the Employers' Association led to competitive wage bidding, and many associated employers

[8] Socialdepartmentet, *Ot. prp. nr. 162,* 1945–46, p. 5.

[9] Socialdepartmentet, *Ot. prp. nr. 162,* 1945–46, p. 7.

complained that their workers were being pirated away. The problem was submitted to the Central Coördinating Council for its advice; the following recommendation was made on July 5, 1947:

A temporary wage stop should be introduced for the remainder of the current year. Effective measures are needed to prevent the payment of excessive wages and to prevent increases or fluctuations in wages and piece rates within contract periods aside from customary adjustments in the minimum wage trades and adjustment of piece rates in connection with labor saving and time study.[10]

The principle of a wage stop was approved unanimously by a tripartite labor-disputes committee, and a temporary law to that effect was enacted in September 1947, to run for the remainder of the year.[11] Wage increases were defined comprehensively to include the following actions: (a) increases in money wages, gifts, payments in kind; (b) filling vacancies on better terms than stipulated in existing collective agreements, or in the absence of agreement, in excess of customary terms; (c) intra-establishment transfer of a worker at an increased wage, unless the new position carried a higher contract rate than the old; (d) "to provide in piece-rate agreements which do not specify definite rates, a piece-rate surplus over time-rate earnings in excess of that contained in permanent agreements between the Employers' Association and the Federation of Labor for corresponding work"; (e) guarantee that piece rates will yield minimum hourly earnings in excess of contract time rates; (f) awarding of production premiums without corresponding increases in output.

Certain exceptions to the general control order were made in the interest of preserving customary wage practices. Thus, contracted cost-of-living index increases, age and experience upgrading, and personal rate increases based upon demonstrably regular schedules were permitted. New collective agreements could be adopted only with the approval of the State Mediator, who also had the power to reduce wages that he considered "obviously unreasonable," after consultation with the two central collective bargaining organizations.

Because of internal trade union opposition to the wage-stop legislation, it proved politically impossible to extend it into 1948,

[10] Socialdepartementet, *Ot. prp. nr. 103*, 1947, p. 3.
[11] Socialdepartementet, *Ot. prp. nr. 103*, 1947, pp. 7–8.

as had been planned originally. As a substitute, the representative council of the Federation of Labor adopted a resolution calling upon its affiliates not to seek any general wage increases during 1948, and exercised its constitutional power to the effect that "no contract termination may take place and no wage demand made without the prior consent of the secretariat [of the Federation of Labor]." [12] At the same time the government introduced legislation extending the compulsory arbitration features of the original act of 1944, with some sharpening of the wage control provisions that had been in effect prior to the wage-stop law. The new provision read:

For the duration of this law, affiliates and members of the Norwegian Employers' Association or the Norwegian Federation of Labor cannot terminate their collective agreements without the permission of those central organizations.

Employer associations or employers independent of the Norwegian Employers' Association and trade unions independent of the Norwegian Federation of Labor cannot terminate their agreements for the duration of this law without permission of a board named by [the Ministry of Labor].[13]

The first paragraph of this proviso merely confirmed legislatively the authority which the two central organizations already enjoyed under their own constitutions. The journal of the Employers' Association pointed out that "of course the central organizations have always had the opportunity to impose such denial [of the right to terminate agreements], even if they did not use it to the extent that might have been desirable. Now the Federation of Labor desires to put it into law in order to give it more authority." [14]

The second paragraph of the above-quoted proviso represented a compromise between the strict control over nonmember collective agreements exercised by the central organizations under the Provisional Act of 1944 and subsequent amendments which stripped those organizations of such control and placed nonmember agreements under the general supervision of the State Mediator. The presumption was that the special board named to pass

[12] *Arbeiderbladet,* November 29, 1947.
[13] *Arbeidsgiveren,* December 19, 1947.
[14] *Arbeidsgiveren,* February 6, 1948.

upon nonmember applications for changes in terms of collective agreements would base its decisions upon the collective agreements negotiated by affiliates of the central organizations, in order to prevent competitive wage bidding. The central organizations were restored to a position of primacy with respect to the determination of conditions of labor, but without the anomalous situation whereby they could govern the actions of nonmembers. The pluralism implicit in the Provisional Act of 1944 was thus modified to conform with traditional Norwegian practice respecting the role of the state in industrial relations.

THE PROCESS OF WAGE DETERMINATION

From this review of the Norwegian labor legislation enacted between 1945 and 1948, it would appear that the Labor government was endeavoring to modify sectional and particularistic wage determination in the interest of furthering price and wage stability. The growing belief that untrammeled collective bargaining in its traditional form is incompatible with successful governmental planning[15] has received some substantiation in Norway's postwar experience.

Many of the same considerations entered into Norwegian wage setting under the aegis of the Wage Board as in wartime United States under the National War Labor Board. There were several facets to the determination of those wages which would be most conducive to maximization of output: the general wage level, inter-industry differentials (including the problem of substandard wages), relationships between distinct groups of plants within particular industries, and intraplant wage structure. A complicating factor in the Norwegian situation which was perhaps not present in the United States to the same degree, was the inappropriateness of a wage level and a system of wage differentials based upon prewar conditions to an economy characterized by "overfull" employment and faced with specific and exacting reconstruction requirements.

[15] See Barbara Wooton, *Freedom Under Planning* (Chapel Hill, 1945), p. 102; G. D. N. Worswick, "The Stability and Flexibility of Full Employment," in *The Economics of Full Employment* (Oxford, 1945); Eugene Forsey, "Trade Union Policy Under Full Employment," in Lester and Shister, *Insights into Labor Issues* (New York, 1948). Cf. H. W. Singer, "Wage Policy in Full Employment," *The Economic Journal,* December 1947, p. 438.

The considerations entering into changes in the general wage level were twofold. In the first place, the Wage Board was obliged to consider whether its awards were consistent with the "wages fund" determined specifically by an economic plan or, as in the United States, by the requirements of price stabilization in an inflationary situation.[16] If wages were raised above the planned level, the result could be either a redistribution of income in favor of workers or a proportionate increase in the prices of other factors, leading to a stable level of real wages. Secondly, averting work stoppages remained an important, if not the paramount consideration. In most cases it was deemed cheaper to modify a plan or to permit a moderate price inflation (bend-the-line) than to incur the losses of output entailed in strikes, though this was not always so. Under some circumstances it seemed wiser to uphold certain principles at the expense of current output, particularly where concessions might have led to a multiplier effect upon wages generally.

Modification of inter-industry differentials involved the crucial problem of labor force allocation. Drastic steps were necessary to arrest and reverse the downward secular trend in manpower available to agriculture and lumbering, since the ordinary price mechanism would have been inadequate to provide labor for these industries upon which the country was so immediately dependent, for food and foreign exchange respectively. The only alternative to using the wage mechanism as a lever would have been direction of manpower, which the Labor government was anxious to avoid except as a last resort.[17] Beyond the basic manpower question was the desire, springing from moral as well as economic grounds, to eliminate substandard wage conditions that had become embodied in the national wage structure.

The adjustment of intra-industry and intraplant wage differentials raised similar questions. Because of the complexity and variety of these differentials, however, the Wage Board was disposed to retain the inherited system unless compelling reasons were

[16] Essentially, the Hold-the-Line Order of April 8, 1943 (Executive Order 9328) provided the United States War Labor Board with guideposts similar to those established for the Norwegian Wage Board first by the general stabilization policy pronouncements of the Labor government and later by the economic plans for 1947 and subsequent years.

[17] The manpower controls instituted were considered in Chapter XI.

advanced to the contrary. The equalization of the wage structure that occurred at this level was a consequence less of government wage determination than of worker pressure induced by an over-all shortage of manpower.

Before proceeding to an examination of individual Wage Board decisions, one generalization is in order. Partly because of the state of employment, and partly as a result of deliberate governmental policy, there has been a general narrowing of wage differences in Norway under the Labor government. Within some industries, occupational differentials have become so small as to endanger a continuing flow of labor into the skilled trades. Among industries, permanent retention of the new relative wage structure would seem to be dependent upon an extensive system of governmental subsidies.

THE GENERAL WAGE LEVEL

The major wage level decisions promulgated by the Wage Board had their inception in two trade union demands for general increases in cost-of-living supplements. The first demand was raised in August 1945, under the terms of a preliberation agreement between the central organizations of labor and employers permitting the wage stipulations to be reopened three months after liberation.

The case was certified to the Wage Board with little preliminary negotiation. The chairman of the Federation of Labor admitted that "we meet before this honorable Wage Board under somewhat extraordinary circumstances. From earlier practice we know that a wage dispute was rarely arbitrated before a long period of negotiation and mediation had elapsed. This time there have been no negotiations, while mediation lasted but a few hours." [18] He might well have added that the issue had been blown up into a minor political crisis, and that the government was anxious to settle it before the forthcoming general elections.

The history of the trade union case went back to 1939 when the unions, fearing a wartime inflation, decided to protect living standards by tying wages to the cost-of-living index. Negotiations were initiated in December 1939, and on January 25, 1940, the Federation of Labor and the Employers' Association agreed to adopt September 1939, when the cost-of-living index stood at

[18] Arbeidernes Faglige Landsorganisasjon, *Beretning 1945.*

171, as the point of departure for index-wage adjustments. The unions secured an upward adjustment of one öre per index point from September to December 1939 ("full" compensation for living-cost increases because of the fact that the average hourly earnings of men were 1.71 kroner in September 1939), but consented to adjustments of 0.75 öre per index point based upon the index at March 15, and June 15, 1940, on the theory that in wartime every social group must expect a reduction in real living standards. However, effectuation of this agreement was frustrated by the German invasion of Norway.

As the result of an agreement reached in Stockholm in 1944 between the two central organizations, employers began paying supplements of 38 öre per hour immediately upon liberation. When the trade unions brought their demand for additional compensation before the Wage Board in 1945, the cost-of-living index had reached 268, or 97 points above the September 1939 base. The chief trade union demand was for an additional cost-of-living supplement of 59 öre per hour, which with the 38 öre already given formally would have provided the workers with "full" compensation for the increased cost of living.

A number of subsidiary demands were made as well: (1) A national minimum basic wage of 1.30 kroner per hour for men and 0.90 kroner for women. (2) The wages of all firms paying below the "customary" level in each industry to be adjusted to that level. This was aimed at establishments which had received special dispensation for unique reasons, for example, the Grimstad Conserve Company, whose low wages enabled it to produce a domestic wine in competition with Portuguese wine. (3) Overtime, holiday, and night-shift premiums to be calculated on the basis of total hourly earnings rather than on basic hourly rates. The magnitude of the cost-of-living supplement to basic wage rates made this an important issue.

The employers opposed any upward wage adjustment on the ground of the inflationary danger involved. They pointed out, too, that average hourly earnings had risen during the war through individual adjustments, independent of collective wage schedules, and that this increase should be taken into account.

The Wage Board in a divided vote increased the cost-of-living supplement by 20 öre per hour. The increase was justified in the following terms:

During the war the price level has risen by a greater amount than average wages and most wage earners have suffered a reduction in real wages and living standards. They have, therefore, a just claim for a wage increase. On the other hand, it is clear that the catastrophe which overtook our country has reduced our real capital and weakened our productive ability. The possibility of raising living standards to the prewar level is, therefore, not immediate. As the situation stands today we must reckon that a general wage increase will essentially be compensated through new price increases. The possibility of wage increases without price increases will first occur after an increase in employment, adjustment of work, speedier labor tempo, and with rationalization and cost economy in other factors. But such a development takes time, and today a general wage increase will initiate an inflationary race between wages and prices with serious consequences for the future of our economy, as well as for wage earners, who always lose by inflation . . .

The nation's weakened economic situation sets a limit on the size of the wage supplement. Labor's demand for full compensation for the price increase cannot now be granted without serious consequences . . . We have therefore decided on a supplement which together with previous supplements and the basic wage increases which were put into effect during the war will give on the average three-quarters compensation for the increase in the cost-of-living index from January 1, 1940, to July 15, 1945.[19]

The arithmetic of the board's decision was as follows: three-quarters of the 97 index-point increase from September 1939 to July 1945 amounted to 73 öre. The workers were already receiving a cost-of-living supplement of 38 öre per hour, while the Central Statistical Bureau estimated that average hourly wage rates had risen during the war by 15 öre per hour independent of the cost-of-living supplement, making the total wage increase already received 53 öre. An additional 20 öre per hour brought the total up to the 73 öre per hour required by the "three-fourths compensation" notion.

On the subsidiary issues the parties agreed to negotiate the questions of a national minimum wage and the leveling of substandard firms. This practice of deciding the principal question and returning "fringe" issues to the parties for further negotiation was followed in many later cases, relieving the board of a mass of detail. With the central problem out of the way, the parties were

[19] Wage Board, Case No. 1, September 12, 1945.

usually successful in adjusting subsidiary matters directly. However, the board did specify that premium rates should be calculated on earnings rather than basic rates, thus granting an additional pay boost.

The decision was regarded as a satisfactory solution by the labor leadership. The amount of the award was sufficiently large to allay worker discontent and to prevent any serious inroads by the Communist minority within the trade unions. The Prime Minister expressed the view that the workers should be satisfied with the principle of "three-quarters compensation" in view of the fact that "the country is much poorer and no group in the population can secure the standard of living it had in 1939 before the economy is reconstructed." [20]

In this first general wage case, the principle established by the Wage Board of "three-quarters compensation" for increases in the cost of living was not an invention of the board. It had been accepted by trade unions as a reasonable relationship of wages to the cost of living during a period of reduced consumer-goods output, and appealed to the average worker as a fair compromise. In a sense, the board was codifying a common law principle in the jurisprudence of industrial relations.

From July 15, 1945, the base date of the 1945 cost-of-living award, to May 15, 1946, the official cost-of-living index rose from 155.6 to 158.0,[21] only about half the increase necessary to reopen the wage question under the stipulation of the 1945 award. However, the trade union leadership was faced with a groundswell of discontent with current wages. Reluctantly, the Federation of Labor approached the Employers' Association for a further increase in the cost-of-living supplement.

The Labor government ranged itself firmly against any upward change in the general wage level. In a speech before the 1946 congress of the Federation of Labor, the Minister of Finance warned that any further wage increases would lead inevitably to a rise in the level of prices. The price subsidy program had been stretched to the limit of safety, raw material costs could not be reduced because of inflation in import prices, and profits had reached the

[20] *Arbeiderbladet,* December 29, 1945.

[21] These figures differ from the cost-of-living data cited above by virtue of the recalculation of the entire series on a 1938 base to replace the old 1914 base. There was no change in the method of constructing the index, however.

lowest level compatible with their operation as an incentive factor. He told the delegates:

We must free ourselves of the conception that money provides the basis of well-being and a higher standard of living . . . The question must be approached from the point of view of what correct policy would be from our own movement's interest. I consider it only fair to say openly and frankly that I do not believe that such a policy [of higher wages] is sound at present, when we face the fact — that neither monetary policy nor other artifice can disguise — that our present standard of living, on the average, cannot be raised above 85 to 90 per cent of the 1939 level." [22]

The trade union leadership acknowledged that the approach to wage problems under a labor government must be entirely different from the procedure under a "bourgeois" government. In a forthright article that appeared in the journal of the Federation of Labor, the vice-chairman of the Federation made a significant declaration upon this theme:

No longer, as in the old days, do others decide economic policy and we, through collective bargaining, through conflict or threat of conflict, force employers and the government to change their plans and calculations in conformity with our demands. We are no longer in the position where we can reach our goal only through use of our economic weapons. Neither are wage questions determined through negotiation with employers as a compromise based on mutual strength. Today wage policy is a link in over-all economic policy, in the determination of which the labor movement itself is taking part, in the interest of the workers . . .

We could easily increase money wages, but when the quantity of goods remains the same, this would lead to an increase in prices. The question is, therefore: Shall we carry out a policy that stabilizes the price level, or a policy that forces it up?

A weak government and a weak labor movement could do what has been done in other countries. They could approve all demands for more paper money, and then let inflation have its way . . . We look upon it this way. It is necessary to achieve a policy upon which the whole of the labor movement can agree. We must reach a positive line that goes beyond the old method, where five and ten öre per hour were the most important consideration . . .

[22] *Arbeiderbladet,* May 11, 1946.

We must not make any demands that break the framework of price stabilization and lead to inflation. We must try to regain our standard of living in the course of the next five years, partly through wage policy, partly through price policy and social legislation.[23]

Despite these unequivocal statements by both the political and economic leaders of the labor movement, the demand for higher money wages persisted, and the leadership was forced to yield, not only to protect its own position, but in order to avert strikes. Customary habits of thought proved too strong; the absolute size of the pay check was still a paramount consideration to workers.

The trade union demand for an additional 15 öre per hour was submitted to mediation, in the first instance, as a gesture to orderly procedure. But this was hardly a matter for collective bargaining. Both employers and the trade unions were aware that any substantial wage increase must be accompanied by a price increase, so that the ultimate decision lay with the government. The mediator reported that he was unable to find any basis for compromise, and the dispute was certified to the Wage Board.

The award of the Wage Board granted an increase of 5 öre per hour in the cost-of-living supplement payable beginning September 1, 1946; a second 5 öre to be paid beginning March 1, 1947; and a third 5 öre on September 1, 1947. The trade unions received their full demand, but in installments. Simultaneously, the government announced that it would pay family allowances of 200 kroner per child per annum, beginning with the second child, obviously designed as a further palliative for the workers.

The board's opinion reveals the dilemma in which the conflict of political and economic desiderata placed it:

In its decision of September 12, 1945, the Wage Board pointed out the poor position of the country. Nevertheless, the board favored a cost-of-living increase, which together with the previous cost-of-living increase and the basic wage increase during the war meant three-quarters compensation for increased prices. (In some individual cases full compensation was granted to substandard wage groups.) At that time the board assumed that production would increase as time passed, and in addition the government approved increased subsidies to keep prices down. When, therefore, the workers refer to the rise

[23] Gunnar Braathen, "The Economic Situation," *Fri Fagbevegelse,* March 1946.

of the production index that occurred in the autumn of 1945, that rise was to a large extent discounted in the cost-of-living increase granted in 1945. In addition, the general index covers differences within the individual branches of industry. In several of the industries included in the general production index there is a long way to go before the prewar level is reached. The increase in employment does not mean, in all branches of industry, that there are increased profits. According to government statements we cannot expect large subsidies to keep prices down beyond those already in effect. The situation today, in the opinion of the majority, is that an immediate general wage increase would in all probability result in a corresponding price increase. The result would be no improvement in the standard of living, but it would increase the danger of inflation.

The majority finds reason to expect a further increase in the production of goods if labor productivity and plant efficiency can be raised. Improved conditions of labor can have an important effect. In these circumstances it is possible to make a slight wage adjustment. A promise of future wage increases will hasten the desired development . . .[24]

The labor member of the board voted with the majority because he found reason to believe "that an immediate increase of 15 öre per hour will cause a certain increase in prices and thus partly eliminate the true value of the increase. This factor favors the spreading of the increase on condition that prices do not rise." The employer member of the board, in a minority dissent, pointed out that on the basis of the only current wage statistics available, those of the Employers' Association, average hourly earnings of men had risen to 2.51 kroner per hour. If to this were added the 15 öre awarded, the increase in earnings since 1939 would amount to 55.5 per cent, while the cost of living for the same period rose by 57.8 per cent. He accused the majority of abandoning the principle of "three-quarters compensation."

The board was obviously hard put to justify its award. The only logical argument was that "improved conditions of labor" might act as a spur to labor productivity. Manifestly the decision was a political one. The chairman of the Federation of Labor greeted it with reserved approval. Although it "did not quite come up to our expectations," workers could be pleased that "this is an increase in

[24] Wage Board, Case No. 12, June 7, 1946.

real wages, irrespective of a possible rise or fall in the price index." [25]

These cases illustrate the diverse considerations that influence governmental determination of the general level of wages. The orbit of economic calculation must be broadened to include political factors. Strictly from the viewpoint of economic planning, the government would have preferred to avoid any general wage increase in 1946, yet the solution adopted may actually have served to maximize production by allaying labor unrest and preventing the weakening of trade union discipline. While it proved necessary to revise economic plans to take account of the new data, the resultant position may well have been the optimum one.

INTER-INDUSTRY WAGE DIFFERENTIALS

1. Substandard wages. A long-standing goal of the Norwegian labor movement was to increase wages in the relatively low-paid industries. Even before the war, when economic planning was still a vague future hope, the Federation of Labor had begun to advocate a "solidaristic" wage policy, which implied that stronger unions in the higher-paid trades would forego a portion of the wage gains they could achieve provided that the low-paid workers would benefit thereby. Speaking before the 1945 congress of the Labor Party, the Prime Minister (who was also the party chairman) declared with respect to the lowest income groups:

I think everyone will agree that the standard of living of these [low-paid] groups of the population before the war was so bad that there can be no talk of a further reduction for them. On the contrary, it would be both just and necessary, even in the difficult situation the country and the people now face, to obtain higher standards of living for these people than they had before the war.[26]

A subsequent statement by the vice-chairman of the Federation of Labor ran in the same vein:

Above all, we must have an increase for the lowest wage groups. For example, if it is to be possible for us to obtain a sufficient labor force for the textile industry, wages must be raised.[27]

[25] *Arbeiderbladet,* June 8, 1946.
[26] *Arbeiderbladet,* September 8, 1945.
[27] *Fri Fagbevegelse,* No. 3, March 1946.

Lumber workers were the first to benefit from this policy. They were generally acknowledged to have been poorly paid, particularly when the arduous nature of their work is taken into account. From 1935 to 1939, lumber wages rose between 50 and 60 per cent, with an additional wartime increase of 45 per cent, but in 1945 wages were still so low that they prevented the recruitment of an adequate labor force.

The relatively poor labor conditions in the lumber industry were usually attributed to the fact that the overwhelming proportion of the industry's product is exported, constituting before the war 30 per cent of Norway's total exports, and entering into competition with more efficiently produced lumber.[28] Another reason may be sought in the composition of the industry's labor force, which consisted largely of unskilled workers who were forced to endure the privations of inadequate housing, poor food, and work under difficult climatic conditions, under the spur of chronic unemployment.

It was against this background that the Lumber and Agricultural Workers' Union put forth a demand for a wage increase of 55 per cent in 1945. The Wage Board awarded the workers a 20 per cent increase, a relatively substantial amount, on the ground that substandard conditions requiring correction existed:

The statistical material presented by the parties is very confusing, and does not offer a sound basis for rendering a decision, particularly with respect to the relationship between time and piece rates. Neither has the Central Statistical Bureau any useful data. It is clear, however, that the wages of lumber workers were low before the war, and that the workers by this decision will receive more than full compensation for the wartime price increase.[29]

The decision contained a cost-of-living index regulation clause that was to become more or less standard for future decisions, with appropriate changes in dates:

If the Central Statistical Bureau's cost-of-living index on April 15, 1946, shows an increase or a decrease of 5 points or more in relation

[28] Most of the lumber was produced on small holdings and primarily by hand. The government is currently endeavoring to raise the level of productivity by the introduction of mechanical equipment, power saws in particular.

[29] Wage Board, Case No. 2, September 25, 1945.

to the index figure of September 15, 1945, the Federation of Labor in case of an increase, and the Employers' Association in the event of a decline, has the right to set forth a demand for regulation of wages in accordance with the change in the index.

The lumber industry absorbed this wage increase without difficulty because of favorable export prices. The higher wage level facilitated the recruitment of labor for subsequent cutting seasons. The cost problem may become acute when the world demand for lumber falls, however, and the government may then be faced with the alternative of reducing wages or subsidizing production unless there is a considerable increase in productivity.

Many of the same considerations were involved in the situation of agricultural laborers. In 1939, average daily wages for self-subsisting male agricultural workers, at the harvest season, were 6.05 kroner, while at the same time average industrial daily earnings were 14.04 kroner. About 30 per cent of the Norwegian population was then engaged in or supported by agriculture and forestry, but their share of the national income was 15 per cent. Wages are only part of the problem of Norwegian agriculture, which is handicapped by small unit size and an almost complete lack of mechanization.

The 1945 wage demand of the Agricultural Workers' Union[30] was for an hourly rate of 1.50 kroner (about 13.50 kroner a day on the basis of a six-day, fifty-five-hour summer working week). The employers were willing to go only as high as 9 kroner a day in summer and 8.50 kroner in winter. The Wage Board raised the daily rate to 11 kroner a day in summer and 10.25 kroner in winter, assigning the following reasons:

It is a justifiable claim that the differential between the wages of agricultural and industrial workers should be reduced. If the present price level is held, the leveling of wages cannot be accomplished to any great degree unless the government increases the ability of agriculture to pay the higher wages. It is clear that the increased wages will create great pressure on agriculture. But we believe that an increase in production will be possible. In the light of probable postwar conditions, as well as the new level of consumption which social policy

[30] Although the union's membership among farm laborers was small, probably not in excess of 4000, its wage adjustments affect indirectly many additional thousands of workers.

can create, we believe that a production increase, to a certain extent, will assist in the maintenance of farm incomes.[31]

When this award expired a year later, the parties were again unable to agree upon a contract, and the matter was once more submitted to the Wage Board. Over strong employer objection, the board raised the standard wage to 13.25 kroner in summer and 12.75 in winter because "it is right and necessary that agricultural wages be increased in correspondence with industrial wages." [32]

Had the board been concerned primarily with the wage-paying potentialities of agriculture, the wage increases would undoubtedly have been smaller. But the prime concern was with the social status of farm labor, as well as with the long-run objective of arresting a persistent decline in farm population by moving farm wages into closer proximity to industrial wages. The increased cost was met partly by raising farm prices and partly by additional government subsidies to farmers.

The paper industry was also characterized by relatively low wage standards. Average hourly earnings in 1939 were 1.46 kroner compared with 1.79 kroner in the metal trades. The Paper Workers' Union first came before the Wage Board in 1945 when it received the moderate increase of 5 öre per hour for men whose wage rates were less than 1.30 kroner per hour.[33] This award expired in August 1946 and the matter came up before the Wage Board again. Average hourly earnings of men at that time were 2.15 kroner, representing an increase of 47 per cent over 1939 (this included a cost-of-living supplement). The increase in the cost of living for the same period was about 55 per cent, so that the real wages of paper workers had fallen somewhat more than industrial real wages generally.[34]

The union demands included a 40 öre per hour basic-wage increase, plus 15 öre in the form of a cost-of-living supplement. This was scaled down to the still considerable amount of 21 öre per hour by the Wage Board, which also removed the 1.30 kroner limitation in the previous year's award, so that many workers

[31] Wage Board, Case No. 5, November 10, 1945.
[32] Wage Board, Case No. 50, March 26, 1947.
[33] Wage Board, Case No. 3, October 6, 1945.
[34] See Table I.

actually received an increase of 26 öre per hour. To quote the Wage Board's decision:

When we give this increase — the largest the board has ever given — it is on the ground of special conditions in the paper industry. We have taken the wage reduction in the interwar period into account, and consider that the present prosperity should redound to the advantage of the workers. Augmentation of the labor force in an old industry, where the average age of the workers is high, is as important as an increase in the supply of raw materials in the long run. How great a wage increase can be given under present conditions is a matter of judgment concerning which there may be differences of opinion. The majority has decided upon the amount set forth. Average hourly earnings in the paper industry will come up to a level which will not be out of line with earnings in other industries.[35]

Wage increases were also granted by the Wage Board to workers in the stone and fish-packing industries, both producing primarily for export, on the basis of substandard conditions.[36] In dealing with the stone industry, the board queried (but did not decide) whether some wage differential based upon whether the product was produced for domestic or foreign markets might not be justified, provoking a sharp dissent from the labor member to the effect that "it is not correct to set different conditions of labor for products intended for domestic consumption and for similar products designed for export. If it is necessary in an industry, in order to maintain exports, to provide extraordinary subsidies, that is a broad social question. In my opinion it is unreasonable to force a small labor group to bear this burden alone." [37]

Two principal ideas may be discerned in the substandard wage cases. There was first the moral argument that all workers whose product is essential to the national economy are entitled to a fair wage, regardless of the ability of their industry to pay. The customary justification for minimum wage legislation is thus carried a step further to embrace wage equality.

There was also a real economic basis for the elimination of substandard wage conditions, however. Lumbering and agriculture

[35] Wage Board, Case No. 16, August 19, 1946.
[36] Wage Board, Case No. 21, September 6, 1946; Case No. 54, February 28, 1947.
[37] Wage Board, Case No. 62, April 17, 1947.

experienced a manpower crisis after liberation, at a time when the products of the lumber industry were providing a large portion of the nation's foreign exchange, and a world-wide food shortage intensified the need for greater domestic agricultural output. The unemployment that prevailed in varying degree during the entire interwar period prevented serious drains on the rural labor force, but the tight postwar labor market made it possible for lumber and farm workers to escape the relatively poor financial and physical conditions to which they had been subjected. It is likely that wages in these two industries would have risen relatively even in the absence of governmental determination that they should.

The case with respect to the paper industry is not as clear. A shortage of lumber after 1945 reduced paper mill operation to less than half of capacity and created some unemployment among paper workers. Most of Norway's paper mills, however, are located in small towns where there are few alternative work opportunities, so that transfer of workers to other industries often implied physical transfer. Since paper and pulp constitutes one of Norway's principal exports (almost 25 per cent of total physical exports before the war), it was deemed a sound long-term investment to preserve the labor force intact by raising wages and even paying unemployment benefits, if necessary, until the supply of raw materials once more provided the opportunity for capacity production.

2. Inter-industry wage comparisons. Wage comparisons among industries tend to become important data in centralized wage determination. An obvious means of justifying a wage increase is to demonstrate that the wage level of a particular industry has fallen from its customary rank in the national wage structure. Administratively, there is a temptation to restore the traditional relationship rather than to explore the economic significance of the change.

An interesting example of the use of industry comparisons by the Wage Board arose in a dispute in which 27 breweries figured. Average hourly earnings of male brewery workers during the first quarter of 1946 were 1.846 kroner, whereas average male industrial earnings for the same period were 1.93 kroner. Women brewery workers, on the other hand, were receiving 3 öre per hour more than the general industrial level for women. On behalf of the workers, it was shown that the breweries had always paid above average wages and that the distortion came about as a result of wartime conditions.

The Wage Board accepted this argument, finding that "the establishments, under normal circumstances, are very profitable, and the earnings of male workers were above the average industrial level." It awarded the men an increase of 7 öre per hour but, consistent with the principle laid down, denied the women an increase, since they already had "somewhat above average hourly earnings than in industry generally." [38] Although the men were satisfied with this result, the women were not. They promptly went out on strike, causing the plants to shut down until the employers agreed to adjust their wages as well.

Similar reasons were advanced by the Wage Board in granting wage increases to workers employed in auto repair shops, based upon "the relationship which has hitherto existed between wages in the metal trades and in the auto repair shops." [39] In a case involving workers in the relatively low-wage textile industry, the board made a slight upward adjustment based specifically on similar treatment accorded paper workers a short time previously.[40]

The complications of this approach are not difficult to appreciate. For one, it is not always possible to establish inter-industry wage relationships that have long-run validity, either statistically or from a broader economic point of view. Even if this were possible, it would serve to prevent relative wage shifts that might otherwise normally take place. For example, the Building Workers' Union has endeavored unsuccessfully to secure Wage Board approval for introduction of building rates into previously unorganized prefabricated-house construction plants.[41] Moreover, if the criterion of inter-industry differentials is employed together with a substandard wage doctrine, there will be a perpetual race between the average wage level and the wage rates in each industry. Finally, insistence upon the maintenance of traditional differentials deprives planning authorities of one of the principal means of effecting a reallocation of the labor supply.

Where the Wage Board sought merely to employ inter-industry comparisons as a means of determining wages paid for similar types of work, there was often conflict over the comparisons to be made. Should the fabrication of tin plate for canning pur-

[38] Wage Board, Case No. 13, July 13, 1946.
[39] Wage Board, Case No. 22, September 11, 1946.
[40] Wage Board, Case No. 6, November 17, 1945.
[41] Wage Board, Case No. 44, December 18, 1946.

poses be regarded as part of the canning industry or the metal trades? [42] Is the production of furniture comparable to the production of doors, windows, and stairs? [43] Is the cleaning of fish comparable to canning? [44] In each of these situations there were rational arguments on both sides, and the inter-industry comparisons did not yield objective standards.

INTRA-INDUSTRY WAGE DIFFERENTIALS

The Wage Board also contributed to the elimination of wage differentials by consolidating into larger industrial groupings specialized segments of industry that had previously operated under separate conditions. In one such case the Clothing Workers' Union sought to blanket three manufacturers of oilskin and waterproof garments into a nationwide clothing agreement. The firms contended that they could not be considered identical with the clothing industry by reason of differences in materials, processes, and machinery. It was shown, moreover, that the three plants had always paid wages below the general clothing level.

A majority of the Wage Board, consisting of two public members and the labor member, upheld the union contention that the manufacturing processes were basically similar to those carried on in garment production, and ruled that the same wages should be paid. One of the public members, joined by the employer member, wrote a vigorous dissent that goes to the heart of the question:

The two oilskin plants are engaged in a special productive process with particular technical demands. One of them is currently working with modernization plans and experimenting with new products. I cannot disregard the possibility that the wage system in the three plants may have been built up with particular circumstances in mind, which the board has not appraised fully. Individual working conditions are better than those in the clothing industry, particularly those for young workers. In the circumstances it appears best to me that changes in the structure of the wage system be effected through negotiation between the immediate parties, and that the Wage Board limit itself to appropriate improvements within the framework of the general wage system under which the plants have hitherto paid their workers.

[42] Wage Board, Case No. 36, November 19, 1946.
[43] Wage Board, Case No. 43, December 18, 1946.
[44] Wage Board, Case No. 54, February 28, 1947.

A thoroughly consistent adjustment for the entire country of all wages and working conditions in a branch of industry would obviously facilitate governmental wage regulation. But I cannot discount the fact that special agreements in certain cases can more adequately take into account internal technical matters and individual circumstances. Rationalization would both make it possible for workers to earn more and yield the plants a sufficient profit to pay interest and amortize the cost of rationalization; if special agreements can facilitate rationalization, there should be hesitation in supplanting them by official decree.[45]

However, trade unions have not been permitted to apply the principle implied in the majority decision in any mechanical fashion. In one case, the Building Workers' Union claimed that 160 small shops fabricating window panes, doors, staircases, and so on, for building construction belonged to the building industry, and should pay their workers the wages that prevailed for site work. The employers asserted that they were engaged in a typical manufacturing operation, characterized by regularity of operation in contrast with the seasonality of building construction. The Wage Board, although it gave the workers a wage increase, left their rates substantially below building wages.[46]

A similar result attended the efforts of trade unions to have the knit-goods industry classified as part of the clothing industry rather than the lower-wage textile industry, with which it had always been associated for wage purposes. The union based its argument upon the manner in which the workers were organized: of the 1200 workers in the industry, 750 were members of the Clothing Workers' and 450 of the Textile Workers' Union. When a particular plant used raw yarn as its initial material, even if it carried production to the stage of finished garments, its knit-goods workers came under the jurisdiction of the textile union. On the other hand, if it employed cloth in the first stage of production, jurisdiction belonged to the clothing union. However, the board refused to upset the traditional relationship that had existed between knit-goods and textile wages.[47]

[45] Wage Board, Case No. 8, November 24, 1945. Accord: Case No. 36, November 19, 1946.

[46] Wage Board, Case No. 30, October 12, 1946.

[47] Wage Board, Case No. 14, July 15, 1946. The decision was unanimous, the labor member noting that he believed the question of reclassifying the workers to be a matter for collective bargaining.

Another method by which a certain degree of wage standardization has been attained was by raising to the average level of their industry individual firms that had established wage differentials advantageous to themselves because of size, location, or other factors. In one such case the board simply noted that there was "no basis" for the individual difference.[48]

An inclination to reduce intraplant differentials is exemplified by Wage Board policy on the question of the minimum versus the standard wage rate.[49] In general, the Wage Board favored the introduction of the standard wage to replace minimum wage schedules, and in one case assigned the following reason:

We are agreed upon a standard wage in these plants in order to secure the most uniform wage level possible, which might be difficult to achieve under a minimum wage with personal supplements.[50]

This policy provoked disagreement among the public members of the board. In a case involving the wages of agricultural workers, a public member registered his conviction that the established standard wage should be abandoned in favor of the minimum system:

In scarcely any other activity do workers' abilities vary so, or is the unit of employment so different in terms of location, quality, size, and mode of operation. There are also variations in cost of living, and labor and living conditions . . . Under these widely varying circumstances it is impossible to set any single condition which will not be too low in some cases and too high in others . . . The minimum wage system that I favor will all in all be more favorable for the worker than that provided in the majority award.[51]

In another case where the board refused to substitute standard for minimum wages because "it is a plant in which work is carried on in departments with heterogeneous labor conditions and widely

[48] Wage Board, Case No. 46, January 4, 1947. See also Case No. 10, February 27, 1946; Case No. 25, September 21, 1946.

[49] For the distinction between minimum and standard rates see above, pp. 210–215.

[50] Wage Board, Case No. 41, December 7, 1946. Accord: Case No. 23, September 18, 1946; Case No. 32, October 22, 1946.

[51] Wage Board, Case No. 60, March 26, 1947.

varying wages," it ordered instead that a certain level of average earnings be maintained.[52]

Well established intra-industry differentials based on geography, urban-rural location, size of operation, or occupation were treated more gingerly. The board hesitated to eliminate them altogether, usually confining itself to narrowing the amount of the differential. Thus, where previous collective agreements provided for distinct wage classes based upon type of activity,[53] scale of operation,[54] or geographical location,[55] some degree of differential was retained. The justification for urban-rural differences in wage rates was also acknowledged. In one such case, where the Food Workers' Union had demanded that eleven canning establishments situated in rural communities be required to meet the national average, the Wage Board found

that the establishments concerned have so many extra costs above those of urban establishments that it would not be reasonable to apply the national wage agreement to them . . . It is reasonable that wages lie somewhat lower in rural districts than in cities, first because the cost of living in the country is usually lower, and secondly because production would otherwise be impossible because of the many extra costs involved.[56]

Recognition of the urban-rural differential received its most precise expression where it had been the industrial practice to place Oslo in a wage class distinct from the remainder of the country. In almost every case involving this issue the Wage Board held it justifiable to continue the differential, though usually with a reduced magnitude.[57]

[52] Wage Board, Case No. 47, January 9, 1947.

[53] In Wage Board, Case No. 42, December 1946, the board specified separate wage schedules for local, long distance, and nationwide bus lines.

[54] Wage Board, Case No. 41, December 7, 1946. In this case 67 small shipyards in Western Norway objected to inclusion within a nationwide agreement for the shipbuilding industry. To justify exemption, they pointed out that they were producing small fishing craft, with a labor force consisting largely of part-time farmers, and that they operated with only primitive machinery. The Wage Board narrowed the former differential of 50 öre per hour to 22 öre.

[55] Wage Board, Case No. 53, February 22, 1947; Case No. 58, March 8, 1947.

[56] Wage Board, Case No. 29, October 1946. Accord: Case No. 32, October 22, 1946.

[57] Wage Board, Case No. 20, August 29, 1946; Case No. 30, October 12, 1946; Case No. 45, January 3, 1947; Case No. 61, March 31, 1947.

The board was more willing to grant nationally uniform wages where the minimum wage system was in effect, on the theory that local differences in operating costs and cost of living would be compensated for by adjustments in personal wage rates above the minimum.[58] And in one early case, that might have created an important precedent had it not been for the peculiar character of the enterprise, the Wage Board abolished long-standing geographical wage zones for road workers in government employment, stating:

These zonal divisions are not based upon statistical investigation of living costs in the different districts and localities. Both the zone division and the different wage systems appear originally to have arisen from purely fortuitous circumstances and have therefore always been a matter of dispute.[59]

The problem of occupational differentials did not loom large in the Wage Board's work since neither employers nor employees were disposed to alter them to any significant extent. The board often relied implicitly upon customary differentials of this nature in setting occupational rates,[60] and only in exceptional circumstances deviated from established norms.[61]

OTHER ISSUES

The original intention of the Norwegian legislators was to confine the jurisdiction of the Wage Board strictly to wages. It soon became apparent, however, that the wage aspect of disputes could not be dealt with in isolated fashion. Therefore the board's jurisdiction was broadened to include the entire subject matter of industrial relations. A few of these problems are considered in the following section.

1. The bargaining unit. On several occasions the Wage Board was confronted with demands by craft groups that their wages and working conditions be determined separately from those of production workers. Its response was invariably in the negative,

[58] Wage Board, Case No. 55, March 4, 1947.

[59] Case No. 3, October 3, 1945. Presumably what the board had in mind was that there was opportunity for determination of differentials neither through free market forces nor through scientific investigation.

[60] For example, Wage Board, Case No. 35, November 1946.

[61] For example, Wage Board, Case, No. 59, March 12, 1947.

supported by the industrial union from which the craft desired to be distinguished.

The most clear-cut case was one in which twenty-five employees of a paper mill, engaged in the fabrication of specialized products from the paper produced in the mill, requested that their wage rates be raised above those of other production workers in the same establishment. Until 1940 they had belonged to the Paper Workers' Union, but at that time they formed their own independent association. It was not until 1946 that they were freed of the obligations arising under a collective agreement negotiated by the Paper Workers' Union on their behalf, accounting for their delay in seeking separate treatment.

Their contention was that the work they performed was characteristic of the paper-specialty rather than the paper-production industry, and should be paid in accordance with the higher rates prevailing in the former. In rejecting this claim, the Wage Board cited a decision of the Labor Court to the effect that further processes in connection with paper mill operation constituted a natural extension of such activities, even though similar processes were performed in establishments divorced from paper manufacture. The Wage Board concluded:

We do not find any proof that the work performed in the special department of Drammen Paper Mills is so distinct from work in other departments of the plant or other paper mills that there is ground to deviate from the principle that workers in the same plant should, so far as is possible, have uniform wage and working conditions. The introduction of dissimilar collective agreements within the same plant can have far-reaching consequences not only for the paper industry, but for other industries as well.[62]

The same general conclusion was reached with respect to local unions of bricklayers, electricians, and transport workers which maintained that the wage scales of their members employed in the paper industry should be determined in the light of conditions within their respective crafts, rather than on the basis of wage trends in the paper industry. The Wage Board held that the wages of these craftsmen "ought to be based on the same system, no matter to which union they belong." [63] The labor member of the Wage

[62] Wage Board, Case No. 39, November 28, 1946.
[63] Wage Board, Cases No. 17, 18, and 19, August 19, 1946.

Board, an official of the Federation of Labor, concurred in the decision, emphasizing the industrial unit bias of the Federation.

2. *Role of the mediation proposal.* The often-expressed fear that mediation would be seriously handicapped by operation of compulsory arbitration failed to materialize. If the Wage Board had formulated its policies without regard to the results of mediation, the latter would indeed have become a mere formality, with the real arena of bargaining transferred to the board's hearing room. The fact that the board in all but a few instances chose instead to back the State Mediator in his appraisal of the merits of disputes served instead to augment the importance of the mediation proposal.[64]

In only two cases were mediation proposals submitted to the Wage Board under those provisions of the Act of 1944 (Section 5, first paragraph) restricting the board to the option of ratifying the proposal without alteration, or rejecting it *in toto*. It will be recalled that the State Mediator may employ this section of the law only where there has been prior agreement with the negotiators on both sides that he shall formulate a proposal.

In the first case the Stone Workers' Union had demanded of four companies producing steatite and talc that hourly rates be raised from 1.17 to 1.67 kroner per hour. On June 25, 1946, a district mediator formulated a proposal in which he suggested an hourly rate of 1.37 kroner. When this was rejected by both parties, mediation proceedings were renewed, and a new proposal, this time with the approval of the negotiators, was made. The rate proposed was 1.45 kroner. In a referendum on the proposal, the employers voted to accept it, but the workers rejected it on the express ground that "the hourly rate should have been 1.52 kroner instead of the proposed 1.45 kroner."

The Wage Board, in sustaining the mediator, stated:

The wage question has been under negotiation and mediation since May 20, 1946. The mediator set forth a proposal on June 25, 1946, containing an hourly rate of 1.37 kroner, which was rejected by both parties, and issued a new proposal of 1.45 kroner on August 24, 1946. This proposal had the concurrence of the negotiators on both sides. It is thus clear that the proposal was made by the mediator and recommended by the negotiators on both sides after very thorough considera-

[64] The mediation proposal is discussed above, pp. 102–104.

tion, and after an earlier vain attempt to agree upon a lower figure. There is nothing to indicate that the proposal is based on inaccurate evidence, nor anything to indicate that the board should regard the proposal as unreasonable.[65]

The second instance of this character, in which the workers had also rejected by referendum a mediation proposal approved by their negotiators, was similarly treated, the board merely noting that the mediation proposal "by and large provided a reasonable and equitable solution of the dispute." [66]

On occasions when the mediation proposal had been formulated without the explicit consent of the negotiators, and subsequently rejected either by the negotiators or in balloting, the board was inclined to accept the proposal either without modification or with only minor alterations of no real substantive import.[67] There have been several cases, however, in which the Wage Board granted the workers more favorable terms than the mediator had suggested,[68] and these tended to promote the repudiation of mediation proposals in other negotiations being conducted concurrently.

A dissenting employer board member pointed out that

when the parties' negotiators, after a series of negotiation and mediation meetings, agree upon a proposal that bears the stamp of the State Mediator, the Wage Board should assume that an appropriate conclusion has been reached. The majority judgment signifies so serious a divergence from the State Mediator's proposals as to jeopardize the very institution of mediation.[69]

Despite these exceptions, the mediator appears to have assumed a greater rather than a lesser role in the bargaining process. In fact, an element of compulsion is almost introduced into mediation, for if he chooses to do so the mediator may assume quasi-arbitral functions, secure in the knowledge that the Wage Board will back him up in the absence of unusual circumstances. But

[65] Wage Board, Case No. 26, September 25, 1946.

[66] Wage Board, Case No. 65, May 9, 1947.

[67] Wage Board, Case No. 28, October 4, 1946; Case No. 30, October 12, 1946; Case No. 40, November 30, 1946; Case No. 44, December 18, 1946; Case No. 49, January 18, 1947; Case No. 58, March 8, 1947; Case No. 70, June 23, 1947.

[68] Wage Board, Case No. 15, August 6, 1946; Case No. 33, October 30, 1946; Case No. 42, December 1946; Case No. 57, March 4, 1947.

[69] Wage Board, Case No. 15, August 6, 1946.

since this course would tend to destroy the mediation system in the long run, the three State Mediators since 1945 have wisely refrained from imposing their views on unwilling negotiators, and have confined their formal proposals to situations in which the negotiators were agreed upon a settlement, but could not approve it publicly for tactical reasons.

3. Fringe issues. To lighten the burden of its work, the Wage Board constantly endeavored to avoid the determination of fringe issues in dispute. The parties were urged to stipulate as many points as they could, leaving only the cardinal issues for adjudication. In this way, the work load was kept down to manageable proportions, and thus far it has proved unnecessary to appoint the supplementary arbitration boards originally viewed as a probable necessity.

Nevertheless, the Wage Board was at times obliged to wander far afield when disputants were unable to resolve minor problems. In one such case it refused a thirty-five hour basic night shift to lithographers, and overruled worker objection to a contract clause permitting employers to introduce hourly performance-control cards into their shops.[70] In another, employers were ordered to bear the expense of cleaning the work clothes of their employees, but the board balked at considering the question of appropriate ratios between the number of journeymen and helpers to be employed.[71] In a third instance, the board awarded 450 workers engaged in the construction of power lines a supplement of 10 öre per hour for work performed in mountainous areas.[72]

One additional case is worthy of special note. There was a controversy between the Office and Commercial Workers' Union and the Commercial Employers' Association involving numerous agreements covering employees in offices and retail stores throughout the country. In writing a national contract for the first time, the negotiators were able to agree upon all but a few points. The most important of the unsettled issues were: closing time of stores and offices on the day before holidays; the question of whether individual employees should be required to perform mo-

---

[70] Wage Board, Case No. 28, October 4, 1946.

[71] Wage Board, Case No. 22, September 11, 1946. The employer was ordered to provide working clothes at his own expense in Case No. 53, February 22, 1947.

[72] Wage Board, Case No. 38, November 27, 1946.

notonous machine work full time; length of service required for one extra week of vacation; vacation rights of employees performing compulsory military service; and the number of days of annual sick leave. The Wage Board decided each of these matters in turn, without opinion.[73]

THE EFFICACY OF COMPULSORY ARBITRATION

Two years of experience with compulsory governmental arbitration are not sufficient to provide the basis for final judgment of the practicability of thus determining wages under planning. Nevertheless, analysis of the seventy-odd decisions rendered by the Norwegian Wage Board from 1945 to 1947, together with relevant expressions of opinion by government, labor, and management representatives permit the formulation of tentative conclusions on what is rightly coming to be regarded as one of the most crucial problems of economic planning.[74]

It should be stated parenthetically that the Wage Board's activities had a decisive effect upon the wage level during the period under review. While many, indeed the great majority of collective agreements were negotiated without the board's intercession, its decisions in key disputes set the pattern for private bargaining. The cost-of-living supplement cases of 1945 and 1946, moreover, were universal in their impact upon the remuneration of labor.

The conversion of Norwegian labor leadership to the desirability of government arbitration from long-standing, implacable opposition to it began even before the war, when the Labor government felt obligated to employ *ad hoc* arbitration in several stubborn disputes.[75] The arguments advanced in favor of compulsory arbitration from the trade union side at that time stem directly from the Marxist conception of the state as an instrument of class power, and indicate clearly that arbitration was by no means conceived of as a judicial process:

[73] Wage Board, Case No. 20, August 29, 1946.

[74] For example, "Of all possible points of conflict between conscious planning of priorities and traditional freedom, the regulation of wages is likely to prove the most stormy. Successful planning may indeed be dependent here upon deep changes in social attitudes." Barbara Wooton, *Freedom Under Planning*, p. 102.

[75] In addition to the transportation strike discussed above, p. 110, a dispute in the lumber industry was handled similarly in 1938.

If the influence of the workers is so strong that they can determine the form and legislative framework of compulsory arbitration, the situation is quite different than under a bourgeois government. If important social interests with respect to particular groups of workers and trade unions make it desirable to have a dispute adjudicated by compulsory arbitration, we ought to leave the way open. Our opponents have always used their political strength. The workers must do the same. Or we will make no progress . . .

People are fearful of certain consequences. If a labor government exercises its political power, will not bourgeois governments do the same? That is the objection usually raised, and it is apparently quite convincing. But does not the employer use his political power in any event? He reasons and acts cold-bloodedly, no matter what we do. We must learn that.[76]

The appropriateness of compulsory arbitration for something more than averting crises was borne upon the Labor government soon after it decided in 1945 to attempt stabilization of prices and wages, and even more so when comprehensive economic planning was introduced. For it became apparent that planned production involved the planning of wages, that until trade unions were able to shift their functional orientation from the quest for higher money wages to an identification of increased output with worker welfare, "the price of planning must either be compulsory industrial direction or compulsory arbitration backed by legal sanctions. If it comes to that, compulsory arbitration is much to be preferred to industrial direction." [77]

But it was a far cry from advocacy of compulsory arbitration by the planning authorities to its acceptance by those immediately responsible for determining wages. The system of collective bargaining developed before the war was deeply ingrained in the habits of thought of both workers and employers, and commanded universal respect. There was no disposition on either side to abandon it in favor of administrative wage fixing. Workers still felt that if their demands could not be achieved through regular trade channels, the wielding of economic weapons should be the last resort. The employers were fearful of government intervention in the regulation of labor conditions, particularly when the government was run by their adversaries.

[76] *Landsorganisasjons Meddelelseblad,* 1938, No. 2. See also an interesting article by Gunnar Ousland, *ibid.,* 1938, No. 5.
[77] Barbara Wooton, p. 120.

In an effort to render government arbitration more palatable, and more effective, its regulatory aspects were played down. Instead, emphasis was placed upon a more limited conception of it as a court of last resort when the regular collective bargaining mechanism had failed. All the forms of collective bargaining were carried out faithfully as a preliminary to arbitration, even though much of the substance may have been missing; in many situations both trade union leaders and employer representatives were aware from the beginning that agreement by direct negotiation was impossible. Arbitration was presented as a temporary necessity during a period of industrial reconstruction, and to affirm its transitory character each renewal of arbitration legislation was limited to a maximum period of one year.

For similar reasons it was insisted that the Wage Board was a judicial rather than an administrative body. Nominally, the board enjoyed complete independence of the executive branch of government, and was theoretically free to dispense justice impartially without regard to other consequences. Actually, it functioned in close coöperation with the Ministry of Labor and other interested agencies of government. Almost every decision indicated an awareness of the practical implications that flowed from the government's economic plans, and often there was explicit acknowledgment of the binding nature of current governmental policy. While it would be an exaggeration to say that the Wage Board consulted with members of the government in every case and on every issue, there is little doubt that major decisions were made after joint consideration by members of the board — a majority of whom, incidentally, were chosen from among "friends" of labor — and government officials.

The nominal independence of the Wage Board served further to enhance its utility as a regulatory agency, from the point of view of the Labor government, by enabling the board to effectuate governmental wage policy without directly implicating the administration and its trade union allies. Direct denial by the government of wage demands might well have led to the development of a rift between the leadership and the rank and file of the labor movement, particularly in the face of a militant Communist minority seeking every pretext to undermine the position of the Labor Party. Interposition of the Wage Board in a sense shielded the labor leadership from importunate rank and file demands that were manifestly incompatible with national economic policy. The onus of making unpopular decisions was shifted to an apparently impartial agency; and the effect was furthered by the almost invariable expressions of disagreement and dissatisfaction with Wage Board awards uttered by the union leadership concerned.

Although there were a few instances of defiance, in the main workers — and employers invariably — accepted the outcome of arbitration with good grace. The enforcement of arbitration awards by a labor government is essentially a problem of trade union discipline, which is dealt with in the following chapter. Suffice it to say that the problem cannot be solved simply by declaring certain strikes illegal, fixing appropriate penalties, and imposing those penalties when violations occur. In a democracy, a labor government cannot enforce penal sanctions against its constituents individually in controversies arising out of industrial relations and expect to remain in office very long. Nor can the dilemma be solved by limiting penalties to collective defiance, since the trade union bodies which constitute the obvious targets will ordinarily be doing their utmost to secure compliance. Unless there is firm and widespread conviction that arbitration is just and equitable, it will not work.

No responsible Norwegian official has even intimated that compulsory arbitration of labor disputes may have to be prolonged beyond the emergency period of postwar reconstruction. On the contrary, numerous declarations can be found to the effect that once normal production is restored, final responsibility for the fixing of wages and other conditions of labor will be returned to the collective bargaining parties.[78] But it is difficult to understand how the task of reconciling individual wage bargains with the national plan will then be accomplished unless the trade unions themselves are willing and able to undertake it. In the short run, at least, it seems likely that "the doctrine that planned production implies planned wages will find readier acceptance if it becomes

[78] A recent trade union release declares: "Our leading trade union officers have now expressed the view that time for abolishing the Wage Board has come. The trade unions want the machinery of negotiation and mediation to be reinstituted on the same basis as before." *Trade Union News Bulletin from Norway,* November 1948. Cf., "Some form of arbitration as an alternative to industry-wide strikes will undoubtedly become a permanent feature of industrial relations in a Labour Britain." J. B. Jeffreys, *Trade Unions in a Labour Britain* (London, 1947), p. 6.

the rule for wages to be fixed by public authorities than if we rely on a changed spirit in collective bargaining." [79]

The institutional background of Norway's most recent experience with compulsory arbitration renders dubious the application of any generalizations therefrom to the contemporary American scene. Government arbitration undoubtedly weakened collective bargaining, but is that not inevitable anyway when labor achieves political power? Arbitration as practiced in Norway was accompanied by a period of labor peace when neighboring countries were experiencing a great deal of conflict; but how much credit should be given to arbitration per se, and how much to the fact that behind the arbitration system stood a government and a trade union movement enjoying the confidence of the workers? If any inference can be drawn, it is the futility of debating the merits of particular institutional means of solving labor problems *in vacuo*.

[79] Wooton, p. 119.

CHAPTER XIII

TRADE UNIONS UNDER A LABOR GOVERNMENT

THE NORWEGIAN LABOR MOVEMENT finally achieved in 1945 the long-sought goal of its political activities, an absolute parliamentary majority. The Labor government that assumed office in that year was virtually assured of a four-year term under Norwegian parliamentary practice. Moreover, prospects for a longer tenure appeared bright in the absence of some unforeseen catastrophe.

Although recent years have witnessed a diminution of the revolutionary ardor that prompted affiliation with the Comintern in the years following World War I, the Labor Party has never renounced its ultimate goal of transforming Norway into a socialist state. "The Norwegian Labor Party stands for democratic socialism," read the draft of a new statement of principles prepared in 1948, "and the party will employ democratic means in the construction of a new society." [1]

In practice, the Labor Party has been cautious. Preoccupied with immediate administrative tasks, and fearful of interfering with production, there has been little disposition thus far to nationalize industry from doctrinaire considerations alone. A thoroughgoing system of economic planning through government regulation has been adopted, but there have been only hesitant steps toward the socialist state in its classical conception.

But despite a desire to postpone institutional change until the economic ravages of the war could be made good, certain fundamental problems involving trade unions and their functions manifested themselves from the start. Ideologies and worker attitudes that had proved successful in the struggle for power no longer sufficed once power was achieved. It became increasingly evident, when the Labor government had commenced its ambitious program of economic planning, that a reorientation of political and economic thinking on the part of trade union workers was essential if disastrous failure was to be averted.

[1] Norwegian Information Services, *Nytt fra Norge,* New York, March 25, 1948.

In response to the requirements of the new situation, basic changes have begun to take place in the entire character of Norwegian trade unionism. An analysis of this experience is of interest not only for its own sake but also as an illustration of the possible course that trade unionism may take under democratic socialism in other Western-European countries.

Trade unionism has been nurtured on the doctrine that its primary function is the protection of workers in an inevitable clash of interest with employers. Consequently, its major preoccupation has been with bargaining and combat. The Norwegian trade union movement was no more prepared than would be its counterparts in other countries to assume the functions of government suddenly thrust upon it.

Part of the difficulty lies in the nature of a democratic transition to socialism. When a revolution occurs, and the entire institutional fabric must be rewoven, the reformulation of objectives becomes an obvious necessity. But when the process of change is gradual, conscious adaptation is a much less simple matter.

An added difficulty is the transitory nature of political power in a democratic state. Not only must current circumstances be taken into account, but the factor of expectations regarding future contingencies is an important datum as well. Thus trade unions — and workers — might be more willing to consider seriously fundamental modifications of policy if they felt confident of long-run power, even though the immediate economic structure were predominantly private capitalism.

This may in part account for the relatively slight impact of the prewar minority Labor government upon trade union structure and function, although the inability of that government to effectuate its plans for far reaching social change, in view of its reliance upon nonsocialist political parties for continued existence, was undoubtedly a major factor. That some shift in the trade union theory of its own future role was beginning to occur, however, is evidenced by the following statement from the then chairman of the Federation of Labor in a printed symposium designed for the use of workers' education groups:

In their own interest, and in the interest of the masses of the population, workers must take into account broad social considerations in their collective bargaining. Each controversy must be judged in the light of its effects upon the over-all policy of the trade union movement and the party. Otherwise we will tear down with one hand what we are engaged in building with the other.

Obviously this does not mean that, in general, workers yield the right to strike. Strikes have occurred frequently even under the Labor government . . . A cold-blooded analysis of the operation and results of lengthy labor strife, however, yields the conclusion that it is rarely worth while.[2]

But there was little tangible evidence of change beyond such words of caution. At any time it might again be necessary to enter the arena of industrial conflict; the combative apparatus and psychology of trade unions had to be maintained intact against such eventuality. More than that, the contemporary rise of fascism on the continent of Europe meant that momentarily the labor movement might become involved in a struggle for its very existence. In the circumstances it is little wonder that theoretical discussions of future trade union forms aroused little interest. This was true not only of Norway but of Europe generally.

The stability of Norwegian labor's parliamentary majority after 1945 and the optimism that prevailed within the labor movement regarding its future were more conducive to a broader approach to the problems of trade unionism under a labor government. While the debate was still in its infancy, however, the pressure of immediate problems forced functional adaptation almost without conscious awareness on the part of even the trade union leadership. The average worker remained scarcely cognizant of either the need for or the fact of innovation in the trade union sphere.

The trade unions found themselves obliged to reconsider time-honored doctrine regarding wage policy, industrial disputes, collective bargaining and labor's share in the managerial function. The requirements of economic planning and, beyond that, of nationalized industry, often ran directly counter to some of the most firmly held preconceptions in the trade union mentality. The stresses and strains produced by the tug between institutional conservatism and economic reality proved to be one of the critical elements upon which success of the planning experiment hinged.

[2] Olav Hindahl, "Fagbevegelsens samfundsmessige stilling," *Fagbevegelsens Økonomiske Problemer* (Oslo, 1938), p. 267.

WAGE POLICY

Even under the system of industry-wide collective bargaining that had been developed in prewar Norway, individual national unions were not much concerned with the wider economic repercussions of their wage demands. Employers could be expected to bring out all the relevant arguments against wage increases and to offer sufficient resistance to wage rates that were excessive. Very little economic research was sponsored by the unions, the few staff members hired for this purpose being engaged mainly in statistical work bearing directly on contract negotiation. The chairman of the Federation of Labor summed up the situation in the following terms:

There is a long way to go before we can say that trade unions are sufficiently realistic when it comes to making demands and voting on new contracts. The individual is inclined above all to take a position based upon the interests of his own group or the district he represents. And so it is forgotten that such matters must be judged from a class and a social point of view.[3]

With the institution of stringent price control after 1945 and the deliberate paring of profit margins to what was acknowledgedly a bare minimum, as part of the postwar program of Norwegian labor, the trade unions found themselves obliged to assume responsibility for price as well as wage movements, whether they wanted to or not. In view of the manpower shortage employers had little objection to wage increases provided they were able to secure appropriate price relief. Unions were thus placed in the anomalous position of pressing for wage changes which, if granted, would upset the very price policy which they themselves had initiated as the most consistent with the interests of workers.

If the view that trade unions cannot change the focus of their wage policy or the means of negotiating wage changes without endangering their future were accurate,[4] the Norwegian planning

[3] Olav Hindahl, "Fagbevegelsens samfundsmessige stilling," *Fagbevegelsens Økonomiske Problemer,* p. 270.

[4] This is essentially the argument advanced with respect to the British unions by H. W. Singer, "Wage Policy in Full Employment," *The Economic Journal,* December, 1947.

experiment would probably have died stillborn. Fortunately for their aspirations, the Norwegian trade unions were able to make the necessary adjustments in both these matters, facilitating the evolution of methods whereby deviations of actual from expected wage developments, which could attain any magnitude in particularistic wage determination, were kept within the limits consistent with economic planning.

Adoption of a national wage policy determined in consultation with government was a means by which it was sought to balance worker income with the availability of consumer goods. This was facilitated by the degree to which authority had already become centralized in the Federation of Labor as opposed to its constituent unions.[5] The Federation was thus in a position at the beginning of 1948 to warn its affiliates not to seek wage increases except for unreasonably low-paid workers, and to require all prospective wage demands to receive its prior approval. The individual wage movements of 1946 and 1947 were also coördinated, partly through the efforts of the Federation of Labor and partly as a result of the operation of compulsory arbitration.

Another major change in trade union wage outlook was induced by the possibility, under the Labor government, of operating on two fronts — money wages and prices. Without political power, trade unions are confined to the variable of money wages in seeking to increase real wages, although they may be fully aware of the implications of wage-price relationships. But when they can

---

[5] See Chapter II. The problem has proved much more difficult in Great Britain, where the Trades Union Congress traditionally enjoyed very little power over the policies of its affiliates. At the now famous debate on wage policy at the Margate Conference of the Labor Party, Mr. Arthur Deakin, chairman of the powerful Transport and General Workers' Union, stated unequivocally: "Under no circumstances at all will we accept the position that the responsibility for the fixation of wages and the regulation of conditions of employment is one for the Government . . . It would be disastrous, it would create chaos among the rank and file, and this would be destructive of the economy of the country, and of the effort so vitally necessary at this time." In reply, a delegate from the political side of the labor movement said: "I will say without hesitation—and I am sure that my Party will back me up—that I have never before heard such an irresponsible and pernicious speech as we heard from Arthur Deakin today . . . Yes, there will be trouble until some of our Trade Union leaders begin to think on Socialist lines for the first time." *Report of the Forty-Sixth Annual Conference of the Labour Party*, 1947, pp. 144, 148.

exercise control over prices through government, unions are able to pursue the goal of higher real wages through alternative means.

The Norwegian labor leadership decided in 1945 that a stable price level was the most efficient avenue of approach to an improvement in worker living standards. This entailed moderation in money wage demands, a policy which was not palatable to the average worker. The following proclamation, issued by the representative council of the Federation of Labor on November 28, 1947, is typical of the efforts that were made to gain widespread member understanding and support for the altered wage policy:

We must realize that a general increase in current money wages cannot be accomplished without an increase in prices and a consequent increase in the cost of living . . .

To protect the position we have achieved, safeguard the nation's economic independence and prevent the disasters of inflation, the main task of the trade union movement today must be to coöperate in increasing production, and through sharpening of price control to force the cost of living down and thereby further raise the wage earner's living standards.[6]

While relegation of the customary quest for higher money wages to a secondary position obviously does not imply renunciation of basic trade union goals, it does mean drastic modification of an aim always regarded as synonymous with economic progress in trade union thinking. Workers may appreciate intellectually the rationale of the new policy, but it will require a long period of indoctrination before they accept wholeheartedly its application to their own pay envelopes. However, the almost universal recognition among Norwegian trade union leaders that a change in policy was desirable, and their willingness and ability to act upon this conviction, to seek major reforms under circumstances that often entailed considerable risk to their personal political status, indicate that effective leadership may overcome the conservative propensities inherent in worker attitudes toward their conditions of labor.

INDUSTRIAL DISPUTES

Trade union function in the area of industrial controversy is also undergoing a metamorphosis. The view is gaining currency

[6] *Arbeiderbladet,* November 29, 1947.

that political pressure is more effective than economic action in coercing recalcitrant employers. Labor sponsorship of compulsory arbitration offers a case in point; the chairman of the Federation of Labor admitted quite frankly that it was "conditioned upon the political power situation in the country . . . With the shift in political power that occurred after the parliamentary elections in 1945 it was natural that we solve interest disputes in industrial relations through social intervention, without work stoppages." [7]

Even more important is the tendency on the part of trade unions to identify maximum output with labor welfare, which leads logically to the view that strikes are contradictory to the purposes of the labor movement. The following quotation from a workers' education pamphlet is indicative of this new philosophy:

In a planned economy, where the labor movement has political leadership, it is unthinkable that wage disputes should lead to great conflicts between workers and employers, with the public a sort of unwilling middleman . . . A planned economy is not the same as socialism. But it does mean that society plays an active role in the development, coördination, and conduct of economic life toward a goal set by itself . . .

It is outmoded and uneconomic to demonstrate by wasting labor time and stopping work. We must seek other and equally effective means of expressing our discontent, rather than have the production on which we ourselves are dependent reduced or halted entirely.[8]

It is proving more difficult for the Norwegian worker to make the mental adjustment required by this attitude toward strikes than in the case of the new wage policy. Reared in the tradition of Marxism, with its emphasis upon class conflict, and subjected to constant communist propaganda extolling direct action as the only means of redressing alleged grievances, he is somewhat resentful that his own leaders condemn strikes, particularly when the existence of a labor government has removed most of the risks involved in striking. Regardless of the political change, he still finds himself in the employ of private interests. It requires a good deal of sophistication to appreciate the underlying shifts in economic power that have occurred.

The gap between the leadership and the rank and file that tends

[7] *Arbeiderbladet,* December 31, 1947.
[8] Gunnar Ousland, *Se samfunnet gjennom verkstedet* (Oslo, 1946), pp. 21–22.

to develop from this aspect of trade union outlook constitutes one of the most serious threats to the socialist program. In recognition of the urgency of bridging this gap, an intensive educational program was undertaken by both the trade unions and the government. Members of the cabinet visited the larger factories during lunch hours and discussed with the workers the requirements of planning. The radio, the extensive labor press, and the resources of the well developed Workers' Education Association were employed to the same end. The following statement taken from a pamphlet distributed widely among workers indicates the type of argument that is being advanced:

We must come to regard open conflict as an archaic stage in trade union development, and attain a policy in which collective bargaining will more and more assume the character of general social and economic accounting in which the wages and conditions of all wage earners will be determined in relation to production and the supply of goods, and the requirements of other social classes . . .

We were once uncertain whether it would be possible to shape a new social order by democratic means. Yes, there were times when it was dogma that a new society could not be established without revolution. It was then that we looked upon the strike as "revolutionary gymnastics" . . .

Both the objective and subjective situation after World War II have led the working class to declare its belief that the road forward to socialism can be achieved by democratic means. The strike has thus lost the justification it had in a revolutionary situation. We must only retain our preparedness in the event that new reactionary movements manifest themselves . . .

Too many trade unionists are still of the belief that the work stoppage is the only effective union weapon. It is to them the most radical and purest mode of expression, a blow on the table with the fist against the employer and society as a whole—the only thing reaction understands and respects. They will not understand that the strike represents a bygone point of view, a weapon belonging to a period when capitalists sat with complete power in the government, in municipalities and in the economy as a whole. Today a strike may result in greater harm to the labor movement and to socialism than to capitalists . . .

What was perhaps radical during the class conflict of the twenties is no longer radical today. It is reactionary because it interferes with the basic aims of the labor movement . . . We are no longer under a tyranny, either of the Gestapo or of capitalism. We live in an epoch of change, in which the form of production is shifting from private capitalism to coöperation and socialism . . . We must not be held back by methods and weapons that originated in the days of tyranny.[9]

There is a significant sentence in the quoted passage, reserving the possibility of the strike as an ultimate contingency, that recalls the lurking fear of an uncertain future. As long as industry remains predominantly in private hands, reversion to unrestricted capitalism would be relatively easy, should labor lose its electoral majority. Therefore it may be dangerous to oversell workers on the notion that they are automatically benefiting themselves by refraining from striking; a sharp distinction is made between the labor and the "bourgeois" state, leaving the door ajar for a return to the earlier trade union militancy should the latter replace the former.

Even beyond that, however, there is the question of how far it is possible to go in condemning the use of the strike without endangering political democracy. This problem has not yet been faced squarely, but the Soviet experience has convinced the socialists of Western Europe that the right to strike, not merely as a constitutional maxim, but as a political reality backed by organizational means, is the cornerstone of democracy regardless of the prevailing form of economic structure.

It is utopian to anticipate complete termination of work stoppages in a democratic society. Neither compulsory arbitration legislation nor the antistrike policies of the Norwegian Federation of Labor and its national affiliates have ushered in a period of absolute industrial peace. Since 1945 Norway has experienced numerous "unofficial" stoppages, most of them involving small numbers of workers and of short duration, but in the aggregate representing a not inconsiderable loss of working time to the economy.[10]

These stoppages have been of two kinds: those arising spontaneously over real or fancied grievances that workers felt were not being prosecuted with sufficient vigor by their unions, and those stimulated by the communist opposition to the socialist trade

[9] Gunnar Ousland, *Fagorganisasjons problemstilling i dag* (Oslo, 1946), pp. 20–40.

[10] Government statistics covering this type of stoppage are not available. The Employers' Association indicated that during the first nine months of 1947, there were forty-two such stoppages reported to it. *Arbeidsgiveren,* January 2, 1948.

union leadership for political reasons. A fertile source of controversy was employee objection to the continued employment of managerial and supervisory personnel whose patriotism during the period of German occupation was suspect.

Both the government and the trade unions formally expressed condemnation of such strikes when they occurred. Speaking before the first postwar Labor Party Congress, the Prime Minister declared:

The feeling of responsibility which I said must be brought home to each individual must, among other things, end illegal strikes. They are most unreasonable at a time like this when we are all supposed to be coöperating in building our country up again. Here in Norway we lack many of the commodities most necessary for daily use; we must purchase from foreign countries and pay for the commodities with our exports. Therefore it is tragic to see enterprises close down, for example in the cellulose industry, which through its exports could supply us with food, clothing, and necessary raw materials. It is tragic when we consider that we live in a democratic state. We will never win complete victory as long as we do not abide by the law. The majority of the people will not trust a movement which does not fully respect the country's laws.[11]

But repressive measures were out of the question. Nothing would be better calculated to evoke widespread sympathy for the strikers than the imposition of fines or imprisonment, or the use of the military. Norwegian socialists are of the firm conviction that the use of governmental force against workers engaged in industrial disputes is the most hazardous enterprise upon which a labor government could embark, regardless of the merits of the disputes.

They believe that the only effective course, in the long run, is persuasion exercised through individuals and organizations enjoying the confidence of the workers, that is, through officials and committees of their own and related trade unions. This procedure has been denounced as demagogic and opportunistic by employers,[12] who failed to perceive that repression would tend to under-

[11] *Arbeiderbladet,* September 8, 1945.

[12] For example, "If public opinion, which is in the first instance represented by the majority party in this country, does not insist that an unlawful strike is an *unlawful* strike, all the admiration within the ranks of employers for the

mine that sector of the political labor movement which is seeking to protect the democratic state.

A few examples may serve to make clear how this method of handling illegal strikes worked in practice. In the fall of 1946 the Oslo plumbers struck for a wage increase, a valid collective agreement then being in effect. Although the strike was instigated by communist elements within the local union, the men felt genuinely aggrieved by what they considered relatively low take-home pay. The effect of the stoppage was to halt completion of desperately needed housing units.

A few days after the plumbers had left their jobs, officials of the Building Workers' Union, with which the plumbers are affiliated, met with the strikers and urged that the stoppage be terminated, but to no avail. The strike dragged on for almost a month, intermittent attempts at settlement proving equally fruitless. There was vigorous debate in the labor press over responsibility for the strike, the socialists charging that the communists had instigated the walkout for political purposes while the communists denied complicity and termed the strike a genuine expression of rank and file dissatisfaction. However, no attempt was made to threaten or coerce the workers themselves.

At the end of a month enthusiasm among the strikers was on the wane and it was necessary to find a face-saving formula that would permit them to return to work. This was afforded by a meeting of the Oslo building trades, which resolved that the plumbers had a justifiable grievance that would be prosecuted expeditiously through regular trade union channels. On this promise the strike was called off.

While the costs of refraining from direct intervention were undoubtedly great, it is questionable whether any other measures would have been more effective in bringing the strike to an end. By its policy of abstention the Labor government avoided the politically dangerous label of "strikebreaker." By refusing to make

---

capable and devoted work being done within the labor movement will be replaced by new conceptions of demagogic indolence and slavish custom." *Arbeidsgiveren*, January 31, 1947. Again, "One can obviously not discount the fact that labor organizations have sought to prevent or bring to an end illegal strikes, but on the other hand there are also instances in which it is clear that the responsible trade union was playing the game of the illegally striking workers." *Arbeidsgiveren*, January 2, 1948.

concessions during the strike, it put workers on notice that similar wildcat stoppages were not likely to be productive of real gains.

Another serious illegal strike, in January 1947, involved the drivers of gasoline trucks serving the Oslo area. A nationwide collective agreement had been concluded shortly before the strike was called, in which the workers outside Oslo were given a relatively greater increase than the Oslo workers in order to eliminate a long-standing wage differential. Although the Oslo group voted against the agreement, it was adopted by a preponderance of the votes nationally.

The strike, which deprived the city of gasoline and paralyzed a good part of its economic life, was clearly in violation of law and of the collective agreement, but neither government nor trade union officials voiced outright condemnation. Instead, a conciliatory mien was adopted which employers characterized as "the old tone from prewar days." The labor press, as a tactical matter, assigned part of the blame to employers despite the fact that the legal position of the latter was unassailable. An editorial in the Labor Party newspaper commented:

> The current transport strike could undoubtedly have been prevented by slight flexibility on the part of the new leadership of the Employers' Association. The strike is clearly illegal, and obviously regrettable, but it is not sufficient to refuse a demand on purely formal grounds. Men in responsible positions, with sound judgment, should seek to determine the legitimacy of the demand and correct injustices . . .
>
> When one considers what has happened since liberation, the good will shown by workers and their leaders, greater understanding is to be expected, more human feeling, and a different social outlook from those who lead the Employers' Association. If the abruptness and shortsightedness that characterize this case signalize a new course, there is great danger ahead for the nation.[13]

Concurrently, repeated efforts were made from all sides to induce a return to work. It was impressed upon the strikers that their irresponsibility was affecting the livelihood of thousands of fellow workers. After a week of intense pressure from their own union leaders and prominent government officials, the strikers capitulated. They resumed work on the basis of a formula proposed by the Federation of Labor that involved no wage adjust-

[13] *Arbeiderbladet,* January 30, 1947.

ment but promised the inception of negotiations looking toward the introduction of a pension system.[14]

In a few cases involving small groups of strikers, trade unions have threatened to expel workers from membership. But since the union shop is not practiced in Norway, this would be a moral rather than an economic sanction since it would not lead to loss of employment.

The Labor government, in its dealings with "unofficial" strikers, has enjoyed the support of the regular trade union bodies. With a single short-lived exception, the postwar chairmen of all national unions have been members of the Labor Party, and could always be counted on to coöperate with the government in the last analysis. The strongly centralized character of the Norwegian trade union movement offered further insurance against defiance by official trade union action. Whether a policy of "sweating it out" could have been employed with equal effect if the trade unions were divided along factional lines, or where national unions enjoyed virtual autonomy, is highly problematical. Open trade union warfare against a labor government under such circumstances might well require repressive action, whatever the ultimate political cost, for the methods of persuasion employed in Norway would hardly be applicable.

What are the remedies open to an employer in the event of an illegal strike? He may file a complaint with the Labor Court against the individual strikers, charging them with breach of contract and requesting damages. Almost invariably, however, such suits have been withdrawn as part of the back-to-work agreement. Trade unions might even welcome the imposition of fines against illegal strikers, but the practical difficulties involved in collection appear insurmountable.

The employer also enjoys the legal right to terminate the employment relationship. As a practical matter, however, he would be reluctant to do so because of the difficulty or impossibility of securing replacements. This would be true regardless of the state of the labor market, for even with less than full employment, trade unions are not likely to consent to the employment of strikebreakers save in the exceptional case in which they desired to make an example of a recalcitrant group of strikers. Even

[14] Although this was done, nothing came of the negotiations.

then, prevailing worker solidarity would complicate the search for willing replacements.

Nor has the employer any recourse against the union, for almost invariably the latter will have complied with its statutory duty in discouraging the strike. Moreover, if an employer is a member of the Employers' Association he may not even offer to negotiate with the strikers without the approval of the association, and the likelihood is that the latter would insist that no concessions be granted the strikers beyond the terms of existing contracts. The position of employers faced with illegal strikes has been summarized by the chairman of the Employers' Association in these terms:

The employer can do nothing. The strike can be solved only by the workers and their organizations. The latter must now demonstrate that they have authority over the workers, and that agreements will be respected.[15]

The transfer of political power to the labor movement appears to vest trade unions with a preponderance of the responsibility for maintaining industrial peace and enforcing collective agreements. The role of the trade union as a militant representative of the worker is overshadowed by its new function as disciplinarian. Trade union leaders are less concerned with taking economic action against employers who refuse their demands than with the enforcement of terms of employment which, on the basis of information secured with the assistance of the government, are the most favorable that can be obtained. The social responsibility of trade unions, a matter of so much controversy in the past, becomes explicit; the alternative to adequate discharge of that responsibility seems to be nothing less than relinquishment of the long cherished goal of socialism.

COLLECTIVE BARGAINING

What is the future of collective bargaining in an economy evolving on the Norwegian pattern? The term bargaining implies an area of discretion within which either party is free to make or reject an offer. To what extent is an employer whose prerogatives

[15] *Arbeiderbladet,* February 1, 1947.

are sharply limited by price control, rationing of industrial goods, and profit limitations, able to enter into meaningful bargaining relationships with a trade union?

True bargaining requires, moreover, an element of indeterminacy in the results. If it is known at the start that the outcome of negotiations must correspond generally with a predetermined economic plan, precisely what is the scope of the negotiating function?

A case against probable continuance of traditional collective bargaining under planning has been made as follows:

> . . . the familiar methods of adjusting wages are quite inappropriate to the demands of economic planning. If we retain completely free collective bargaining, we should have somehow to induce a quite revolutionary change in the attitude of the parties to those bargains. It would, moreover, be a change which would completely do away with bargaining in the present sense of a tussle of economic strength and wits; and which would do violence to the fundamental *raison d'être* of the organizations which now make these bargains. Trade Unions, and their counterparts on the employer side, exist, as we have said, to get all they can for their members. They would be turned upside down and inside out, if they renounced this function in favor of the task of helping to regulate wages and conditions of employment in such a way as to match labor supply with the requirements of public plans.[16]

There is not yet sufficient experience with planning in Norway to provide a basis for conclusive judgments on the future of collective bargaining. It seems clear, however, that while collective bargaining is likely to persist for some time to come, it is undergoing modification in substance if not in form.

Wage determination through collective bargaining has certain important advantages, even at the expense of precision in planning estimates and goals. In the first place, workers are accustomed to regulation of their labor conditions by the somewhat stylized mechanism of collective bargaining. Contract reopening, preliminary negotiation, mediation, arbitration if necessary, and finally conclusion of a written agreement may be as important in themselves as in the results they produce. Certainly Norwegian trade union officials are convinced, to judge by their actions, that devi-

[16] Wooton, *Freedom Under Planning*, p. 113.

ation from habitual bargaining patterns would complicate enforcement of the ensuing agreements.

Secondly, it is recognized that as long as any substantial part of the economy remains in private hands, differential profits will have to be permitted in order to provide an efficiency incentive. Price regulation, for example, has not been designed to produce uniform operating results; on the contrary, it is premised on the theory that efficient producers should earn higher profits. Minimization of cost, including labor cost, remains a valid entrepreneurial objective.

The ability of an individual firm to secure relatively favorable wage rates is limited in Norway by the prevalent practice of industry-wide bargaining. Even where individual bargaining persists, trade unions are apt to demand standard contracts of employers to prevent competitive underbidding (since 1945, overbidding) of the union scale. Nevertheless, within the framework of national agreements there are often exceptional clauses bargained for on the basis of peculiar local circumstances, specified in the agreements themselves.

Moreover, through bargaining with respect to plant occupational structure, incentive systems, and piece-rate determination, and rates for new and changed jobs in dynamic situations, all of which are determined largely on the plant level *after* the collective agreement has been negotiated, a perspicacious entrepreneur might gain a real advantage over his less acute rival. Employers are encouraged to produce as cheaply as possible, and this type of collective bargaining provides one avenue for the exercise of managerial ability to that end.

A third point is that the function of collective bargaining is by no means limited to wage setting. Most non-wage conditions of employment, often as important as wages, continue to be determined by negotiation on the historical pattern. Despite the tendency, predating the Labor government, to transfer such non-wage subjects as the length of vacation periods from collective bargaining to government legislation, there is a widespread belief within the trade union movement itself that it would be unwise to bureaucratize the collective agreement. It is felt that methods of handling grievances, seniority, specific shop rules, and kindred matters are best decided at the local level by the individuals most familiar with the details, as a guarantee against inflexibility and the creation of situations in which workers feel obliged to strike in order to secure hearings of their complaints.

Finally, to the extent that nationalization of industry precludes further bargaining with private employers, collective bargaining between trade unions and government agencies may emerge as a substitute. This is not a novel conception for Norwegians, since civil servants and employees of state-owned enterprises have long enjoyed by law the right to bargain collectively, including the right to strike, and many are represented by the standard trade unions.[17] Although the precise manner in which nationalized industry will be organized has not yet been decided, it is certain that worker participation in industrial control will be through the government rather than by direct trade union participation in management.[18] Thus the unions will not be bargaining with themselves; factory management will be likely to have different immediate interests, and maintain a different point of view on labor conditions, in spite of its ultimate responsibility to the labor movement.

But if it is incorrect to assume that the assumption of office by a stable labor government pursuing a policy of economic planning eliminates the logical basis for collective bargaining, it is equally erroneous to expect that the traditional system will remain unaltered. Particularly when the unit within which uniform decisions are made is a broad one, covering entire industries or multi-industrial groups, certain limits will have to be imposed by the state upon wage setting in both an upward and downward direction. Provided the trade unions are able to maintain their independent identity, a species of supplementary bargaining may arise between them and the government, "a new type of indirect bargaining through government for redistribution of real income," [19] in the process of which such limits will be established. Employers must expect, however, that in the event of real interest conflicts the power of the state will inevitably be thrown into the balance on the side of the worker.

Even in this altered scheme of things the employer retains an

[17] See above, pp. 117–120.

[18] On this point see Robert A. Dahl, "Workers' Control of Industry and the British Labor Party," *American Political Science Review,* October 1947, p. 875.

[19] Forsey, "Trade Union Labor Policy Under Full Employment," in *Insights Into Labor Issues,* p. 312.

important bargaining function; as one of the Labor government ministers put it, "let us not be too sure that one fine day we shall not get a law, whether through negotiation or otherwise, which will make employer associations effective and useful cogs in the social machinery." [20] Presumably, the more effectively an employer represents his own interests, the more useful the social function he performs. The employer who readily grants wage increases when they are demanded of him, and immediately runs to the price authorities for relief, is contributing neither to efficient production nor to the maintenance of labor discipline. To quote an employer source, the employer becomes "a watchful sparring partner, a fourth wall which can be used to dam up irresponsible demands." [21]

Whatever the future may hold, it seems clear that Norwegian collective bargaining has already undergone substantive changes of no little import. The experience of two years under the postwar Labor government was summed up by the Employers' Association in the following terms:

In the collective bargaining that has taken place since the war, it has been, practically speaking, the workers' own shop stewards and trade union officials who have drawn up the main lines of new agreements. The workers have had dominant parliamentary strength — if not always in the foreground, at least as a final trump card — and they could always threaten to establish one-sided arbitration boards and pass one-sided laws. It is certainly accurate to say that they have determined the development of the last years in accordance with the policies they considered provident.[22]

THE MANAGERIAL FUNCTION AND PRODUCTIVITY

With the advent of a planned economy, novel concepts of ownership and management are created. Maximization of individual profit is no longer considered to be a valid social end. The entrepreneur tends to lose his right to dispose of his resources at

[20] *Arbeidsgiveren,* January 16, 1948.

[21] *Arbeidsgiveren,* January 16, 1948.

[22] *Arbeidsgiveren,* September, 26, 1947. The import of this quotation is not that individual workers and union officials, as contrasted with the Labor government and the Federation of Labor, have determined labor policy, but rather that the working group taken as a whole, vis-à-vis the employer group, was in a position to make final decisions.

will, and becomes instead a social steward who holds property in trust on condition that he operate it in the general interest, even if it should mean running at a loss or at a profit below the former incentive level.

The historian of the Norwegian trade union movement, a veteran socialist, has given expression to the relevant current views of the Norwegian labor leadership as follows:

In our society the power of the capitalist is sharply reduced. There are already large sectors of the economy that are either socialized or coöperatively managed. But the private capitalistic sector is also thoroughly regulated. Capitalists hold their property rights in trust . . .

We must understand that through the shops we work indirectly for society. In reality the capitalists are only intermediaries between us and society. In the present situation it is of little significance whether we work for a nationalized, a coöperative, or a private factory. The output is in all cases equally necessary for society . . . To delay or reduce production is a crime against society, our own society, in which we ourselves have taken power.[23]

From this standpoint, management efficiency becomes a matter of direct and immediate trade union concern. The Norwegian trade unions have demanded some voice in management with the object of assuring the best possible utilization of resources. Their aspirations have been satisfied, at least for the time being, by an agreement with the Employers' Association providing for the establishment of labor-management production committees.[24]

This agreement made compulsory the organization of a production committee in every enterprise employing twenty full-time workers during a calendar year; committees were also to be set up in smaller enterprises upon demand of the employer or a majority of the employees. The production committee is conceived as an advisory body with the right to receive information from management on production, sales, and economic problems gen-

[23] Ousland, *Se samfunnet gjennom verkstedet,* pp. 9–11.

[24] Similar bodies were set up in Norway after World War I pursuant to legislation designed to curb the revolutionary ferment within the labor movement. The 163 factory committees then established were short lived and proved to be of little influence. For a discussion of the production committee movement in Europe since 1945, see Henry Grünbaum, *Industrielt Demokrati* (Copenhagen, 1946). The text of the Norwegian agreement of 1946 is contained in Appendix B.

erally; to consider means of rationalizing production and improving health and safety conditions; and to supervise in-plant training. However, it may not deal with matters involving wages and hours, which continue to be adjusted through collective bargaining. The problem of drawing the jurisdictional line between the trade union and the production committee is left to union shop stewards and the local production committee itself.

Each committee consists of representatives of management, technical and office employees, and manual workers. The number of representatives of labor and management may be equal, though not necessarily, for there is no formal voting on disputed issues. Labor representatives are elected by secret ballot of all workers in the establishment, usually for a term of two years. Meetings are held monthly, with regular agendas distributed to committee members at least three days in advance of the meeting.

To coördinate the work of individual production committees, a national advisory committee was established, composed of two representatives each of the Employers' Association and the Federation of Labor, having final authority to adjudicate such disputes as may arise from the operation of the system. In the event that this committee cannot agree, the chairman of the Labor Court serves as arbitrator.

Although they felt obliged to conclude the agreement, employers were not overly enthusiastic about it. The Employers' Association found a ray of hope in the implicit recognition it gave to the idea that progress lay in increased production rather than redistribution of income, and that feather-bedding and the slowdown were harmful to labor's interests. But it was feared that the production committees were intended to give workers technical insight into management problems as a preliminary to nationalization of industry. More specifically, employers have objected to the requirement that the committees are to be supplied with information relating to the establishment's affairs. The agreement is vague on the precise nature of the information to be furnished, and the Employers' Association has taken the position that the employer has "considerable discretion with reference to the information of an economic nature that must be submitted." It is not unlikely, however, that the worker representatives will demand data which under ordinary circumstances would not be divulged to anyone outside of management.

If they are interested in achieving greater participation in the conduct of managerial affairs, the Norwegian trade unions have also evidenced their willingness to assume a share of the responsibility for operating results. Campaigns have been undertaken by the unions, with the moral and financial support of the government, to raise labor productivity. Workers are exhorted to increase their output by more intensive application to their tasks, overtime work, decreased absenteeism and production competitions.[25]

Another illustration of trade union interest in productivity is afforded by an agreement concluded in 1947 between the Federation of Labor and the Employers' Association setting forth a procedure for joint time and motion studies. Management agreed "to provide the time study steward or stewards elected [by the workers] the theoretical and practical training necessary to enable them satisfactorily to fulfill their tasks," and to pay them regular wages for both the training period and the time spent in actual time study work. The unions agreed in return "to coöperate loyally to obtain accurate results." [26]

However, this sharp break with traditional trade union antipathy to the techniques of scientific management by no means received the automatic approval of rank and file workers. It proved necessary, before the rationale of the new policy could even begin to seep down to the base of the trade union pyramid, to engage in intensive educational activities designed to convince workers that their habitual modes of thought were no longer appropriate. It is interesting to find official publications of the trade unions explaining sympathetically the work of Frederick Taylor and other

---

[25] In a public address, the Prime Minister commented on such a campaign: "Many will remember the 'overtime action' which began last year on the initiative of the Information Committee for Reconstruction Work. A study tour was arranged for shop stewards in plants playing an important role in the reconstruction program. When they came home they resolved to set in motion 'overtime actions' . . . As a result of the campaign I can cite the fact that a large foundry was able to increase its deliveries to Finmark by 25 per cent during the period of the campaign. Another establishment increased its production 15 per cent, and in all plants absenteeism was reduced significantly." *Arbeiderbladet,* December 15, 1947. References to similar achievements have appeared in the labor press with increasing frequency.

[26] The text of the agreement is contained in Appendix C.

American efficiency engineers,[27] and arguing against the idea that technological advance results in unemployment.[28] The Employers' Association was led to the wry comment that "when the labor movement suddenly found itself shouldered with political and economic responsibility it was forced to adopt a different propaganda line, one which earlier had been more popular in *other* circles, those circles which had been fighting such slogans as sabotage and reduction of labor tempo." [29]

LONG-TERM PROSPECTS

That a radical transformation of Norwegian economic institutions is occurring despite the absence of such an obvious manifestation as industrial nationalization on any considerable scale, is hardly to be doubted. The chairman of the Federation of Labor referred to postwar events as "a quiet revolution;" [30] the Employers' Association agreed that "we live in an era characterized by peaceful revolution. Significant changes in concepts of property rights are taking place, and a new ethic is in the making." [31]

This development has had a considerable impact upon trade union function. Even in the brief period since the Norwegian Labor Party obtained its parliamentary majority, it became evident that trade unions would be obliged to assume unprecedented responsibilities and virtually to undergo a functional revolution. Since the trend has been away from particularism and toward centralized decision making, similarly drastic effects upon union

[27] See, for example, Egil Einarsen, *Rasjonaliserings-Spørsmålet* (Oslo, 1946) ; Einar Hågå, "Rasjonalisering og arbeidsstudier," in *Arbeideren og Bedriften* (Oslo, 1946).

[28] "Workers raise the objection that rationalization leads to unemployment. It is true that one of the effects of rationalization is to increase output per labor hour, or to decrease the labor cost per unit of production. Thus in a single plant there will be unemployment through rationalization. But that is only in the first instance, for on the second level rationalization increases employment. It makes that production profitable which was not profitable before. It opens the way for new production. It calls for a greater amount of transport labor and increases jobs in selling and distributing . . .

"Those who are made idle must remember that if rationalization had not been undertaken the establishment might be forced to shut down entirely because of inability to compete." Einarsen, pp. 20–21.

[29] *Arbeidsgiveren*, December 19, 1947.

[30] *Arbeiderbladet*, August 25, 1947.

[31] *Arbeidsgiveren*, September 26, 1947.

structure would probably have manifested themselves had it not
been for the already great concentration of power within the Federation of Labor.[32]

But beyond the immediate functional problems lies the interesting and crucial question of the relationship between state and trade
unions in a socialist society. Upon the manner in which this relationship is conceived may hinge the direction of further trade
union evolution as the present form of economic organization
gives way to one in which the state increasingly replaces individual enterprise as the chief employer of labor.

Many years ago Martin Tranmael, the outstanding figure in the
history of Norwegian labor, formulated a solution which, though
influenced by syndicalism, allowed for dualism in social structure:

Trade unions representing social groups will continue to be necessary under socialism. They will then be administrative divisions of
society rather than, as now, defensive and combative organizations.[33]

This statement, and the context from which it is drawn, represent a position approximating that which Lenin reached with
respect to Russian trade unionism under communism. At the 1919
Russian trade union congress, Lenin supported a resolution that
committed the Russian trade unions "to take an active part in the
work of the Soviet government by directly working in all government bodies, by organizing mass control over their activities, etc.,
and by setting up new organs for the registration, control and
regulation of all production and distribution." [34] It is in this sense
that he regarded it as "inevitable that the trade unions be gov-
ernmentalized . . . that they be fused with the organs of state

[32] The problems of British trade union evolution are more complicated in
this respect. "The increased participation of the trade union in industry and
national policy-making bodies has added urgency to the problem of the cen-
tralisation and co-ordination of the trade union movement. Here the first
problem is that of the powers, function and authority of the General Council
of the Trades Union Congress. A glance at the Reports of the General Council in the last ten years reveals a rapid increase in both the number and importance of the tasks undertaken by the Council although its limited constitutional powers have remained unchanged. This trend cannot continue without
a breakdown, and a full-time General Council with greater powers, accompanied by some limitation of the rights of individual affiliated unions would
appear inevitable." Jeffreys, *Trade Unions in a Labour Britain*, p. 7.

[33] Aksel Zachariassen, *Martin Tranmael,* p. 50.

[34] Lenin, *Collected Works* (American edition), XXIII, 511.

power," [35] for two years later, in opposing those who proposed a complete merger of trade unions with the state, he declared: "Our present government is such that the proletariat, completely organized, must protect itself against it. And we must use the workers' organizations for the protection of the workers against their government." [36]

Without at all assuming that Norwegian trade union evolution will parallel that of trade unionism in the Soviet Union, it may be suggestive to catalogue briefly the current functions of Soviet trade unionism: (1) Enforcement of centrally determined wage plans, and the adaptation of general wage plans to local conditions. (2) Conclusion of collective agreements relating to local conditions of labor. (3) Adjustment of grievances. (4) Stimulation of production through competitive drives, participation in plant rationalization, and so on. (5) Promotion and supervision of in-plant training. (6) Enforcement of protective labor legislation. (7) Administration of the social security system. (8) Promotion of cultural and welfare activities. (9) Trade unions, although guaranteed the right to strike by the Soviet constitution, do not exercise it in practice, regarding it as incompatible with their social responsibilities.[37]

From the foregoing analysis, it would seem that Norwegian trade unions are beginning to take on some of the functional characteristics associated with contemporary Soviet trade unionism. But it is decidedly premature to conclude that the Norwegian trade unions will ever go the way of their Soviet counterparts, to become in effect administrative divisions of the state with little real autonomy.

It is important to recall that trade unionism was almost non-existent in pre-revolutionary Russia, and that in its rapid expansion after 1917 control was firmly exercised by a single political party. In Norway, on the other hand, trade unionism developed slowly out of the basic economic needs of workers and has rich democratic traditions both in terms of the relationship of the individual worker to the union organization and of the organization as such to political groups. The Labor Party may constitute the

[35] *Ibid.*, p. 514.

[36] Lenin, *Collected Works* (Russian edition), XXVI, 81.

[37] See Maurice Dobb, "The USSR," in *Organized Labor on Four Continents* (New York, 1939).

political voice of the majority, but an individual worker or a union may affiliate with a rival political party with impunity.

Moreover, it is quite possible that socialism and genuine trade union independence are reconcilable. When the goal of socialism, as in Norway, is a mixed rather than a completely nationalized economy, there will be a continuing need for nongovernmental trade unions to deal with the private sector of the economy. Nor is assignment to trade unions of autonomous authority over wage determination, labor allocation, and related functions incompatible with economic planning, provided the unions are able to change traditional worker attitudes which had their origins in the private employment nexus. To quote the chairman of the Federation of Labor: "It takes time to educate the membership to the [new] economic policy. But do it we must. If not, trade unions may be the rock on which the new economic policy will founder. And in the long run that would harm most the people represented by the trade unions." [38]

Although surprisingly little attention has been devoted to the future of trade unionism by Norwegian socialists, on one point there is general agreement: the significance of independent unionism in affording the individual worker protection against the arbitrariness of the state.[39] Without minimizing the difficulties involved, confidence is expressed that if this elementary democratic criterion is accepted as a first principle, it will be possible slowly to evolve an arrangement whereby the trade union movement is neither a puppet nor master of the state, but a free partner in a coöperative endeavor to maximize social welfare.

Norwegian labor has embarked upon an experiment to determine whether a socialist economy can be achieved gradually and without force. The future of this experiment should be of concern to Americans, for it may well be that the course which the Norwegians are pioneering represents Western Europe's only alternative to the monolithic state of Soviet communism. The deeply-rooted democratic traditions of Norway give promise that whatever the social modifications that may occur, the right of the individual to state his opinions freely and without fear will be respected.

[38] *Arbeiderbladet,* December 21, 1946.
[39] For a similar expression from a British source, see Ben Roberts, *Trade Unions in the New Era* (London, 1947), p. 10.

APPENDIX A

BASIC AGREEMENT OF 1947
BETWEEN

The Norwegian Employers' Association (NEA) and the Norwegian Federation of Labor (NFL) covering on the employer side the Norwegian Employers' Association, affiliated national employer associations, local employer associations and individual plants, and on the employee side the Federation of Labor and affiliated national and local unions. (To constitute Part I of all collective agreements between the Norwegian Employers' Association and the Norwegian Federation of Labor).

RIGHT TO ORGANIZE

Par. 1

The Norwegian Employers' Association and the Federation of Labor recognize the mutual right of employer and employee to organize freely.

SHOP STEWARDS

Par. 2

In each establishment shop stewards shall be elected to represent the organized employees, if either the management or the employees desire it.

Par. 3

In each establishment employing up to and including twenty-five workers, two shop stewards may be elected.

In each establishment employing: from 26–50 workers, 3 shop stewards; from 51–150 workers, 4 shop stewards; from 151–300 workers, 5 shop stewards; from 301–500 workers, 6 shop stewards; from 501–750 workers, 8 shop stewards; over 750 workers, 10 shop stewards.

If so desired, election of shop stewards can take place groupwise. Each group of employees which management recognizes as such, and which averages at least twenty-five members, then has the right to select one shop steward to the shop committee. This holds even if the number of shop stewards resulting therefrom should exceed the scale fixed in the preceding section.

If the establishment employs members of a single local trade union only, and such local union's jurisdiction is confined to that establishment, committee members of the local union may be selected as shop stewards to the number permitted by this agreement.

If the employees are affiliated with several local unions, there shall be joint meetings at which the organized employees shall select shop stewards.

The election shall provide an expression of the will of the majority of the organized employees.

Par. 4

Shop stewards shall be over twenty-one years of age. They shall be elected from among the employees generally acknowledged to be the most capable, with experience and insight into the problems of the establishment. So far as possible stewards shall be elected from among the employees who have been employed in the plant during the preceding two years, but employees under nineteen years of age shall be privileged to elect one shop steward under twenty-one years of age to the shop committee. The number fixed in Par. 3 must not be exceeded, however.

Elections shall be valid for one calendar year at a time.

If a shop steward loses his employment, he ceases to function as such.

The establishment shall be notified in writing of the names of those elected, within eight days. An employee cannot demand to be recognized as a shop steward before such notice is given. Until the establishment receives notice of the new election, those shop stewards elected previously shall continue to be recognized.

Note: If one of the parties believes that the election has been conducted in conflict with these rules, the matter may be submitted to the central organizations for negotiation.

Par. 5

1. Shop stewards shall be recognized as representatives of and spokesmen for the organized employees.

Shop stewards together with employers and the representatives of employers are pledged to do their best to maintain peaceful and effective coöperation at the place of work. This holds true during work, during conferences between the employer and the shop stewards, in giving information to their organizations and in their demeanor toward the other party.

2. Shop stewards have the right to take up and seek to settle minor grievances that individual employees raise against management, or management against individual employees.

3. Shop stewards have the right, within the terms of agreements, to commit employees on matters that concern the entire labor force or groups of workers. It is assumed that the shop stewards, if they deem it necessary, will submit the matter to their constituents before committing themselves.

4. Shop stewards shall see to it that the obligations of the parties under agreement and law and, where there is not a production committee, under the provisions of labor protection legislation, are fulfilled. It is incompatible with the shop steward's position of trust to stimulate or coöperate in unlawful work stoppages.

Par. 6

Before reaching a final decision, the employer is obligated to confer with the shop stewards: (1) in preparing working rules or additions or changes therein (see Secs. 34, 35, and 38 of the Labor Protection Act of 1936); (2) concerning changes in conditions of labor which may result from significant changes in productive methods; (3) if reduction of output may lead to a reduction in the labor force (this shall not include discharge of individual workers or of workers hired for specific jobs or seasonally); (4) in the event of significant transfers of groups or workers within the establishment.

Par. 7

1. In negotiating with shop stewards the employer may either be present in person or appear through a representative. The employer or his representative may request other members of management to participate in the negotiations. With the consent of the employer the shop stewards may call upon other employees involved in the negotiations.

2. The employer shall have a responsible representative present daily to whom the shop stewards may address themselves.

Par. 8

1. When shop stewards have something to propose, they shall address themselves directly to the employer or to his representatives at the place of work.

2. The chairman of the shop committee shall have unhindered access to the various departments in the establishment to the extent necessary to discharge his obligations. He must give prior notice to his immediate superior, and inform him of the reason for which it may be necessary to leave his place of work.

3. In discharging their obligations the other shop stewards must not leave their work without permission of their immediate superiors.

Note: The parties are agreed that shop stewards must take due caution that production is interfered with as little as possible, and that as far as possible machines shall not be stopped during their regular operation.

The parties are also agreed that the rule of section 3 is not intended to interfere with shop stewards in the performance of their duties as shop stewards.

Par. 9

Discharge or layoff of shop stewards may not take place without just cause. The employer, in individual discharge of a shop steward, must give him four weeks' notice. In general, shop stewards shall have no special privileges in the establishment.

If a layoff is due to lack of work, the notice to shop stewards shall be the same as for other employees.

Before the employer discharges or lays off a shop steward, he shall confer with the shop stewards concerning the cause if the shop stewards desire that he do so.

RIGHT AND DUTY TO NEGOTIATE

Par. 10

1. Where there is a collective agreement, a work stoppage or other labor dispute shall not occur. If a dispute should arise concerning the interpretation of a collective agreement or a demand based upon a collective agreement, the dispute shall be adjudged by the Labor Court, if the parties cannot agree under the rules in sections 2 to 4.

2. Disputes between an establishment and its employees shall first be submitted to negotiation between the establishment and the shop steward or shop stewards. Minutes shall be taken of these meetings.

3. If agreement is not obtained, the parties involved, and the central organizations, agree to continue negotiations at the place of work, in the presence of a responsible representative of each of the central organizations.

The central organizations or their subordinate bodies may not contact their opposite numbers with respect to wage and working conditions without the permission of the other organization.

4. If agreement is not reached through the negotiations provided for in sections 2 and 3, or if such negotiations do not take place, each of the parties is obligated to bring the dispute to the national organizations concerned or the Federation of Labor and the Employers' Association or properly authorized subordinate organizations.

5. Negotiations shall be held within eight days of a written demand therefor by either of the parties.

New Members of the NEA and NFL

Par. II

1. Establishments which affiliate with the Employers' Association in the course of a collective agreement period:

Such establishments are covered by the existing agreement between the organizations for establishments of the same character if the NEA or the NFL requests it. A dispute over what is an establishment of the same character shall be decided by the Labor Court. In determining the character of an establishment, account shall be taken of its operation and working conditions and the type and execution of the work which comes under the agreement. The firm name is not deciding, and first and foremost that agreement shall be considered which from a production point of view is most natural for the plant.

Contract wage provisions (hourly, daily, weekly, monthly, or percentage or piece wages) that cannot be applied directly shall be subject to negotiation as provided in section 2. There shall be similar negotiation where the collective agreement lacks wage provisions for categories peculiar to the new establishment or where special circumstances in the new plant make it necessary to introduce new provisions not found in existing agreements.

In the event that there are several agreements in existence, they shall be applied in the following order: (a) a national agreement; (b) an agreement covering groups of plants in the city or district in which the newly affiliated plant lies; (c) an agreement covering a single plant in the same locality; (d) any other agreement for establishments of a similar character.

This order may be departed from where necessary to place an establishment under that collective agreement to which the establishment is naturally adapted, on the basis of the whole complex of agreements between the central organizations. If the parties are unable to agree which agreement shall be binding, this shall be decided by a board set up as provided in the next section.

If the newly affiliated establishment is bound by any special terms, they shall remain in effect until the agreement expires.

Should there be any prospective layoffs upon the affiliation of an establishment in consequence of revision of the establishment's agreement, the labor organizations may oppose the automatic application of existing agreements between themselves and the Employers' Association.

Provisions in existing agreements that the State Mediator shall set wages for newly affiliated establishments, or for already affiliated establishments where wage conditions have not yet been set, shall continue to be valid until specifically terminated.

Note: The above provisions shall also cover the situation in which a member of the Employers' Association begins work not yet covered by a collective agreement.

2. Employees who join the Federation of Labor during a contract period:

When employees are newly organized within an establishment covered by a collective agreement, and their work is performed at the place bound by the agreement without actually covering their work, either party may demand that their wage and working conditions be negotiated under the provisions of Par. 10. In the event of failure to agree, the dispute shall be adjudicated by a board consisting of one representative of each of the parties together with a neutral chairman named jointly. If they cannot agree on the neutral, he shall be named by the State Mediator.

The board shall take into consideration the wage and working conditions fixed by agreement for the other employees in the same establishment. When it determines the relationship between the new conditions and those already fixed by agreement, it shall base its decision upon corresponding relationships within the same locality. If there are similar establishments affiliated with the Employers' Association, their agreements should be considered first in determining the differentials.

The term "employees" as used in this paragraph shall not include foremen in administrative positions.

Leaves of Absence and Work Certificates

Par. 12

1. When lack of work or materials result in employees being laid off temporarily without the customary dismissal notice, they shall remain attached to the establishment. They therefore have the right and duty to seek reëmployment at the establishment so long as the employee relationship is not formally terminated. This includes employees in seasonal establishments during the slack season.

2. Shop stewards in the establishment and employees holding official positions in trade unions shall not be denied leave without compelling reason when called to meetings and negotiations by their organizations.

3. When an employee leaves an establishment after due notice, at his own request or through action of the employer, regardless of the reason therefor, he shall receive a work certificate covering the period during which he was employed at the establishment.

The certificate shall include only: (1) name and date of birth, (2) date of commencement at the establishment, (3) date of termination (without any stated reason therefor), (4) trade, (5) wage rate at termination, (6) date of his last vacation.

> *Note:* The parties agree that Par. 12, section 1, shall not in itself establish any authority for laying employees off without notice. The basis for shorter notice must be found in law, collective agreement, or custom.

Par. 13

1. Employees are not obligated to work together with or under the supervision of persons who displayed such conduct [during the occupation] that general social opinion could justify a demand for their discharge. If there is a dispute over such matter, there must be no work stoppage or other form of labor dispute. Negotiation shall take place under the rules of Par. 10, with final judgment by the Labor Court in the event of failure to agree.

2. If a shop steward is guilty of a serious breach of his obligation under the Basic Agreement, the NEA or the NFL can demand his resignation as shop steward. In the event that the Federation of Labor does not acknowledge the correctness of the demand, the matter shall be submitted to the Labor Court. If a shop steward must resign, the employees shall immediately elect a successor.

COLLECTIVE NOTICE OF TERMINATION
Par. 14

The NEA and the NFL will, at the time of contract revision or with respect to notice concerning a work stoppage under the labor disputes act, accept as valid a notice of termination of employment exchanged between the two organizations or between affiliated national associations and unions, when the central organization has received notice of such. Both parties agree that they will give at least fourteen days' notice of termination.

Notice of termination shall conform in form and content to Par. 28 of the labor disputes act.

VOTING RULES
Par. 15

A. Employee Voting Rules.

I

In voting on proposed collective agreements, those having the right to vote shall be called to a meeting, where the proposal shall be explained, and a secret written ballot taken. The ballots shall be collected either by the executive committee of the local union or by a specially appointed committee. The ballots shall be sealed and held either by the local executive or the special committee until the voting in the electoral district is concluded. The executive or the committee shall then count the ballots and enter the results in the minutes. The results shall be sent to the national union concerned, and must not be published in any form until the central organizations have given their permission. If requested, the ballots shall be sent to the national union.

The national unions shall send the local unions a summary of the combined results of the voting.

II

(a) All employees in an establishment who will be covered by a proposed agreement have the right to vote on it.

(b) In local unions the members of which constantly shift their place of work (building workers, transport workers, lumber and agricultural workers, workers in seasonal plants, and so on), all members have the right to participate in voting.

(c) When there is submitted to a local union an agreement which in fact determines wages and working conditions for the entire trade, all its members have the right to participate in voting.

(d) All members enjoying the right to vote have the duty to vote.

III

(a) If so few vote that the results do not provide an adequate expression of majority opinion, the national union executive may order a new vote. The new vote shall cover all interested local unions and enfranchised members.

(b) In establishments where there is shift work, in the absence of dispute the meeting or meetings shall so be held as to afford all members the opportunity to vote.

IV

Members who are receiving financial assistance from a union and who fail to vote on proposed agreements shall lose the right to continued assistance. Disputes between the local union and its members concerning this provision shall be decided by the national union executive.

V

These rules for voting on contract proposals shall be followed by all organizations affiliated with the Federation of Labor.

VI

Should a dispute arise within the trade unions concerning the voting rules, it shall be decided finally by the secretariat of the Federation of Labor.

VII

These rules do not alter the right of national unions and the secretariat to conduct and terminate contract negotiations and conflicts under the constitution of the NFL.

VIII

These rules do not apply to voting among seamen.

B. Employer Voting Rules.

When proposed agreements are submitted to referendum, those members of the Employers' Association covered by the agreement shall participate. Voting shall be secret and by written ballot. Before a proposal submitted to a referendum vote shall be considered defeated, at least half of those entitled to vote shall have voted for its rejection.

If a proposed agreement for an individual or several individual members of a national association of employers contains provisions that may affect the labor conditions of other members of the association, all members of the latter shall have the right to participate in the voting.

These rules do not affect the right of the central executive committees [of the NEA] and the national associations to conduct and terminate contract negotiations and conflicts under relevant constitutional provisions.

Sympathetic Actions

Par. 16

The obligation to maintain peaceful relations shall not limit the right of either employers or employees to participate in a work stoppage in support of a lawful conflict, when consent of the Employers' Association or the Federation of Labor is obtained. Negotiations between the latter organizations must precede the granting of permission.

Negotiations shall commence within four days of a request therefor.

Notice of the work stoppage shall be given as provided in Par. 14.

In the event of a sympathetic strike affecting a member of the NEA in support of workers employed at establishments that are not affiliated with any association of employers, three weeks' notice shall be given.

If the NFL declares a sympathetic strike among members of the NEA because of a dispute at an establishment not affiliated with the NEA, the NFL shall simultaneously declare a sympathetic strike at corresponding unaffiliated establishments, if there are such; and the number of workers participating in the sympathetic strike at the un-affiliated establishments shall be approximately equal to the number at the affiliated establishments.

The central organizations can agree upon exceptions to this rule. The NFL may except state, communal, coöperative, and worker-owned undertakings.

The right of the NFL to declare sympathetic strikes at establish-ments affiliated with the NEA in support of demands raised against unaffiliated employers is contingent upon such demands not going beyond the conditions contained in NEA collective agreements for similar establishments.

Notice of termination of employment under the rules of this para-graph shall be unconditional, unless the underlying dispute involves the right to have conditions of labor embodied in a collective agree-ment in an establishment where at least half of the workers employed are organized in a union affiliated with the NFL. If the purpose of the dispute is to protect the right to organize, the NFL or an affiliated union has the right to employ conditional notice of termination of employment regardless of degree of membership.

DISPUTES OVER INTERPRETATION
Par. 17

Either party may bring a dispute concerning the interpretation of this Basic Agreement before the Labor Court.

DURATION
Par. 18

This Basic Agreement shall remain in effect until December 31, 1950, and for further periods of two years unless one of the parties submits six months' notice in writing of its intention to terminate the Agreement.

NOTES

1. The Basic Agreement shall constitute the first part of all collec-tive agreements entered into between members of the signatory or-ganizations and/or their members.

Special conditions in individual collective agreements shall not be disturbed or altered in any way by the Basic Agreement.

2. Par. 1, first sentence, in the current shop steward regulations for the building trades shall be altered thus: "Shop stewards together with employers and the representatives of employers are pledged to do their best to maintain peaceful and effective coöperation at the place of work."

Otherwise the current shop steward rules for the building trades shall remain unchanged.

3. Longshoremen — Present practice with respect to shop stewards, controlmen, and so on, paid or elected by the local union, shall remain unchanged.

4. This Basic Agreement does not cover shipping activity covered by the Basic Agreement between the NEA and the Norwegian Seamen's Union.

Oslo, September 4, 1947

APPENDIX B

AGREEMENT ON PRODUCTION COMMITTEES

In accordance with the political parties' joint program of 1945, and with reference to the proposal of the Production Committee Preparatory Board of 1945, the following agreement has been concluded between the Norwegian Employers' Association (NEA) and the National Federation of Labor (NFL).

Par. 1

A production committee shall be established at every industrial and handicraft establishment in which, during the last year, 46,000 hours of work have been performed (equivalent to 20 years of full-time work by one person) by the establishment's employees.

A production committee may also be formed at smaller establishments if the employer or a majority of the employees desire it. This shall also apply to all establishments which begin to function during the time the agreement is in force.

Par. 2

The production committee is an advisory and informational body which shall consider the following matters: (a) Information and confidential reports from the management on the establishment's economic status, production and sales possibilities. Such reports are to be made quarterly. (b) Information and confidential reports on industrial techniques with a view to the promotion of effective production. The committee is to aim at the rationalization of production and, through educational work, the promotion of understanding of the importance of such for the establishment and the community as a whole. (c) Suggestions for improving employee security, working, and health conditions. The committee must see to it that the requirements of the workers' health-protection law are met by all parties. (d) Vocational training.

The committee is also to establish effective supervision over all trainees, to ensure that they receive comprehensive training so that they can pass their tests, and to ensure that employees are given the opportunity to specialize in order to achieve the highest possible skill in their trades.

When matters which have been included under (a) and (b) of this paragraph are under discussion, the information that is given by the establishment is to be regarded as strictly confidential, if management so desires.

Par. 3

The committee is not to discuss wages and hours.

Par. 4

The committee is to be composed of representatives of the following groups: (a) responsible management. (b) technical and office employees. (c) [production] workers.

In establishments where not more than fifty man-years of work (115,000 hours of work, *vide* Par. 1) have been performed annually, the management can select a maximum of three representatives, and the technical and office employees and workers together a maximum of three representatives.

Where there is more than one representative of the employees, one must represent the technical and office employees.

In establishments where more than fifty man-years of work have been performed, the management can select up to five members and the employees five members. Where the employees select more than three representatives, one must represent the technical and one the office employees.

A deputy is to be appointed for each group of members.

Par. 5

The committee is authorized to call on individual members of the establishment for advice on matters in which they are especially competent.

The committee may, if the parties agree, refer the discussion of certain matters to special representatives or subcommittees which will then make verbal or written reports to the main committee.

Par. 6

The management is to select its own representatives.

The elections within the respective [employee] groups are to be written and secret, and conducted under the direction and control of the appropriate shop stewards.

The elections are to be held in such a manner that all those entitled to vote are able to do so.

One of the employee representatives on the committee shall be chosen from among the shop stewards.

Par. 7

Elections are to be held before the end of the calendar year. The members of the committee will begin to serve from the first day of the new year. The period of service is two years.

When the production committee is first established, it is to take office immediately after the election. The committee is to function up to the end of the calendar year which brings the period of service as nearly as possible to two years.

In newly established committees where there is more than one representative of each group, one-half is to retire one year after the election and new representatives chosen for two years. Where the committee is not established on January 1, half the committee shall resign at the end of that calendar year which brings their length of service as nearly as possible to one year.

Par. 8

Members of the production committee must be over twenty-one years of age and are to be chosen from among the most qualified employees in the establishment, if possible from among those who have worked in the establishment for the preceding two years (see the Basic Agreement between the NEA and the NFL, Par. 4).

Should a member of the production committee leave the establishment, he will cease serving as a member of the committee, and a deputy will take his place.

Notice of dismissal of members of the production committee cannot be effected without good cause. The employer must give four weeks' notice of dismissal to a member of the production committee. The members of the production committee are not to be accorded preferred treatment within the establishment.

If a layoff is due to lack of work, the members of the production committee are to be given the same notice as other employees.

When the employer gives notice or dismisses a member of the production committee, he must, if the member of the production committee desires it, confer with the members of the production committee on the grounds for his action.

All employees in the establishment shall have the right to vote for the members of the committee.

Par. 9

The committee's work is to be directed by a chairman and a secretary, each elected for one year.

The chairman is to be elected alternately by the management and the employee representatives, unless the parties agree on another arrangement. Where an employer representative is the chairman, the employee representatives are to select the secretary.

Where the employee representatives have selected the chairman, the management is to choose the secretary.

Par. 10

The production committee is to hold regular meetings monthly, unless the chairman and the secretary agree that a meeting is not necessary. The agenda is to be prepared by the chairman and secretary jointly, and distributed to the members at least three days in advance of the meeting.

Should one of the parties so desire, extraordinary meetings can be held on three days' notice if matters of special importance arise. The employee members of a production committee are entitled to their normal wages for the time spent at committee meetings.

Par. 11

A record is to be kept of the committee's decisions. Copies of the record are to be submitted to management, the members of the production committee and the shop committee chairman.

The committee is to keep the interested parties informed of the results of its work in a manner which will increase interest in the committee's work, but must ensure that confidential reports are kept secret (see Par. 2).

Par. 12

To serve as liaison between the production committees of various establishments and the organizations which have signed the agreement, a national advisory committee is to be established. This is to consist of two representatives selected by the NEA and two representatives selected by the NFL. In disputes in which the parties' representatives cannot come to an agreement, the chairman of the Labor Court is to serve as arbitrator.

Deputies are to be appointed for the members of the national advisory committee.

The committee, in coöperation with the organizations which have signed the agreement, is to direct informational activities and assist the production committees in their work.

The committee will make final and binding decisions in disputes arising out of the interpretation of this agreement.

The committee is to have full power to call qualified persons to meetings. The expenses arising from the advisory committee's activities are to be shared equally by the employers and trade unions signatory to the agreement.

Par. 13

This agreement has been effected between the NEA and NFL and has been agreed to by . . .

The agreement shall remain in effect for two years from the date of signature, and for further two-year periods if neither party has given notice in writing six months prior to the end of a contract period.

This agreement shall not affect the building and construction industry until the central organizations, after further negotiation, have agreed on the question of committee structure therein. Such negotiation will take place as soon as possible.

Notes on the individual paragraphs

The following remarks are not intended to give reasons for the provisions of the agreement. The intent is merely to clarify certain points where this may be necessary.

Par. 1. The paragraph's second section is to be understood to mean that production committees are to be established in those cases where either the management or employees demand it. It is assumed that in either case the appropriate central organization will support the establishment of a production committee. "A majority of the employees" means in this connection a majority within the different employee groups taken together.

The third part of this paragraph is to be understood to mean that the establishment of production committees in new enterprises — regardless of size — is only to occur on the demand of one of the parties. After the establishment has been in operation for one year, and a better estimate can be made of its size, where at least 46,000 hours of work have been performed, the formation of production committees is compulsory in accordance with the provisions of the paragraph's first part.

Par. 2. The intention of this paragraph's last section is that information the secrecy of which it is important for the individual establishment to preserve, must not be divulged to anyone not concerned.

Par. 3. The intent of this paragraph is that questions regarding wages and working hours will continue to be handled exclusively by the regular negotiating bodies functioning under wage or collective agreements. These questions are, therefore, not to be considered by the production committees.

If the shop stewards have already taken up, within the framework of the collective agreement, other matters than wages and working hours, practical considerations will determine which body will in the future consider such matters.

It is assumed that the question of division of work will be solved by agreement between the shop stewards and the production committee so that jurisdictional disputes and duplication can be avoided.

See paragraph 6, last section, which should ensure effective coöperation.

Par. 4. The expression "responsible management" is to be understood to mean that the representatives selected by the establishment are to be persons who have authority, and knowledge of conditions within the establishment. The management of the establishment, therefore, cannot nominate a subordinate employee as its representative.

According to this paragraph both parties—the management on the one side, and the employees on the other—have the right to demand equal representation on the production committee.

The parties are, however, free to decide whether they will fully utilize this privilege, as there is no question involved requiring deciding of issues by vote.

It has been assumed that, in the selection of representatives and deputies, there will be an attempt to have the various crafts and trades within the establishment represented.

Par. 7. It is assumed that elections will generally be held a short time before the new year.

At the start, elections are to be held as soon as it has been decided to establish a production committee, without waiting for the next new year.

The provision of the third part of this paragraph does not prevent reëlection.

Par. 9. According to this paragraph, the parties have equal right to assume administrative direction of the committee.

The parties must agree between themselves on which of them shall elect the chairman for the first time. In those cases where the management of the establishment elects the chairman for the first year, the employees have the right to elect the chairman the following year. The parties are free in each individual case, however, to agree to another arrangement.

The first year the chairman should, for practical reasons, be selected by the management, which will more easily be able to provide clerical personnel, and so on.

It is assumed that in those cases where management has only one representative on the committee, he will be allowed to select a secretary from among the employees. This secretary must be given the opportunity to take part in the work of the committee, but without any of the rights enjoyed by members.

Par. 12. It is assumed that the advisory committee will inform the individual committees of the work that is being done by other committees. It is also assumed that the collection of information, in those cases where that is advisable, will be effected through the central organizations. The advisory committee shall, however, have direct access to the individual production committees.

Oslo, December 7, 1945
Norwegian Federation of Labor
Konrad Nordahl
Norwegian Employers' Association
Finn Dahl

APPENDIX C

RULES FOR THE CONDUCT OF LABOR STUDIES

Approved by the Norwegian Employers' Association and the Norwegian Federation of Labor [1947].

With reference to the agreement on production committees in industrial and handicraft establishments, Par. 2, section b, where it is stated, *inter alia:* "The committee is to aim at the rationalization of production," the parties agree to coöperate in carrying through labor studies to further industrial rationalization and the setting of correct task rates.

Labor studies shall be conducted in consonance with the following rules so that labor conditions and earning potentialities shall not be diminished in relationship to their level before rationalization. In this connection individual departments or groups shall be considered as a single unit.

Before labor studies are commenced at an establishment contact shall be established with the shop stewards and the production committee to present information and draft the proposed measures.

It is assumed that during the studies all parties will coöperate loyally to secure correct results.

In order to confer with management on questions concerning labor studies and to assist those employees who may desire help regarding task rate calculations, the employees shall elect one or more labor-study shop stewards, depending upon the nature and size of the establishment. The provisions of the Basic Agreement regarding shop stewards shall apply to these. It is assumed that these stewards will have good technical knowledge of and interest in labor studies. Their period of service shall be two years. This period may be prolonged unless there is valid reason to change stewards. If the parties are in agreement, a new election can be held within a shorter period.

The establishment shall assist in giving the elected shop steward or stewards the necessary theoretical and practical training so that they can carry out their duties in a satisfactory manner. During training and actual performance of their work as labor-study shop stewards they shall receive full pay from the establishment.

By labor studies the following are understood: I. method studies, II. lost-time studies, III. task-time studies.

Depending upon the purpose of the labor study, one or more types of study will be employed, although, in general, studies of types I and II will be made before task-time studies of type III are begun.

I. *Method studies* are intended to arrange work, investigate the work place, machinery, materials, transportation, and production methods in order to undertake changes and improvements and install the most economical means of performing the work. In connection with these studies conferences shall be held with the employees concerned.

II. *Lost-time studies* can be undertaken for two different purposes, namely: (a) to determine all the time lost in a place of work or a department in order that it may be eliminated, (b) to determine the various lost-time supplements. Such supplements are divided into the following groups: (1) technical production lost-time supplements, (2) personal lost-time supplements, (3) special supplements.

1. *Technical production lost time* means the total time which in the course of a long period it proves necessary to take into consideration as a percentage supplement to the performance of a particular labor operation. Such lost time is a concomitant of piece work, the factory, machinery, materials, and so on, and cannot be significantly affected by the employee. This supplement is to be determined by a lengthy, coördinated lost-time study, and must be determined separately for each machine, work place, or department.

2. *Personal lost time* means the time that each individual employee shall have at his disposition daily for purely personal needs. This time shall also be expressed as a percentage supplement to the task, and will be determined in most cases through negotiation, after study, at the establishment.

3. *Special supplements.* In addition to the customary technical and personal lost-time supplements it may be necessary in individual labor operations to give special supplements. For example, there may be special idle time because of heavy labor, particularly intense work, unhealthful temperature or ventilation conditions, or other causes beyond the usual and normal working pattern in comparable work. The percentage supplement shall be determined on the basis of the experience and theoretical knowledge of time-study engineers, in conjunction with employee time-study shop stewards.

III. *Task-time studies* shall be undertaken to determine the normal time required by a fairly proficient worker to perform a labor operation through the exertion of normal effort.

1. By normal effort is meant the work performed by an experienced employee familiar with production methods, the materials, and machinery, working at a tempo that he can maintain for years without injury to himself.

2. During the study the employee's skill and intensity of labor shall be evaluated in order that the time may be regulated up or down, if necessary.

3. Work involved in the study shall be performed by an experienced employee and, if necessary to secure a more reliable base, by several employees experienced in the operation concerned. It is assumed that the expanded studies can be accomplished without unduly affecting production plans.

4. The lost and normal time determined shall hold for the conditions and the methods used during the studies.

Task-Rate Calculation

1. All task rates shall be fixed on the basis of normal time. Normal time shall be determined through labor studies and/or through systematic review of earlier labor studies in the establishment.

2. Task time shall be determined, in general, by adding to the normal time the previously determined technical, personal, and special supplements.

3. All task rates shall be calculated either as time rates or as money piece rates with a premium for excess production, as determined in the collective agreement proper.

Task Negotiations — Task Lists

1. When the task is calculated it shall be submitted to the employee or group of employees who are to perform the work for their approval, and shall be signed by the regular shop steward, if this does not conflict with existing agreements.

2. If the employee so desires, the time studies and calculations on which the task is based shall be submitted to him.

3. If there is agreement on a task, it comes into effect immediately. All piece rates adopted shall be entered into a rate book.

Shop stewards, if they so desire, are entitled to secure copies of task rates, signed by management.

4. In the event of failure to agree on a rate, the establishment, together with the time-study shop steward, may institute control studies. Whether and how such studies shall be commenced shall be judged by the time-study engineer and the time-study shop steward jointly. If no agreement results, the regular collective agreement provisions regarding rate disputes shall be employed.

Basis for Changing Task Rates

A revision of task rates may take place when one or more of the following conditions prevail: (1) A general increase or decrease in the wage level through revision of collective agreements; (2) Changes in methods, machinery, or materials; (3) Changes in the establishment's (or department's) general degree of rationalization which are reflected in altered personal or technical lost time; (4) Rates that are obviously incorrect, as, for example, when arithmetical errors occur in their calculation. Both parties are obligated to give notice if they discover such errors.

Above-normal piece earnings, on the basis of rates fixed through labor study, do not create any right to reduce rates if the higher earnings result from an increase in intensity of labor and skill.

SELECTED BIBLIOGRAPHY

Books and Pamphlets

Aukrust, Odd, and Bjerve, Petter Jacob, *Hva Krigen Kostet Norge,* Oslo, 1945.

Berg, Paal, *Loven av 5 Mai om Arbeidstvister og Tvungen Voldgift,* Oslo, 1928.

—— *Arbeidsrett,* Oslo, 1930.

—— *Arbeidskonflikter,* Sarpsborg, 1938.

Bull, Edvard, *Arbeiderklassen i Norsk Historie,* Oslo, 1947.

Delegations for the Promotion of Economic Coöperation, *The Northern Countries in World Economy,* Finland, 1939.

Engh, Arnljot, *Fagorganisasjonen og Loven,* Oslo, 1934.

Frydenberg, Alf, *Kollektive arbeidstvister og deres bileggelse i Norge,* Oslo, 1927.

—— *Norwegian Labor Disputes Legislation as of 1940,* Norwegian Information Services, New York, 1946 (mimeographed).

Jeffreys, J. B., *Trade Unions in a Labour Britain,* London, 1947.

Koht, Halvdahn, and others, *Det Norske Arbeiderpartis Historie,* Vols. I and II, Oslo, 1937.

Koht, Halvdahn, and Skard, Sigmund, *The Voice of Norway,* New York, 1944.

Krefting, Axel, *Norsk Arbeidsgiverforening 1900–1910,* Oslo, 1910.

Lange, Halvard, *Fagorganisasjonens Historie i Norge,* Oslo, 1934.

Larssen, Olav, *Under Arbeiderregjeringen,* Oslo, 1938.

Lie, Trygve, and Hansteen, Viggo, *Den Nye Arbeidstvistlov,* Oslo, 1933.

Meyer, Håkon, *Den politiske Arbeiderbevegelse i Norge,* Oslo, 1931.

Moe, Finn, *Does Norwegian Labor Seek the Middle Way?* New York, 1937.

Nordskog, John Eric, *Social Reform in Norway,* Los Angeles, 1935.

Norsk Forening for Socialt Arbeide, *Social Håndbok for Norge,* Oslo, 1937.

Ousland, Gunnar, *Fagorganisasjonen i Norge,* Oslo, 1927.

Øvergaard, J., *Arbeidstvist og Boikott-Loven,* Oslo, 1934.

Reutz, Johanne, *Indeksregulering,* Oslo, 1928.

Roberts, Ben, *Trade Unions in the New Era,* London, 1947.

Rømcke, Ferdinand, *Lov om Arbeidervern,* Oslo, 1947.

Skeie, Jon, *Ulovlige midler i Kampen om Arbeidsvilkaar,* Oslo, 1931.

Tuveng, Morten, *Arbeidsløshet og Beskjeftigelse i Norge før og under Krigen,* Bergen, 1946.

Wooton, Barbara, *Freedom Under Planning,* Chapel Hill, 1945.

Zachariassen, Aksel, *Martin Tranmael,* Oslo, 1939.

ARTICLES IN PERIODICALS AND BOOKS

Debes, Inge, "Erfaringer med Tvungen Voldgift i Norge," *Samtiden,* 1923.

Forchheimer, Karl, "The Role of Relative Wage Differences in International Trade," *The Quarterly Journal of Economics,* November 1947.

Forsey, Eugene, "Trade Union Policy Under Full Employment," in *Insights Into Labor Issues,* New York, 1948.

Lorentzen, Sigurd, "Oversikt over norsk prisregulering," *Socialt Arbeid,* 1946.

Olsen, Halvard, "Arbeidernes syn om lovforslagene om boikott," *Socialt Arbeid,* 1933.

Singer, H. W., "Wage Policy in Full Employment," *The Economic Journal,* December 1947.

Worswick, G. D. N., "The Stability and Flexibility of Full Employment," in *The Economics of Full Employment,* Oxford, 1945.

GOVERNMENT PUBLICATIONS

Arbeidsdirektoratet, *Arbeidsmarkedet* (monthly statistical report), 1945–1947.

Det Økonomiske Samordningsråd, *Beretning for året 1945.*

Domstolen for Boikottsaker, *Dommer og Kjennelser,* 1933–1940.

Finans- og tolldepartementet, *Ot. prp. nr. 152,* 1945–46 (Lov om prisregulering).

——— *St. meld. nr. 10,* 1947 (Om nasjonalbudsjettet 1947).

Handelsdepartementet, *St. meld. nr. 1,* 1948 (Om nasjonalbudsjettet 1948).

——— *Ot. prp. nr. 153,* 1945–46 (Lov om bransjeråd).

Justis- og Politidepartementet, *Ot. prp. nr. 85,* 1933 (Lov om forhandlingsrett for statstjenestemenn).

——— *Ot. prp. nr. 70,* 1947 (Lov om boikott).

Lønnsnemnda, *Kjennelser,* 1945–1947 (mimeographed).

Norwegian Information Services, *Nytt fra Norge,* New York, 1940–1948.

Socialdepartementet, *Ot. prp. nr. 54,* 1925 (Lov om arbeidstvister).

——— *Ot. prp. nr. 35,* 1929 (Lov om arbeidstvister).

——— *Ot. prp. nr. 6,* 1933 (Lov om arbeidstvister).

——— *Ot. prp. nr. 71,* 1933 (Lov om arbeidstvister).

—— *Ot. prp. nr. 31*, 1934 (Lov om arbeidstvister).

—— *Ot. prp. nr. 14*, 1938 (Lov om voldgift i transportkonflikten).

—— *Ot. prp. nr. 149*, 1945–46 (Lov om arbeidsdirektoratet).

—— *Ot. prp. nr. 162*, 1945–46 (Lov om arbeidstvister).

—— *Ot. prp. nr. 63*, 1947 (Lov om arbeidskraft).

—— *Ot. prp. nr. 73*, 1947 (Lov om arbeidstvister).

—— *Ot. prp. nr. 103*, 1947 (Lov om forbud mot lønnsauke).

—— *Ot. prp. nr. 104*, 1947 (Lov om ferie).

Statistisk Sentralbyrå, *Statistisk Årbok for Norge* (annual volumes).

—— *Industristatistisk*, 1915 and 1918.

—— *Statistisk Oversikter*, 1926.

—— *Arbeidslønninger*, 1940–1945.

—— *Tariffavtaler og Arbeidskonflikter*, 1927–1938.

—— *Statistiske Meddelelser* (monthly volumes).

—— *Statistisk-Økonomisk Utsyn over Krigsårene*, 1945.

Trade Union Publications

Arbeidernes Faglige Landsorganisasjon, *Lover*, 1946.

—— *Kongressen 1927, Dagsorden og Protokoll.*

—— *Kongressen 1931, Dagsorden og Protokoll.*

—— *Kongressen 1934, Dagsorden og Protokoll.*

—— *Kongressen 1938, Protokoll.*

—— *Protokoll over Kongressen 1946.*

—— *Beretning 1945.*

—— *Fagorganisasjonens Arbeidsprogram 1941.*

—— *Rasjonaliserings-Spørsmålet*, Oslo, 1929.

—— *Industrien i Oppgangskonjunkturen 1932–1937*, Oslo, 1939.

—— *Fri Fagbevegelse* (monthly journal, titled *Landsorganisasjons Meddelelseblad* prior to 1940).

Jacobsen, Albert, *En oversikt over lønnsfastsettelsen*, Oslo, 1946 (mimeographed).

Norges Arbeidslederforbund, 1910–1935, Oslo, 1935.

Norsk Papirindustriarbeiderforbund, *Opmarsjen 1878–1938*, Olso, 1938.

Publications of the Workers' Education Association

ABC i Fagforenings Kunskap, Oslo, 1946.

Arbeideren og Bedriften, Oslo, 1946.

Bøe, Gunnar, *Produksjons-Utvalgene*, Oslo, 1946.

Einarsen, Egil, *Rasjonalisering-Spørsmålet*, 1946.

Evensen, Lars, *Tariffavtalen*, Oslo, 1935.

Fagbevegelsens Økonomiske Problemer, Oslo, 1938.

Fagbevegelsens samfundsmessige stilling, Oslo, 1938.

Hansteen, Viggo, *Arbeidsgiverforeningen,* Oslo, 1935.
Lange, Halvard, *Fagbevegelse og Politikk,* Oslo, 1938.
Norsk Naeringsliv og Dets Problemer, Oslo, 1938.
Ousland, Gunnar, *Fagorganisasjons problemstilling i dag,* Oslo, 1946.
────── *Se samfunnet gjennom verkstedet,* Oslo, 1946.

OTHERS

Arbeiderbladet (daily newspaper published by Oslo Labor Party).
Arbeidsgiveren (monthly journal of the Norwegian Employers' Association).
Det Norske Arbeiderparti, *Landsmøter 1912–1933, Beslutninger og resolusjoner,* Oslo, 1934.
────── *Arbeidsprogram,* 1945.